American

Regional Cuisine

SECOND EDITION

Ai THE ART INSTITUTES

Michael F. Nenes, CEC, CCE

Photography by Joe Robbins

WILEY

JOHN WILEY & SONS, INC.

Published by John Wiley & Sons, Inc., Hoboken, New Jersey.

Published simultaneously in Canada

For general information on our other products and services or for technical support, please contact our Customer Care Department within the United States at (800) 762-2974, outside the United States at (317) 572-3993 or fax (317) 572-4002.

Wiley also publishes its books in a variety of electronic formats. Some content that appears in print may not be available in electronic books. For more information about Wiley products, visit our web site at www.wiley.com.

LIBRARY OF CONGRESS CATALOGING-IN-PUBLICATION DATA:

Nenes, Michael F.
  American regional cuisine / the Art Institutes ; Michael F. Nenes ; photography by Joe Robbins.-- 2nd ed.
     p. cm.
  Rev. ed. of: American regional cuisine. 2002.
  Includes bibliographical references and index.
  ISBN-13 978-0-471-68294-3 (cloth)
  ISBN-10 0-471-68294-2 (cloth)
 1. Cookery, American. I. Art Institutes. II. American regional cuisine. III. Title.
  TX715.A50847 2007
  641.5'973--dc22
                            2005019107

Printed in the United States of America

10 9 8

Book design by Richard Oriolo

Contents

Foreword

by Martin Yan

In my travels, I've crisscrossed the world, experiencing different cultures and tasting their dishes. And I must say that the United States is one of the most diverse nations with respect to culture, people, history, and food. Some say the American national cuisine is a melting pot of ethnic cuisines; others describe it as a mixed salad with distinct ingredients. Regardless of which analogy you prefer, each American regional cuisine is a special treat, combining its unique local history and culture with distinct regional ingredients. It's not by chance that certain parts of the country maintain a particular taste or flavor in their dishes. Regional cuisines reflect the characteristics of the locale.

From one U.S. coast to the other, from ocean to mountain, valley to plain, I've noticed that each region's dishes tell a story and are like mirrors. A recipe evolves along with the community and, with each adaptation, the dish absorbs and reflects much of the environment. For example, the cuisine of New England is an adaptation of English cuisine, with local ingredients such as turkey, lobster, and clams giving the region its well-known Boston brown bread, clam chowder, and Maine boiled lobster. In the Great Plains, where wheat is the staff of life, you'll find wheat and honey buns, colaches, and wheat beer. You can actually taste the wet weather typical of the Pacific Northwest in its apples and berries. In the Southwest, you'll find food flavored by fiery spices because of their abundance in the region. Head over to my home state of California and you'll taste the freshness of the seasons and the experimental spirit of the people, whose recipes use a wide range of readily available ingredients—asparagus, lettuce, artichoke, bok choy, lemongrass, tomato, and more.

I've had the pleasure of gaining an illuminating perspective on each region I've visited just from taking a bite of its food. The Cajun and Creole region, home of my good friend Paul Prudhomme, is a marvelous blend of French, Spanish, Italian, German, Native American, African, and West Indian traditions. For a taste of the Asian blends, such as Chinese, Japanese, Filipino, Korean, Indian, and Thai, it's back to California and the Pacific Northwest. It's an enjoyable journey for the mind and taste buds when traveling the United States.

Travel among these pages—enjoy! What follows is insight into and details of what makes each American culinary region unique. Each chapter contains not only recipes but also historical and cultural information, as well as a guide to ingredients specific to that region. And to top it off, once you prepare these dishes and take a bite, the flavors and tastes will reinforce everything you read. It's a history, anthropology, and cooking class all in one!

MARTIN YAN is a master chef and corporate chef of Chef Martin Yan's CreAsian. He has written more than 24 cookbooks and is the host of *Yan Can Cook* on PBS. Chef Yan is the founder of the Yan Can International Cooking School, located in the San Francisco Bay area.

Acknowledgments

The Art Institutes wish to thank the following contributors for their effort on behalf of *American Regional Cuisine:*

Author Michael F. Nenes, CEC, CCE. The second edition of *American Regional Cuisine* is the result of intensive cooperative effort by many people. Thanks to Lois Nenes, M.Ed., who taught at the Art Institute of Houston for eight years. Lois is a relentless and incredibly creative researcher, who had to become part explorer, part student and teacher. She rewrote the manuscript, attempting to include only information that could be supported by at least two documented sources. Lois was a supportive colleague and we both had fun on the *American Regional Cuisine* adventure.

Photographer Joe Robbins of Joe Robbins Photography, Houston, Texas. Joe taught at The Art Institute of Houston for over 15 years, helping to shape the careers of students in the visual arts. This project gave Mr. Robbins the opportunity to influence students in the field of culinary arts. Joe's collaboration and outstanding photography contribute to the effectiveness of this book.

Certified Master Chef Klaus Friedenreich, the Culinary Program Chair of The Art Institute of Fort Lauderdale, contributed his tremendous talent for food styling for the photographs. Chef Friedenreich supervised the preparation and purposely plated the food in a style that students could duplicate. We also wish to thank Helene Hatfield for her assistance and contributions to the organization and her preparation of the food during the photography sessions.

Chef Peter Lehr, CEC, CCE, and his spring 2004 and summer 2004 American Regional Cuisine students merit special thanks for their outstanding work in testing the recipes. Chef Lehr handled the detailed and demanding work of calculating the weights and writing the measurements for each recipe.

In addition, we are grateful for the contributions of The Art Institutes' Culinary Programs across the country. Culinary Arts is offered at the following Art Institute locations:

The Art Institute of Atlanta

The Art Institute of California—Los Angeles

The Art Institute of California—Orange County

The Art Institute of California—San Diego

The Art Institute of Charlotte

The Art Institute of Colorado

The Art Institute of Dallas

The Art Institute of Fort Lauderdale

The Art Institute of Houston

The Art Institute of Las Vegas

The Art Institute of New York City

The Art Institute of Philadelphia

The Art Institute of Phoenix

The Art Institute of Pittsburgh

The Art Institute of Seattle

The Art Institute of Tampa

The Art Institute of Vancouver—Dubrulle International Culinary Arts

The Art Institute of Washington

The Art Institutes International Minnesota

The Illinois Institute of Art—Chicago

American Regional Cuisine, **Second Edition,** is written with great pride in our country, the professionalism of our culinarians, and the incredible foods that are bountiful from coast to coast. Few countries can boast the diverse selection of high-quality ingredients found in the United States. Our indigenous ingredients, combined with America's varied cultures and colorful history, have led to a worldwide reputation for creative and purposeful cuisine. The geographical diversity represented by The Art Institutes' culinary programs and their associated culinary educators provides a unique breadth of knowledge of American regional cuisine. The recipes, specialized skills, and procedures presented in this book are authentic and unique to each region. They have been, in many cases, handed down from generation to generation among our faculty of professional chefs. We are pleased to present this book to professional culinarians, students, and home gourmets. It documents the history and culture that led to the development of American regional cuisine, and it identifies the vast and wide variety of foods available in our great country.

The cuisine of the United States is not homogenous. It is a blending of many cultures and ethnic backgrounds found in specific regions. Each region possesses a unique history and culture and has a variety of ingredients that make its cuisine distinct.

The principles and foundations of cooking were developed and practiced in Europe, Asia, Africa, and other countries long before the development of American regional cuisines as we know them today. The European immigrants who came to America applied their basic culinary skills to the ingredients at hand. In the 1900s, as the palate of the typical American became more sophisticated, many European-trained chefs emigrated to the United States to take jobs in the growing restaurant and hotel industries. In time, Americans began to cook professionally, and in many cases they trained under these European chefs. Thus, even today, French is the language of cooking taught to students of the culinary arts. A glossary of cooking terms used in this book can be found at the back of the book.

A knowledge of basic cooking principles is essential to proper presentation of the recipes in this book. When learning to play a musical instrument, you must first learn how to read music. Likewise, when learning to cook, you must first learn how to prepare stocks and sauces and to become proficient in the fundamental techniques before being able to create attractive and tasty dishes.

The chapters that follow present the cuisines of 11 culinary regions of the United States. These regional chapters are presented in an order that follows the arrival of the first colonists and the approximate routes they took as they explored and settled what eventually became the United States. The states covered in each chapter have been selected based on the similar cultures and backgrounds of their residents and their cuisines, as well as on how the indigenous ingredients are utilized in that cooking.

Here are some important tips for using this book:

- **It is important to understand that to yield a superior dish, you must start with high-quality ingredients. Good results cannot be obtained with substandard ingredients.**

- **Some ingredients are highly specific to a region and may be difficult to obtain elsewhere. These recipes are followed by Chef Tips, which indicate suitable substitutions.**

- **All herbs called for in recipes should be fresh unless specified as dried.**

- **All butter called for in recipes should be lightly salted unless specified as unsalted.**

- **It is recommended that both white and black pepper be ground fresh to the level of coarseness called for in the recipes. Ground pepper loses strength over time, making it difficult to judge the quantity needed.**

- **When citrus juice is called for in the recipes, it should be squeezed from fresh fruit rather than reconstituted from concentrate.**

- **Many of the cooking times indicated in the recipes are approximations. The altitude, type of cookware used, and amount of heat applied are all variables that affect cooking time. Professional cooks use these times as a guide but determine doneness by appropriate means.**

An *Instructor's Manual* (0-471-78131-2) is also available to qualified adopters of this book. It contains lecture notes for each chapter along with expanded definitions of the terms contained within the text to support classroom discussion.

The Cuisine of New England

The New England region is known for the rocky coastlines of Maine, the White Mountains of New Hampshire, the rolling green mountains and dairies of Vermont, and the fertile farms and orchards of Connecticut. From New England's rivers, bays, and oceans comes seafood of great variety and high quality. The hills and valleys of New England are home to some of America's oldest fruit orchards and vegetable farms. Sugar maple trees and fiddlehead ferns are abundant. The swampy bogs found in Cape Cod and Nantucket make this area home to the cranberry.

Perhaps more than any other of the area's natural resources, the Atlantic cod is recognized as a symbol of the region's natural heritage. This species is so much a part of the early history of the settlement of the coastal regions, that a model of the "sacred cod" hangs in the Massachusetts statehouse.

Connecticut "The Nutmeg State." The state shellfish is the Eastern oyster, the state animal is the sperm whale, the state bird is the American robin, the state flower is the mountain laurel, and the state song is "Yankee Doodle."

Maine "The Pine Tree State." The state animal is the moose, the state fish is the landlocked salmon (a freshwater fish available only to sports fishermen), the state insect is the honeybee, and the state flower is the white pine cone and tassel.

Massachusetts "The Bay State." The state fish is the cod, the state tree is the American elm, and the state bird is the chickadee.

New Hampshire "The Granite State." The state saltwater fish is the striped bass, the state freshwater fish is the brook trout, the state tree is the white birch, and the state animal is the white-tailed deer.

Rhode Island "The Ocean State." The state shell is the quahog, a clamshell that Native Americans used as money; the state bird is the Rhode Island red chicken; and the state tree is the red maple.

Vermont "The Green Mountain State." The sugar maple tree is the state tree, and its sap is gathered at the beginning of spring in an activity known as "sug'rin"; the sap is then boiled down to make delicious maple syrup. The state fishes are the brook trout and walleye pike, the state flower is the red clover, and the state insect is the honeybee.

History

THE FIRST COLONISTS

Most people who initially came to the New World hoped to find treasure of one kind or another and return home. But in the New England region, religious motives brought the first settlers. A small group of English separatists, the Pilgrims, arrived in 1620 and founded the Plymouth Colony. Unprepared for the hardships of their first winter, their concern was survival. With help from the Native Americans, the Pilgrims lived through the winter.

Native American influence on colonial cookery was incalculable—primarily in terms of the kinds of produce used, leading off with maize, which the settlers called "Indian corn." One tribe of natives, the Wampanoag, shared their seeds of native corn plants and instructed the settlers in how to plant and fertilize their crop by planting a tiny fish along with each seed. The harvested corn could be steamed, roasted, or pounded into cornmeal. Cornmeal "mush" became a staple of the colonists' diet and was served hot or cold, with milk and butter. The colonists learned to adapt their own traditional recipes, substituting cornmeal for hearth cakes—puddings with a different flavor, but a similar cooking method. Americans now have johnnycakes, boiled and baked Indian puddings, and other English recipes using Indian corn. This use of maize is the most important and original aspect of American cookery, and the nation is known for its many corn recipes.

In addition to corn, Native Americans subsisted beans and squash. This "triad" of corn, beans, and squash was referred to as the "three sisters." Kidney beans, string beans, snap beans, butter beans, lima beans, navy peas, and pole beans were planted. Many varieties of squash, including acorn, zucchini, pumpkins, and gourds, were adopted by the colonists. The squash could be eaten fresh or could be dried and stored. The squash seeds could be dried and used as well. The vegetables combined together were known as "succotash," a term that today describes a mixture of corn, with any type of beans and squash.

The Native Americans taught these newcomers how to hunt and fish, and how to cure and smoke their food to preserve it through the winter. Bean pods could be left on the vine until they were thoroughly dry, and then used through the winter. The colonists learned to cook dried beans and depended on them as a staple food. The Indians of New England flavored their beans with maple sugar and bear fat and slow-cooked them in underground pits inside deer hides. This preparation evolved into today's baked beans that are very slowly cooked in a bean pot with salt pork and molasses. The Puritans' observance of the Sabbath led to the widespread practice of making beans on Saturday to be eaten on Sunday.

NEW IMMIGRANTS

In the 1880s, when immigrants, particularly those from Ireland, Italy, and Portugal, began to arrive en masse in New England, the culinary customs they brought from their homelands were incorporated into the regional cuisine and cooking style. Single-pot dishes such as meat and seafood stews, which were commonly eaten in Europe, were adapted to the local ingredients. Braised and pickled beef, a mainstay of Britain and Ireland, became the popular dish called New England Boiled Dinner.

The New England Pantry

EARLY FARMERS

Native New England ingredients formed the basis of the developing cuisine. Root vegetables such as beets, celeriac, carrots, parsnips, rutabagas, turnips, onions, and white and sweet potatoes saw them through the winters. Apples were brought over by the English colonists, and over 150 varieties were planted. They established apricot, plum, and pear orchards and cultivated strawberries, blueberries, blackberries, and raspberries.

The early settlers of New England also brought many animals with them to their new

Lobsters

Maine lobster, also known as the American lobster, is found in the North Atlantic from Laborador to North Carolina, with Maine contributing to more than half of all lobsters caught in the United States. Maine lobster is distinguished from the "spiny" lobster, or rock lobster, caught along the southern Atlantic coast and the coast of California, by its large heavy claws. Live Maine lobster is available year-round, with the bulk of the catch harvested in the summer in fall. June and July is the peak molting season.

Lobsters grow by molting, or shedding their shells. Just after they molt, they are soft and fragile until their new shell has hardened. It takes about 25 molts over 5 to 7 years for a lobster to grow to a minimum legal size, 1 pound. Newly molted lobsters are called "soft-shell" lobsters. It is important to be aware of the quality and price of these lobsters, as soft-shell lobsters have less meat in proportion to total body weight than hard-shell lobsters. Hard-shell meat is firmer, while soft-shell meat is softer and tends to have more water.

The New England states have very strict laws governing lobstering. In Maine, it is illegal to sell lobsters under and over a certain size. Lobstermen use a special gauge to accurately measure the length of the lobster's carapace (body). The legal minimum length of the carapace is 3 1/4 inches. Lobsters under this length are called "shorts" or "snappers" and must be thrown back into the ocean. Minimum sizes are enforced to make sure that lob-

homeland. As livestock were useful and easy to feed and care for, they could be found on nearly every New England farm. Farmers raised cattle for milk and beef, sheep for mutton and wool, chicken for eggs and meat, and oxen and horses for pulling carts and plows. Pigs were widely owned because they could fend almost entirely for themselves by foraging in the woods for food.

Wheat and rye could be planted once the livestock was available to plow the rocky land. The colonists brought their techniques of stone-ground milling for their grains.

Cider and ale were the main beverages of the early settlers. Hard fermented cider, the standard drink for both adults and children, was generally made from apples, although pears were also used. Wines from mulberries, cherries, and grapes were also produced.

sters are mature enough to breed at least once before they are harvested. The maximum legal length of the carapace is 5 inches; these lobsters are called "jumbo." The maximum size limit is regulated to protect the breeding stock. A minimum-size lobster will weigh around 1 pound, while a maximum-size lobster will weigh between 2 and 4 pounds.

Lobster is referred to in the industry by different names depending on its weight. Market sizes range from "chickens" (1 to $1^1/_8$ pound) to jumbos (over $3^1/_2$ pounds). The most plentiful and most popular size of Maine lobster is between $1^1/_4$ and $1^1/_2$ pounds each.

Other terminology regarding lobsters includes:

CORAL The roe inside the female lobster that, when cooked, turns from black to orange. The coral is frequently chopped and used in the stuffing for baked lobster or eaten plain with steamed or boiled lobster.

CULL A lobster with only one claw.

PAQUETTE A female lobster with black, fertilized eggs under the tail.

TOMALLEY The liver of the lobster. Many New Englanders consider tomalley a delicacy. Opinions vary on how best to cook lobster. Some say steaming is best because it is gentle heat, which will not toughen the meat. Others say boiling seals the flavor into the lobster. Baking is another option, but the lobster should be quickly boiled or steamed beforehand.

THE INFLUENCE OF THE SEA ON THE ECONOMY

Eventually, settlers arrived who understood fishing. Coming mainly from Italy and Portugal, they discovered the immense resources of the Georges Bank, an underwater plateau southeast of Boston that is the richest fishing area off the east coast of North America. Fishing and fish became an important part of the lifestyle and history of the peoples of coastal New England. The abundance of cod and other fish made it possible to survive in the New World. It was not long after this region was settled that the first fisheries came into existence and the New England economy flourished through the exportation of cod. Before the invention of refrigeration, salted cod was not only an important export item, but also the only fish available in inland areas.

The ocean fish that can be caught year round in this area include cod, haddock, pollock, and silver hake. Also popular are the flatfish, halibut, flounder, fluke, and dabs. Monkfish, eels, wolffish, sea trout, perch, and sea bass are less familiar but readily available. Small ocean fish like mackerel, porgies, butterfish, and smelts are also in abundant supply. Swordfish, shark, tuna, bluefish, Atlantic salmon, and striped bass come north in the spring and leave before winter arrives. Shellfish such as lobsters, crabs, scallops, oysters, clams, mussels, periwinkles, sea urchins, and even shrimp live in the icy waters.

In New England, the cooking of the earlier era was plain, resting on simple ingredients and skilled hands. But today, the culinary traditions of New England grow ever richer as more cultures are integrated and add diversity to the cuisine. New influences currently come from the Middle East, Asia, and Latin America. However, the roots of the region run deep and they are the source from which the rest of our nation has sprung.

Typical New England Ingredients and Dishes

Anadama Bread A yeast bread made from cornmeal and molasses.

Apple A tart fruit with firm flesh. About 40 varieties of apples are commonly grown in New England. The most popular today are McIntosh, Cortland, New England Red Delicious, Empire, and Rome. Apples have a long and vital tradition in New England. Many varieties were discovered here and have been grown for centuries. The New England apple industry is still largely family owned and orchards are an important community resource.

Barbecue To a New Englander, "barbecue" means to grill quickly over a fire made from charcoal briquettes, lump charcoal, or hardwood, or simply to cook on a gas or propane grill. In this region, the terms "barbecue" and "grill" are used interchangeably.

Blueberry A small, round, blue-skinned berry. In Maine, there is a thriving industry for processing both wild and cultivated blueberries. Before the arrival of Europeans to North America, the Native Americans gathered and dried the fruit for use in winter. The most popular variety is the highbush blueberry because of the larger size of its berries. Also popular is the wild lowbush blueberry, with smaller fruit that is prized for its intense flavor and color.

Bluefish A round saltwater fish ranging in size from 3 to 6 pounds, common to the coast of Cape Cod and Nantucket in the summer. The bluefish has a blue-silver skin and dark, oily flesh. It is well suited for smoking, broiling, and sautéing, but it must be used quickly, as its freshness decreases rapidly. It is known as a sportsman's "trophy fish" because of its fierceness and fighting nature.

Boston Brown Bread A traditional colonial sweet bread served on Saturday evenings with baked beans. Boston brown bread is made from cornmeal, molasses, and both rye and whole wheat flours. It is steamed in a large can or mold.

Boston Baked Beans A dish of navy beans baked a long time with molasses and salt pork or bacon.

Boston Cream Pie A pie with two layers of white cake, custard filling, and chocolate topping. Considered a pie instead of a cake because colonists did not have cake pans and baked this in a pie pan. Boston cream pie is also considered a pudding pie cake.

Chowder From the French *chaudeau,* literally meaning "hot water," the term broadly applies today to a hot soup. In this region, it refers to a seafood soup such as New England clam chowder, a creamy mix of clams, onions, and potatoes. (New England clam chowder differs from Manhattan clam chowder, in that the latter has a tomato base and sometimes vegetables added to a broth, and from Vermont clam chowder, which is simply a clear broth with clams, onions, and potatoes.)

Cider An alcoholic beverage made from apples. It was common until the 19th century, when the temperance movement campaigned against alcohol consumption. Early settlers consumed cider and beer instead of the unreliable and sometimes polluted local well water.

Clams Hardshells, or quahogs, are the hard-shell gray clams that vary in size, from small littlenecks, to cherrystones, to chowder clams. Littlenecks are the choice for raw, half-shell clams; they are mild, sweet, and briny. Clams are slow growers. Littlenecks—the most tender, most expensive, and most sought after—are two to three years old. Cherrystones are five to six years old. Large chowder clams can be 30 years old. Soft-shell clams have an oval shell that is thin and brittle. These clams average $1^1/_2$ to 3 inches in length, and their shells cannot close completely because of a protruding siphon. The main commercial sources of both types of clams are Maine and Cape Cod. The soft-shell clam has delicate meat that is sweet and slightly salty. The shell should be clean and the siphon firm and plump, not flaccid and dry—it should retract when touched. The siphon is covered with a dark membrane that is removed before the cooked clam is eaten. Soft-shells are not eaten raw, but are used for steaming or frying.

Clambake A traditional outdoor cooking method used for festive occasions along the coastal regions of New England. The clambake is typically done on a beach, where a pit is dug in the sand and lined with rocks. It typically takes 2 to $2^1/_2$ hours to prepare the fire, which is built on top of the rocks to get them to cooking temperature, then the ashes of the fire are then removed from the pit. Cleaned seaweed is laid down to protect the food from the heat of the hot rocks. Regional seafood such as lobster, clams, and mussels are placed on top of the seaweed. Side dishes such as potatoes, corn on the cob, onions, and lemons are added as well. The food is then covered with more seaweed. A liquid such as beer is poured on top to provide steam for the cooking process. A sheet of canvas protects the contents and the pit is covered with a bed of sand. The cooking time is roughly 45 minutes, after which the steamed food is dug up and served. Today, most people cook this dish in a large pot.

Cobbler A baked, unlined, deep-dish fruit pie with a biscuit or piecrust topping.

Cod A fish so important to New England that the region's largest peninsula, Massachusetts's Cape Cod, was named after it. This fish is in a family that includes haddock, pollock, hake, and hoki. Market size is $2^1/_2$ to 10 pounds. Large cod weigh 10 to 25 pounds; jumbos are 25 pounds and over. The term "scrod" generally refers to cod under $2^1/_2$ pounds. Raw Atlantic cod is translucent, ranging from white to pinkish. The lean meat has a mild, clean flavor and large, tender flakes.

Common Crackers Round, nuggetlike crackers originally from Vermont. Country stores that sold cheese provided these crackers to their customers in "cracker barrels." They are typically eaten with aged cheese or crumbled into a bowl of clam chowder.

Concord Grape A robust and aromatic grape from a native species found growing in the rugged New England soil. It ripens early, escaping the killing frosts. Concord grapes were used in the first unfermented grape juice known to be produced by Dr. Thomas Welch. It is also used for grape jelly and wine.

Cranberry A fruit from the northern bogs and one of the few fruits native to North America. Cape Cod and the island of Nantucket are known for their cranberries.

Fiddlehead Fern The edible, young, coiled frond of a fern that emerges in spring, so named because they look like violin scrolls. In New England, fiddleheads are available for about two weeks in April and early May.

Indian Pudding A pudding made with cornmeal, milk, and molasses.

Johnnycake (Journey Cake) An unleavened cornmeal pancake made without eggs or butter, so-called because it could be carried on long trips in a traveler's saddlebag and baked along the way. Cornbread, also known as "hoecake," "ashcake," and "spidercake," was a staple of any traveler during this period, since cornbread didn't spoil as easily as other breads.

Mackerel A saltwater fish with a rich, pronounced flavor. The meat is soft, flaky, and moist. The outer bands of dark, strong-tasting meat along the midline may be cut out for a milder flavor. Immature mackerel, called "tinkers," are available in spring and weigh less than a pound. They are a traditional seasonal treat in New England.

Maple Sugar The crystallized form of maple syrup.

Maple Syrup By tapping the sap of sugar maple trees and boiling it down to a thick syrup and then to a sugar, Native Americans were able to produce this sweet treat and use it for flavor and for trade. It takes 60 gallons of sap to produce $1^1/_2$ gallons of syrup. Real maple syrup differs markedly from maple-flavored syrups, which may contain 10 percent or less of actual maple syrup.

Molasses A syrup derived during the processing of sugarcane into sugar. Molasses was first imported to America from the West Indies. It is commonly found in two varieties: light and dark. Light molasses is used as a syrup, while dark or blackstrap molasses is used primarily as an ingredient.

Mussel A bivalve mollusk found in shallow coastal waters. Blue mussels from New England have a rich, sweet taste, like a blend of oysters and clams. At one time held in low esteem, blue mussels both grow wild on rocks and pilings and are farmed. Maine is the largest U.S. producer. Mussels are farmed on ropes or in mesh tubes suspended from rafts. Farmed mussels have thin, dark shells, while wild mussels have thicker, silvery shells. Mussels have beards, or byssus threads, which they use to anchor themselves to a growing medium. The beard should be removed prior to cooking. Bags or containers of mussels should display the license number of the shipper to assure they have been purchased from certified growers who harvest in approved, clean areas.

New England Boiled Dinner This traditional meal is similar to many one-pot meals. Meat, fresh or cured, is simmered for hours, and then vegetables are added. The meat flavors the vegetables, and they both flavor the broth. The New England boiled dinner uses gray or salt-cured brisket of beef as well as parsnips and beets. A regular corned brisket is a good substitution.

Oyster A bivalve mollusk found in shallow coastal areas. The native East Coast oysters are named according to the bay or town they are associated with—Pemaquids, Wellfleets, and Sheepscotts are a few. The large Belon oyster, also called the "European flat," was brought to America from France and thrives in New England waters. Oysters in New England are enjoyed on the half shell, smoked, in turkey stuffing for Thanksgiving, and in casseroles.

Periwinkle Small, black or gray snaillike marine mollusk found attached to rocks and seawalls in New England coastal waters. Periwinkles usually are cooked in salted boiling water for 5 to 10 minutes, or until the black cap, used as a lid by the mollusk, can be lifted and removed easily. Periwinkles are extracted with a needle or a sharp toothpick, and served with lemon or garlic butter.

Popover An American variation on English Yorkshire pudding, popovers are a type of muffin or bread made by pouring a batter of eggs, milk, and flour into butter that has been heated in a muffin pan. They puff up when baked and form a crisp crust and moist center.

Pumpkin A winter squash introduced to the colonists from the Native Americans. This long-keeping squash is one of the foods that helped the colonists survive their first winter in the New World.

Red Flannel Hash The leftovers from a New England boiled dinner are chopped and mixed with beets to make a fried mush for the next morning's breakfast. The hash is cooked slowly to form a crusty bottom and served with a poached egg on top.

Scallops A family of bivalves with fan-shaped shells. The adductor muscle, which allows scallops to "swim" by clicking their shells together, is eaten. This mobility helps scallops escape pollutants that immobile bivalves like mussels, clams, and oysters can't avoid. There are three types of scallops in this region. They are:

Bay Scallops Small scallops that average 70 to 100 per pound. Mild and sweet, bay scallops are considered the best-tasting of the scallops.

Cape Scallops Found around Nantucket Island during the winter months, cape scallops are noted for their sweet flavor and are best served raw.

Sea Scallops Large scallops that range from 20 to 40 per pound. Since sea scallops die out of water, they are always shucked at sea and kept on ice. New Bedford, Massachusetts, is the largest sea scallop port in the country. Sea scallops are farmed in New England, but production is limited. Sea scallops have a sweet, rich taste that ranges from mild to briny. Always remove the little moon-shaped strap that held the muscle to the shell.

Sea Urchin A green, saltwater animal that looks like a spiny pincushion. It is abundant along the New England coast; the center, soft part that is eaten is referred to as "urchin roe." To serve, cut around the mouth, or bottom, of the urchin using wire cutters or scissors. Rinse gently and remove the viscera that surround the creamy golden roe attached to the top of the urchin. Invert, place on crushed ice, and serve with toast and lemon or lime wedges. The roe can also be used to flavor and garnish sauces.

Shrimp Maine shrimp are relatives of the northern European prawn. They are small, about 50 to 60 count per pound, and sweet. They are available only from November to March.

Turkey A large fowl indigenous to the New World. The conquistadors took them to Europe; from there, they were introduced in other parts of the world. Today's domesticated turkeys differ from wild turkeys, with the exceptionally large breasts that breeding produces.

Vermont Cheddar Cheese A firm yellow or orange cheese made from cow's milk. One of the most difficult and most expensive cheeses to make, owing to the need for consistent milk quality and the process of cheddaring, whereby curds are stacked to force out the whey. True Cheddar cheese is made only in the summer months from the milk of one herd, from one specific farm. Other Cheddar cheese is called "factory Cheddar." It ranges from mild to extra sharp.

Menus and Recipes from the Cuisine of New England

MENU ONE

New England Clam Chowder

Marinated Tomato and Zucchini Salad

New England Boiled Dinner with Horseradish Sauce

Peach and Blueberry Cobbler

MENU TWO

Clams Casino

Cod Cakes with Tartar Sauce

Roasted Turkey Roulade with Giblet Gravy and Cranberry Sauce

New England Bread Stuffing

Glazed Turnips

Mashed Sweet Potatoes

Green Beans with Fried Onions

Gingerbread

MENU THREE

Butternut Squash Soup

Boston Baked Beans

Boston Brown Bread

Mesclun Salad with Cranberries and Apples

Bluefish with Clams and Fresh Corn Cakes

Cole Slaw

OTHER RECIPES

Johnnycakes

Popovers

Baked Boston Scrod

Summer Squash Noodles

New England Clam Chowder   4 SERVINGS

AMOUNT	MEASURE	INGREDIENT
10 or		Cherrystone clams, washed
2 cups	16 ounces, 470 ml	Shucked clams, chopped
2 cups or	16 ounces, 470 ml	Water
1 1/2 cups	12 ounces, 325 ml	Clam juice
1/4 cup	2 ounces, 56 g	Salt pork, minced to a paste
1/2 cup	2 ounces, 56 g	Onion, 1/4 inch (.6 cm) dice
1/2 cup	2 ounces, 56 g	Celery, 1/4 inch (.6 cm) dice
1 1/2 teaspoons	1.5 g	Thyme, chopped
1 tablespoon	1/3 ounce, 10 g	All-purpose flour
2 cups	16 ounces, 470 ml	Milk, scalded
4 cups	16 ounces, 453 g	All-purpose potatoes, peeled, 1/4 inch (.6 cm) dice
1/2 cup	4 ounces, 117 ml	Heavy cream
2 tablespoons	16 g	Parsley, chopped
1/2 teaspoon or to taste	2 ml	Tabasco
1/2 teaspoon or to taste	2 ml	Worcestershire sauce
to taste		Salt and white pepper

PROCEDURE

1 Steam the whole clams in a covered pan using the 2 cups (16 ounces, 470 ml) water until they open.

2 Strain the broth through a filter or cheesecloth and reserve.

3 Remove from the shell, chop, and reserve clams.

4 Render the salt pork slowly.

5 Add the onion and celery and cook slowly until translucent. Add the thyme; cook 1 minute.

6 Stir in the flour and cook to make a blond roux.

7 Add reserved broth or clam juice and milk gradually, and incorporate to a smooth consistency. Bring to a simmer and simmer for 25 to 30 minutes.

8 Add the potatoes and cook until tender.

9 Add reserved clams and the cream; bring to a simmer.

10 Add remaining ingredients and correct seasoning.

Marinated Tomato and Zucchini Salad 4 SERVINGS

AMOUNT	MEASURE	INGREDIENT
For the Dressing		
1 tablespoon	10 g	Shallot, minced
1 teaspoon	5 ml	Dijon mustard
2 tablespoons	6 g	Basil leaves, chopped
1/4 cup	2 ounces, 56 ml	Extra-virgin olive oil
2 tablespoons	1 ounce, 28 ml	Vegetable oil
2 tablespoons	1 ounce, 28 ml	Red wine vinegar
to taste		Salt and black pepper
For the Salad		
2 cups	16 ounces, 453 g	Plum tomatoes, peeled, seeded, cut into wedges
2 cups	8 ounces, 226 g	Zucchini, julienned
1/2 cup	1 1/2 ounces, 42 g	Red onion, very thinly sliced
1 cup	2 ounces, 56 g	Romaine leaves, chopped
2 tablespoons	20 g	Parmesan cheese, freshly grated

PROCEDURE

1 Combine the shallots, mustard, basil, and olive oil; mix well.

2 Add vegetable oil, vinegar, and salt and pepper; stir well and allow to rest 1 hour for the flavors to combine.

3 Marinate the tomatoes, zucchini, and red onion in three-quarters of the dressing for 1 hour.

4 Toss romaine with the remaining dressing, then divide among 4 plates.

5 Arrange the vegetables on romaine and sprinkle with the Parmesan cheese.

New England Boiled Dinner 4 SERVINGS

AMOUNT	MEASURE	INGREDIENT
2 pounds	907 g	Corned beef brisket, trimmed
1 tablespoon	3 g	Pickling spices
2		Garlic cloves, peeled
12 ounces	340 g	Turnips, pared, shaped, 2 per serving
8		Pearl white onions, peeled
8		Red Bliss potatoes, peeled, cut in half if large
12 ounces	340 g	Carrots, pared and shaped, 2 per serving
20 ounces	567 g	Green cabbage, cut into 4 wedges
1 tablespoon	3 g	Parsley, chopped
		Cheesecloth

PROCEDURE

1. Place the corned beef in a large pot with enough cold water to cover it by 1 inch (2.5 cm); add the pickling spices tied in cheesecloth and the garlic, and bring to a boil.

2. Lower the heat and cover; simmer very gently 2 to 3 hours or until the meat is fork-tender.

3. About 30 minutes before the meat is done, add the turnips, onions, potatoes, and carrots. Continue simmering until the vegetables are tender, 25 to 30 minutes. Remove the corned beef and wrap it in foil (along with any tender vegetables) to keep warm. Remove the pickling spices and discard.

4. Add the cabbage and cook until tender.

5. Drain the vegetables and reserve the liquid.

6. Slice the corned beef against the grain into $1/4$-inch (.6 cm) slices.

7. Serve the corned beef with hot vegetables and cooking liquid.

8. Garnish with parsley.

9. Serve each portion with Horseradish Sauce (page 16).

Horseradish Sauce, Version I   4 SERVINGS

AMOUNT	MEASURE	INGREDIENT
2 tablespoons	1 ounce, 28 g	Prepared horseradish
1 cup	8 ounces, 235 ml	Sour cream
1 tablespoon	1/2 ounce, 15 ml	Lemon juice
Dash	Dash	Tabasco
1 teaspoon	5 g	Salt

PROCEDURE

Combine ingredients, mix until smooth, and chill.

Horseradish Sauce, Version II   4 SERVINGS

AMOUNT	MEASURE	INGREDIENT
2 tablespoons	1 ounce, 28 g	Prepared horseradish
1/4 cup	2 ounces, 55 ml	Dijon mustard
2 teaspoons	10 ml	Lemon juice
1/2 cup	4 ounces, 115 ml	Whipping cream

PROCEDURE

1   Combine the horseradish, mustard, and lemon juice.

2   Beat cream until soft peaks form. Fold in horseradish mixture. Cover and chill 1 hour.

Peach and Blueberry Cobbler 4 SERVINGS

AMOUNT	MEASURE	INGREDIENT
1 1/2 cups	9 ounces, 255 g	Peaches, sliced
1 cup	5 ounces, 141 g	Blueberries, picked over, washed
1 tablespoon	9 g	Granulated sugar

For the Shortcake

AMOUNT	MEASURE	INGREDIENT
1 cup	4 ounces, 112 g	All-purpose flour, sifted
2 tablespoons	18 g	Granulated sugar
2 teaspoons	8 g	Baking powder
1/4 teaspoon	2 g	Salt
4 tablespoons	2 ounces, 56 g	Unsalted butter
1		Egg, beaten
2 tablespoons	1 ounce, 28 ml	Milk

PROCEDURE

1 Preheat the oven to 350°F (175°C).

2 Toss the peaches and blueberries with sugar to coat evenly.

3 Place the fruit in a baking dish.

4 Sift together the flour, sugar, baking powder, and salt.

5 Cut the butter into small pieces about the size of a hazelnut, and add to the flour mixture. Mix gently.

6 Whisk the egg and milk together.

7 Add to the flour mixture and mix just until dough sticks together; knead gently.

8 Divide into 8 small or 4 large biscuits and cover the top of the fruit.

9 Bake for 25 to 30 minutes, or until the fruit is tender and the shortcake is lightly browned.

10 Allow the cobbler to cool slightly before serving.

11 Serve warm with cream, whipped cream, or ice cream.

Clams Casino 4 SERVINGS

AMOUNT	MEASURE	INGREDIENT
¹/₄ cup	2 ounces, 56 g	Bacon, ¹/₄ inch (.6 cm) dice
2 tablespoons	1 ounce, 28 g	Shallots, minced
1 tablespoon	12 to 15 g	Garlic, minced
¹/₄ cup	1 ounce, 28 g	Red bell pepper, ¹/₄ inch (.6 cm) dice
¹/₄ cup	1 ounce, 28 g	Green bell pepper, ¹/₄ inch (.6 cm) dice
1 teaspoon	1 g	Flat-leaf parsley, minced
1 teaspoon	5 ml	Lemon juice
¹/₂ cup	4 ounces, 113 g	Unsalted butter, melted
1 cup	4 ounces, 113 g	Bread crumbs, dry
to taste		Salt and black pepper
24		Littleneck or Cherrystone clams
as needed		Rock salt
2		Lemons, cut in half, wrapped in cheesecloth

PROCEDURE

1   Preheat the oven to 400°F (205°C).

2   Cook the bacon over medium heat until fat is completely rendered and bacon is crisp.

3   Add the shallots, garlic, and peppers to the bacon and sauté over medium heat for approximately 2 to 3 minutes or until peppers are tender.

4   Add the parsley, lemon juice, butter, and bread crumbs; combine well and season to taste.

5   Cool the bread-crumb mixture, set aside.

6   Open the clams with a clam knife and discard the top half of the shell. Loosen the meat from the lower shell with the clam knife. Leave the clams in the shell. (Alternatively, steam the clams for about 5 minutes until their shells just begin to open. Set aside to cool. When cool enough to handle, remove the top shells and discard. Slide a knife under each clam to loosen it in the shell.)

7   Place the clams on a baking sheet and top each clam with 1 tablespoon (¹/₂ ounce, 15 ml) of the bread-crumb mixture.

8   Bake the clams until they are thoroughly cooked and the bread-crumb mixture is crisp, approximately 5 to 8 minutes.

9 To serve, place 6 clams on each warmed plate atop some rock salt to anchor it in place.

10 Garnish each portion with lemon half wrapped in cheesecloth.

Clams Casino

Cod Cakes 4 SERVINGS

AMOUNT	MEASURE	INGREDIENT
8 ounces	226 g	Codfish fillets
2 cups	12 ounces, 340 g	All-purpose potatoes, peeled, cooked, mashed
1 teaspoon	1 g	Parsley, minced
1 teaspoon	1 g	Chives, minced
Pinch	Pinch	Mace
1		Egg
1 tablespoon	$^1/_2$ ounce, 14 g	Unsalted butter, softened
2 tablespoons	1 ounce, 28 ml	Heavy cream
to taste		Salt and white pepper
$^1/_2$ cup	2 ounces, 56 g	Bread crumbs, dry
$^1/_4$ cup	2 ounces, 56 g	Butter, clarified
1 teaspoon	1 g	Parsley, minced, for garnish

PROCEDURE

1 Poach the codfish until just cooked; drain and cool. Chop into $^1/_2$-inch (1.2 cm) pieces.

2 Add the mashed potatoes, parsley, chives, mace, and white pepper and mix well.

3 Add the egg and mix again.

4 Form into 8 patties about $^3/_4$ inch (1.9 cm) thick.

5 Dip both sides of each patty into bread crumbs to coat.

6 Heat butter and fry patties about 4 minutes on each side, until brown and crisp.

7 Drain on paper towels, garnish with parsley, and serve with Tartar Sauce (page 22).

For Codfish Balls Prepare the same recipe but roll mixture into 1-inch (2.54 cm) balls. Fry in hot oil and serve as hors d'oeuvre.

Cod Cakes

Tartar Sauce 4 SERVINGS

AMOUNT	MEASURE	INGREDIENT
1/2 cup	4 ounces, 113 g	Mayonnaise
2 tablespoons	1 ounce, 28 g	Dill pickles, finely diced
2 tablespoons	1 ounce, 28 g	Capers, finely diced
1		Egg, hard-boiled, chopped
1 tablespoon	1/2 fl ounce, 15 ml	Lemon juice
to taste		Salt and black pepper
Dash		Worcestershire sauce
Dash		Tabasco

PROCEDURE

1   Mix the mayonnaise, dill pickles, capers, hard-boiled egg, and lemon juice in a bowl.

2   Blend until all ingredients are thoroughly incorporated.

3   Season to taste with salt, pepper, Worcestershire sauce, and Tabasco.

4   Chill mixture thoroughly before serving.

Roasted Turkey Roulade 4-8 SERVINGS

AMOUNT	MEASURE	INGREDIENT
1	47 ounces, 1.33 kg	Turkey breast, bone in, skin on

For the Filling

AMOUNT	MEASURE	INGREDIENT
1¼ cups	6 ounces 170 g	Turkey leg meat, trimmed, cubed
1		Egg white
to taste		Salt and white pepper
1 teaspoon	1 g	Thyme, chopped
1 teaspoon	1 g	Parsley, chopped

To Roast

AMOUNT	MEASURE	INGREDIENT
1 cup	4 ounces, 113 g	Onion, peeled, roughly chopped
½ cup	2 ounces, 56 g	Celery, roughly chopped
⅓ cup	2 ounces, 56 g	Carrot, peeled, roughly chopped
2 cups	16 ounces, 470 ml	Chicken stock
to taste		Salt and black pepper

PROCEDURE

1 Remove the skin from the turkey breast, being careful to keep the skin in one piece.

2 Lay out the skin in a rectangle on a covered sheet pan and put in the refrigerator to chill.

3 Bone the turkey breast and reserve the bones.

4 Butterfly the turkey breast into a rectangle and place between 2 pieces of parchment paper or plastic film; tap the breast gently with a mallet until it is approximately ¼ inch (.6 cm) thick, then season and set aside to chill.

5 Place the leg meat and any breast meat trimmings in a chilled food processor bowl.

6 Add the egg white and chop until smooth.

7 Add the seasoning and herbs, and combine well. Cook a small portion to taste for seasoning and adjust if necessary.

8 Preheat the oven to 450°F (232°C).

9 Lay the turkey breast meat onto the turkey skin.

10   Top the breast meat with the chopped leg meat; leave a $^1/_2$-inch (1.2 cm) margin on all sides.

11   Roll up the turkey breast to form a tight roll. Truss the roll as you would a roast. Season to taste.

12   Place the reserved turkey bones and the chopped vegetables in a roasting pan.

13   Place the turkey roll on top and roast for 15 minutes to sear the meat. Turn the oven down to 350° (176°C), add the chicken stock to the pan, and roast until the turkey reaches an internal temperature of 165°F (74°C).

14   Remove the roast from the oven. Place the turkey on a platter and keep warm. Strain the pan juices and use to make Giblet Gravy (page 24).

Giblet Gravy   4 SERVINGS

AMOUNT	MEASURE	INGREDIENT
2 tablespoons	1 ounce, 28 g	Butter, melted
$^1/_4$ cup	1 ounce, 28 g	All-purpose flour
to taste		Salt and white pepper
1 tablespoon	$^1/_2$ ounce	Turkey giblets
		Turkey neck and wing tips
$1^1/_4$ cups	10 ounces, 290 ml	Turkey or chicken stock

PROCEDURE

1   While the turkey is roasting, simmer the turkey giblets, neck, and wing tips in stock for 2 hours. Remove giblets and dice. Strain stock.

2   Melt the butter in a saucepan, add the flour, and make a pale roux.

3   Add the stock and bring to a simmer. Whisk vigorously until smooth, then simmer on low heat for 30 minutes. Season with salt and pepper.

4   Add diced giblets as garnish.

New England Bread Stuffing 4 SERVINGS

AMOUNT	MEASURE	INGREDIENT
1/4 cup	2 ounces, 56 g	Butter
1 cup	4 ounces, 113 g	Onion, 1/4 inch (.6 cm) dice
1/2 cup	2 ounces, 56 g	Celery, 1/4 inch (.6 cm) dice
1/2 cup	3 ounces, 85 g	Ham, cooked 1/4 inch (.6 cm) dice
1/2 cup	3 ounces, 85 g	Chicken meat, cooked, 1/4 inch (.6 cm) dice
1/4 cup	2 ounces, 56 g	Sage sausage, cooked, chopped
3 cups	3 ounces, 85 g	Bread (day-old), 1-inch (2.5 cm) cubes
2		Eggs
1/2 teaspoon	1/2 g	Sage, crumbled
1/8 teaspoon	1/8 g	White pepper
1/8 teaspoon	1/8 g	Thyme (dried)
1/8 teaspoon	1/8 g	Mace
1/8 teaspoon	1/8 g	Marjoram (dried)
1/2 teaspoon	4 g	Salt
1/4 cup	2 ounces, 55 ml	Chicken stock

PROCEDURE

1   Heat the butter and sauté the onion and celery until very soft.

2   Add the ham, chicken meat, and sausage; cook 5 minutes, stirring occasionally.

3   Mix with the bread cubes and cool.

4   Beat the eggs with the spices, salt, and stock.

5   Combine with the bread and meat; mix well. Add more stock if necessary.

6   Bake in 375°F (190°C) oven, uncovered, until top is brown and dressing reaches 165°F (74°C) internal temperature.

Cranberry Sauce 4 SERVINGS

AMOUNT	MEASURE	INGREDIENT
¹/₂ cup	3¹/₂ ounces, 100 g	Granulated sugar
2 tablespoons	1 ounce, 28 ml	Orange juice
¹/₄ cup	2 ounces, 55 ml	Water
3 cups	8 ounces, 226 g	Cranberries, fresh or frozen
Pinch		Cinnamon

PROCEDURE

1   Combine the sugar, orange juice, and water in a pan and bring to a boil.

2   Add the cranberries and cinnamon. Simmer until cranberries burst, approximately 15 minutes. Simmer for 5 more minutes or until reduced to desired consistency.

3   Remove from heat, cool, and refrigerate.

chef tip   **White cranberries are the same variety as the familiar red ones except that they are harvested about 3 weeks earlier, before they become crimson. Some say the white berries are smoother and milder in taste than the red berries.**

Glazed Turnips 4 SERVINGS

AMOUNT	MEASURE	INGREDIENT
3 cups	12 ounces, 340 g	Turnips, peeled, 1 inch (2.5 cm) dice
$^1/_2$ cup	4 ounces, 115 ml	Chicken stock
2 tablespoons	1 ounce, 28 ml	Unsalted butter
2 tablespoons	1 ounce, 28 ml	Maple syrup
to taste		Salt and white pepper

PROCEDURE

1 Combine the turnips with the chicken stock, butter, and maple syrup.

2 Bring to a simmer and cover the pan. Stir occasionally. Simmer until the liquid has evaporated; do not overcook turnips. If turnips cook before liquid has reduced, remove and continue to reduce the liquid to a glaze, then return turnips and toss to coat.

3 Season with salt and white pepper.

Mashed Sweet Potatoes 4 SERVINGS

AMOUNT	MEASURE	INGREDIENT
5 cups	20 ounces, 567 g	Sweet potatoes, peeled, quartered
$^1/_2$ teaspoon	4 g	Salt
6 tablespoons	3 ounces, 84 ml	Heavy cream, hot
$^1/_4$ cup	2 ounces, 56 g	Butter, softened

PROCEDURE

1 Cover the sweet potatoes with water and season with salt. Bring to a boil, reduce the heat and simmer until fork-tender, approximately 25 minutes.

2 Drain sweet potatoes and let the steam escape. Put them through a food mill.

3 Add cream and butter. Mix and correct seasoning.

Green Beans with Fried Onions 4 SERVINGS

AMOUNT	MEASURE	INGREDIENT
2 cups	8 ounces, 226 g	Green beans, washed, trimmed
1/2 cup	2 ounces, 56 g	Onions, thinly sliced
1/2 cup	2 ounces, 56 g	All-purpose flour
to taste		Salt and black pepper
2 cups	16 ounces, 450 ml	Corn oil
2 tablespoons	1 ounce, 28 g	Unsalted butter
1 cup	2 1/2 ounces, 70 g	White mushrooms, sliced

PROCEDURE

1 Cook the green beans in boiling salted water until tender. Shock the green beans in an ice-water bath and reserve.

2 Soak the onions in ice water for 1 hour.

3 Heat the oil in a deep-fryer to 375°F (190°C).

4 Drain and dry the onion thoroughly.

5 Combine the flour and salt and pepper. Toss the onion in the seasoned flour until coated. Shake off the excess flour.

6 Deep-fry the onion until golden brown and crisp.

7 Melt the butter and sauté the mushrooms over medium-high heat until tender.

8 Add the reserved beans to the mushrooms and heat thoroughly.

9 Top beans with the fried onions just before serving.

Gingerbread 4 SERVINGS

AMOUNT	MEASURE	INGREDIENT
1/2 cup	4 ounces, 113 g	Butter
1/2 cup packed	4 ounces, 113 g	Brown sugar
1 cup	11 1/2 ounces, 235 ml	Molasses
1		Egg
1 1/2 cups	11 ounces, 311 g	All-purpose flour
1 teaspoon	2 g	Ground ginger
1/2 teaspoon	1 g	Ground cinnamon
1/4 teaspoon	1/2 g	Ground cloves
1/2 teaspoon	2 g	Salt
1 teaspoon	4 g	Baking soda
1 cup	8 ounces, 235 ml	Hot water
1 cup	8 ounces, 235 ml	Heavy cream, whipped

PROCEDURE

1 Preheat the oven to 350°F (175°C).

2 Grease and flour an 8-inch (20.3 cm) square baking pan.

3 Cream the butter and brown sugar until light and fluffy.

4 Beat in the molasses and egg.

5 Sift the flour and spices together and then sift over the mixture, blend until smooth.

6 Dissolve the baking soda in hot water, then add gradually stirring into batter; the mixture will be thin.

7 Pour batter into baking pan and bake for 40 to 45 minutes, or until a toothpick inserted in center comes out clean and the cake is light and springy.

8 Serve warm with whipped cream.

Butternut Squash Soup 4 SERVINGS

chef tip

Cooking the leeks, squash, and apples until they caramelize gives the soup its depth of flavor.

AMOUNT	MEASURE	INGREDIENT
2 tablespoons	1 ounce, 28 g	Unsalted butter
1 cup	3 ounces, 85 g	Leeks, white and pale green parts only, sliced thin
1 teaspoon	4 g	Garlic, minced
3 cups	18 ounces, 510 g	Butternut squash, peeled, seeded, $^1/_4$ inch (.6 cm) dice
1 cup	6 ounces, 170 g	McIntosh or Gala apples, peeled, seeded, $^1/_4$ inch (.6 cm) dice
1 teaspoon	2 g	Curry powder
pinch		Nutmeg
3 cups	24 ounces, .71 l	Chicken or vegetable stock
$^1/_2$ cup	4 ounces, 115 ml	Heavy cream, hot
to taste		Salt and white pepper
1		McIntosh or Gala apple, peeled and cored
1 tablespoon	$^1/_2$ ounce, 14 ml	Lime or lemon juice
2 tablespoons	6 g	Chives, chopped

PROCEDURE

1. Melt the butter over moderate heat until it turns nut brown; reduce heat to low.
2. Add leeks; cook until slightly softened, about 5 minutes.
3. Add garlic; cook 30 seconds.
4. Turn up heat to high.
5. Add squash and apples; cook, stirring, until the vegetables begin to caramelize.
6. Stir in curry powder and nutmeg; cook 1 minute.
7. Add stock and bring to a boil. Reduce heat; simmer 30 minutes or until squash is tender.
8. Purée the soup through a food mill or blender (the soup should have a coarse texture).
9. Bring the soup back to a simmer; add hot cream and correct seasoning (salt and white pepper).

10   To serve, coarsely grate the apple into a small bowl. Toss with lime fuice. Ladle the soup into bowls; place a small mound of apples in the center of each serving.

11   Sprinkle with chives

Boston Baked Beans 4 SERVINGS

chef tip

The Indians of New England slow-cooked beans in underground pits inside deer hides, with maple sugar and bear fat. The Puritans' belief in minimal work on the Sabbath led to the widespread practice of making beans on Saturday, to be eaten on Sunday.

AMOUNT	MEASURE	INGREDIENT
I cup	8 ounces, 226 g	Navy beans, pea beans, or other small white beans, dry
3/4 cup	4 ounces, 113 g	Salt pork, rind removed
I cup	4 ounces, 113 g	Onion, 1/2 inch (1.2 cm) dice
2		Garlic cloves, minced
1/2 cup	3 ounces, 85 g	Tomato, peeled, seeded, diced
1/2 teaspoon	3 g	Salt
I teaspoon	2 g	Black pepper
2 tablespoons	1/2 ounce, 14 g	Dry mustard
1/4 cup	2 ounces, 55 ml	Molasses
1/4 cup	2 ounces, 56 g	Brown sugar
I		Bay leaf
1 1/2 tablespoons	21 ml	Cider vinegar

PROCEDURE

1   Rinse the beans, pick over to remove any small stones, and cover with cold water. Let stand overnight. Drain.

2   Add half of the salt pork to the beans, add water to cover; cover and simmer till beans are tender, about 1 hour.

3   Drain, reserving 2 cups (16 ounces, 470 ml) of the liquid, adding more water if necessary.

4   Dice the salt pork. Set the beans aside.

5   Preheat the oven to 300°F (149°C).

6   Place cooking liquid in large saucepan with the garlic, tomato, salt and pepper, mustard, molasses, brown sugar, bay leaf, and vinegar. Simmer 2 minutes.

7   Cut remaining salt pork into thin slices and score crosswise so they will not curl during cooking.

8   Line the bottom of a 2-quart (64 ounces, 2 l) bean pot or casserole with the diced salt pork and the onion. Place the drained beans on top.

9   Pour the simmered mixture over. Top with the sliced salt pork.

10   Cover and bake for 3 hours, checking occasionally to be sure the liquid is just barely covering the beans. After 2 hours, remove the cover and cook for 1 hour more. Remove the strips of salt pork and stir the pot before serving.

Note: **By precooking the beans, you should save 2 to 3 hours of cooking time. Traditionally, step 2 is not included.**

Boston Brown Bread 4 SERVINGS

AMOUNT	MEASURE	INGREDIENT
I tablespoon	$^1/_2$ ounce, 14 g	Unsalted butter, for greasing the mold
$^1/_2$ cup	$2^1/_2$ ounces, 70 g	Bread flour
$^1/_2$ cup	$2^1/_4$ ounces, 63 g	Whole wheat flour
$^1/_2$ cup	3 ounces, 83 g	Cornmeal
I teaspoon	4 g	Baking soda
$^1/_2$ teaspoon	3 g	Salt
$^1/_3$ cup	3 ounces, 85 ml	Molasses
$^1/_2$ cup	4 ounces, 115 ml	Buttermilk
$^1/_2$ cup, loose	$2^1/_2$ ounces, 70 g	Raisins

PROCEDURE

1 Preheat the oven to 350°F (175°C).

2 Butter a 1-quart (32 ounces, 1 l) pudding mold or a 1-pound (453 g) coffee can.

3 Combine the flours, cornmeal, baking soda, and salt.

4 Stir in the molasses and buttermilk. Fold in the raisins.

5 Fill the mold or coffee can with batter. It should come up about two-thirds of the way. Cover the top with foil and tie securely with a string to make it airtight.

6 Place the mold or coffee can in a deep pan and fill the pan with boiling water to come halfway up the side of the mold.

7 Place in oven and steam for 2 hours, checking the water level after 1 hour. Add more water if needed.

8 Check for doneness by sticking a skewer into the bread; it will come out clean when done.

9 Remove string and foil and allow bread to cool for 1 hour before unmolding.

10 Serve warm.

Mesclun Salad with Cranberries and Apples 4 SERVINGS

AMOUNT	MEASURE	INGREDIENT
For the cider vinaigrette		
2 tablespoons	1 ounce, 30 g	Shallot, minced
2 teaspoons	1/3 ounce, 10 g	Dijon mustard
1/4 cup	2 ounces, 55 ml	Apple cider
3 tablespoons	1 1/2 ounces, 42 ml	Cider vinegar
1/4 cup	2 ounces, 55 ml	Vegetable oil
to taste		Salt and black pepper
For the salad		
1 teaspoon	1/4 ounce, 7 g	Dried cranberries
1/4 cup	1 ounce, 28 g	Carrot, finely julienned
1/2 cup	2 ounces, 56 g	Granny Smith apple, finely julienned
2 cups	4 ounces, 113 g	Mesclun (baby field greens), cleaned
1/4 cup	1 ounce, 28 g	Almonds, sliced or slivered, toasted

PROCEDURE

1 Combine all the ingredients for the Cider Vinaigrette, whisking together. Correct the seasoning.

2 Marinate the cranberries, carrots, and apples in the cider vinaigrette for at least 15 minutes.

3 When ready to serve, add the mesclun and toss.

4 Garnish with the toasted almonds.

Mesclun Salad with Cranberries and Apples

Bluefish with Clams　4 SERVINGS

chef tip

Bluefish has a strong and distinctively rich taste, and it takes well to strong flavors. Small mackerel can be substituted for bluefish.

AMOUNT	MEASURE	INGREDIENT
4	4–6 ounces, 113–170 g each	Bluefish fillets, skin on
2 tablespoons	1 ounce, 28 ml	Vegetable oil
to taste		Salt and black pepper
3 tablespoons	1 1/2 ounces, 42 ml	Olive oil
2		Bay leaves
6		Garlic cloves, finely minced
1 cup	6 ounces, 170 g	Onion, 1/4 inch (.6 cm) dice
1/4 cup	2 ounces, 55 ml	Dry white wine
1/4 cup	2 ounces, 55 ml	Fish stock or water
24		Littleneck clams, scrubbed
1 teaspoon	5 g	Rosemary, chopped
1 teaspoon	1 g	Basil, chopped
1/4 cup	1 ounce, 28 g	Flat-leaf parsley
6 tablespoons	3 ounces, 84 g	Unsalted butter

PROCEDURE

1　Preheat the broiler or oven to 400°F (205°C).

2　Trim the bluefish and remove any scales or bones.

3　Rub the fish fillets with oil and season with salt and pepper.

4　Cook the bluefish in broiler or oven until just done, 5 to 7 minutes.

5　Heat the olive oil in a medium saucepan over medium heat and add bay leaves. When the bay leaves begin to brown, add the garlic and onion.

6　Cook until the onion is lightly browned.

7　Turn heat to high and add the wine and stock.

8　When the sauce begins to boil, add the clams and cover the saucepan.

9   When the clams open, remove them from the sauce. Remove the bay leaves and add the rosemary, basil, and parsley. Swirl in the butter and season with more pepper. (The clams provide enough salt.)

10   To serve, place one fillet on each plate, place 6 clams around the fillet, and spoon sauce over both.

Cole Slaw 4 SERVINGS

AMOUNT	MEASURE	INGREDIENT
1 1/2 pounds	680 g	Green cabbage
1/2 cup	2 ounces, 56 g	Red onion, grated
1/2 cup	2 ounces, 56 g	Carrot, grated
2 tablespoons	6 g	Parsley, chopped
1 1/2 teaspoons	3 g	Dry mustard
1 1/2 tablespoons	3/4 ounce, 22 g	Mayonnaise
1/4 cup	2 ounces, 55 ml	Cider vinegar
1/4 cup	2 ounces, 55 ml	Vegetable oil
1 tablespoon	1/2 ounce, 15 g	Sugar
to taste		Salt and black pepper

PROCEDURE

1   Remove the core from the cabbage. Soak the cabbage in cold water for 1 hour in refrigerator to mellow the flavor.

2   Drain the cabbage well and shred very fine.

3   Combine the cabbage, onion, carrot, and parsley in a bowl.

4   Combine the mustard, mayonnaise, vinegar, oil, and sugar in another, larger bowl. Add the vegetables and mix well.

5   Season to taste with salt and pepper. Mix and chill.

6   Check seasoning before serving.

Fresh Corn Cakes 4 SERVINGS

AMOUNT	MEASURE	INGREDIENT
3 ears		Corn on the cob, shucked
1/4 cup	1 ounce, 28 g	Onion, 1/4 inch (.6 cm) dice
1 1/2 tablespoon	3/4 ounce, 20 g	Unsalted butter
1/4 cup	1 ounce, 28 g	Red bell pepper, 1/4 inch (.6 cm) dice
1/4 cup	1 ounce, 28 g	Green bell pepper, 1/4 inch (.6 cm) dice
2		Eggs
1/2 cup	4 ounces, 115 ml	Milk
1/3 cup	2 ounces, 56 g	Yellow cornmeal
3/4 cup	3 ounces, 85 g	All-purpose flour
1/2 teaspoon	3 g	Salt
1/2 teaspoon	2 g	Black pepper
1 tablespoon	3 g	Chives, chopped
as needed		Vegetable oil, for frying

PROCEDURE

1 Remove the kernels from cobs (yield: 1 1/2 cups or 8 ounces, 352 ml). Scrape down the cobs to extract the sweet milk from the corn.

2 Combine the corn, corn milk, and onion and make a coarse puree. (Pass the mixture through the medium blade of a grinder, use a food processor, or chop by hand.)

3 Heat the butter and sauté peppers for 2 minutes. Add the butter and peppers to the corn batter.

4 In a separate bowl, mix the eggs and milk. Add the cornmeal, flour, salt and pepper; mix until smooth.

5 Stir cornmeal mixture into the corn batter. Add the pepper and chives.

6 Heat a nonstick or well-seasoned pan over medium heat until very hot; this takes up to 5 minutes. Lightly grease the pan and make the pancakes. Serve warm.

Johnnycakes 4 SERVINGS

AMOUNT	MEASURE	INGREDIENT
I cup	6 ounces, 170 g	Cornmeal
$^1/_4$ cup	$1^3/_4$ ounces, 49 g	Granulated sugar
$^1/_2$ teaspoon	2 g	Baking soda
I teaspoon	4 g	Cream of tartar
$^1/_4$ teaspoon	2 g	Salt
I cup	8 ounces, 235 ml	Buttermilk
I		Egg, beaten
I tablespoon	$^1/_8$ ounce, 10 g	Molasses
I tablespoon	$^1/_2$ ounce, 14 g	Butter, melted

PROCEDURE

1   Preheat the oven to 350°F (175°C). Butter a 9-inch (22.5 cm) pie pan.

2   Sift together the dry ingredients into a mixing bowl.

3   Add the buttermilk, beaten egg, molasses, and melted butter and mix until smooth.

4   Pour the mixture into the pie pan and bake for 30 minutes or until cooked.

5   Slightly cool, unmold, and cut into wedges.

Popovers   4 SERVINGS

AMOUNT	MEASURE	INGREDIENT
I cup plus I tablespoon	8 ounces, 226 g	All-purpose flour
I teaspoon	5 g	Salt
2¹/₂ cups	20 ounces, 587 ml	Milk
2		Eggs
as needed		Vegetable oil

PROCEDURE

1   Preheat the oven to 450°F (225°C).

2   Place the flour and salt in a bowl. Gradually add the milk, and mix until a smooth batter is formed.

3   Add the eggs, one at a time. Mix until the batter is frothy, about 5 minutes.

4   Brush a medium muffin pan with oil and place in oven for 5 minutes or until very hot.

5   Remove the pan and fill each compartment three-fourths full with batter.

6   Place back in the hot oven and bake for approximately 15 minutes.

7   Reduce the heat to 350°F (175°C) and bake for an additional 15 to 20 minutes, until the popovers are browned and crisp on the outside.

8   Remove the popovers from the pan and serve immediately.

Baked Boston Scrod · 4 SERVINGS

AMOUNT	MEASURE	INGREDIENT
1/2 cup	2 ounces, 56 g	Bread crumbs, dry
I teaspoon	2 g	Paprika
I teaspoon	5 g	Lemon zest, grated
to taste		Salt and black pepper
4	5 ounces, 141 g each	Boston scrod or orange roughy fillets
1/2 cup	2 ounces, 56 g	All-purpose flour
I		Egg, beaten with I tablespoon water
1/4 cup	2 ounces, 56 g	Butter, melted

PROCEDURE

1 Preheat the oven to 400°F (205°C).

2 Combine the bread crumbs, paprika, lemon zest, salt, and pepper.

3 Dredge the fillets in flour, then shake to remove excess.

4 Dip the presentation side of fillets into egg wash, then into the bread-crumb mixture (one side only).

5 Drizzle melted butter evenly over the bread crumbs.

6 Bake for 10 to 15 minutes, or until fish begins to flake.

7 Serve with tartar sauce or lemon wedges.

Summer Squash Noodles 4 SERVINGS

AMOUNT	MEASURE	INGREDIENT
2 tablespoons	1 ounce, 28 ml	Unsalted butter
1 tablespoon	1/2 ounce, 14 ml	Olive oil
1 cup	4 ounces, 113 g	Yellow squash, cut into long, thin "noodles"
1 cup	4 ounces, 113 g	Zucchini squash, cut into long, thin "noodles"
1 cup	4 ounces, 113 g	Carrot, cut into long, thin "noodles" and blanched
1 tablespoon	3 g	Parsley, chopped
1 tablespoon	3 g	Basil, chopped
to taste		Salt and pepper

PROCEDURE

1. Heat the butter and oil over medium heat.

2. Add the vegetables and cook until heated through.

3. Add the herbs and correct the seasoning.

The Cuisine of the Mid-Atlantic

The Mid-Atlantic region, with its mild climate, abundance of river valleys with rich soil, and extensive coastline, was a perfect environment for the orchards and farms established by the early settlers who emigrated to American from England, Germany, the Netherlands, and other Western European countries. People from all over the world who have been attracted to the large cities of the Mid-Atlantic have, over the years, played an important role in the cuisine of this region.

New York. The apple is the state fruit of the "Empire State," so it makes sense that the apple muffin is the state muffin. The state tree is the sugar maple.

New Jersey "The Garden State" has the brook trout as its state fish and its state tree is the red oak.

Pennsylvania "The Keystone State" adopted the ruffled grouse as its state bird; its state tree is the hemlock.

Delaware Known as the "First State," Delaware chose the blue hen as the state bird. The state flower is the peach blossom and sweet goldenrod is the state herb.

Maryland The Maryland blue crab is the "Old Line State" state crustacean. The rockfish is the state fish.

Virginia While the state is often referred to as "Old Dominion," "Virginia Is for Lovers" is the popular state slogan. The oyster is the state shell.

West Virginia Known as the "Mountain State," West Virginia has the golden delicious apple as the state fruit. The sugar maple is the state tree and the honeybee is the state insect.

History and Major Influences

Throughout the 1600s and 1700s, more British colonies were founded in the New World, each for a different reason. Together, the colonies represented a wide variety of people, skills, motives, industries, resources, and agricultural production. This diversity continues to be seen in the distinct features found in each area of the Mid-Atlantic states.

NEW YORK, AMERICA'S FIRST "MELTING POT"

New York's ethnic heritage began in the 17th century, when it was founded as New Amsterdam colony by the Dutch. Before long the colony's population reached 1,000, and its residents spoke more than 15 different languages. For many immigrants, the new colony meant religious freedom. New York's first religious refugees were French Huguenots who settled in what is now considered the Catskills. Religious persecution in the 18th century brought a wave of German immigrants who settled in the Hudson and Mohawk Valleys. Later, Pogroms in Eastern Europe brought hundreds of thousands of Jewish people to New York.

Other immigrants arrived later in search of a better living. A potato famine in Ireland sent thousands of Irish people to New York in the mid-19th century. These Irish laborers helped build the Erie Canal and the state's first railroads. In the early 20th century, Italian immigrants settled in central New York. Poles, Lithuanians, Romanians, and Russians were drawn to the industrial towns of Buffalo, Syracuse, and Schenectady.

Today, the diverse ethnic makeup of New York City significantly influences the city's cuisine. The Italian and Chinese influences are seen all over the city but especially in Little Italy and Chinatown, while the Lower East Side remains the traditional home of Russian, Polish, German, and Ukrainian Jews, who introduced the delicatessen to

America. Just north of Central Park in Manhattan is Harlem, where the culinary influences of African Americans, Caribbeans, and Puerto Ricans are seen. Queens has one of the largest foreign-born populations of any county in the United States. The many ethnic enclaves are attractive to immigrants looking to live among people of the same background. Originally a haven for Italians, Germans, and other working class immigrant populations, the area now includes large numbers of Koreans, Chinese, South Asians, Caribbeans, Africans from all different nations, and people from India, Pakistan, and Bangladesh. Russian immigrants are centralized in the borough of Brooklyn in Brighton Beach, which is sometimes called Little Odessa.

New York State is one of the top dairy producers in the nation. Dairy products account for over half of the state's total farm income, with more than 10,000 dairy farms in operation. New York farmers also raise beef cattle, hogs, pigs, sheep, chickens, turkeys, and ducks. More than half of the farm-raised ducks in the country come from Suffolk County on Long Island. Apples are New York's major fruit, and there are over 3,000 apple orchards in the state.

NEW JERSEY, "THE GARDEN STATE"

New Jersey's official nickname derived from its having so many farms. The name dates back to its early European settlers who were so pleased with the fertile soil that they wrote letters to family in Europe, calling their new home a "garden spot." Rich soil and plentiful rain make this state one of the most productive farmlands in the nations. New Jersey ranks among the top ten states in its production of blueberries, peaches, lettuce, tomatoes, and apples.

Indeed, food products are one of the state's leading enterprises. Popular brand-name food items made in New Jersey include M & M's candy, Campbell's soups, Oreo cookies, Lipton tea, Heinz ketchup, and Budweiser beer. Along the coast, the fishing industry is also active. New Jersey, once known as the "Clam State," is still a leading producer of clams. The catch off New Jersey's shores also includes scallops, swordfish, tuna, squid, lobster, and flounder.

PENNSYLVANIA

Pennsylvania, and Philadelphia in particular, are known as the birthplace of American independence and *Philadelphia* is Greek for "City of Brotherly Love." Toward the end of the 17th century, William Penn, a member of the Society of Friends (also known as the

Quakers), was granted the right to begin a North American colony as a Quaker province. He invited Europeans seeking religious freedom to settle in his colony and many people, beginning with the Mennonites, accepted his invitation. The Mennonites were followed by the Amish and the Moravians, who first arrived in Philadelphia. These German-speaking people soon became known as the best farmers in the region. Over time, many of these settlers continued their migration west; however, those who remained in Pennsylvania became known as the "Pennsylvania Dutch." Called "Dutch" owing to a mispronunciation of the name of their language, "Deutsche," they settled in and around Lancaster, where their descendants still live today. In a life marked by simplicity and peace, these people prepare food referred to as "plain and plenty." Homemade bread, dumplings, doughnuts, and chicken pot pie are specialties. Hearty soups and stews utilize all foods. Home gardens provide fresh fruits and vegetables, and excess from the garden is preserved as pickles, preserves, relishes, and fruit butters.

Food is one of Pennsylvania's most important products. The Hershey factory is the world's biggest producer of chocolate. The world's largest pretzel factory is located near Lancaster, and Lancaster's Central Market is the country's oldest continuously operating farmers market. Milk is the state's most important farm product, and Pennsylvania is one of the country's leading dairy states. Apples, peaches, cherries, and grapes grow well in the region. Pennsylvania leads the nation in production of mushrooms, and Kennett Square houses the world's largest mushroom facility. White button mushrooms and exotic mushrooms such as portobellos, chanterelles, and cepes are harvested; Pennsylvania hosts an annual Mushroom Festival in the Brandywine Valley each September.

MARYLAND AND DELAWARE

When the colonists arrived in the Mid-Atlantic region, they discovered that over 40 rivers fed into the Chesapeake Bay, where the mix of fresh and salt water was home to an amazing quantity and variety of seafood. The colonists quickly learned from the Native Americans how to gather oysters and blue crabs from Chesapeake Bay, which in the local language meant "great shellfish bay." Oysters, a familiar food to the European settlers, were found in such quantities that not only were they consumed but the shells were used for brickmaking and for lining paths. Maryland's waters still produce more oysters than any other state, and the total commercial seafood catch drives the state's economy.

Historically, the main occupation of Delaware citizens has been agriculture. The original settlers concentrated on growing wheat and corn, and in the early 1800s the area was known for its peach trees. Unfortunately, in the late 1800s, a disease killed more than

Oysters

Two-thirds of the nation's oyster harvest is of Eastern oysters. They are harvested from natural beds as well as farmed along the East Coast. Because of different conditions in coastal areas—nutrients in the water, salinity levels, temperature, and so on—oysters vary in taste from one location to the next and often bear the name of the region where they were grown as a means of distinguishing their flavor. The Blue Point oyster is originally from Long Island Sound, but this is now a generic term for all Atlantic oysters. Other names include Chesapeake Bay, Chincoteague, Kent Island, Pine Island, St. George, and Cape Cod oysters. Oyster farming has been practiced for years in Long Island Sound, Delaware Bay, and the Chesapeake Bay. Harvesters try to avoid the parasites that often destroy natural beds by growing them under controlled conditions in commercial hatcheries.

Oysters are typically consumed only during months that have the letter *r* in them—generally the cooler months. Although oysters are edible in the non-*r* months, this is their spawning season and the production of glycogen is excessive at this time, giving the meat a milky appearance, bland taste, and flabby texture.

Oysters are tender creatures and should never be heated too quickly or too long. As soon as the mantle starts to curl, the oyster is done. Though oysters are often served on the half shell, people in high-risk health categories, such as the young, the elderly, or people with chronic illnesses, should avoid raw shellfish. Oysters may be baked, fried, grilled, sautéed, smoked, or steamed.

Note: Chefs in commercial restaurants should never buy oysters that do not bear the harvester's name, address, date, and certification number, and they should keep the tag for at least 90 days. In the event of a food-borne illness determined to be caused by eating raw oysters, inspectors will be able to use the tag to trace the origin of the harvest and take appropriate actions. The liquid in which shucked fresh oysters are packed should be clear. To test for live oysters, tap the shell; it should close. A sulfur odor indicates a dead oyster.

half of those trees. The next agricultural milestone was laid in 1920 by Cecile Steele of Sussex County. She started raising chickens for retail sale instead of just for their eggs. Today, broiler chickens are the state's most valuable agricultural product, and Perdue Farms, which is headquartered in nearby Maryland, is the nation's second largest poultry producer. Breeder Frank Perdue was known for successfully crossbreeding chickens, as well as for having developed a special all-natural feed that combined corn and soybeans with minerals from ground oyster shells and marigold petal extract. Although the marigold petal extract does not add vitamins to the chicken's diet, it is responsible for its distinctive yellow-gold skin color. The company processes approximately 50 million pounds of chicken and turkey per week and the industry continues to grow.

VIRGINIA AND WEST VIRGINIA

In its earliest years, Virginia's entire economy was plantation-based. Early plantations lay along one of the state's major rivers, and the tobacco grown on that land was shipped to England. Luxury goods and other items that the colony could not produce were imported from Europe. Tobacco was the mainstay of the state, and even after the Civil War it was tobacco that kept Virginia's economy alive for many years. But as early as the 1840s, newcomers to Virginia had begun to show local farmers that they didn't have to depend on tobacco. Gradually, the Tidewater region became a major source of fresh fruits and vegetables for the nation. This truck farming continued because it did not require slave labor. Today, Virginia remains a major producer of potatoes, peanuts, and apples.

During the 19th century, many Scotch Irish and Germans arrived in what is present-day West Virginia by way of Pennsylvania. Later, immigrants from Ireland and eastern and southern Europe came to the state. Because West Virginia has very little flat land, growing crops is difficult. Livestock is the leading agricultural product, and broiler chickens bring the greatest income. Apples and peaches are grown in the eastern panhandle, and West Virginia farmers were first in the nation to produce Golden Delicious apples.

Typical Mid-Atlantic Ingredients and Dishes

Angel Food Cake A light puffy cake made without yeast or egg yolks, and leavened with beaten egg whites. Considered to be from the thrifty Pennsylvania Dutch as a sensible use of leftover egg whites.

Apple Butter A butterlike spiced apple spread made by the Pennsylvania Dutch. This type of spread can be made with any fruit, but making apple butter is often a traditional Pennsylvania Dutch fall social event involving women.

Bagel A small round yeast bread with a hole in the center. The only bread dough to be boiled and then baked, which results in a chewy texture. Bagels may be made with a variety of ingredients or toppings, and today are fashioned by machine and cooked in a modified process.

Beef on Weck A sandwich is of thinly sliced, very lean roast beef, served on a German caraway-seed roll encrusted with salt, topped with the beef juices, and accompanied with horseradish. The German name for the roll is *kummelweck,* which is shortened in the name for the sandwich.

Beefsteak Tomato A tomato of any variety that grows to at least 3 inches in diameter. Large beefsteak tomatoes are prized for the excellent balance of sweetness and tartness, achieved by being vine-ripened during the hottest days of summer.

Beet Egg An Amish preparation in which eggs are hard-boiled in a seasoned liquid derived from cooked beets. When done, the eggs turn a purplish-red color. Beet eggs were considered to be the first use of colored eggs for the Easter holiday, a tradition brought to America by the first Amish immigrants.

Bialy A chewy round roll made from wheat flour, salt, yeast, and water. It has an indentation in the center, sprinkled with either chopped onion or poppyseed, and is baked until crisp and golden brown. The name derives from the Polish town of Bialystock.

Blue Crab A common species of crab found in abundance in the Chesapeake Bay, harvested April through December. Blue crabs are marketed and sold in both their hard- and soft-shell stages. The meat from the crab is available as (*lump*) large pieces from the leg (*flake*) small pieces from the body and (*claw*) small pieces. The following terminology is associated with blue crabs:

> **Apron** The flap located on the underside of the body. The apron is pried away from the body to remove the intestinal vein, which is normally pulled out.

> **Dead Man's Fingers** The spongy yellow matter found in the crab's body. The gills and intestines, along with the dead man's fingers, should be discarded.

> **Jimmies** Male crabs, considered a little meatier than female crabs.

> **Peelers** Crabs that have grown their new soft shell underneath and have split the hard shell on top. The new shell will begin to harden within a few hours if the crab is left in the water after molting.

> **Soft Shell** The stage when the crab begins to molt and shed its shell. Both male and female crabs lose their shells and form new ones as they grow. Blue crabs molt up to

22 times before reaching full maturity, between 5 and 7 inches across. Soft-shell crabs are graded by the size of the shell span. Hotel crabs are 4 to $4^1/_2$ inches, prime crabs are $4^1/_2$ to 5 inches, jumbo crabs are 5 to $5^1/_2$ inches, and whale crabs are $5^1/_2$ inches and larger. Soft-shell crabs are generally pan-fried and eaten whole.

Sooks Female crabs.

Tomalley The yellow-colored liver. The tomalley is edible and considered by many to be a delicacy.

Boova Shenkel A Pennsylvania Dutch beef stew with potato dumplings. The literal translation is "boys' legs" for the dumplings that resemble short, thick legs.

Borscht A beef, beet, and cabbage soup of Russian and Polish origin, popular among Jewish people. Served hot or cold, garnished with a dollop of sour cream.

Button Mushrooms The most common mushrooms consumed in America. They are recognized by a firm white exterior and smooth skin.

Challah A traditional Jewish braided white yeast bread. This holiday bread is enriched with eggs and sprinkled with poppyseeds.

Chicken The different names for chickens refer to stages of growth, and sometimes to the cooking method. They are:

Poussin A baby chicken weighing 14 to 18 ounces.

Hen An egg-laying female not used for cooking until egg production has ended. Good for broths, stock, and soup.

Pullet A young female used for meat. Often sold as broilers (weighing from $1^1/_4$ to $2^1/_2$ pounds) or as fryers (from $2^1/_2$ to $3^1/_2$ pounds).

Roasters Young males not sold as broilers and fryers, often raised to be roasters (4 to 6 pounds).

Capons Males that have been castrated. They are plump and juicy and weigh between 7 and 12 pounds.

Roosters or cocks Males that are used primarily for breeding. They can be used for broths, stocks, and soups.

Chicken Pot Pie A Pennsylvania Dutch chicken stew similar to Southern chicken and dumplings. The dumplings are flat squares made from a dough that resembles pie dough and are boiled in a pot of broth, then added to stew.

Clams Surf clams are the clam variety most frequently found in New Jersey and New York. Too big and too coarse to be eaten whole like other clams, these are processed and are often the "fried clams" featured on menus. The meat is also ground or chopped and used for chowders, bisques, and sauces.

Crab Boil A special mix of herbs and spices used to season blue crabs when steaming them.

Crab Cake A patty of crab meat mixed with fresh bread crumbs, eggs, herbs, and spices. It may be pan-fried or sautéed.

Fastnacht A rectangular piece of dough slit down the center and deep fried, much like a doughnut. It may be filled with jam or topped with molasses.

Foie Gras The "fat liver" of ducks and geese. The Moulard duck is especially bred for its liver, and in the Mongaup Valley in the Catskill Mountains of New York, this prized duck is now raised to provide America's first French-style foie gras.

Funnel Cake A crisp, squiggly pastry made by pouring batter through a funnel into hot fat, then swirling it into strips. Funnel cakes are typically sprinkled with powdered sugar or topped with molasses or syrup. Pennsylvania Dutch farmers eat these as a midmorning snack.

Gyro A Greek-American sandwich made from slices of rotisserie-roasted, seasoned lamb, served in the pocket of pita bread. Sold at Greek lunch counters in New York City and pronounced "JEER-o."

Kosher Food prepared according to strict Jewish dietary laws. According to kosher laws, meat and milk may not be eaten together at the same meal; even separate dishes, pots, pans, and utensils must be used. Also, consuming pork or shellfish is prohibited. In order for meats to be called "kosher," the animals must be slaughtered a certain way, under the supervision of a rabbi.

Kugel A baked noodle or potato pudding served on the Jewish Sabbath.

Latke A Jewish fried pancake usually made from grated potatoes and traditionally served at Chanukah.

Lebkuchen A Pennsylvania Dutch spiced drop cake made especially at Christmastime.

Lox A salt-cured (but not smoked) side of salmon, sliced paper-thin and frequently served on a bagel half spread with cream cheese.

Maryland Stuffed Ham A ham larded with a mix of cabbage, onions, mustard, hot pepper, and other seasonings, wrapped tightly in a cloth bag, covered with water, and simmered for several hours. The ham is cooled, the bag is cut away, and the ham is served, usually cold, the next day. This is a dish found in southern Maryland and served at Easter.

Matzo A plain unleavened bread in thin sheets, traditional at the Jewish Passover.

New York Cheesecake A dense cream cheese cake with a graham cracker crust, sometimes topped with fresh fruit.

Pastrami Beef brisket that has been brine-cured and seasoned for one to three weeks, then smoked and finally steamed. Served sliced on rye bread, often with mustard.

Philadelphia Pepperpot A soup of tripe, pepper, and seasonings.

Philly Cheese Steak A sandwich of shaved slices of rib eye steak and grilled onions, served on a hard roll topped with Cheez Whiz. Additional toppings include relish, peppers, ketchup, and hot sauce.

Pumpernickel A rye bread with the addition of molasses or caramel to give its dark brown color.

Reuben Sandwich A grilled sandwich of corned beef, Swiss cheese, sauerkraut, and Russian dressing on rye bread.

Rivel Rice-shaped bits of dough, formed by rubbing a ball of pasta dough through a sieve, cooked in simmering broth.

Rye Bread Jewish-style rye bread is a mixture of rye grain and wheat flour, and uses a sourdough starter as a leavening agent, giving it a distinctive, slightly sour flavor. German-style rye bread contains only rye flour; caraway seeds may be either sprinkled on top of the dough or mixed into it before baking.

Sauerbraten Beef roast that has been cured with sugar and vinegar, then braised, served in a gravy thickened with crushed gingersnaps. The long marinating makes a flavorful, tender roast. A Mennonite and Amish dish.

Schmaltz A Yiddish-American term for rendered chicken fat. It may be used as a cooking ingredient or flavored with apples, onions, and seasonings and used as a spread.

Schmear A Yiddish term for a dab or smear of a condiment like cream cheese spread on a bagel, or mustard on a roll.

Schnitz und Kneppe A Pennsylvania-Dutch dish of smoked ham with dried apples and dumplings.

Scrapple A pan pudding of boneless pork simmered with cornmeal or buckwheat flour and flavored with sage. The pudding is chilled, sliced, and pan-fried until golden brown.

Shad A member of the herring family, a coastal and river fish with a rich, oily flesh and delicate flavor. Boning shad can be tedious, owing to the "floating ribs" that lie in two rows paralleling the backbone on each fillet. Available in the spring, when the fish returns from the ocean to spawn. The annual yield of shad has decreased at an alarming rate owing to pollution.

Shad Roe The roe produced by shad just before spawning. Considered a delicacy with a distinctive, nutty flavor, it can be poached, pan-fried, or sautéed.

Shoofly Pie The most famous of all Pennsylvania Dutch pies. Also referred to as pie cake or molasses, it is a crumbly mixture of brown sugar, flour, cinnamon, and butter baked over a layer of molasses in a pie shell.

Stromboli A specialty of Philadelphia, this sandwich is pizza dough folded over a variety of ingredients, usually mozzarella cheese and sliced pepperoni.

Smithfield Ham Ham cured and smoked via a patented process, a product of Smithfield, Virginia. The hams are cured for 6 to 12 months; before they can be used, they must be soaked in water for 12 to 24 hours to remove excess salt.

Smoked Sable A smoked black codfish found in New York City–style delicatessens, it is sliced thin and served on bread with onions, black olives, and sweet butter.

Tzimmes Any of a wide variety of Jewish-American casserole dishes made of various sweetened vegetables or fruits.

Vichyssoise A creamy potato and leek soup served cold.

Waldorf Salad A salad of apples, celery, and walnuts, with a mayonnaise dressing.

Menus and Recipes from the Cuisine of the Mid-Atlantic States

MENU ONE

Spicy Crab Soup with Crab Puffs

Egg, Cucumber, and Tomato Salad

Buffalo Chicken Wings

Roast Duck with Garlic and Honey

Roasted Potatoes and Pearl Onions

Applesauce Cake with Caramel Glaze

MENU TWO

Vichyssoise

Beets, Belgian Endive, and Feta Salad

Scallops with Mushrooms and Asparagus

"Shaker-Style" Turkey Cutlet

Croquette Potatoes

Potatoes Parmentier

Green Beans

Spaghetti Squash

Ginger Pound Cake with Warm Cranberries

MENU THREE

Navy Bean Soup

Waldorf Salad

Sautéed Soft-Shell Crabs on Fennel Salad

Braised Short Ribs

Buttered Homemade Noodles

Red Swiss Chard and Spinach Sauté

OTHER RECIPES

Beef Potpie with Rich Biscuit Topping

Caprese Salad

Chicken with Dill Dumplings

Spicy Crab Soup 4 SERVINGS

AMOUNT	MEASURE	INGREDIENT
2 tablespoons	1 ounce, 28 g	Unsalted butter
1/2 cup	2 ounces, 56 g	Onion, 1/2 inch (1.2 cm) dice
1/2 cup	2 ounces, 56 g	Celery, 1/2 inch (1.2 cm) dice
1 cup	4 ounces, 113 g	Potato, 1/4 inch (.6 cm) dice
2 cups	12 ounces, 340 g	Tomatoes, peeled, seeded, 1/2 inch (1.2 cm) dice
1/2 cup	2 ounces, 56 g	Corn kernels
2 cups	16 ounces, 0.473 l	Chicken stock
1 teaspoon	2 g	Old Bay seafood seasoning
1/2 teaspoon	3 g	Salt
1/4 teaspoon	2 g	Black pepper
1 cup	6 ounces, 170 g	Crab meat, lump, thoroughly picked of shell
1/2 cup	2 ounces, 56 g	Green peas
1 teaspoon	5 ml	Lemon juice

PROCEDURE

1 Heat the butter over medium heat and cook onion 4 minutes.

2 Add the celery and cook 3 minutes.

3 Add the potato, tomatoes, corn, and chicken stock.

4 Add the seasonings and cook 25 minutes.

5 Add the crab meat and peas, then simmer 10 minutes.

6 Correct the seasoning with salt, pepper, and lemon juice. Serve with Crab Puffs (page 58).

Egg, Cucumber, and Tomato Salad

Egg, Cucumber, and Tomato Salad 4 SERVINGS

AMOUNT	MEASURE	INGREDIENT
$1/2$ teaspoon	2 g	Black pepper
$1/8$ teaspoon	1 g	Salt
1		Garlic clove, minced
3 tablespoons	$1 1/2$ ounces, 42 ml	Olive oil
1 tablespoon	$1/2$ ounce, 14 ml	Red wine vinegar
1 tablespoon	$1/2$ ounce, 14 ml	Lemon juice
$1/4$ cup	1 ounce, 28 g	Green onions, finely diced
4		Eggs, hard-cooked, sliced
$1/2$ cup	2 ounces, 56 g	Celery stalk with leaves, $1/4$ inch (.6 cm) dice
$1/2$ cup	2 ounces, 56 g	Cucumber, peeled, seeded, $1/4$ inch (.6 cm) dice
6		Red radishes, sliced
1 head	6 ounces, 170 g	Boston (Bibb) lettuce, shredded
2		Tomatoes, ripe, thinly sliced (16 slices)

PROCEDURE

1 Mix the pepper, salt, garlic, olive oil, vinegar, lemon juice, and green onions.

2 Combine the eggs, celery, cucumber, radishes, and lettuce with most of the dressing.

3 Fan some tomato slices on each plate and top with egg/lettuce mixture.

4 Drizzle remaining dressing on top.

Crab Puffs   4 SERVINGS

AMOUNT	MEASURE	INGREDIENT
3 ounces	85 g	Crab meat, claw and back, thoroughly picked of shell
1/4 cup	1 ounce, 28 g	Cheddar cheese (sharp), grated
1 tablespoon	3 g	Green onion, minced
1/2 teaspoon	2.5 ml	Worcestershire sauce
1/2 teaspoon	1 g	Dry mustard
1/2 cup	4 ounces, 115 ml	Water
1/4 cup	2 ounces, 56 g	Unsalted butter
1/8 teaspoon	1 g	Salt
1/2 cup	2 ounces, 56 g	All-purpose flour
2		Eggs (large)

PROCEDURE

1. Preheat the oven to 400°F (205°C).

2. Combine the first 5 ingredients and mix well.

3. Combine the water, butter, and salt over medium-high heat and bring to a boil. Immediately remove from heat and add the flour, beating until mixture leaves sides of pan and forms a ball.

4. Add the eggs, one at a time, beating thoroughly after each addition.

5. Thoroughly blend in crab mixture.

6. Drop by small teaspoonfuls onto ungreased baking sheet.

7. Bake 15 minutes, reduce heat to 350°F (175°C), and bake 10 minutes longer.

Buffalo Chicken Wings 4 SERVINGS

Buffalo wings are so ingrained in our national food culture that it is hard to remember life before wings. They have been around for a lot shorter time than most people think. From their origin in 1964 to today, however, wings are a prime example of a food that incorporates many of our cultural traits. For example, *thrift* (wings, after all, come from the part of the chicken most people throw away or use only for soups and stocks), *ingenuity* (the preparation uses simple, at-hand materials to make a new item), and *eating with your hands* (there is a childlike satisfaction in eating with your fingers, especially when there is a flavorful sauce to lick off). Buffalo wings offer something for almost everyone, and that's why the food spread so rapidly from its home in Buffalo, New York, to become part of our national food culture.

AMOUNT	MEASURE	INGREDIENT
12–14	3 pounds, 1.36 kg	Chicken wings
6 cups	1.4 l	Vegetable oil, for frying
1/4 cup	2 ounces, 55 ml	Unsalted butter
3 tablespoons	1 1/2 ounces, 42 ml	Hot sauce such as Franks or Tabasco
2 tablespoons	1 ounce, 28 ml	Cider vinegar
to taste		Salt
2 cups	8 ounces, 226 g	Celery sticks

For the Blue Cheese Dressing

1/2 cup	4 ounces, 115 ml	Mayonnaise
1/4 cup	2 ounces, 55 ml	Yogurt
1/2 cup	2 ounces, 56 g	Blue cheese, crumbled

PROCEDURE

1 Cut off chicken wing tips, reserving for another use, and halve chicken wings at joint.

2 Heat oil to 375°F to 380°F (190°C to 193°C), pat wings dry, and fry until cooked through, golden and crisp, 5 to 8 minutes.

3 Drain on paper towels.

4 Combine butter, hot sauce, vinegar, and salt over medium heat, and warm until butter is melted.

5 Add chicken wings and toss to coat.

6   Combine the mayonnaise and yogurt, and stir in the blue cheese; dressing will not be
     smooth.

7   Serve chicken wings warm or at room temperature, with celery sticks and dressing.

Buffalo Chicken Wings

Roast Duck with Garlic and Honey 4 SERVINGS

AMOUNT	MEASURE	INGREDIENT
I	5 pounds, 2.26 kg	Long Island duck, whole
8		Garlic cloves, peeled
to taste		Salt and black pepper
³/₄ cup	6 ounces, 170 ml	Orange or tangerine juice, fresh, save the peels
6 tablespoons	3 ounces, 84 g	Unsalted butter
2 cups	8 ounces, 226 g	Red onions, ¹/₂ inch (1.2 cm) dice
I cup	4 ounces, 113 g	Parsnips, peeled, I inch (2.5 cm) dice
I cup	4 ounces, 113 g	Turnips, peeled, I inch (2.5 cm) dice
2 cups	8 ounces, 226 g	Carrots, I inch (2.5 cm) dice
I ¹/₂ cups	12 ounces, 352 ml	Dry red wine
¹/₄ cup	4 ounces, 113 g	Honey
2 teaspoons	2 g	Thyme, chopped
I teaspoon	2 g	Black pepper

PROCEDURE

1 Preheat the oven to 400°F (205°C).

2 Rinse the duck inside and out with cold water, reserving the neck and liver. Trim the excess fat and skin.

3 Pat dry and make 8 incisions in the duck breast and thighs, inserting a garlic clove into each incision. Prick the duck skin all over with a fork, but don't pierce the meat.

4 Rub the duck inside and out with orange or tangerine peels.

5 Truss the duck and place breast side down on a rack in a roasting pan. Roast for 20 minutes.

6 Turn duck breast side up and baste with fat; reduce heat to 350°F (175°C) and continue roasting and basting occasionally until desired doneness is achieved, 10 to 15 minutes more.

7 Heat 1¹/₂ tablespoons (³/₄ ounce, 21 ml) butter over medium-low heat, add the onions, and cook until they begin to soften, 2 minutes.

8   Add the duck liver and cook, stirring until liver is firm, about 5 minutes. Remove and cut liver into $1/2$-inch (1.2 cm) dice, then return to pan with onions.

9   Add the parsnips, turnips, and carrots; cook 1 minute.

10   Add the remaining butter and $1/2$ cup (4 ounces, 115 ml) orange juice. Cook until just tender and liquid is almost gone, then set aside.

11   While duck is roasting, make the sauce base. Bring the duck neck, remaining orange juice, wine, honey, thyme, and 1 teaspoon (2 g) pepper to a boil over high heat. Reduce the heat to very low and simmer 10 to 15 minutes, until the liquid is reduced to 1 cup (8 ounces, 235 ml).

12   When duck is cooked, remove and let stand 10 minutes before carving.

13   Meanwhile, pour the fat and pan juices into a container. Let stand until the clear yellow fat separates and rises to the top. Pour or skim off the yellow fat (which can be cooled, covered, and refrigerated to use as cooking fat) and pour pan juices back into roasting pan.

14   Return pan to heat and add sauce base. Bring to a boil, scraping up the browned bits on the bottom of the pan. Reduce to sauce consistency and pour into a sauceboat. (Sauce may need to be thickened.)

15   Carve the duck and serve with the vegetable mixture and sauce.

Roasted Potatoes and Pearl Onions 4 SERVINGS

AMOUNT	MEASURE	INGREDIENT
12		Red potatoes
12		Pearl onions, peeled
1 tablespoon	$^1/_2$ ounce, 14 g	Unsalted butter, melted
3 tablespoons	1 $^1/_2$ ounces, 42 ml	Balsamic vinegar
$^1/_2$ teaspoon	3 g	Salt
to taste		Black pepper
4		Thyme sprigs

PROCEDURE

1 Preheat the oven to 350°F (175°C).

2 Starting at the top of each potato, pare away a $^1/_4$-inch (.6 cm)-thick band of skin in a spiral. This not only makes them look appealing but also allows the vinegar to penetrate during the slow cooking process.

3 Combine the onions and potatoes in a baking dish just large enough to hold them.

4 Add the butter and vinegar, and toss to coat.

5 Add salt and pepper. Bury the thyme springs in the vegetables.

6 Bake for 1 hour or until tender, stirring the vegetables every 15 minutes. (It is important to turn the vegetables every 15 minutes if they are to brown evenly.)

Applesauce Cake with Caramel Glaze SERVES ONE 10-INCH CAKE

AMOUNT	MEASURE	INGREDIENT
I cup	8 ounces, 226 g	Unsalted butter, at room temperature
2 cups	16 ounces, 453 g	Brown sugar, packed
I		Egg
3 cups	13 ounces, 368 g	All-purpose flour
2 teaspoons	8 g	Baking soda
1/4 teaspoon	2 g	Salt
I teaspoon	2 g	Ground cinnamon
I teaspoon	2 g	Ground nutmeg
I teaspoon	2 g	Ground cloves
2 cups	17 ounces, 482 g	Applesauce, unsweetened
2 cups	12 ounces, 340 g	Raisins
I cup	4 ounces, 113 g	Walnuts, coarsely chopped

For the glaze

AMOUNT	MEASURE	INGREDIENT
I cup	8 ounces, 226 g	Brown sugar, packed
1/4 cup	2 ounces, 56 g	Unsalted butter
1/4 cup	2 ounces, 55 ml	Evaporated milk

PROCEDURE

1 Preheat the oven to 350°F (175°C). Grease and flour a 10-inch (25.4 cm) tube pan.

2 Cream the butter until smooth. Gradually add the brown sugar, beating until light and fluffy.

3 Add the egg; beat well.

4 Sift together 2¹/₂ cups (10 ounces, 283 g) of the flour, the baking soda, salt, and spices. Add to the creamed mixture in batches alternating with the applesauce. Beat well after each addition.

5 Dredge the raisins and walnuts in the remaining flour; fold into the batter.

6 Pour the batter into the prepared pan. Bake for 1 hour and 15 minutes or until cake tests done.

7   Cool cake in pan 15 minutes, then invert onto a cake rack to cool completely.

8   Meanwhile, prepare the glaze. Combine the brown sugar, butter, and milk.

9   Heat, stirring constantly, until the mixture comes to a boil and the sugar is dissolved.

10 Continue cooking, stirring constantly, until the mixture reaches soft-ball stage (240°F or 115°C). Remove from the heat, and beat about 5 minutes or until thick.

11 Drizzle the hot sauce over the cooked cake.

Beets, Belgian Endive, and Feta Salad   4 SERVINGS

AMOUNT	MEASURE	INGREDIENT
4 cups	16 ounces, 453 g	Beets, mixed red and golden if available, whole
7 tablespoons	3¹/₂ ounces, 98 ml	Walnut oil
2 tablespoons	1 ounce, 28 ml	Tarragon vinegar
to taste		Salt and black pepper
¹/₄ cup	1 ounce, 28 g	Walnuts, chopped
2		Belgian endive, firm and white
1 cup	2 ounces, 60 g	Feta cheese, crumbled

PROCEDURE

1   Preheat the oven to 400°F (205°C).

2   Leaving on the tails and 1 inch (2.5 cm) of the stem on the beets, rinse them, put them in a baking pan with ¹/₄ inch (.6 cm) of water, cover, and bake until tender when pierced with a knife, 25 to 40 minutes depending on the size of the beets.

3   Cool beets, then peel and dice into ¹/₂-inch (1.2 cm) cubes.

4   Mix 6 tablespoons of the oil, the vinegar, salt, and pepper.

5   Toss beets in half of the vinaigrette.

6   Toss the walnuts with remaining walnut oil, salt, and pepper. Bake in 350°F (175°C) oven for 5 to 7 minutes or until they smell toasty. Set aside to cool.

7   Just before serving, quarter the endive, cut out the cores, and break into leaves.

8   Arrange endive leaves in a spoke pattern on individual plates. Spoon beets in the center.

9   Lightly dress endive with vinaigrette. Sprinkle the feta cheese over the salad and top with walnuts.

Note: If walnut oil is unavailable, use olive oil and 1 teaspoon Dijon-style mustard.

Beets, Belgian Endive, and Feta Salad

Vichyssoise 4 SERVINGS

Most food historians generally attribute the creation of this cold soup in 1917 to Louis Diat, chef at the Ritz-Carlton Hotel in New York. There are, however, some conflicting facts that make this story interesting. Was Mr. Diat the first to make French-style cream of leek and potato soup? Culinary evidence suggests not. Recipe 696 in Escoffier's *Guide Culinaire* (circa 1903) provides instructions for *purée parmentier*. The difference? Mr. Escoffier's soup was served hot; Mr. Diat's vichyssoise was served cold. If there is a connection to Vichy (beyond the name), it has not been preserved for posterity.

AMOUNT	MEASURE	INGREDIENT
3 cups	12 ounces, 340 g	Leeks, use white part only
1/4 cup	2 ounces, 56 g	Unsalted butter
1/2 cup	2 ounces, 56 g	White onions, 1/2 inch (1.2 cm) dice
2 cups	10 ounces, 283 g	All-purpose potatoes, peeled, 1/2 inch (1.2 cm) dice
3 cups	24 ounces, 705 ml	Chicken stock
to taste		Salt and white pepper
3/4 cup	6 ounces, 170 ml	Milk
1 cup	8 ounces, 235 ml	Heavy cream
1/3 cup	1/2 ounce, 14 g	Chives, snipped

PROCEDURE

1 Split the leeks lengthwise, wash well to remove all sand and grit, then slice them.

2 Heat the butter over medium heat and add the leeks and onions. Cook slowly, browning them very lightly.

3 Add the potatoes and chicken stock, season with salt and pepper, and bring to a simmer. Simmer until the leeks and potatoes are very tender, approximately 45 minutes.

4 Puree the soup in a food processor, blender, or food mill, then run through a fine strainer.

5 Return puree to the heat and add the milk and 1/2 cup (4 ounces, 115 ml) cream. Season to taste and return to a boil. Strain again through a fine strainer.

6 Let cool, then add remaining cream. Chill thoroughly before serving, garnished with snipped chives.

Scallops with Mushrooms and Asparagus 4 SERVINGS

AMOUNT	MEASURE	INGREDIENT
4 tablespoons	2 ounces, 56 g	Unsalted butter
2		Shallots, minced
3 cups	8 ounces, 226 g	White mushrooms, sliced
2¹/₂ cups	16 ounces, 453 g	Asparagus, peeled, cut into 2-inch (5 cm) pieces, blanched
¹/₄ cup	2 ounces, 55 ml	Sherry wine
2 tablespoons	1 ounce, 28 ml	Olive oil
12 ounces	340 g	Scallops, sea or bay
to taste		Salt and black pepper
4 tablespoons	1 ounce, 28 g	Parmesan cheese, grated
2 tablespoons	6 g	Parsley, chopped

PROCEDURE

1. Heat 2 tablespoons (1 ounce, 28 ml) butter and cook the shallots 1 minute.
2. Add the mushrooms and cook 2 minutes, stirring.
3. Add the asparagus, cook 1 minute, add the sherry, and set aside.
4. Using a nonstick pan, heat the oil until very hot.
5. Season the scallops, and sear until golden brown.
6. Add the remaining butter halfway through cooking to achieve a nutty flavor.
7. Divide mushrooms and asparagus among plates and top with scallops.
8. Sprinkle with Parmesan cheese and parsley, and serve.

"Shaker-Style" Turkey Cutlet 4 SERVINGS

AMOUNT	MEASURE	INGREDIENT
8	3 ounces, 84 g, each	Turkey cutlets
to taste		Salt and black pepper
as needed		Unsalted butter
I tablespoon	15 g	Shallot, $^1/_4$ inch (.6 cm) dice
$^1/_2$ cup	4 ounces, 115 ml	Dry white wine
$1^1/_4$ cups	10 ounces, 293 ml	Fond de veau de lie (brown stock)
I cup	6 ounces, 170 g	Tomato, peeled, seeded, $^1/_4$ inch (.6 cm) dice
I tablespoon	3 g	Parsley, chopped

PROCEDURE

1   Pound the turkey cutlets to approximately $^1/_4$ inch (.6 cm) thick. Pat dry. Season to taste with salt and pepper.

2   Dredge cutlets in flour and shake off the excess.

3   Heat the butter over medium-high heat. Sauté the cutlets approximately 2 to 3 minutes on each side, until golden brown. Remove and keep warm.

4   Discard the excess fat from the pan and return to medium-high heat. Add the shallots and cook 1 minute, stirring often.

5   Add the white wine and scrape up the pan drippings, reducing liquid by half.

6   Add the brown stock and reduce to sauce (nappé) consistency.

7   Add the tomato and cook for 1 minute or until hot.

8   Return cutlets to the pan and reheat, then remove to plates, 2 cutlets per serving.

9   Stir 2 tablespoons butter into pan drippings, correct the seasoning, and add the parsley. Spoon sauce over cutlets.

Croquette Potatoes 4 SERVINGS

AMOUNT	MEASURE	INGREDIENT
3 cups	16 ounces, 453 g	Russet potatoes, peeled, quartered
2 tablespoons	1 ounce, 28 g	Butter, softened
1		Egg yolk
to taste		Salt and white pepper
1/2 cup	2 ounces, 56 g	All-purpose flour
2		Eggs, beaten with a pinch of salt (egg wash)
3 cups	3 ounces, 85 g	Bread crumbs, dry
as needed		Vegetable oil, for deep-fat frying

PROCEDURE

1 Place the potatoes in cold water, bring to a boil, turn down heat, and simmer for about 30 minutes, until potatoes are tender.

2 Drain and dry the potatoes, run them through a food mill, then add the butter and egg yolk. Season with salt and pepper.

3 Shape the croquettes as required. Dredge in flour, then egg wash, and coat with bread crumbs.

4 Deep-fry in 375°F (190°C) oil until golden brown. Drain on paper towels and serve immediately.

Potatoes Parmentier 4 SERVINGS

AMOUNT	MEASURE	INGREDIENT
3 cups	16 ounces, 453 g	Russet potatoes, peeled, $1/2$ inch (1.2 cm) dice
2 tablespoons	1 ounce, 28 ml	Vegetable oil
$1/4$ cup	2 ounces, 55 ml	Unsalted butter
to taste		Salt and black pepper
2 teaspoons	2 g	Parsley, chopped

PROCEDURE

1   Heat the oil and butter.

2   Add the potatoes and sauté over medium heat for 10 to 12 minutes, or until an even golden color. Keep in warm oven.

3   When ready to serve, season with salt and pepper, and sprinkle with parsley.

Green Beans 4 SERVINGS

AMOUNT	MEASURE	INGREDIENT
2 cups	8 ounces, 226 g	Green beans, trimmed
2 tablespoons	1 ounce, 28 g	Butter
Pinch		Mace
$1/4$ teaspoon	1 ml	Lemon juice
to taste		Salt and white pepper

PROCEDURE

1   String and parboil the green beans in salted boiling water for 6 to 8 minutes; check for tenderness.

2   Shock the beans in ice water, drain, and chill until needed.

3   Heat a sauté pan, add the butter, let it get light brown, then toss in the green beans. Season with mace, lemon juice, salt, and pepper.

Spaghetti Squash 4 SERVINGS

AMOUNT	MEASURE	INGREDIENT
¹/₂ small	2 pounds, 907 g	Spaghetti squash, cooked
¹/₄ cup	2 ounces, 56 g	Unsalted butter
to taste		Salt and black pepper

PROCEDURE

1 Melt the butter over medium heat.

2 Add the cooked strands of squash and cook until heated thoroughly.

3 Season to taste with salt and pepper.

How to Cook Spaghetti Squash

BAKE IT. Pierce the whole shell several times with a large fork or skewer and place in baking dish. Cook squash in preheated 375°F (190°C) oven approximately 1 hour or until flesh is tender.

BOIL IT. Heat a pot of water large enough to hold the whole squash. When the water is boiling, drop in the squash and cook for 20 to 30 minutes, depending on its size. When a fork goes easily into the flesh, the squash is done.

MICROWAVE IT. Cut the squash in half lengthwise; remove seeds. Place squash cut sides up in a microwave dish with ¹/₄ cup (2 ounces, 55 ml) water. Cover with plastic wrap and cook on high for 10 to 12 minutes, depending on size of squash. Add more cooking time if necessary. Let stand covered, for 5 minutes.

Once the squash is cooked, let it cool for 10 to 20 minutes so it will be easier to handle. Cut in half (if it wasn't already) and remove the seeds. Pull a fork lengthwise through the flesh to separate pulp into long strands. You can do these steps ahead of time.

Ginger Pound Cake 4–6 SERVINGS

AMOUNT	MEASURE	INGREDIENT
2 cups	8 ounces, 226 g	All-purpose flour
1/2 teaspoon	2 g	Baking powder
1/4 teaspoon	2 g	Salt
1 cup	8 ounces, 226 g	Unsalted butter, at room temperature
1/2 teaspoon	2.5 g	Orange zest, minced
1 1/4 cups	9 ounces, 255 g	Granulated sugar
3		Eggs, at room temperature
2 tablespoons	1/4 ounce, 20 g	Ginger, grated
1/2 cup	4 ounces, 115 ml	Milk

PROCEDURE

1 Preheat the oven to 350°F (175°C). Butter and lightly flour a loaf pan or line it with parchment paper.

2 Sift together the flour, baking powder, and salt. Set aside.

3 Cream the butter and zest until light and fluffy, about 5 minutes.

4 Gradually add the sugar and beat until the mixture is fluffy again.

5 Add the eggs 1 at a time, being sure that they are well incorporated after each addition.

6 Mix in the ginger.

7 Add the flour mixture alternately with the milk, beginning and ending with the flour.

8 Pour the batter into the pan and bake for 1 3/4 to 2 hours, until a skewer inserted in the center comes out clean.

9 Serve cake warm with Warm Cranberries (page 75).

Warm Cranberries 4 SERVINGS

AMOUNT	MEASURE	INGREDIENT
³/₄ cup	5 ounces, 142 g	Granulated sugar
³/₄ cup	6 ounces, 165 ml	Water
1		Orange
3 cups	8 ounces, 226 g	Cranberries

PROCEDURE

1. Combine the sugar and water over medium heat and bring to a boil, making sure all the sugar is dissolved.

2. Cut a 2-inch (5 cm) zest strip from the orange using a vegetable peeler; do not include any of the bitter, white pith.

3. Add the zest and cranberries to the syrup and reduce to a low simmer.

4. Simmer for 6 to 8 minutes or until the cranberries begin to pop, but do not overcook. The berries should be soft but still retain their shape.

5. Remove from the heat and leave in the syrup to cool.

Waldorf Salad 4 SERVINGS

chef tip

This simple salad has become victim of too many ingredients, including sugar, whipped cream, grapes, dates, raisins, and so on. Well-flavored ripe apples do not need to be sweetened. Use Red Delicious, Winesap, or any other eating apple.

AMOUNT	MEASURE	INGREDIENT
3 cups	12 ounces, 340 g	Apples, unpeeled or peeled, cored, julienned
1 tablespoon	1/2 ounce, 14 ml	Lemon juice
1 cup	4 ounces, 113 g	Celery, julienned
1/2 cup	2 ounces, 56 g	Walnuts, chopped
1/4 cup	2 ounces, 55 ml	Mayonnaise
		Lettuce leaves, for garnish

PROCEDURE

1   Combine the apples and lemon juice; make certain the apples are well coated so they will not turn dark.

2   Add the celery and walnuts.

3   Add mayonnaise; use just enough to bind the ingredients together—no more.

4   Arrange salad on lettuce and serve immediately.

Waldorf Salad

Navy Bean Soup   4 SERVINGS

AMOUNT	MEASURE	INGREDIENT
3 1/4 cups	1 1/2 pounds, 680 g	Navy beans, picked over
1/4 cup	2 ounces, 56 g	Bacon, 1/4 inch (.6 cm) dice
1 cup	4 ounces, 113 g	Carrot, 1/4 inch (.6 cm) dice
1 cup	4 ounces, 113 g	Celery, 1/4 inch (.6 cm) dice
1 1/2 cups	6 ounces, 170 g	Onions, 1/4 inch (.6 cm) dice
1 tablespoon	15 g	Garlic, minced
1/2 teaspoon	1/2 g	Sage, chopped
1 teaspoon	1 g	Thyme, chopped
3 cups	24 ounces, 705 ml	Chicken stock
1	5 ounces, 141 g	Smoked ham hock
1 tablespoon	3 g	Chives, minced

PROCEDURE

1   Soak the beans in water overnight and drain.

2   Cook the bacon over low heat until almost crisp.

3   Add the carrot, celery, and onions; cook 5 minutes.

4   Add the garlic, cook 1 minute. Add the herbs.

5   Add the chicken stock, ham hock, and white beans and bring to a simmer.

6   Cook until the beans are tender. Remove ham hock, cut off meat into small bits, and return meat to soup, discarding the bone.

7   To thicken the soup, crush some of the beans.

8   Taste and adjust seasoning.

9   Garnish each serving with chives.

Braised Short Ribs 4 SERVINGS

AMOUNT	MEASURE	INGREDIENT
3 pounds	1.36 kg	Beef short ribs, bone-in English-style, trimmed of excess fat and silver skins
to taste		Salt and black pepper
as needed		Flour, for dusting
$^1/_4$ cup	2 ounces, 56 ml	Vegetable oil
1 $^1/_2$ cups	6 ounces, 170 g	Onions, $^1/_2$ inch (1.2 cm) dice
$^3/_4$ cup	3 ounces, 85 g	Carrots, peeled, $^1/_2$ inch (1.2 cm) dice
$^1/_4$ cup	2 ounces, 56 g	Celery, $^1/_2$ inch (1.2 cm) dice
1 teaspoon	5 g	Garlic, minced
2 tablespoons	$^1/_2$ ounce, 14 g	All-purpose flour
$^1/_2$ cup	3 ounces, 84 g	Tomato, peeled, seeded, $^1/_2$ inch (1.2 cm) dice
1 $^1/_2$ cups	12 ounces, 352 ml	Dry red wine
2 cups	16 ounces, 470 ml	Beef stock
1 tablespoon	3 g	Thyme leaves, chopped
1 teaspoon	1 g	Rosemary leaves, chopped
2		Bay leaves
1 teaspoon	5 g	Tomato paste

PROCEDURE

1 Season beef with salt and pepper. Dust with flour and shake off excess.

2 Heat oil in a large braising pan or Dutch oven over high heat.

3 Brown short ribs on all sides; transfer to platter and reserve.

4 Reduce heat to medium and cook the onions and carrots in same pan until golden brown.

5 Add the celery and cook until soft.

6 Add the garlic and cook until fragrant, about 30 seconds.

7 Stir in the flour until vegetables are coated, about 1 minute.

8 Add the tomato, wine, beef stock, thyme, rosemary, bay leaves, and tomato paste.

9   Bring to a boil and return short ribs; ribs should be almost covered with liquid. Return to a boil, cover, and place in oven at 350°F (175°C). Simmer until ribs are tender, about 2 hours.

10 Remove ribs from pot; remove excess vegetables that may cling to meat; discard loose bones that have fallen away from meat.

11 Strain the braising liquid, pressing out liquid from solids; discard solids. Degrease.

12 Heat the braising liquid to a boil and thicken to desired consistency; correct seasoning.

13 Return short ribs to sauce and cook, partially covered, until ribs are heated through.

14 Divide ribs and sauce among serving plates.

Sautéed Soft-Shell Crabs on Fennel Salad 4 SERVINGS

AMOUNT	MEASURE	INGREDIENT
1	16 ounces, 453 g	Fennel bulb
2 tablespoons	1 ounce, 28 ml	Raspberry vinegar
6 tablespoons	3 ounces, 84 ml	Olive oil
4	3 ounces, 84 g, each	Soft-shell crabs, prime grade, cleaned
1/2 cup	2 ounces, 56 g	All-purpose flour
1/2 teaspoon	3 g	Salt
1/4 teaspoon	2 g	Black pepper
1/4 teaspoon	1/4 g	Oregano (dried)
as needed		Vegetable oil, for sautéing
1 tablespoon	15 g	Garlic, minced

PROCEDURE

1   Trim the stalks and feathery tops from the fennel. Cut the bulb in half from top to root. Slice into very thin slices.

2   Combine the raspberry vinegar and olive oil; toss with the fennel. Correct the seasoning (can be held up to 1 hour before serving).

3   Combine the flour, salt, pepper, and oregano.

4   Dredge the crabs in the seasoned flour; shake off excess flour.

5   Heat oil over medium heat and cook garlic 1 minute.

6   Add crabs to pan; add more oil if necessary. Cook until golden brown on both sides. When done, there should be very little or no oil left in the pan and the crabs should be covered with garlic and flour scrapings.

7   Divide the fennel salad among 4 plates and top each salad with 1 crab.

To Clean Soft-Shell Crabs

With sharp scissors or a knife, snip off the "face" of the crab, from behind the eyes—this will kill the crab instantly. Flip the crab over and you will see a triangular "tail" piece folded up against the body of the crab. Unfold it and snip it off, too. Turn the crab right side up and unfold each of the sides. Remove the sandbags and gills either with your scissors or your hands.

Soft-shell crabs are one of America's favorite seafood delicacies. While all crabs shed their shells to grow, only a few species of crab can actually be eaten in this form. The blue crab is the only commercially available soft-shell product. The scientific name, *Callinectes sapidus*, is derived from Latin and Greek (*calli* = beautiful; *nectes* = swimmer; *sapidus* = savory). The translation is not only accurate but surprisingly poetic—the beautiful, savory swimmer.

Buttered Homemade Noodles 4 SERVINGS

AMOUNT	MEASURE	INGREDIENT
4		Eggs (large)
I teaspoon	5 g	Salt
3¹/2 cups	14 ounces 397 g	All-purpose flour
1/2 cup	4 ounces, 115 ml	Water, cold
4 tablespoons	2 ounces, 56 g	Unsalted butter
2 tablespoons	6 g	Parsley, chopped
to taste		Salt and black pepper

PROCEDURE

1. Beat the eggs and salt together.

2. Place the flour in a bowl; make a well in the center.

3. Combine the eggs with half the water and place in center well.

4. Gradually mix in the surrounding flour with a wooden spoon or spatula. Beat to make a stiff dough.

5. Turn out onto a floured work surface and knead vigorously with the heel of the hand, adding droplets of water to unblended bits. Dough should just form a mass—the pasta machine will do the rest.

6. Cut the dough in half and cover one piece with plastic.

7. For the other piece, flatten into a cake the size of your palm. Pinch one edge so it will fit into the pasta machine.

8. Set the smooth rollers to their widest opening. Crank the dough through, fold dough in half end to end, and crank through several more times until dough is smooth and a fairly even rectangle; as necessary, brush the dough with flour before passing it through rollers, since it will stick to the machine if it is too damp.

9. When the dough is smooth, reset the rollers to the next lower setting and crank it through, then to the next lower, and the next. By this time, the dough will be long; you may want to cut it in half.

10. Continue rolling until it achieves the correct thickness for noodles ($^{1}/_{8}$ inch or .3 cm).

11. Hang each strip as it is finished to dry briefly (but not to stiffen)—4 to 5 minutes.

12. Repeat the process with the remaining dough.

13   For each strip of dough, dust the top with a little flour and roll it up like a jelly roll. Slice the dough crosswise into noodles $^1/_4$ inch (.6 cm) thick.

14   Cook the noodles in boiling salted water for approximately 2 to 3 minutes or until tender. Drain thoroughly.

15   Heat the butter over medium heat.

16   Add the noodles and toss to coat with melted butter and heated thoroughly.

17   Add the parsley, salt, and pepper and toss to incorporate.

Red Swiss Chard and Spinach Sauté   4 SERVINGS

AMOUNT	MEASURE	INGREDIENT
6 cups	12 ounces, 340 g	Spinach leaves, ribs removed, washed thoroughly
6 cups	12 ounces, 340 g	Red Swiss chard, ribs removed, washed thoroughly
2 tablespoons	1 ounce, 28 ml	Olive oil
$^1/_4$ cup	1 ounce, 28 g	Onion, minced
1 tablespoon	$^1/_2$ ounce, 14 g	Garlic, minced
4 tablespoons	2 ounces, 56 ml	Unsalted butter
to taste		Salt and black pepper

PROCEDURE

1   Bring about 3 quarts (96 ounces) of salted water to a boil.

2   Blanch the chard for 2 minutes and the spinach for about 30 seconds (depending on how old the spinach is).

3   Drain and refresh in ice water; squeeze the leaves dry by hand.

4   Heat the oil over medium heat and cook the onion for 3 minutes. Add the garlic and cook 1 minute more.

5   Add the butter and let melt.

6   Add the spinach and chard. Cook until the liquid from the greens has evaporated and the chard is tender, 5 to 7 minutes.

7   Adjust seasoning.

Beef Potpie 4 SERVINGS

chef tip

The potpie—the real, old-fashioned **American** potpie made of chicken, veal, or a combination of meats and fowl—was made in a large, black iron kettle using leftover stew. Strips of dough were placed in the greased kettle, the cooked meat and uncooked vegetables were put in with broth around them, and biscuits were placed on top, the cover weighted down, and the whole mass simmered for an undetermined length of time. Individual potpies with a savory top crust are not only more appealing to the eye but also more appetizing to the palate. Biscuits, plain or with herbs and special flavors, are used mostly in making **New England** potpies. **Southerners** are more apt to make potpies with a rich pastry topping.

AMOUNT	MEASURE	INGREDIENT
2 cups	12 ounces, 340 g	Cooked beef, $^3/_4$ inch (1.9 cm) dice
$^3/_4$ cup	3 ounces, 85 g	Carrots, $^1/_2$ inch (1.2 cm) dice, parboiled
8		Pearl onions, peeled, parboiled
1 $^1/_2$	8 ounces, 226 g	All-purpose potatoes, peeled, $^1/_2$ inch (1.2 cm) dice, parboiled
1 cup	2 $^1/_2$ ounces, 71 g	White mushrooms, sliced, sautéed
3 tablespoons	1 $^1/_2$ ounces, 42 ml	Chicken fat or butter
3 tablespoons	$^1/_2$ ounces, 44 g	All-purpose flour
1 $^1/_4$ cups	10 ounces, 293 ml	Beef stock
$^3/_4$ cup	6 ounces, 170 ml	Light cream or half-and-half
to taste		Salt and black pepper
Rich Biscuit Topping		

PROCEDURE

1 Arrange the beef and vegetables in 4 individual, lightly buttered, ovenproof casseroles.

2 Melt the chicken fat and blend in the flour; cook 3 minutes, stirring.

3 Add the beef stock and whisk to a smooth consistency; let cook 10 minutes.

4 Add the cream and cook 5 minutes; correct consistency by reducing or adding more stock.

5 Correct seasoning and pour over beef and vegetables.

6 Place potpies in oven or on top of the stove and bring mixture to a boil.

7 Cover with biscuit topping and serve.

Rich Biscuit Topping 4 SERVINGS

AMOUNT	MEASURE	INGREDIENT
2 cups	8 ounces, 226 g	All-purpose flour, sifted
2 1/2 teaspoons	10 g	Baking powder
3/4 teaspoon	4 g	Salt
6 tablespoons	3 ounces, 84 g	Unsalted butter, cold, 1/2 inch (1.2 cm) dice
2/3 cup	5 1/3 ounces, 140 ml	Milk

PROCEDURE

1. Preheat the oven to 425°F (220°C).

2. Combine the flour, baking powder, and salt.

3. Mix the cold butter into the flour until the mixture looks like coarse cornmeal.

4. Stir in the milk and mix until it starts to form a ball.

5. On a lightly floured surface, knead gently for 30 seconds to shape into a ball (takes about 15 turns).

6. Roll or pat the dough to a 1/3-inch (.8 cm) thickness.

7. Cut dough to fit tops of casseroles or into diamond shapes.

8. Bake about 25 minutes, or until browned and heated through. (Do not immerse biscuit dough in liquid, or they will not brown well.)

Caprese Salad

Caprese Salad 4 SERVINGS

AMOUNT	MEASURE	INGREDIENT
16 slices	12 ounces, 453 g	Tomatoes (3 large), peeled
12 slices	6 ounces, 170 g	Fresh mozzarella
20		Basil leaves
$^1/_4$ cup	2 ounces, 55 ml	Extra-virgin olive oil
to taste		Sea salt
to taste		Black pepper

PROCEDURE

1. On individual plates, layer alternating slices of tomatoes (4 each serving) and mozzarella (3 each serving), adding a basil leaf between each.

2. Drizzle the salads with oil and season with salt and pepper.

Chicken with Dill Dumplings

Chicken with Dill Dumplings 4 SERVINGS

AMOUNT	MEASURE	INGREDIENT
I	2¹/₄ pounds, 1.02 kg	Chicken, boned, cut into 8 pieces
¹/₂ cup	2 ounces, 56 g	All-purpose flour
to taste		Salt and white pepper
2 tablespoons	I ounce, 28 ml	Peanut oil
I tablespoon	¹/₂ ounce, 14 g	Unsalted butter
¹/₂ cup	2 ounces, 56 g	Celery, ¹/₂ inch (1.2 cm) dice
¹/₂ cup	2 ounces, 56 g	Onion, ¹/₂ inch (1.2 cm) dice
I		Bay leaf
I teaspoon	I g	Thyme leaves, chopped
I teaspoon	I g	Parsley, chopped
2 cups	16 ounces, 470 ml	Chicken stock
I cup	8 ounces, 235 ml	Heavy cream

For the Dumplings

AMOUNT	MEASURE	INGREDIENT
I cup	4 ounces, 113 g	All-purpose flour, sifted
2 teaspoons	8 g	Baking powder
¹/₂ teaspoon	3 g	Salt
I tablespoon	3 g	Dill, chopped
¹/₂ cup	4 ounces, 115 ml	Milk

PROCEDURE

1 Dry the chicken pieces. (Skin may be removed from chicken if desired, but the dish will have more flavor if not removed.)

2 Combine flour with salt and pepper.

3 Heat oil and butter over medium-high heat until hot but not smoking. Dredge chicken pieces in flour and shake off excess.

4 Brown chicken pieces on all sides until golden brown.

5 Add the celery and onion; cook 2 minutes.

6   Add the bay leaf, thyme, parsley, and chicken stock. Bring to a boil, cover, and reduce heat. Simmer 15 minutes.

7   Stir in cream and continue to simmer for 5 minutes.

8   Prepare dumplings. Mix ingredients together to form a thick batter. Drop a tablespoon at a time into the simmering chicken stew. Cover tightly and cook chicken and dumplings an additional 20 minutes without removing cover.

9   Remove bay leaf and serve immediately.

The Cuisine of the South

Southern hospitality: Big family Sunday dinners, fish frys and fish boils, barbecues, oyster roasts, and public feasts. Throughout the region's history, Southern hospitality has meant open doors, welcoming smiles, and a feast for family, friends, and strangers. Southern cooking came from a blend of English, Native American, and African influences, with a mix of French and Spanish. Today it represents the comfort food that has survived the conflicts of an emerging nation.

Alabama "The Yellowhammer State," named after the nickname for the state bird, a colorful woodpecker called the northern flicker. The blackberry is the state fruit, and the State Barbeque Championship takes place in Demopolis at Christmastime.

Arkansas "The Natural State," where the state fruit and the state vegetable are the South Arkansas vine-ripe pink tomato.

Georgia "The Peach State." Georgia is known for producing the highest-quality peaches. The state vegetable is the Vidalia onion. Peanuts are the largest cash crop in the state.

Kentucky "The Bluegrass State." The Kentucky spotted bass is the state fish, and Old Kentucky blue grass and the Georgetown pattern are the state silverware patterns.

Mississippi "The Magnolia State," where the town of Belzoni is known as the Catfish Capital of the World.

North Carolina "The Tarheel State." The Scuppernong grape is the state fruit, and the state vegetable is the sweet potato.

South Carolina "The Palmetto State." The sabal palmetto is the state tree; one can sit under a palmetto tree sipping tea—the state hospitality beverage.

Tennessee "The Volunteer State." Tennessee river pearls are the state gem. The state tree is the yellow poplar, or tulip tree.

History

The roots of Southern cuisine predate the arrival of the English and Spanish in the Americas. As in most other areas of the United States, Native Americans of the region heavily influenced the cuisine. When the settlers founded Jamestown, in the Virginia Colony, they encountered the Powhatan tribe of the Algonquian Native Americans and shared a dish of succotash, venison, and berries. The Native Americans' diet included meat and seafood cooked over open fires, thought of by many as the original barbecue. Game stews, sweet potatoes, squash, pumpkins, and corn were also staples of this region.

NEW SETTLERS

After the Carolinas were founded in 1670, the first wave of settlers moved south and west, eventually crossing the Appalachian Mountains into Kentucky. The Great Philadelphia Wagon Road, called the Philly Road, was completed in the 1750s and linked Philadelphia to South Carolina. The immigrants traveling down the Philly Road were typically of Irish, Scottish, Welsh, English, and German descent. From Augusta, Georgia, wagons left the Philly Road and followed the nation's second road, the Upper Federal Road, through Georgia and Alabama to bring goods to market towns like Columbus, Mississippi. A second wave of immigrants split off from the Philly Road in North Carolina in the 1790s to settle in the Blue Ridge Mountains and the valleys and plateaus of Tennessee.

THE OLD SOUTH

The Old South can be defined as the states of the pre–Civil War period from 1820 to 1860 and consisted of North Carolina, South Carolina, Georgia, Mississippi, and Alabama. Arkansas became part of the United States with the Louisiana Purchase in 1803 and received statehood in 1836. Its tie to the South was its main crop, cotton. During the pre–Civil War period, the main cash crop in all of the Southern states, from North Carolina to Texas, was cotton. The tobacco and cotton plantations led the economic growth of the South and, in turn, provided the materials for the industrialization of the North.

THE NEW SOUTH

The Reconstruction era began with the emancipation of the slaves after the Civil War. Cotton plantations, small family farms, subsistence farming, and sharecropping defined the region's economy. By 1900, the expansion of Southern railways, cotton textiles, tobacco and forest products, and the iron, steel, and coal industries were the benchmarks of the New South. During the 1920s cotton was still the region's main cash crop, others being rice, sugar, and tobacco.

The cultivation of apples, peaches, peanuts, pecans, and soybeans also began about this time. President Roosevelt's New Deal in 1933 allowed Southern farmers to replace 50 percent of the topsoil depleted by cotton acreage with soybeans, peanuts, hay, wheat, and truck crops. Truck crops included fruits such as peaches, apples, grapes, watermelon, cantaloupe, and blueberries.

Major Influences

WHEN RICE WAS KING

The introduction and successful cultivation of rice was a significant development in colonial South Carolina. From the mid-1700s to the late 19th century, South Carolina was the nation's leading rice producer and rice was exported by the ton. Rice cultivation, which required intensive labor, provided the basis for an extensive slave-based plantation economy. Charleston was an affluent port serving wealthy plantation owners in rice production. Rice became a staple used frequently in the cooking of the Low Country—an area of swampy marshes, inlets, and bayous that extends from Orangeburg, South Carolina, to the coast, and the length of the state from the North Carolina border to Georgia's Savannah River. Southerners added rice to casseroles, soups, breads, and puddings.

Although the production of cotton and tobacco eventually surpassed that of rice in South Carolina in the first half of the 19th century, rice culture had a significant impact on the landscape, economy, and society. The Civil War, hurricanes, and the end of slavery took their toll on the rice industry in South Carolina, and by the end of the 1800s, most rice production had moved to Texas, California, Arkansas, and Mississippi.

SOUTHERN PLANTATIONS

The agricultural economy and much of life in the South revolved around plantations. Magnificent estate houses and extensive gardens reflected the gracious living, hospitality, and elegance of plantation life in the South. A complete plantation complex as it existed in the 18th and 19th centuries functioned as a small self-sustaining town. The mansion for the owner and his family was generally flanked by a number of outbuildings including the overseer's house, slave quarters, summer kitchen, smokehouse, icehouse, poultry house, cotton barn, and corn house. Slaves raised crops, tended livestock, and cultivated gardens. The smokehouse was an integral component of every plantation and a cured ham represents one of the original elements of the Southern diet. Poultry was also an important part of the Southerner's diet. Most plantations kept a variety of domesticated fowl, including chickens, ducks, geese, pigeons, and turkeys. Chickens were the most popular, and Southern fried chicken is a mainstay of the traditional Sunday dinner.

Wealthy planters enjoyed the finest of everything and served elegant, elaborate, labor-intensive meals to guests. They had the financial resources to import costly spices, wines, and fine European foods. Controversial as it was, this lifestyle became known as "Southern hospitality," and even those who lived in humble circumstances prided themselves on being gracious and welcoming to guests.

THE AFRICAN INFLUENCE

The food and style of cooking in the South was profoundly influenced by the African slaves. Not only did African-American slaves introduce many now basic foods, such as okra, yams, black-eyed peas, collard greens, sesame seeds, and watermelon, they also brought cooking techniques that had been familiar to them in West Africa, such as deep-fat frying. Working as plantation cooks both during and after slavery, they were considered to be even better cooks than the French chefs who had been brought to America.

Southern food replaced the plain, bland English cooking and African Americans developed much of what is now thought of as Southern regional cooking.

But the slave cooks had to be creative and inventive when they cooked for their own families. They were provided only the waste products after preparing the finer cuts of meat for their owners. Pork was the staple meat of the region, and it was rendered into lard while the hog's skin was fried and called "cracklings." Other ingredients commonly used by slaves included hoofs, ears, tails, brains, and intestines. With food supplies limited to the vegetables that they could grow, and only a limited amount of free time for hunting or fishing, slaves relied on their African traditions to combine complementary ingredients with small portions of meat stretched to flavor vegetable dishes. The term *soul food* referred to food made with feeling and care, and that came from the soul, or one's memory. Recipes were typically handed down through the generations by word of mouth. When millions of African Americans migrated to northern industrial cities in the 20th century, soul food became a way to recognize and celebrate their African-American identity.

For many years, Fripp Island, St. Helena's Island, and the nearby Sea Islands were cut off from mainstream South Carolina. As a result, a small group of freed African-American slaves, known as "Gullahs," were able to preserve their culture. The Gullahs came from what is now Sierra Leone in West Africa. Most notable was their language— a mixture of contemporary English, older English, and African. They developed their own music and their own rice and fish dishes, and they wove grass baskets that were both sturdy and colorful. Food in this culture took the form of one-pot meals and are represented by recipes such as Frogmore stew, a blend of shrimp, blue crab, sausage, potatoes, and corn. Red rice, hoppin' John, okra soup, shrimp and grits, pilau, peanut soup, and red beans and rice have their origins in these islands as well.

MOUNTAIN COOKING

When the first pioneers came to the Southern Appalachian Highlands that now are made up of the states of Kentucky, Tennessee, and Alabama, they faced a constant struggle against known and unknown dangers. But the hardy English, Scotch, Irish, Germans, and others tamed the wilderness and left their mark on the region. Industrious and ingenious, these early settlers cultivated fruit, berries, and nuts, as well as grew vegetables, collected honey, and had livestock. By necessity, tastes were simple, food was plain, and thrift was a natural way of life. With neighbors living miles apart, trails rugged, and communications slow, they learned to make the most of what they

Barbecue

In her book *Celebrating Barbecue,* Dotty Griffith differentiates the traditional barbecue regions in the United States. Within the debate of barbecue, all cooks agree that true barbecue is slow cooking distinguished by the cut of meat and the technique used to cook it.

In the Carolinas, pork is the traditional barbecue meat. Generally, the whole hog or shoulder is pit-cooked using direct heat. Slow-cooking at a low temperature ensures that the pig is cooked thoroughly. The resulting pulled and chopped pork may be served with a sauce based on vinegar, water, salt, and pepper. Tomato sauce or ketchup may be added depending on the cook's preferences.

Memphis barbecue also relies on pork, especially the ribs and shoulder. The meat is smoked over indirect heat and then finished over direct heat. With parts rather than the whole hog, cooking requires less time, space, and fuel. There is considerable debate in this region as to whether the meat or ribs are better when coated with a tomato-based sauce during the cooking process, resulting in a wet, or sticky, barbecue, or seasoned and served with sauce on the side, known as "dry barbecue."

Texans depend on beef for their barbecue, and the preferred cut is the brisket. Long, slow cooking over indirect heat results in very tender meat that is cut across the grain, rather than pulled or chopped. The meat may be seasoned with a dry rub, but the smoke is what provides the flavor. A wet mop is a sauce that is used during cooking and does not include sugar or tomato sauce, which might burn during cooking. A savory, slightly sweet tomato-based sauce is served on the side, with pickles and sliced onions. Glazed pork ribs or sausage with sauce on the side may also be included in a traditional Texas barbecue.

Tradition in Kansas City calls for both beef and pork (especially the ribs) cooked over indirect heat, but the emphasis is on the sauce. The preference is for a thick, tomato-based sauce with a sweet-and-sour flavor. The sauce is brushed on the meats as a finishing coat during cooking, as well as served on the side.

Traditional dishes to serve with barbecue include beans, coleslaw, and potato salad. The style of potato salad, whether mayonnaise-based or mustard-based, the type of slaw—grated, chopped, or shredded—with a creamy or vinegar dressing using red or green cabbage, and the choice of sweet or savory beans depends on the cook and the region and further individualizes a barbecue meal.

had on hand. Cooking was done by early settlers in open fireplaces and brick ovens and was more of an art than a science. Fruits and vegetables were preserved in brine or sugar, or both, in order to have foods for the winter months. A great variety of sweet-and-sour preserves, pickles, chow-chows, and relishes were put out at every meal. Ducks, quail, doves, wild turkeys, and geese were the most sought-after game birds. Other small quarry such as rabbit, squirrel, and raccoon were also used and often roasted, fried, stewed, or smothered in a sauce or gravy.

SOUTHERN LIVING

Rich or poor, native or immigrant, the South's style of cooking made food a central feature of Southerners' lives. Throughout the region's history, Southern hospitality has revolved around Sunday dinners and public feasts, and the tradition of getting together is taken seriously. It is worth noting that what the rest of the country refers to as "lunch," Southerners call "dinner" and their evening meal is called "supper." No matter the purpose, Southerners are known for their abundant food and timeless, gracious hospitality.

Typical Southern Ingredients and Dishes

Ambrosia A chilled salad or dessert made with diced fruit, nuts, marshmallows, and coconut.

Benne Wafer Benne is another name for sesame seed, the main ingredient in this crisp, nut-flavored cookie.

Bibb Lettuce A small, round lettuce with loosely formed heads and soft, buttery-textured leaves. It is named for Judge Jack Bibb, who developed it in his greenhouse in Frankfort, Kentucky, in 1865. It is also known as "limestone lettuce" because the alkaline limestone soil of the area was credited with helping produce this lettuce.

Biscuit A small, round quick bread leavened with baking powder or baking soda and cream of tartar. Biscuits should be tender, light, and flaky and are usually served for breakfast, smothered in gravy, or as an accompaniment to fried chicken at dinner.

Black-Eyed Peas Also known as "cowpeas," these small, tan beans with a distinctive black eye, were brought by African slaves. They are sold fresh, dried, frozen, and canned.

Brunswick Stew This stew traditionally used squirrel as its primary meat. Today, it may contain smoked pork or chicken and is sometimes seasoned with a ham bone. Brunswick stew is hearty and thick, somewhere between soup and stew in its consistency. The traditional vegetables included are tomatoes, onions, celery, carrots, potatoes, lima beans, and corn.

Burgoo A thick stew made from barbecued meat or mutton and vegetables. Burgoo is often associated with Kentucky.

Butter Bean A regional name for lima bean.

Catfish A freshwater, bottom-feeding fish found in the rivers and lakes of the South. The wild variety has been replaced by the farm-raised variety, now popular across America. Belzoni, Mississippi, is recognized as the Catfish Capital of the World and is famous for its high-quality, farm-raised catfish, which have a fresh, subtle taste and no fishy odor. Traditional catfish recipes call for the fish to be dredged in cornmeal and fried, served with hush puppies and coleslaw on the side.

Chicken Country Captain A traditional Low Country dish made by simmering chicken in tomato gravy flavored with curry. It is served over rice.

Chitterling The small intestine of a hog. After being cleaned, chitterlings are simmered until tender, then fried, added to soups, or served with sauce. They are also used as a casing for sausage.

Chow-Chow A relish that typically includes cabbage and green tomatoes, which are boiled in pickling brine and flavored with a hint of mustard.

Corn The Native Americans introduced this staple to the colonists. At the time, corn was tough and required slow cooking to become edible. Now every part of the corn plant can be used. The kernels are the most versatile part—used whole in side dishes and popcorn, cooked in ground forms such as cornmeal and cornstarch, and transformed into corn syrup, bourbon, and whiskey. The stalks and cobs are fed to cattle and other animals. The husks are the only authentic wrap for tamales. Corn is primarily a summer crop, but it is readily available throughout the year, frozen and canned. White cornmeal is used more often than yellow in the South, but the two can be interchanged in recipes.

Cornmeal Ground dried corn kernels. The old-fashioned grinding technique involved water-powered stone mills. The modern approach employs steel rollers. Both methods can be controlled to vary the texture of the resulting meal. Cornmeal is sold in several color varieties—white, yellow, and blue—each of which has its own characteristic flavors.

Corn Pone The word *apone* is Native American, meaning "baked." These cakes are made from water and cornmeal and baked in ashes. From this simple recipe, an assortment of breads was developed, including hush puppies, spoonbread, cracklin' bread, johnny-cakes, and hoecakes.

Country Ham A dry ham that is salt-cured for up to 3 months, then aged for up to 12 months. Country hams are produced in Virginia, Kentucky, Tennessee, North Carolina, and Georgia. After the curing process, the salt is rinsed off and the ham is slowly smoked over a hardwood fire before being aged. The salt used to cure country ham draws out the moisture in the meat, yielding a firm, flavorful finished product.

Cowpeas A broad category of peas that includes black-eyed peas and purple-hulled peas.

Cracklings The crisp fried, brown skin of roasted pork. Cracklings are sold packaged and eaten as a snack. They are also used as an ingredient in cornbread.

Deviled In the South, "deviled" indicates a dish that contains mustard, Worcestershire sauce, Tabasco, and peppers. Deviled eggs are a commonly served appetizer or hors d'oeurve.

Divinity A regional confection made from white fudge, corn syrup, or molasses combined with stiffly beaten egg whites.

Fatback A fresh, unsmoked, and unsalted layer of fat from a hog's back.

Frogmore Stew Named after a town on St. Helena Island, South Carolina, Frogmore Stew is a Gullah dish of crab, shrimp, sausage, and corn cooked with spicy seasonings.

Greens The edible leaves of plants such as collard, mustard, turnip, beet, watercress, poke sallet, spinach, kale, ramp, and dandelion. Greens are usually sautéed with salt pork or bacon or steamed.

Grits Ground from hominy to a course, medium, or fine texture, grits are typically made into a soft, savory cornmeal mush. Grits are often served as a breakfast, but also as a side dish. Shrimp and Grits is a traditional Carolina dish.

Hoecakes Also referred to as "johnnycakes," these flat griddle cakes are made from corn-meal, salt, and boiling water. It is said they were created by slaves, who cooked the mixture on their hoe under the hot sun while they worked in the fields.

Hominy Corn kernels boiled in a lye solution, then hulled, washed, and dried. Hominy is usually sold whole in cans. It is an ingredient commonly found in succotash. When ground, hominy is referred to as "hominy grits."

Hoppin' John Made from black-eyed peas cooked with salt pork and combined with rice, this dish was a staple of the African slaves who populated the plantations, especially those of the Gullah country of South Carolina. Hoppin' John was traditionally served on New Year's Day to ensure good luck and prosperity, but it is now served year-round. Collard greens and cornbread usually accompany Hoppin' John. The greens are said to represent money and the cornbread signifies gold.

Hush Puppies A cornmeal dumpling that is fried. They are the traditional accompaniment to fried catfish.

Muscadine A native American grapevine that grows well in the Southeast. It is eaten as a fruit but was the grape used for the first American-made wine made in North Carolina.

Okra A vegetable first brought to America by African slaves who used it in stews, soups, or as a side dish. It can be prepared by several methods—frying, boiling, stewing, and baking. Okra's characteristic property is that, when cooked, it exudes a gooey substance that acts as a thickening agent. Okra is available frozen, canned, breaded, and frozen breaded.

Oyster Roast A popular Low Country event similar to a clambake in the Northeast. Bushels of oysters are dumped into a roasting kettle and covered with a burlap sack, and then placed over hot coals to cook. Once cooked, the oysters are served on newspaper-lined picnic tables and are pried open with special knives.

Peanut South Americans originally cultivated this groundnut over 5,000 years ago. They were taken from South America to Africa by the Spanish explorers. The African slaves, in turn, brought the high-protein peanuts to North America. Slave traders used peanuts to provide sustenance to the Africans on the long overseas voyage. Today, peanuts are grown primarily in the South. The peanuts grown in Georgia are used primarily for peanut butter and peanut oil. The peanuts grown in Virginia are for eating raw or as cocktail nuts.

Pecan This relative of the hickory nut has a fat content of over 70 percent, which is higher than any other nut. The trees were brought east from Texas by Thomas Jefferson to his estate in Monticello, Virginia. Most pecans are grown in Georgia now, but they can also be found in Oklahoma, Texas, and Virginia.

Pilau A rice dish associated with South Carolina. Long-grain rice is simmered in an aromatic broth until cooked and nearly dry. Some pilaus call for meat or seafood in a manner similar to Spanish paella.

Poke Sallet The leaves of the perennial pokeweed plant, which grows wild in the eastern United States. The plant can reach a height of 10 feet and bears small, white flowers that become purple berries. The berries and roots are poisonous. The young leaves must be washed, boiled, and then washed again. Once cooked, poke sallet resembles spinach but tastes like asparagus.

Potlikker The liquid left over from a meal of greens, field pea, pork, or other items. Often served as a broth, potlikker was a staple among the field hands of the South.

Ramp A wild onion that resembles a large scallion. Found between February and June over a considerable range—from the Carolinas to Canada—it has an assertive garlic and onion flavor. Ramps are used both raw and cooked.

Red-Eye Gravy This gravy is made from pan drippings and flecks of ham, a few spoonfuls of coffee, and water. It is cooked until thick and is usually served with ham, biscuits, or cornbread, or used as a sauce with grits or other breakfast food.

Salt Pork A salt-cure layer of fat from a hog's sides and belly. Salt pork should be blanched before using.

She-Crab Soup A flour-thickened cream soup prepared exclusively from immature female crabs, resulting in a superior flavor. The roe (crab eggs) is usually added to enhance the flavor. Hard-boiled eggs can be used as a substitute for the crab roe.

Silver Queen Corn A hybrid corn that is sweet, tender, and white in color. Silver Queen corn matures beginning in July and remains in season for only about 30 days. It is the preferred corn in the South.

Spoonbread A type of cornbread that is similar to a soufflé.

Succotash A dish Native Americans served to the first American colonists. It is a cooked dish of lima beans, corn kernels, sweet peppers, and, sometimes, meat. The name is a contraction of a Native American word meaning "boiled whole kernels of corn."

Sweet Potato A large edible root found by European colonists in America. Sweet potatoes belong to the morning glory family and come in two varieties. The first has a light yellow skin and a pale yellow flesh. Despite its name, it is not sweet. Its texture is crumbly. The second variety has a thicker, dark orange skin and an orange, sweet flesh that cooks to a moist texture. Prepare them by baking, boiling, sautéing, or frying.

Vidalia Onion Sweet onion brought from Texas and grown only in a small number of counties around Vidalia, Georgia. The sulfur-deficient soil in this region yields a milder, sweeter onion than those grown in Texas or Hawaii. The peak growing season is late spring, and every onion is set, clipped, harvested, and sized by hand.

Menus and Recipes from the Cuisine of the South

MENU ONE

Grilled Quail with Spicy Eggplant Relish

Tomato Aspic on Bibb Lettuce Salad

Pecan-Encrusted Catfish with Orange-Scented Sweet Potatoes

Succotash of Corn, Hominy, and Baby Lima Beans

Slow-Cooked Greens

Hush Puppies

Peanut Brittle

MENU TWO

Hoppin' John Salad with Pecan Vinaigrette

Vidalia Onion Tart with Roasted Tomato Sauce and Green Onion–Basil Oil

Shrimp Perloo

Carolina Pulled Pork Barbecue Sandwich

Sandwich Slaw

Potato Salad

Banana Pudding

MENU THREE

Watermelon and Watercress Salad with Shallot-Citrus Dressing

Fried Green Tomatoes with Blue Cheese and Roasted Red Pepper Sauce

Southern Fried Chicken with Cream Gravy

Pan-Roasted Butternut Squash and Turnips

Peach Cobbler

OTHER RECIPES

Cauliflower with Curry

Smothered Pork Chops

Frogmore Stew

Rutabagas with Bacon and Thyme

Grilled Quail with Spicy Eggplant Relish   4 SERVINGS

Brining poultry (soaking in a saltwater solution) before cooking serves two purposes: it helps the flesh retain moisture and it seasons all the way through. To make the brine, stir kosher salt into cold water until dissolved, in the proportion of $1/4$ cup (15 g) salt to 1 quart (1 l) water. (Don't use table salt in this formula or it will be too salty.)

AMOUNT	MEASURE	INGREDIENT
4		Semi-boneless quail, brined for 30 to 45 minutes
to taste		Salt and black pepper
$1/2$ teaspoon		Thyme (dried)
6 tablespoons	3 ounces, 84 ml	Olive oil
1 teaspoon	5 g	Granulated sugar
$1/4$ teaspoon	2 g	Salt
$1/2$ teaspoon	5 g	Dijon mustard
2 tablespoons	1 ounce, 28 ml	Cider vinegar
1 tablespoon	3 g	Parsley, minced
2 cups	8 ounces, 226 g	Yellow squash and zucchini, in long, thin noodles

PROCEDURE

1   Rub the quail with salt, pepper, thyme, and 2 tablespoons (1 ounce, 28 ml) oil.

2   Grill quail to desired doneness, 6 to 8 minutes per side, remove, and set aside.

3   Combine the sugar, salt, mustard, vinegar, remaining oil, and parsley.

4   Toss the squash with the dressing.

5   Divide squash among 4 plates and place 1 warm quail on top of squash. Serve with relish.

Spicy Eggplant Relish 4 SERVINGS

AMOUNT	MEASURE	INGREDIENT
1/3 cup	2 ounces, 56 g	Raisins
1/4 cup	2 ounces, 55 ml	Cider vinegar
2 pounds	907 g	Eggplants
2 tablespoons	1 ounce, 28 ml	Olive oil
1/2 cup	2 ounces, 56 g	Onion, 1/2 inch (1.2 cm) dice
1 cup	4 ounces, 113 g	Green bell pepper, 1/2 inch (1.2 cm) dice
1/2 teaspoon	3 g	Salt
1/4 teaspoon	1 g	Black pepper
3		Garlic cloves, minced
1		Jalapeño pepper, seeded, minced
1/2 cup	3 ounces, 85 g	Tomato, peeled, seeded, 1/2 inch (1.2 cm) dice
1 tablespoon	1/3 ounce, 10 g	Honey

PROCEDURE

1 Preheat the oven to 425°F (220°C).

2 Plump the raisins in the vinegar for 15 minutes.

3 Bake the eggplants (prick skin) for 1 hour or until the skins are shriveled and eggplants are soft. Remove and let cool.

4 Peel eggplant and cut into 1/2-inch (1.2 cm) dice.

5 Heat the olive oil over medium heat, add onion and green pepper, and cook 8 minutes or until soft.

6 Add the salt and pepper, garlic, and jalapeño; stir well and cook 4 minutes.

7 Add the tomato, the raisins with their soaking liquid, the honey, and eggplant. Simmer 15 minutes, stirring often.

8 Correct seasoning and let set overnight for flavors to blend. May be served warm, at room temperature, or cold.

Tomato Aspic on Bibb Lettuce Salad 4 SERVINGS

The traditional accompaniment is mayonnaise.

AMOUNT	MEASURE	INGREDIENT

For the base

AMOUNT	MEASURE	INGREDIENT
2 cups	12 ounces, 340 g	Tomatoes, very ripe, peeled, seeded, roughly chopped
1/2 cup	2 ounces, 56 g	Onion, 1/4 inch (.6 cm) dice
1/2 cup	2 ounces, 56 g	Celery, 1/4 inch (.6 cm) dice
1		Garlic clove, smashed
2		Bay leaves
3		Whole peppercorns
2		Whole cloves
1/2 teaspoon	3 g	Kosher salt
1 cup	8 ounces, 235 ml	Water

Flavoring

AMOUNT	MEASURE	INGREDIENT
1/2 tablespoon	7 g	Granulated sugar
1/2 tablespoon	7 ml	Cider vinegar
1/2 tablespoon	7 ml	Lemon juice
1/2 teaspoon	2 g	Kosher salt

For the Gelatin

AMOUNT	MEASURE	INGREDIENT
1 tablespoon	9 g	Unflavored gelatin
2 tablespoons	1 ounce, 28 ml	Water

PROCEDURE

1 Combine the base ingredients in a nonreactive pan. Bring to a simmer, uncovered, over medium heat.

2 Simmer for 20 minutes or until tomatoes have broken down (to maintain a fresh flavor, do not cook longer than necessary).

3 Strain through a fine-mesh strainer, pressing gently to extract all the juice.

4   Measure to 2 cups (16 ounces, 480 ml) of liquid. Adjust seasoning after tasting, depending on the ripeness and flavor of the tomatoes. Tomatoes can very greatly in sweetness and acidity; also, aspic is a cold dish, and cold temperature will dull the seasoning slightly. When seasoned correctly, return to a simmer.

5   Mix the gelatin with the water until softened.

6   Add the gelatin to the simmering tomato juice and stir for 2 minutes.

7   Remove from heat and transfer to a pan in a bowl of ice water, stirring constantly until the liquid chills and begins to thicken. This is an important step to ensure an even color and texture.

8   Pour into 4-ounce (113 g) lightly oiled molds. Cover and refrigerate several hours until set.

Bibb Lettuce Salad 4 SERVINGS

AMOUNT	MEASURE	INGREDIENT
1 1/2 tablespoons	3/4 ounce, 21 ml	Lemon juice
1 tablespoon	1/2 ounce, 14 ml	Red wine vinegar
1 tablespoon	1/2 ounce, 15 g	Granulated sugar
1 teaspoon	5 g	Dijon mustard
1/4 cup plus 1/2 tablespoon	2 ounces, 62 ml	Olive oil
to taste		Salt and black pepper
2 heads	8 ounces, 226 g	Bibb lettuce, washed, dried, torn

PROCEDURE

1   Combine lemon juice, vinegar, sugar, and mustard; whisk together.

2   Slowly whisk in 1/4 cup (2 ounces, 58 ml) olive oil.

3   Season and set aside.

4   Toss the lettuce with the vinaigrette to coat.

5   Remove the aspic from the molds. Serve the salad on chilled plates and top with the aspic.

Pecan-Encrusted Catfish 4 SERVINGS

AMOUNT	MEASURE	INGREDIENT
I cup	4 ounces, 113 g	Pecans, chopped
1/3 cup	2 ounces, 56 g	Cornmeal, fine-grained
1/2 cup	2 ounces, 56	Bread crumbs, dry
2 tablespoons	6 g	Parsley, chopped
4	(4–6 ounces, 113–170 g)	Catfish fillets, skinless
I		Egg, beaten with I tablespoon (14 ml) water
to taste		Salt and white pepper
I cup	4 ounces, 112 g	All-purpose flour, for dredging
as needed		Vegetable oil, for pan-frying

PROCEDURE

1 Place the pecans, cornmeal, bread crumbs, and parsley in a food processor and blend until chopped. (This can be as fine as you would like.)

2 Season the catfish fillets and dip fillets in flour; shake off excess, dip in egg wash, and let excess drip off. Place fillets in the pecan cornmeal mixture, pat and turn until completely breaded, then set aside until needed.

3 Heat the oil to 350°F (175°C).

4 Pan-fry the fillets 2 to 3 minutes on first side, turn and cook 1 to 1 1/2 minutes more until golden brown; drain on paper towels.

Orange-Scented Sweet Potatoes 4 SERVINGS

AMOUNT	MEASURE	INGREDIENT
16 ounces	453 g	Sweet potatoes, washed
2 tablespoons	3/4 ounce, 20 g	Honey
3 tablespoons	1 1/2 ounces, 42 g	Unsalted butter, melted
1		Egg, lightly beaten
2 tablespoons	1 ounce, 28 ml	Orange juice
1 teaspoon	5 g	Orange zest
1 teaspoon	5 g	Salt
1/4 teaspoon	1 g	White pepper

PROCEDURE

1 Preheat the oven to 400°F (205°C).

2 Pierce the potatoes with a fork. Bake 35 minutes or until tender.

3 Cool potatoes slightly, halve lengthwise, and scoop out the pulp.

4 Combine potato pulp with the honey, 2 tablespoons (1 ounce, 28 ml) butter, egg, juice, zest, salt, and pepper. Mix until smooth (use a food processor for very smooth consistency).

5 Reduce the oven to 350°F (175°C).

6 Place mashed sweet potatoes in baking pan, dot top with remaining butter. Bake 20 to 30 minutes.

Succotash of Corn, Hominy, and Baby Lima Beans 4 SERVINGS

AMOUNT	MEASURE	INGREDIENT
2 cups	5 ounces, 141 g	Baby lima beans
2 tablespoons	1 ounce, 28 g	Bacon, 1/4 inch (.6 cm) dice
2 tablespoons	1 ounce, 28 g	Butter
1 cup	5 ounces, 141 g	Corn kernels, fresh
3 tablespoons	1 ounce, 30 g	Shallots, chopped
1 cup	6 ounces, 170 g	Hominy, canned, drained
2 tablespoons	1 ounce, 28 ml	Dry white wine or chicken stock
1/2 cup	4 ounces, 115 ml	Heavy cream
to taste		Salt and black pepper
1 tablespoon	3 g	Parsley, chopped

PROCEDURE

1 Parboil the lima beans 1 minute, until just tender; drain.

2 Over medium heat, render the bacon until crisp; add half the butter.

3 Add the shallot, cook for 2 minutes or until soft, add the corn, and cook 3 minutes longer or until corn is tender.

4 Add the hominy and lima beans; stir to combine.

5 Add the white wine; cook 3 to 5 minutes to reduce most of the liquid.

6 Add the cream and reduce until it begins to thicken.

7 Stir in remaining butter.

8 Season with salt and pepper, and toss in the parsley.

Slow-Cooked Greens 4 SERVINGS

AMOUNT	MEASURE	INGREDIENT
2 bunches	24 ounces, 680 g	Mixed greens (turnip greens, collard greens, mustard greens, beet greens, kale, or sorrel)
3/4 cup	6 ounces, 170 g	Bacon, 1/4 inch (.6 cm) dice
1/2 cup	2 ounces, 56 g	Celery, 1/4 inch (.6 cm) dice
2 cups	8 ounces, 226 g	Onions, 1/4 inch (.6 cm) dice
1 cup	4 ounces, 113 g	Green bell pepper, 1/4 inch (.6 cm) dice
1	8 ounces, 226 g	Ham hock
2 tablespoons	1 ounce, 28 ml	Red wine vinegar
1/8 teaspoon	1 g	Red pepper flakes
1 cup	8 ounces, 235 ml	Water
to taste		Salt and black pepper

PROCEDURE

1 Pick over the greens to remove any tough stems, veins, and yellow leaves. Wash and drain thoroughly.

2 Cut into 2-inch (5 cm) pieces and set aside.

3 Cook the bacon over medium-high heat until fat has been rendered, brown but not crisp, 3 to 5 minutes.

4 Add the celery, onion, and bell pepper and cook 5 minutes.

5 Reduce the heat to medium and add the greens. Cover and cook, stirring occasionally, until greens are wilted, about 10 minutes.

6 Add the ham hock, vinegar, and red pepper flakes; cover and cook 15 minutes.

7 Add the water, cover, and simmer for 1 1/2 hours, stirring occasionally.

8 Correct the seasoning.

Hush Puppies 4 SERVINGS

chef tip

Hush puppies are an essential component of fried-fish plates. There are many stories on how they were named, the most common referring to the scrapes of fried corn dough thrown to hungry hounds to "hush" them.

AMOUNT	MEASURE	INGREDIENT
I cup	6 ounces, 170 g	Cornmeal, fine-grained
I tablespoon	8 g	All-purpose flour
1/2 teaspoon	2 g	Baking soda
1/2 teaspoon	2 g	Baking powder
1/2 teaspoon	2 g	Kosher salt
1/4 cup	I ounce, 28 g	Onion, grated or finely minced
2 tablespoons	6 g	Green onion, green part only, minced
I		Egg yolk
I cup	8 ounces, 235 ml	Buttermilk
2		Egg whites

PROCEDURE

1   Preheat the deep-fryer to 350°F (175°C).

2   Combine the cornmeal, flour, baking soda, baking powder, and salt; whisk to blend.

3   Add the onion, green onion, egg yolk, and buttermilk; stir to combine (should be the consistency of loose mashed potatoes—if necessary, add more buttermilk).

4   Whip the egg whites to soft peaks. Fold egg whites into cornmeal mixture.

5   Drop mixture by rounded tablespoons into hot oil. Cook to golden brown. Puppies usually roll over on their bellies when they are done, but they may need to be turned to ensure they cook completely.

6   Remove to paper towels to drain. Serve immediately.

Peanut Brittle YIELDS 2 POUNDS (907 G)

chef tip This great treat came out of the South in the late 19th century, when people were searching for new products and ideas for using the peanut crop.

AMOUNT	MEASURE	INGREDIENT
2 cups	14 ounces, 396 g	Granulated sugar
¹/₂ cup	6 ounces, 170 g	Light corn syrup
¹/₂ cup	4 ounces, 115 ml	Water
1 cup	5 ounces, 141 g	Peanuts, raw
¹/₂ teaspoon	3 g	Salt
1 tablespoon	¹/₂ ounce, 14 g	Unsalted butter
¹/₈ teaspoon	1 g	Baking soda
¹/₂ teaspoon	2 ml	Vanilla extract

PROCEDURE

1 Combine the sugar, corn syrup, and water over medium heat and cook to dissolve sugar.

2 Continue to cook to soft-ball stage (238°F, 114°C).

3 Add the peanuts and salt; cook, stirring constantly, until mixture reaches the hard-crack stage (300°F, 149°C).

4 Remove from heat and stir in butter, baking soda, and vanilla.

5 Pour the mixture into a generously buttered shallow pan or cookie sheet. Let cool.

6 When hardened, break into irregular 2-inch (5 cm) pieces. Store in an airtight container.

Hoppin' John Salad with Pecan Vinaigrette
4 SERVINGS

AMOUNT	MEASURE	INGREDIENT
For the Salad		
1/2 cup	3 ounces, 85 g	Long-grain white rice, cooked
2 1/2 cups	13 ounces, 368 g	Black-eyed peas, cooked, chilled
1/2 cup	2 ounces, 56 g	Red bell pepper, seeded, 1/8 inch (.3 cm) dice
1/2 cup	2 ounces, 56 g	Green beans, blanched, shocked, cut 1 1/2 inches (3.8 cm) long on bias
1/2 cup	2 ounces, 56 g	Green onions, chopped
2 cups	4 ounces, 113 g	Mixed baby field greens
For the Vinaigrette		
2 tablespoons	1 ounce, 28 ml	Cider vinegar
1/2 teaspoon	2 g	Brown sugar
1/3 cup	1 1/2 ounces, 42 g	Pecans, chopped, toasted
1/2 teaspoon	1 g	Thyme, chopped
1/2 teaspoon	4 g	Salt
1/2 cup	4 ounces, 115 ml	Vegetable oil
to taste		Salt and black pepper

PROCEDURE

1 Combine the rice, black-eyed peas, bell pepper, green beans, and green onions. Set aside.

2 Puree the vinaigrette ingredients except oil in a food processor.

3 Slowly drizzle in the oil. Adjust seasoning.

4 Toss all but 6 tablespoons (3 ounces, 84 ml) of the vinaigrette with the black-eyed pea mixture.

5 Toss mixed greens with remaining vinaigrette and place as a bed on cold plates.

6 Mold 1 cup (4 ounces, 112 g) of hoppin' john mixture onto each plate of greens.

Vidalia Onion Tart   YIELDS 9-INCH TART

AMOUNT	MEASURE	INGREDIENT
1 sheet	6 ounces, 170 g	Frozen puff pastry dough, thawed
2	10 g	Shallots, peeled, left whole
1		Garlic clove, peeled
1/4 cup	2 ounces, 55 ml	Olive oil
1	4 ounces, 113 g, each	Red onion, peeled, sliced thinly
1 cup	4 ounces, 113 g	Vidalia onion or sweet onion, peeled, julienned
1 cup	4 ounces, 113 g	Leeks, white part only, cleaned, julienned
2 each		Eggs, beaten
3/4 cup	6 ounces, 165 ml	Heavy cream
to taste		Salt and black pepper
1 tablespoon	3 g	Chives, finely diced

PROCEDURE

1   Preheat the oven to 375°F (190°C).

2   Line a 9-inch (22.9 cm) tart pan with puff pastry; prick the dough all over with a fork.

3   Top with a second pie pan; trim the overhang to 1/2 inch (1.2 cm) beyond the rim. Par-bake the unfilled pie shell in a preheated oven for 10 to 15 minutes or until the shell is cooked. Remove from oven, remove second pie pan, and cool.

4   Turn oven to 350°F (175°C).

5   Toss shallots and garlic in 1 tablespoon (1/2 ounce, 15 ml) olive oil and wrap loosely in foil; roast for 20 minutes, or until soft.

6   Heat 1 tablespoon (1/2 ounce, 15 ml) oil over medium heat and slowly caramelize the whole slices of red onion. Handle gently so that they retain their round shape. When well-browned and soft, place slices on bottom of prepared shell.

7   Smash the roasted shallots and place around the red onion.

8   Heat remaining oil over medium heat and cook the Vidalia onions and leeks for 10 minutes or until very soft and slightly brown. Scatter evenly over red onion rings in tart shell.

9   Mash roasted garlic in a bowl and add eggs, cream, salt, pepper, and chives. Mix to combine.

10 Pour over onions and bake for about 15 minutes, until brown on top; loosely cover with foil and bake until set, 45 minutes.

11 Remove tart from oven and discard foil. Cool slightly—at least 10 minutes—before cutting and serving.

12 Serve with Green Onion–Basil Oil and Roasted Tomato Sauce (page 116).

Vidalia Onion Tart

Green Onion–Basil Oil 4 SERVINGS

AMOUNT	MEASURE	INGREDIENT
1/4 cup	2 ounces, 56 ml	Olive oil
1/2 cup	2 ounces, 56 g	Green onions, chopped
1 cup	1 ounce, 56 g	Basil leaves, loose packed

PROCEDURE

Puree all ingredients in blender until smooth.

Roasted Tomato Sauce 4 SERVINGS

AMOUNT	MEASURE	INGREDIENT
3 cups	16 ounces, 453 g	Plum tomatoes, quartered
1 cup	3 ounces, 85 g	Red onion, quartered
1/2 teaspoon	1 g	Thyme, chopped
1/2 teaspoon	1 g	Rosemary, chopped
1 tablespoon	1/2 ounce, 14 ml	Olive oil
to taste		Salt and black pepper

PROCEDURE

1 Preheat the oven to 350°F (175°C).

2 Toss the tomatoes, onions, and herbs with oil.

3 Place on parchment-lined sheet pan and roast for 45 minutes.

4 Puree in a food processor to desired consistency (slightly lumpy, coarse texture).

5 Correct seasoning with salt and pepper.

Shrimp Perloo 4 SERVINGS

AMOUNT	MEASURE	INGREDIENT
1/4 cup	4 ounces, 113 g	Bacon, 1/2 inch (1.2 cm) pieces
1 1/2 cups	6 ounces, 170 g	Onions, 1/2 inch (1.2 cm) dice
2 cups	12 ounces, 340 g	Tomatoes, peeled, seeded, chopped
1/2 teaspoon	1 g	Red pepper flakes
3/4 cup	5 ounces, 141 g	Long-grain rice
2 cups	16 ounces, 470 ml	Clam juice
16 ounces	453 g	Shrimp (16–20 count), peeled, deveined
1/4 cup	1/2 ounce, 14 g	Parsley, chopped
1 1/2 tablespoons	3/4 ounce, 21 ml	Lemon juice
to taste		Salt and black pepper

PROCEDURE

1 Render the bacon over medium heat and cook until crisp. Remove to paper towel–lined plate.

2 Drain all but 2 tablespoons (1 ounce, 28 ml) of fat from pan.

3 Add the onion and sauté, stirring occasionally, 10 minutes.

4 Add the tomatoes and red pepper flakes, and cook 5 minutes.

5 Stir in the rice and clam juice. Bring to a boil, reduce to a simmer, and cover. Cook 20 minutes.

6 Stir in the shrimp and fluff the rice. Remove from the heat and cover; let set 10 minutes (the heat from the rice should cook the shrimp).

7 Add the parsley, lemon juice, and reserved bacon. Correct seasoning and serve.

Carolina Pulled Pork Barbecue Sandwich 4 SERVINGS

AMOUNT	MEASURE	INGREDIENT
For the Dry Rub		
1 1/2 tablespoons	1/3 ounce, 10 g	Black pepper, ground
1 1/2 tablespoons	3/4 ounce, 21 g	Dark brown sugar, packed
1 1/2 tablespoons	1/3 ounce, 10 g	Paprika
2 tablespoons	1 ounce, 28 g	Coarse salt
1/2 teaspoon	1 g	Cayenne pepper
2 pounds	907 g	Pork shoulder (Boston butt), boneless
For the Mop		
1/2 cup	4 ounces, 115 ml	Apple cider vinegar
1/4 cup	2 ounces, 55 ml	Water
1 tablespoon	1.2 ounce, 14 ml	Worcestershire sauce
1/2 tablespoon	3 g	Black pepper
1/2 teaspoon	3 g	Coarse salt
1 teaspoon	5 ml	Vegetable oil
1 cup	8 ounces, 23 ml	Carolina Barbecue Sauce
4		Hamburger buns, toasted

PROCEDURE

1 Mix the ingredients for the dry rub.

2 Sprinkle the dry rub over the pork and press into the meat. Cover and let set 1 hour at room temperature.

3 Combine ingredients for the mop and set aside.

4 If possible, hot-smoke the pork until fork-tender, brushing with cold mop every 45 minutes; or roast the pork at 300°F (150°C) for 3 hours or until fork-tender, brushing with cold mop every 45 minutes.

5 Remove from oven or smoker and let rest 30 minutes.

6 Pull the meat apart or shred using 2 forks.

7   Combine the shredded pork with barbecue sauce, cover tightly, and simmer 20 to 30 minutes. Add more water if needed.

8   Serve pork on toasted bun with coleslaw, potato salad, and additional barbecue sauce.

Carolina Pulled Pork Barbecue Sandwich

Carolina BBQ Sauce

YIELDS 1 1/2 CUPS (12 OUNCES, 336 ML)

AMOUNT	MEASURE	INGREDIENT
1 teaspoon	2g	Dry mustard
1 teaspoon	5 g	Coarse salt
1 tablespoon	1/4 ounce, 7 g	Sweet Hungarian paprika
1 tablespoon	1/2 ounce, 15 g	Granulated sugar
1 tablespoon	1/2 ounce, 15 g	Brown sugar
1/2 teaspoon	1 g	Cayenne
1/2 teaspoon	1 g	Black pepper
2/3 cup	6 ounces, 141 ml	Water
1/4 cup	2 ounces, 55 ml	Worcestershire sauce
1/2 cup	4 ounces, 115 ml	Red wine vinegar

PROCEDURE

1 Combine the dry ingredients in a saucepan. Stir in the water; heat to boiling, then remove from heat.

2 Stir in the Worcestershire sauce and vinegar.

Sandwich Slaw 4 SERVINGS

AMOUNT	MEASURE	INGREDIENT
2 cups	7 ounces, 198 g	Green cabbage, shredded
2 tablespoons	1/2 ounce, 14 g	Onions, minced
2 tablespoons	1 ounce, 28 ml	Cider vinegar
2 tablespoons	1 ounce, 28 ml	Mayonnaise
1		Garlic clove, minced
2 teaspoons	1/3 ounce, 10 g	Granulated sugar
1 teaspoon	2 g	Black pepper
to taste		Salt

PROCEDURE

Mix the ingredients and refrigerate for 1 hour. Place a generous portion on each sandwich or serve alongside.

Potato Salad 4–6 SERVINGS

AMOUNT	MEASURE	INGREDIENT
3 cups	18 ounces, 510 g	All-purpose potatoes, cooked, in 1-inch (2.5 cm) cubes
2		Eggs, hard-cooked
1/2 cup	2 ounces, 56 g	Celery, 1/4 inch (.6 cm) dice
1/4 cup	1 ounce, 28 g	Green onions, chopped
1/3 cup	2 ounces, 56 g	Bread-and-butter pickles, chopped
1/2 cup	2 ounces, 56 g	Red onion, 1/4 inch (.6 cm) dice
1/2 cup	2 ounces, 56 g	Red bell pepper, 1/4 inch (.6 cm) dice
3/4 cup	6 ounces, 170 ml	Mayonnaise
1 teaspoon	5 ml	Worcestershire sauce
1 teaspoon	5 ml	Dijon mustard
to taste		Salt
to taste		Pepper

PROCEDURE

1 Boil the potatoes in their skins until tender, then peel and cube.

2 Separate the yolks from the whites of the eggs. Mash yolks and chop whites.

3 Combine the potatoes, chopped egg white, celery, green onions, pickles, red onion, and bell pepper

4 Combine the egg yolks, mayonnaise, Worcestershire sauce, and mustard; mix well.

5 Combine dressing with potatoes and stir gently to coat.

6 Correct seasoning with salt and pepper. Chill.

Banana Pudding 4 SERVINGS

AMOUNT	MEASURE	INGREDIENT
For the custard		
1 cup	8 ounces, 235 ml	Milk
1 cup	8 ounces, 235 ml	Heavy cream
1/2		Vanilla bean
6		Egg yolks
1/3 cup	2 1/2 ounces, 70 g	Granulated sugar
2 tablespoons	1 ounce, 28 g	All-purpose flour
pinch		Salt
1 teaspoon	5 ml	Vanilla extract
For the Meringue		
6		Egg whites, at room temperature
1/4 teaspoon	2 ml	Vanilla extract
1/2 cup	3 1/2 ounces, 100 g	Granulated sugar
For the Filling		
2 cups	8 ounces, 226 g	Angel food cake, 1-inch (2.5 cm) cubes, lightly toasted, or vanilla wafers
2	13 ounces, 368 g	Bananas, 1/2-inch (1.2 cm)-thick slices

PROCEDURE

1 In a nonreactive pan, combine the milk, 1/2 cup (4 ounces, 115 ml) cream, and the vanilla bean. Heat to just below a simmer, cover, and remove from heat; let set for 15 minutes to develop the vanilla flavor. Remove vanilla bean, wipe off, and retain for another use.

2 Whisk together the egg yolks, sugar, flour, and salt until smooth.

3 Whisk the warm milk into the egg yolk mixture, return to the heat, and cook until the custard thickens and begins to bubble. Cook for 1 minute after the custard comes to a boil. (It should be thick at this point.)

4 Strain through a fine-meshed sieve into a bowl and immediately whisk in the remaining cream and the vanilla.

5 Preheat the oven to 400°F (205°C).

6 Beat the egg whites until they begin to froth and add the vanilla. Continue beating until they make soft peaks. Gradually add the sugar a tablespoon at a time, and beat until egg whites are moist and very glossy.

7 Spoon a thin layer of custard onto the bottom of a 4-cup (32 ounces, 946 ml) oven-proof baking container. Top with layer of cake cubes and sliced bananas. Spoon more custard over and continue layering, ending with custard on top.

8 Top with meringue, making sure there is a good seal at the edges of the baking pan.

9 Bake for 5 minutes, until golden brown. Serve warm or at room temperature.

Watermelon and Watercress Salad with Shallot-Citrus Dressing 4 SERVINGS

AMOUNT	MEASURE	INGREDIENT

For the Dressing

AMOUNT	MEASURE	INGREDIENT
1 1/2 tablespoons	3/4 ounce, 21 g	Shallots, minced
1 teaspoon	5 ml	Dijon mustard
1/2 teaspoon	3 ml	Honey
2 tablespoons	1 ounce, 28 ml	Apple cider vinegar
1 tablespoon	1/2 ounce, 14 ml	Orange juice
1 tablespoon	1/2 ounce, 14 ml	Lime juice
1/4 cup	2 ounces, 55 ml	Extra-virgin olive oil
1/4 cup	2 ounces, 55 ml	Vegetable oil
to taste		Salt and black pepper

For the Salad

1¹/₂ tablespoons	¹/₃ ounce, 10 g	White sesame seeds
¹/₄ teaspoon	1 ml	Roasted sesame oil
2 cups	11 ounces, 311 g	Watermelon, seeded, 1-inch (2.5 cm) pieces
3 cups	6 ounces, 170 g	Watercress leaves, washed, dried
¹/₄ cup	¹/₂ ounce, 14 g	Flat-leaf parsley
¹/₂ cup	2 ounces, 56 g	Green onions, white and green parts, sliced
¹/₄ cup	1 ounce, 28 g	Chervil tops, fresh (fresh oregano may be substituted)

PROCEDURE

1   Combine all the dressing ingredients except the oils and salt and pepper in a blender. Blend until smooth and add the oils slowly to make an emulsion. Correct seasoning.

2   Toast the sesame seeds in sesame oil until lightly toasted, and let cool.

3   Combine half of the seeds with the watercress, parsley, green onions, and chervil. Toss with half of the dressing.

4   Toss the watermelon with the remaining dressing.

5   Divide the greens among cold plates and top with watermelon.

6   Sprinkle with remaining sesame seeds.

Fried Green Tomatoes with Blue Cheese · 4 SERVINGS

AMOUNT	MEASURE	INGREDIENT
8 slices	16 ounces, 453 g	Green tomatoes or firm red tomatoes
1/2 cup	4 ounces, 115 ml	Buttermilk
1		Egg, beaten
1/2 tablespoon	8 ml	Tabasco
1/2 cup	2 ounces, 56 g	All-purpose flour
1 cup	6 ounces, 170 g	Yellow cornmeal, medium-grind
1/2 teaspoon	3 g	Salt
1/8 teaspoon	1 g	Black pepper
as needed		Peanut oil, for pan-frying
1/4 cup	56 g	Blue cheese
as desired		Roasted Red Pepper Sauce

PROCEDURE

1 Core the top of each tomato and cut into 1/4-inch (.6 cm)-thick slices.

2 Combine the buttermilk, egg, and Tabasco.

3 Place the tomato slices in the mixture and marinate for 30 minutes, turning occasionally.

4 Combine the flour, cornmeal, salt, and pepper.

5 Drain the tomato slices and dredge in the breading mixture.

6 Place the slices on a baking sheet and refrigerate for 30 minutes to allow the breading to dry.

7 Heat the oil to 350°F (175°C).

8 Pan-fry for 45 seconds to 1 minute on each side or until they are golden brown. Do not overcrowd the pan or the temperature of the fat will drop and you will end up with greasy tomatoes.

9 Drain on paper towels.

10 To serve, place 2 tomato slices on each warm plate. Spoon on Roasted Red Pepper Sauce (page 128) and sprinkle with blue cheese.

Fried Green Tomatoes with Blue Cheese

Roasted Red Pepper Sauce   4 SERVINGS

AMOUNT	MEASURE	INGREDIENT
20 ounces	567 g	Red bell pepper, 3–4 whole
2 tablespoons	1 ounce, 28 ml	Olive oil
1		Garlic clove
2	2 ounces, 56 g	Shallots, chopped
3 tablespoons	1¹/₂ ounces, 42 ml	Dry red wine
¹/₄ cup	2 ounces, 56 ml	Chicken stock or vegetable stock
¹/₂ teaspoon	1 g	Oregano, chopped
¹/₂ teaspoon	3 ml	Balsamic vinegar
1 teaspoon	5 g	Granulated sugar
as needed		Salt and pepper

PROCEDURE

1   Roast the peppers over an open flame and turn as needed to char the surface of each pepper. Remove from the fire and wrap each pepper in plastic wrap for 10 minutes. Remove the charred skin, stem, seeds, and then dice. (Do not wash or you will lose the roasted flavor.)

2   Heat the oil over medium heat, add the garlic and shallots, and cook 2 minutes.

3   Add the red pepper and cook 2 minutes more.

4   Add the wine, stock, oregano, vinegar, and sugar; cook 1 minute.

5   Remove from the heat and puree with peppers until smooth. Strain through a fine strainer (optional).

6   Adjust seasonings if necessary.

Southern Fried Chicken with Cream Gravy 4 SERVINGS

chef tip

For a true Southern pan-fried chicken, combine 1 pound (453 g) lard, ¹/₂ cup (4 ounces, 115 ml) butter, and ¹/₂ cup (4 ounces, 113 g) diced country-style ham over low heat and simmer for 30 minutes, skimming as needed, until the butter is clarified. Strain and use for frying chicken.

AMOUNT	MEASURE	INGREDIENT
1	3 pounds, 1.36 kg	Chicken, cut into 8 pieces, brined
1 quart	1 l	Buttermilk
1 cup	4 ounces, 113 g	All-purpose flour
2 tablespoons	²/₃ ounce, 18 g	Cornstarch
to taste		Salt and black pepper
as needed		Vegetable oil, for frying

For the Cream Gravy

AMOUNT	MEASURE	INGREDIENT
2 tablespoons	1 ounce, 28 ml	Vegetable oil
¹/₄ cup	1 ounce, 28 g	All-purpose flour
2 cups	16 ounces, 470 ml	Milk
to taste		Salt and black pepper

PROCEDURE

1 Drain the chicken and soak in buttermilk for 1 hour at room temperature or 4 hours under refrigeration.

2 Combine the flour, cornstarch, salt, and pepper.

3 Remove the chicken from the buttermilk and drain. Dredge in the flour mixture, then pat well to remove all excess flour. Let sit until the flour is pastelike. This is crucial for crisp chicken.

4 Heat oil to 335°F (168°C).

5 Add chicken pieces, skin side down; do not overcrowd the pan—fry in batches, if necessary. Cook 8 to 10 minutes on each side, until the chicken is golden brown and cooked.

6 Drain on rack and paper towels.

7   If shallow frying in a skillet, drain off all the oil from the skillet except 2 tablespoons (1 ounce, 28 ml).

8   Make a roux with the oil and flour and cook the roux to a light tan.

9   Add the milk and cook 5 minutes. Add the seasoning and cook until thick and smooth. Taste and adjust the seasoning.

Pan-Roasted Butternut Squash and Turnips 4 SERVINGS

When roasting vegetables, it is important to give the vegetables lots of room so that they will color nicely and not just steam on top of each other.

AMOUNT	MEASURE	INGREDIENT
2 cups	10 ounces, 283 g	Butternut squash, peeled and seeded, 1 inch (2.5 cm) dice
2 cups	10 ounces, 283 g	Turnips, peeled, 1 inch (2.5 cm) dice
1 tablespoon plus 1 teaspoon	2 ounces, 56 g	Honey
2 tablespoons	1 ounce, 28 ml	Vegetable oil
1/4 teaspoon	2 g	Salt
1/4 teaspoon	1 g	Black pepper
1 teaspoon	1 g	Thyme, chopped
1/3 cup	1 ounce, 28 g	Pumpkin seeds, toasted
1 tablespoon	3 g	Chives, finely chopped

PROCEDURE

1   Preheat the oven to 425°F (220°C).

2   Toss the squash and turnips in the honey, oil, seasonings, and thyme. Place on a parchment-lined sheet pan with a sprinkle of water.

3   Roast, covered loosely for 30 minutes; gently turn the vegetables and cook 20 minutes uncovered or until vegetables are tender.

4   Toss with the toasted pumpkin seeds and chives.

Peach Cobbler 4 SERVINGS

AMOUNT	MEASURE	INGREDIENT
For the Pastry		
1 1/2 cups	6 ounces, 170 g	All-purpose flour
3/4 teaspoon	4 g	Kosher salt
1/2 teaspoon	3 g	Granulated sugar
1/2 cup	4 ounces, 113 g	Unsalted butter, in 1/2-inch (1.2 cm) pieces, cold
1/4 cup	2 ounces, 56 ml	Water, very cold
For the Filling		
4 cups	24 ounces, 680 g	Peaches, firm but ripe, peeled, in 1/2-inch (1.2 cm)-thick slices
1/4 cup	2 ounces, 56 g	Granulated sugar
1 tablespoon	7 g	All-purpose flour
1/8 teaspoon	1 g	Salt
1/4 teaspoon	1 g	Nutmeg, freshly grated
2 tablespoons	1 ounce, 28 g	Butter
as needed		Granulated sugar to sprinkle top

PROCEDURE

1 Combine the flour, salt, and sugar. Cut in butter until it resembles coarse meal. Add the cold water and knead the dough about 15 times.

2 Shape into a flat disk, wrap, and let rest, at least 1 hour.

3 Preheat the oven to 425°F (220°C).

4 Roll out half the dough 1/8 inch (.3 cm) thick. Line 1 quart (32 ounces, 1 l), 2-inch (5 cm)-deep baking dish. Trim the edges as needed, leaving 1/2 inch (1.2 cm) of pastry hanging over rim. Cut any trimmings of pastry into 1-inch (2.5 cm) pieces and reserve.

5 Mix the sugar, flour, salt, and nutmeg and toss with peaches.

6 Fill the pastry-lined dish with peaches. Dot 1 tablespoon butter over peaches.

7 Roll out the second half of the dough 1/8 inch (.3 cm) thick—large enough to cover the top of the cobbler. Moisten the rim of the dough in the baking dish with water, and lay the top dough over. Gently press the edges together to seal, then fold the edge over inside the rim.

8   Cut a few 1-inch (2.5 cm) slits in top dough to allow steam to escape. Sprinkle top with sugar and dot with remaining butter.

9   Bake 20 minutes, then reduce heat to 375°F (190°C) and cook 30 minutes longer, until the crust is deep golden brown and the filling begins to bubble through the slits.

10   Cool on a rack until warm; may be served with whipped cream or ice cream.

Cauliflower with Curry 4 SERVINGS

AMOUNT	MEASURE	INGREDIENT
4 cups	16 ounces, 453 g	Cauliflower, cut into 1-inch (2.5 cm) pieces
1/4 cup	2 ounces, 55 ml	Olive oil
2		Garlic cloves, peeled
2 tablespoons	6 g	Parsley, chopped
to taste		Salt
1 tablespoon	1/4 ounce, 7 g	Curry powder
2 tablespoons	1 ounce, 28 ml	Sherry vinegar
1/4 cup	2 ounces, 55 ml	Chicken stock or vegetable stock

PROCEDURE

1   Steam or parboil the cauliflower until just tender.

2   Heat the oil over medium heat with the garlic until the garlic has turned light brown. Remove from heat. Keep the oil; mash the garlic with half the parsley and few pinches of salt.

3   Return pan to low heat and add the curry powder; cook 1 minute. Add the vinegar, stock, and garlic-parsley mixture.

4   Toss cauliflower in the curry mixture and serve.

Smothered Pork Chops 4 SERVINGS

AMOUNT	MEASURE	INGREDIENT
4	5 ounces, 141 g each	Pork chops, $^3/_4$ inch (1.9 cm) thick
$^1/_2$ cup	2 ounces, 56 g	All-purpose flour
4 tablespoons	2 ounces, 56 ml	Bacon fat or vegetable oil
2 cups	8 ounces, 226 g	Leeks, white and light green parts only, halved lengthwise, cleaned, thinly sliced
6		Garlic cloves, slivered
$^3/_4$ cup	6 ounces, 170 ml	Chicken stock
$^3/_4$ cup	6 ounces, 170 ml	White wine
to taste		Salt and black pepper

PROCEDURE

1 Dredge the pork chops in the flour, shaking off excess.

2 Heat the bacon fat over medium heat. Add the pork and cook until golden brown on both sides.

3 Remove pork chops and add leeks and garlic. Cook for 10 minutes, stirring occasionally, until they just begin to brown.

4 Add chops back to leek mixture. Add stock and wine. Stir and smother the chops with leek mixture.

5 Reduce heat to a simmer and cover. Cook until chops are very tender, 30 to 45 minutes.

6 Season with salt and pepper.

Frogmore Stew 4 SERVINGS

AMOUNT	MEASURE	INGREDIENT
I		Vidalia onion, peeled, halved
2		Garlic cloves, minced
I tablespoon	$^1/_4$ ounce, 7 g	Old Bay seasoning
I quart	I l	Clam juice
2 cups	16 ounces, 470 ml	Water
I teaspoon	5 g	Salt
2		Ears of corn, shucked, cut into 3-inch (7.6 cm) pieces
I pound	453 g	New potatoes, scrubbed, cut in half
12 ounces	340 g	Kielbasa or andouille sausage, cut into 1-inch (2.5 cm) pieces
12 ounces	340 g	Crawfish
12 ounces	340 g	Shrimp, unpeeled (20–24 count)
$^1/_4$ cup	I ounce, 28 g	Green onions, thinly sliced
$^1/_2$ cup	3 ounces, 85 g	Tomato, peeled, seeded, $^1/_4$ inch (.6 cm) dice

PROCEDURE

1 Combine the onion, garlic, Old Bay seasoning, clam juice, water, and salt; bring to a boil.

2 Add the corn and cook until tender.

3 Lower to a simmer and add the potatoes and sausage; cook until tender.

4 Add the crawfish and shrimp. Cook until shrimp and crawfish are just done, about 4 minutes.

5 Divide the shellfish, corn, sausage, and potatoes evenly into the bowls. Ladle broth evenly over mixture.

6 Garnish with sliced green onions and tomato.

Rutabagas with Bacon and Thyme   4 SERVINGS

AMOUNT	MEASURE	INGREDIENT
4 cups	16 ounces, 453 g	Rutabaga, peeled, 1-inch (2.5 cm) cubes
1/4 cup	2 ounces, 56 g	Bacon, 1/4 inch (.6 cm) dice
1		Garlic clove, minced
1 teaspoon	1 g	Thyme, chopped
1/2 teaspoon	3 g	Salt
1/2 teaspoon	2 g	Black pepper
1 tablespoon	1/2 ounce, 14 ml	Butter

PROCEDURE

1   Par-boil the rutabaga in salted water; drain.

2   Over medium heat, render the bacon until crisp.

3   Add the rutabaga, garlic, thyme, salt, and pepper. Cook over low heat until tender, approximately 10 minutes.

4   Season to taste and toss in butter.

Floribbean Cuisine

Floribbean cuisine, also known as *new era cuisine,* has emerged as one of America's new and most innovative regional cooking styles. The fresh flavors, combinations, and tastes of Floribbean cuisine are representative of the variety and quality of foods indigenous to Florida and the Caribbean Islands. Regional chefs often make a commitment to using locally grown foods and the fish and seafood of the abundant fresh and salt waters of the area.

The cooking style and techniques used in Florida today are highly influenced by those of Cuba, Jamaica, and the Bahamas, but they are lighter, with less frying and fewer oils involved in the preparation. This current movement is, however, only a little more than a decade old. The roots of Floribbean cuisine trace back to the exploration of the New World by the Spanish.

Florida "The Sunshine State" is one of the world's strongest tourist magnets due to the abundance of sunny days. The state tree is the sabal palm, from which hearts of palm or *swamp cabbage*—is harvested. The state reptile is the alligator, which lives in the streams and swamplands. The state freshwater fish is the largemouth bass, and the state saltwater fish is the sailfish. The state beverage is orange juice, and the state flower is the orange blossom.

History and Influence of the Immigrants

Juan Ponce de Leon first landed on the Atlantic Coast in 1513, and shortly thereafter Spain began to colonize the area, building forts and missions. But with Florida's rough terrain and the Spaniards' supply problems and weakening empire in Europe, all of their expeditions failed. They did, however, establish a settlement at St. Augustine in northeast Florida in 1565, and this became the first permanent European settlement in the United States. The French disputed Spain's right to Florida, so they began to settle the area, too. Both sides attacked the other's settlements, often completely destroying them. Farther north, the English became worried that the Spanish and French would threaten the Carolinas and Georgia. When the French and Indian War ended in 1763, Spain gave Florida to England. After the Revolutionary War, England gave Florida back to Spain. Finally, in 1819, Spain sold Florida to the United States.

FLORIDA DEVELOPMENT

During the final quarter of the 19th century, large-scale commercial agriculture in Florida, especially cattle raising, grew in importance. Industries such as cigar manufacturing took root in the immigrant communities of the state. Potential investors became interested in enterprises as diverse as sponge harvesting in Tarpon Springs, and the Florida citrus industry grew rapidly.

The development of industries throughout Florida prompted the construction of roads and railroads on a large scale. The citrus industry benefited now that oranges could travel to the northern states in less than a week. Beginning in the 1870s, residents from the northern states visited Florida as tourists to enjoy the state's natural beauty and mild climate. This tourism industry drove the development of lavish winter resorts from Palm Beach to Miami Beach, nicknamed the "Gold Coast."

By the early 1900s, Florida's population and per-capita wealth were increasing rapidly, and land developers and promoters marketed the state as a tourist and retirement mecca, resulting in a massive real estate boom in South Florida. This boom ended by 1926, and land prices plummeted. The Great Depression hit the nation and Florida's citrus industry was further devastated by the invasion of the Mediterranean fruit fly.

World War II brought an end to the Great Depression and led the reemergence of economic development in Florida. One of the most significant trends of the postwar era has been steady population growth, resulting from large migrations from within the United States and from countries throughout the Western Hemisphere.

LITTLE HAVANA

Florida's most diverse cities are Tampa and Miami. Before the turn of the century, Tampa was the center of the U. S. cigar manufacturing industry. Many of the cigar makers were Cuban Americans, and southern and eastern Europe provided the rest of the workforce. With so many immigrants from Cuba, Spain, and Italy, Tampa developed a mixed Mediterranean and Latin culture.

Florida's current multicultural center is Miami. In 1959, a revolutionary army led by Fidel Castro seized power in Cuba. Castro's political foes and many professionals and businesspeople fled the island-nation, just 90 miles from southern Florida. Many of these Cuban exiles eventually settled in Miami. In 1980, more than 100,000 people left Cuba for Florida and have developed a Cuban-American economic and political presence in South Florida.

Although Cuban Americans now form South Florida's largest ethnic community, other groups have played a significant cultural role. Northern Jewish retirees moved to South Florida beaches, and today the region has the second largest Jewish population of any U.S. metropolitan area. Large populations from Haiti, Nicaragua, the Dominican Republic, Brazil, and other Central American countries also exist in Florida. In addition, a Southeast Asian influence is beginning to be seen as more people immigrate to Florida from Indonesia, Cambodia, and Vietnam.

The People, Their Ingredients, and Adaptations

THE FLORIDA COASTLINE

When the Spanish arrived in Florida in the early 1500s, they brought cattle and pigs with them to the New World. From this introduction of livestock to Florida, the Spanish are given credit for many recipes using meat in a region that formerly depended entirely on fish and game. In return for livestock, the Native Americans taught the Spanish about local fruits and vegetables, including hearts of palm, malanga, yuca, and plantains.

Later, the abundant finfish attracted Cuban fishermen to the harbors and bays. They salted and dried their catch, and then shipped it to Havana and other Spanish colonial settlements. Before the Civil War in the 1860s, the commercial red snapper and grouper industry was active, as well as industries developed for harvesting and processing clams, scallops, turtles, oysters, and shrimp. The spiny lobster, actually a large sea crawfish with no claws, is found in the waters off lower Florida's west coast. Stone crabs are trapped and fishermen remove one of the two claws, tossing the crabs back into the water to grow the missing claw back. The conch that is found in the spiraled seashell has sweet but tough meat that is chopped up for fritters and chowders. The conch was so popular in Key West that it was hunted to near extinction, leading to dependence on Costa Rica and the Bahamas for harvest.

Greek sponge divers settled at Tarpon Springs in 1905, and other immigrants, including Italians, Chinese, and Cubans, brought their cooking traditions with them.

THE FLORIDA PANHANDLE

Inland toward the center and north of the state, the food is more Southern in character. In the mid-1600s, the Spanish conquistadors brought many thousands of slaves from Africa to Florida and the Caribbean Islands. The slaves brought with them the skills and knowledge to grow, cook, and prepare the types of foods they were familiar with: yams, eggplant, sesame seeds, and okra. Many of the regional specialties, like field peas and okra, came from this period.

In the mid-1700s, a group of Minorcans—people of Catalan descent from the Spanish Balearic Islands—were brought to the Florida region as indentured laborers. Their foods and cooking influenced the existing Florida cuisine, particularly in the use of peppers.

SOUTH FLORIDA AND THE GOLD COAST

Agriculture has fueled much of the area's economic development. Draining the Everglades uncovered rich soil, permitting the development of sugarcane fields, and helped turn the area southwest of Miami into the winter vegetable capital of the country. Today, Florida is the nation's top producer of sugarcane, and Florida trails only California in the production of fresh vegetables such as tomatoes, greens, beans, and peppers. Florida is one of the largest producers of citrus fruits in the world, and Florida oranges

Latin Caribbean Influence

Latin Caribbean cooking offers complex, flavorful ingredients from diverse cultures. Ingredients introduced by ancient Aztecs, Mayans, and Incas are combined with flavors and recipes of its diverse groups of immigrants, including the Spanish, Portuguese, French, Italians, Middle Easterners, Africans, Chinese, Japanese, and Germans. Cooks from regions that include Cuba, Puerto Rico, and the Dominican Republic flavor their foods with relatively mild seasonings—oregano, tomato, garlic, black pepper, and mild chiles. Rice is a staple and seafood, fruits, and root vegetables like cassava, boniato, and malanga are abundant. Ground meat dishes called picadillo, rice and beans, mofongos (mashed plantain with pork crackling), escabeches, seviches, frijoles, and paella are commonly found. Recipes are flavored with adobos, mojos, coconut milk, and cilantro.

Salsas are now the most frequently used condiment in the United States, and are an essential part of Latin regions. Salsas come in many forms and flavors. Spicy and hot with vegetables such as tomatoes, beans, corn, peppers, and cucumbers, or tart and acidic with fruits like mango, pears, pineapple, and grapefruit, they are used extensively to provide flavor. The word *mojo* comes from the Spanish word *mojado,* which means "wet." Mojos are more liquid in consistency than salsas and are used as sauces or marinades. The heat of the salsas and mojos are adjusted with the choice of peppers, from the fiery Scotch bonnets to the milder banana peppers. By using any of the countless vinegars or fruit juices combined with choices of oils that include olive, walnut, hazelnut, and avocado, salsas and mojos can provide a wide range of flavors. In addition, they have the benefit of being very low in calories and cholesterol, making them healthy alternatives to heavier, cream-based sauces. They require little or no cooking and the fresher, more colorful, and more flavorful the ingredients, the better the salsas and mojos are. These sauces are served with chips, or with any type of meat, fish, or poultry.

provide nearly 80 percent of the orange juice consumed in the United States. Florida also produces grapefruit, limes, lemons, and tangerines. Some of the more exotic citrus fruits from the region include kumquats, tangelos, pummelos, and calamondins.

Probably the greatest influence on Floribbean cuisine began in the 1950s, with the large migration of Cubans to South Florida. Caribbean and Latin American immigrants have followed the Cubans and have found that many of their native ingredients are indigenous to Florida. They brought with them all of the rice and legume dishes from the Caribbean, like rice and peas, or beans. Coloring foods, like adding turmeric and saffron to rice, reminded them of the palm oil that is used in West Africa, from where many Caribbean slaves originated. They used cane sugar in oil, caramelized to give a color and flavor to their stews. Dried and smoked ingredients as well as pickled pork and vegetables are important in intensifying their foods. Seasoning pastes, salsa, rubs, and hot sauces are used not only for flavor but also to enhance digestion and encourage perspiration in order to cool off in the hot environment. By balancing the hot spices with cool, tropical fruits, this cuisine has captured the attention of the more adventurous American palate.

In the 1980s, a talented group of local chefs recognized these exotic ingredients and the cooking traditions of the immigrant population. With Miami's explosion as a new and exciting playground for the hip, rich, and famous, they have developed and marketed what has become one of the next acknowledged regional cuisines of America.

Typical Floribbean Ingredients and Dishes

Alcaporado A Cuban-style beef stew cooked with raisins and olives.

Adobo An all-purpose seasoning containing garlic, vinegar, oregano, black pepper, and turmeric. Adobos are used as base seasonings to add flavor to stews, sauces, or rice, and to marinate beef, pork, chicken, or fish. The word *adobo* means "marinade" and dry adobos are used as spice rubs or pastes.

Annatto Small reddish berries (achiote seeds) that serve as a colorant in the cooking of the Caribbean. Mixed with lard or other cooking oils, the foods cooked in them become orange-yellow. It has been suggested that this method of cooking replaces the red palm oil used in West African cooking. Annatto oil can be drizzled over meat and shellfish, or added to salad dressings.

Arroz con Pollo A Cuban chicken and rice dish frequently served in South Florida restaurants. It can be served as an entree with a little broth or as a hearty soup.

Arroz Marillo Cuban-style saffron rice. Typically, long-grain white rice cooked with saffron, but due to the high cost of saffron, turmeric is frequently used as a substitute.

Avocado Originally from Mexico and considered an aphrodisiac by the Incas and Aztecs, avocados grown in South Florida are called "alligator pears" because the skin resembles an alligator hide. Florida avocados typically have a higher water content and milder flavor than avocados from California.

Banana Leaf Found in Latin, Caribbean, and Asian specialty markets, this leaf from the banana tree is used as a wrapper for cooking food in the Florida region. This technique imparts the flavor of the banana to other foods.

Banana Pepper Also known as the Hungarian wax chile, banana peppers are large, usually 3 to 5 inches in length, ranging in flavor from mild to medium hot. Banana peppers are known for their distinctive waxy texture.

Beans The most common beans used in Floribbean cooking are kidney beans, preferred by the Haitians; black beans, preferred by the Cubans; and pink beans, found frequently in Caribbean cooking.

Bolichi A marinated pot roast rolled with hard-boiled eggs, this popular Cuban dish popular in the Florida Keys is similar to the South American preparation for pot roast called *matambre*.

Boniato A tuber similar in appearance to a sweet potato with white or yellow flesh and a somewhat bitter flavor. Drier, fluffier, and a little less sweet than a sweet potato, boniato can be prepared by boiling, baking, deep-frying, roasting, steaming, or sautéing.

Calabeza A large Cuban squash, also known as a West Indian pumpkin, with a round or pear shape. Larger than a honeydew melon, the skin may be orange, green, or striped. The orange flesh has a flavor similar to pumpkin or butternut squash, but is sweeter and moister. Calebeza is typically sold halved or in slices due to its large size.

Calamondins Known as an "acid orange," the fruit is small and orange, about 1 inch (2.5 cm) in diameter, and resembles a tangerine. The tree is often grown as an ornamental, but the fruit is edible and the juice can be used like lemon or lime juice.

Callaloo A vegetable similar to kale, Swiss chard, and spinach, brought to South Florida by the African slaves from the Caribbean.

Cassava Another name for yuca.

Coconut The large, hairy fruit of the coconut palm tree. The flesh of the fruit is white in color and lines the inside of the shell. When selecting coconuts, shake them to ensure that there is liquid inside the shell.

Coconut Milk A combination of equal parts water and shredded fresh coconut meat, simmered until foamy. The mixture is then strained though cheesecloth to retain as much liquid as possible. Canned coconut milk makes an excellent substitute for fresh.

Conch A large mollusk found in the coral reefs off the coast of South Florida and around the Florida Keys. Conch meat has a flavor similar to sweet clams and is typically used to make chowder or fritters. Conch shells are large, attractive, and whorled—the kind that children hold to their ear to hear the sound of the ocean.

Cubanella Pepper A large, lemon-yellow, mild pepper about the size of a green bell pepper.

Flan The Cuban-style preparation of flan flavors the traditional French custard with almonds, coconut, or rum. It is frequently served with plantains or black beans.

Grouper A fish found in the waters of the Caribbean, the Gulf of Mexico, and the North and South Atlantic. There are many species, including black, tiger, yellowmouth, comb, and graysby, ranging in size from 5 to 15 pounds, but sometimes as large as 600 pounds. The flesh is lean, firm, and sweet, making grouper suitable for baking, broiling, frying, poaching, and steaming.

Guava A round fruit with a flavor similar to strawberries. Usually 2 to 6 inches in diameter, with thick greenish-white, yellow, or red edible skin. It has small seeds embedded in the flesh of the fruit that can be removed by passing the flesh through a sieve. Guava can be eaten raw or cooked in jellies, pastes, or chutneys, or used as a base for glazes and custards.

Hearts of Palm Also referred to as "swamp cabbage," hearts of palm are the tender inner parts of the sabal or cabbage palm tree. They have a white to ivory color and many concentric layers with a delicate flavor reminiscent of an artichoke. They are considered rare and are expensive because the palm tree must be destroyed in order to obtain them. Hearts of palm are served in salad preparations and can be eaten raw or cooked.

Jamaican Pimiento Also known as "allspice," this highly aromatic pea-size berry has a flavor that tastes like a combination of cinnamon, nutmeg, and cloves. When the berries are ground, the spice is known as "pimiento."

Jerk Seasoning A dry seasoning used primarily in the preparation of grilled meat. The ingredients can vary depending on the cook, but it is usually a blend of chiles, thyme, spices (such as cinnamon, ginger, allspice, and cloves), garlic, and onions. Jerk seasoning can be either rubbed directly onto the meat or blended with a liquid to create a marinade. In the Caribbean, the most common meats seasoned in this fashion are pork and chicken.

Key Lime One of the two main varieties of lime available in the United States. Small, yellowish fruit with a highly aromatic, tart flavor, similar to very tart lemons, Key lime trees were first planted in the Florida Keys in 1835. The Key lime is smaller than the more common Persian lime, with a color more yellow than green. When substituting Persian limes for Key limes, use one Persian lime for every three Key limes called for in the recipe.

Kumquats These look like small, oblong oranges and have been called "the little gold gems of the citrus family." They have an intensely bitter flavor, but can be eaten whole, used as a garnish, or candied.

Litchi Also spelled *litchee* and *lychee,* this is a small, oval fruit with a hard, red shell; it is frequently referred to as a nut. The fruit contains one large seed surrounded by sweet, white flesh. Litchi is available fresh as well as in cans. The litchi may be eaten fresh or prepared by drying the fruit, which gives it a nutty, raisinlike flavor.

Manchego Cheese A Spanish sheep's milk cheese that has a full, mellow flavor and is ivory to yellow in color and semifirm to hard in texture. Manchego cheese is prepared in a variety of ways, including dry salting, curing, and soaking in olive oil. Each of the preparation techniques used to make Manchego cheese results in a different color, flavor, and texture.

Malanga A root vegetable with a shape like a long yam. It has pinkish flesh and patchy, thin brown or beige skin.

Mango A sweet fruit with a pale to deep yellow flesh with a flavor similar to a very sweet peach. When ripe, the skin of the mango is green to a rosy red color and very aromatic. The surface of the fruit should yield to light pressure, similar to an avocado. Green, unripe mangos are frequently used to prepare chutneys and relishes.

Moros y Cristianos A traditional Spanish dish made with black beans and rice. The name is Spanish for "Moors and Christians" and symbolizes the conflict between the dark-skinned Moors who invaded Spain in the eighth century and the white-skinned Christians, who, after being dominated for hundreds of years, eventually overthrew them. Moros y Cristianos is typically served as a side dish with meat and fried plantains.

Paella The classic Spanish rice dish that became popular in Cuba and South Florida when the Spanish colonized the regions. In Florida, Paella features chorizo and shellfish cooked with Valencia rice in a large cooking vessel commonly referred to as a *pallero* or a *paella.*

Papaya A sweet melonlike fruit with flesh that varies in color from light pink to deep orange. When cut open, the papaya has many small black seeds that have a taste between watercress and pepper. Papaya is usually sliced and served with a wedge of lime. Papaya has the ability to tenderize meat due to the enzyme papain, which also aids in digestion.

Papaya is also used in chutneys, sauces, desserts, and salads. The grayish-black seeds are often used in salad dressings or as a garnish.

Passion Fruit A small, tennis-ball-size fruit with a brownish purple skin that is wrinkled like a walnut. Inside, small black seeds are encased in a yellow or orange-colored translucent flesh that is tart and citrusy. Used more for its juice than its pulp, it is found in sorbets and desserts. To determine whether a passion fruit is ripe, shake the fruit and listen for the sound of liquid moving under the skin.

Picadillo A popular Cuban preparation of highly seasoned and spicy beef hash. It is typically served with black beans, rice, and fried plantains.

Pickapeppa Sauce A bottled sauce made from a blend of tomatoes, onions, sugarcane, vinegar, mangoes, tamarind, and peppers, then aged in oak. It was created in Jamaica in 1921 and is known as "Jamaican ketchup."

Plantain A member of the banana family used extensively in Latin America and the Caribbean. Unlike bananas, plantains are almost never eaten raw, and the ripeness of the plantain determines its cooking use. Green plantains are suitable for chips and adding to stews because of their high starch content. Yellow, medium-ripe plantains are soft but have not lost their starchy taste and can be used as a vegetable. Black-skinned, ripe plantains are these where the starch has turned to sugar and can be used in desserts.

Pummelo A large, thick-skinned fruit resembling an orange, but with the flavor of a grapefruit.

Seville Orange Also referred to as "bitter" or "sour" oranges, they are smaller than regular oranges and have a rough, thin orange and yellow skin. The flesh and juice are darker than typical Florida oranges and have a very tart flavor. Seville oranges are frequently used in the preparation of orange marmalade. The juice is used to marinate meats, and the rind is used to make the liqueur curacao and orange flower water. If Seville oranges are not available, combine regular orange juice with a little lime juice as a substitute.

Sofrito Derived from the Spanish word *sofreir,* meaning "to fry lightly," sofrito is an essential flavoring agent. Though there are many variations, most mixtures are made from salt pork, lard, ham, onion, garlic, and oregano. It can be prepared in large amounts and stored in the refrigerator until needed.

Star Fruit Also referred to as "carambola," this is a small, yellow-green to golden orange fruit named for its star-shaped cross sections. The flesh of the fruit has a tart, crisp flavor somewhat like a tart apple and thin, waxy skin that is edible. Star fruit is frequently used in salad preparations and as a garnish for other dishes.

Tamarind The sticky, dry pod of the tamarind tree with a taste similar to plums, yet much more sour. It is frequently used as an ingredient in chutney but may be used in place of lime or lemon juice in recipes that require a sweet-and-sour tang with extra body. Tamarind paste can be purchased in Caribbean specialty markets. It is also referred to as "Indian date."

Tangelos A hybrid of the mandarin orange and the grapefruit.

Yuca Also referred to as "casava," yuca is a sweet, buttery, and starchy tuber shaped like an elongated sweet potato. It has a barklike skin and hard, white flesh. Yuca is used in preparations much as a potato is, and is frequently prepared as fritters or used in stews. Coating the skin with olive oil helps retain the yuca's moisture, as well as helping it cook faster.

Menus and Recipes from Floribbean Cuisine

MENU ONE

Black Bean Soup

Ceviche of Gulf Shrimp with Floribbean Slaw

Chicken with Tamarind Ginger Sauce

Stewed Pink Beans

Stuffed Chayote with Tomatoes, Mushrooms, and Cheese

Candied Sweet Potatoes

MENU TWO

Key West Conch Chowder

Hearts-of-Palm Salad

Pan-Seared Grouper with Black Bean, Jícama, and Corn Relish or Tropical Fruit Salsa

Corn Custard

Key Lime Pie

MENU THREE

Golden Gazpacho with Puff Pastry Straws

Warm White Beans, Mesclun Salad, and Mango Chutney

Roasted Pork Loin, Cuban-Style

Mango and Jalapeño Mojo

Spicy Orange Carrot Sticks

Fried Plantain Chips

OTHER RECIPES

Rice and Peas

Shrimp with Roasted Garlic and Papaya

Avocado Salsa

Tropical Tuber Torta

Black Bean Soup 4 SERVINGS

AMOUNT	MEASURE	INGREDIENT
2 cups	12 ounces, 340 g	Black beans
1/4 cup	2 ounces, 56 g	Bacon, 1/4 inch (.6 cm) dice
1 1/2 cups	6 ounces, 170 g	Onions, 1/4 inch (.6 cm) dice
2		Garlic cloves, minced
1 teaspoon	2 g	Ground cumin
1 teaspoon	2 g	Oregano (dried)
2 quarts	64 ounces, 2 l	Chicken stock
1		Ham hock
2 tablespoons	1 ounce, 28 ml	Sherry wine
to taste		Salt and white pepper

For the Garnish

AMOUNT	MEASURE	INGREDIENT
1 cup	4 ounces, 113 g	Onion, 1/4 inch (.6 cm) dice
1 tablespoon	1/2 ounce, 14 g	Olive oil
2 tablespoons	1 ounce, 28 ml	Sherry vinegar
2 cups	8 ounces, 226 g	Boiled rice
1 tablespoon	1/2 ounce, 14 g	Sour cream
2 tablespoons	6 g	Green onions, sliced

PROCEDURE

1 Pick over the beans and soak overnight in cold water to cover. Drain.

2 Render the bacon over medium heat, add the onions and garlic, and cook 3 minutes or until soft.

3 Add the beans, cumin, oregano, chicken stock, and ham hock; bring to a simmer, turn down the heat, and simmer for approximately 1 to 1 1/2 hours or until beans are tender.

4 Remove ham hock; cool, remove the meat, dice, and reserve.

5 Puree the soup and bring back to a simmer.

6 Add ham hock, meat, and sherry, and season with salt and pepper. Be sure to check the consistency of the soup; adjust with more chicken stock if too thick.

7 For garnish, marinate onion in olive oil and vinegar for at least 30 minutes.

8 Garnish the soup with rice, marinated onion, sour cream, and sliced green onions.

Ceviche of Gulf Shrimp 4 SERVINGS

AMOUNT	MEASURE	INGREDIENT
$1/2$ cup	2 ounces, 56 g	Red bell pepper, roasted, peeled, seeded, $1/4$ inch (.6 cm) dice
$1/2$ cup	2 ounces, 56 g	Yellow bell pepper, roasted, peeled, seeded, $1/4$ inch (.6 cm) dice
12 ounces	340 g	Shrimp (16–20 count)
$1/4$ cup	2 ounces, 55 ml	Lime juice
2 tablespoons	1 ounce, 28 ml	Lemon juice
1 tablespoon	$1/2$ ounce, 14 ml	Orange juice
2 tablespoons	1 ounce, 28 ml	Olive oil
$1/4$ cup	$1/2$ ounce, 14 g	Cilantro, chopped
pinch		Ground coriander
to taste		Salt and white pepper

PROCEDURE

1   Roast the peppers over an open flame and turn as needed to char surface of each pepper. Remove from the fire and wrap each pepper in plastic; steam for 10 minutes. Remove the charred skin, stem, seeds, and dice. (Do not wash or you lose the roasted flavor.)

2   Peel, devein, and cut the shrimp in half lengthwise; place in a stainless steel bowl.

3   Combine the peppers, and juices with shrimp; add the seasoning and toss the shrimp in the marinade. Marinate for approximately 2 hours. The shrimp will turn pinkish and become firm.

4   Add the olive oil and cilantro; combine thoroughly. Cover and store in refrigerator until needed.

Floribbean Slaw 4 SERVINGS

AMOUNT	MEASURE	INGREDIENT
$^2/_3$ cup	2 ounces, 56 g	Green cabbage, julienned
$^1/_2$ cup	2 ounces, 56 g	Red bell pepper, julienned
$^1/_2$ cup	2 ounces, 56 g	Green bell pepper, julienned
$^3/_4$ cup	3 ounces, 85 g	Carrots, julienned
$^3/_4$ cup	3 ounces, 85 g	Yellow squash, julienned (do not use center)
$^1/_4$ cup	2 ounces, 56 g	Mayonnaise
$^1/_4$ cup	2 ounces, 56 g	Sour cream
$^1/_2$ cup	$^1/_2$ ounce, 14 g	Cilantro, chopped
to taste		Salt and black pepper

PROCEDURE

1 Combine all ingredients and mix thoroughly. Let flavors combine for at least 1 hour.

2 Taste and adjust seasoning; serve cold.

Chicken with Tamarind Ginger Sauce 4 SERVINGS

AMOUNT	MEASURE	INGREDIENT
4	6 ounces, 170 g each	Chicken breasts, boneless, skinless
2 tablespoons	1 ounce, 28 ml	Lemon juice
1 tablespoon	1/2 ounce, 14 ml	Lime juice
2 tablespoons	1 ounce, 14 ml	Vegetable oil
as needed		All-purpose flour, for dusting
2		Garlic cloves, minced
2 cups	8 ounces, 226 g	Onions, 1/4 inch (.6 cm) dice
2 teaspoons	1/3 ounce, 10 g	Ginger, grated
2 tablespoons	1 ounce, 56 g	Tamarind paste
1/2 cup	4 ounces, 115 ml	Chicken stock
3/4 cup	3 ounces, 85 g	Red bell pepper, finely julienned
3/4 cup	3 ounces, 85 g	Yellow bell pepper, finely julienned
1 tablespoon	1/2 ounce, 14 ml	Olive oil
as needed		Salt and black pepper

PROCEDURE

1 Rub the chicken breasts with lemon and lime juices; let marinate for at least 15 minutes.

2 Heat the vegetable oil over medium heat.

3 Season and dust the chicken breasts with flour, shake off excess flour and sauté until lightly browned, 2 to 3 minutes per side.

4 Remove browned chicken and pour off excess oil.

5 Reduce the heat to low, add the garlic and onions, and cook until onions are lightly colored, 3 to 5 minutes.

6 Add the ginger, tamarind, and stock. Return the chicken to the pan and bring to a simmer. Cover the pan and reduce the heat. Simmer until the chicken is cooked.

7 In a separate bowl, toss the peppers in the olive oil and season with salt and pepper.

8 Serve the chicken breast coated with the sauce and topped with the pepper julienne.

Stewed Pink Beans 4 SERVINGS

chef tip

This dish can be made with virtually any variety of dry beans. The West Indian pumpkin is typically available in specialty markets in South Florida. Regular pumpkins are an excellent substitute. If pumpkins are not available, try using yams.

The procedure uses an important element of Latin and Caribbean cooking—sofrito. The term is derived from the Spanish word *sofreir,* meaning "to fry lightly." Sofrito is an essential flavor element and can be prepared in large amounts and stored in the refrigerator until needed.

AMOUNT	MEASURE	INGREDIENT
I cup	7 ounces, 198 g	Pink beans, dried
I quart	I l	Water, cold
I cup	4 ounces, 113 g	Pumpkin, West Indian pumpkin (calabaza) or domestic, peeled, $1/2$ inch (1.2 cm) dice
I cup	5 ounces, 141 g	Russett potato, peeled, $1/2$ inch (1.2 cm) dice

For the Sofrito

I tablespoon	$1/2$ ounce, 14 ml	Vegetable oil
2 tablespoons	I ounce, 28 g	Salt pork, $1/4$ inch (.6 cm) dice
$1/3$ cup	2 ounces, 56 g	Ham, $1/4$ inch (.6 cm) dice
pinch		Oregano (dried)
I cup	4 ounces, 113 g	Onion, $1/4$ inch (.6 cm) dice
2		Garlic cloves, minced
2		Cilantro sprigs, chopped
I cup	6 ounces, 170 g	Tomato, peeled, seeded, $1/2$ inch (1.2 cm) dice
$1/2$		Scotch bonnet or Jalapeño pepper, seeded, minced
2 teaspoons	10 ml	Cider vinegar
to taste		Salt and black pepper

PROCEDURE

1 Rinse the beans under cold running water. Place them in a container, cover with cold water, and soak overnight. Drain and discard any beans that did not swell.

2   Place the beans in a large saucepot and cover with the cold water. Bring to a boil and turn the heat down to a simmer. Simmer for 30 minutes.

3   Add the diced pumpkin and potato and simmer an additional 30 minutes or until the beans are almost tender.

4   Heat the oil for the sofrito, add the salt pork and ham, and cook until browned.

5   Add the oregano, stir, and continue to cook for 30 seconds.

6   Add the onion, garlic, and cilantro; reduce the heat to low and cook, stirring frequently, until the onion is soft.

7   Mash some of the pumpkin and potato against the side of the pan. Add the sofrito mixture, the tomato, and the jalapeño. Simmer for 30 more minutes or until the liquid thickens.

8   Add the vinegar and season with salt and pepper.

Chayote with Tomatoes, Mushrooms, and Cheese 4 SERVINGS

chef tip

Manchego cheese is a Spanish-style sheep's milk cheese. If manchego cheese is not available, a mild feta can be used as a substitute. Goat cheese is also frequently used.

Shiitake mushrooms come from the Orient, but have been grown in Florida since immigrants from China came to Florida.

AMOUNT	MEASURE	INGREDIENT
2		Chayote, split, seeds removed
2 tablespoons	1 ounce, 28 ml	Olive oil
1		Garlic clove, minced
$^1/_4$ cup	1 ounce, 28 g	Red onion, $^1/_4$ inch (.6 cm) dice
$1^3/_4$ cups	4 ounces, 113 g	Shiitake mushrooms, cleaned, stems removed, thinly sliced
$^3/_4$ cup	3 ounces, 85 g	Green bell pepper, $^1/_4$ inch (.6 cm) dice
$^3/_4$ cup	4 ounces, 113 g	Tomato, peeled, seeded, $^1/_4$ inch (.6 cm) dice
1 teaspoon	1 g	Parsley, chopped
to taste		Tabasco
to taste		Salt and black pepper
$^1/_4$ cup	1 ounce, 28 g	Manchego cheese, grated

PROCEDURE

1 Preheat the oven to 350°F (175°C).

2 Put the chayote in a heavy-bottomed pot and add about 1 inch (2.5 cm) of boiling salted water. Cover tightly, reduce the heat, and boil for 10 to 15 minutes or until slightly tender. Remove the chayote and reserve.

3 Heat the olive oil over medium-high heat. Add the garlic and cook for 1 minute. Add the onion, mushrooms, and green pepper; continue to cook until the moisture is evaporated.

4 Turn the heat to low and add the tomato and parsley. Season the stuffing with Tabasco, salt, and black pepper, then let cool slightly.

5 Spoon the stuffing into the chayote halves and top with the grated cheese.

6 Bake until the chayote is tender and thoroughly heated.

Key West Conch Chowder · 4 SERVINGS

chef tip

Celebrity chef Norman Van Aken says, "Conch chowder is to Key West what cioppino is to San Francisco." This unique mollusk is so intwined with the folklore and diet of Key Westerners that the people who were born and raised there in the late 1800s became known as "conchs" (pronounced *konks*).

Conch meat has a rich, exotic, clamlike taste and can be used in salads, fritters, and chowders. Conch meat is almost always purchased frozen, even in Florida. Try to select Grade A quality conch and be sure to check for freezer burn, which can be identified by white spots. Do not buy the conch if you see indications of freezer burn.

Conch meat can be extremely tough, even if you dice it very small. We recommend grinding conch meat in a meat grinder using a medium die. Before grinding, cut away and discard any orange, flaplike meat attached to the conch.

AMOUNT	MEASURE	INGREDIENT
8 ounces	226 g	Conch meat, frozen, thawed
1/2 cup	4 ounces, 115 ml	Lemon juice
1 quart	32 ounces, 1 l	Clam juice
1		Thyme sprig
1		Bay leaf
1/4 cup	2 ounces, 56 g	Bacon, 1/4 inch (.6 cm) dice
1		Garlic clove, minced
1 cup	4 ounces, 113 g	Onion, 1/4 inch (.6 cm) dice
1/2 cup	2 ounces, 56 g	Celery, 1/4 inch (.6 cm) dice
1 cup	4 ounces, 113 g	Carrots, 1/4 inch (.6 cm) dice
1 cup	4 ounces, 113 g	Green bell pepper, 1/4 inch (.6 cm) dice
1 1/2 cups	8 ounces, 226 g	Russet potatoes, 1/4 inch (.6 cm) dice
1/3 cup	2 ounces, 56 g	Tomato, peeled, seeded, 1/4 inch (.6 cm) dice
to taste		Salt and black pepper
to taste		Tabasco

PROCEDURE

1 Thoroughly wash the conch in lemon juice.

2 Grind the conch meat through a medium die in a grinder.

3 Combine the conch meat with the clam juice, thyme, and bay leaf; bring to a simmer and cook over low heat for 30 minutes.

4 Render the bacon in a sauté pan; add the garlic, onion, celery, carrots, and green pepper; cook 5 minutes or until vegetables are soft.

5 Combine the vegetables, conch, potatoes, and tomato. Return to a simmer and cook until the potatoes are tender.

6 Season with salt, pepper, and a dash of Tabasco.

Candied Sweet Potatoes 4 SERVINGS

AMOUNT	MEASURE	INGREDIENT
2	28 ounces, 784 g	Sweet potatoes
4 tablespoons	2 ounces, 56 ml	Butter
$^1/_4$ cup	2 ounces, 56 g	Brown sugar
pinch		Nutmeg
as needed		Water

PROCEDURE

1 Preheat the oven to 350°F (175°C).

2 Wash the sweet potatoes and bake in the oven until tender.

3 Cool and peel the sweet potatoes, cut them into $^1/_2$-inch (1.2 cm) slices.

4 Layer the sliced sweet potatoes in a buttered casserole dish. Dot each layer with the butter, and sprinkle with brown sugar and nutmeg.

5 Add a little water and bake until the top is crisp. Serve immediately.

Hearts-of-Palm Salad 4 SERVINGS

Hearts of palm are also referred to as "swamp cabbage" because they come from the cabbage palm tree and usually grow in swamps in southern Florida. Fresh hearts of palm are frequently available in Cryovac bags and will last up to two weeks in a refrigerator. Canned hearts of palm may be substituted for fresh.

AMOUNT	MEASURE	INGREDIENT
1/4 cup	2 ounces, 55 ml	Lemon juice
2		Oranges, sections and juice
2 cups	12 ounces, 340 g	Hearts of palm, fresh, 1/2 inch (1.2 cm) dice
1/2 cup	2 ounces, 56 g	Red bell pepper, 1/4 inch (.6 cm) dice
1/2 cup	2 ounces, 56 g	Green bell pepper, 1/4 inch (.6 cm) dice
1/2 teaspoon	1 g	Tarragon, chopped
1/4 cup	2 ounces, 55 ml	Mayonnaise
2 teaspoons	1 ounce, 28 ml	Honey
to taste		Salt and black pepper
4		Bibb lettuce leaves, washed and dried
1/4 cup	1 ounce, 28 g	Walnuts, chopped

PROCEDURE

1 Combine the lemon and orange juices with the diced hearts of palm.

2 Add the peppers, tarragon, mayonnaise, and honey; season with salt and pepper.

3 Place a lettuce leaf on each chilled plate, add some hearts-of-palm salad, and garnish with the orange sections and chopped walnuts.

Pan-Seared Grouper 4 SERVINGS

AMOUNT	MEASURE	INGREDIENT
For the Marinade		
1 tablespoon	$^1/_2$ ounce, 15 g	Ginger, grated
1 tablespoon	$^1/_2$ ounce, 15 g	Garlic, minced
1 tablespoon	$^1/_2$ ounce, 15 g	Shallots, minced
1 tablespoon	$^1/_3$ ounce, 10 g	Lemon zest
$^1/_2$ cup	4 ounces, 115 ml	Olive oil
2 tablespoons	1 ounce, 28 ml	Lemon juice
to taste		Salt and black pepper
For the Fish		
4	6 ounces, 170 g each	Grouper fillets, skinless and boneless
2 tablespoons	1 ounce, 28 ml	Olive oil
4		Cilantro sprigs

PROCEDURE

1 Combine marinade ingredients in a food processor or blender and process to a paste.

2 Spread over the grouper fillets and let rest for at least 1 hour.

3 Heat a pan with the oil until it begins to smoke.

4 Add the fish skin side down; sauté until it browns, 2 to 3 minutes, then turn over and brown other side for 1 minute. Finish in oven if necessary.

5 Serve with lime wedge, cilantro sprig, and Black Bean, Jícama, and Corn Relish (page 160) or Tropical Fruit Salsa (page 161).

Black Bean, Jícama, and Corn Relish 4 SERVINGS

AMOUNT	MEASURE	INGREDIENT
I cup	4 ounces, 113 g	Red onion, 1/4 inch (.6 cm) dice
I		Garlic clove, minced
I cup	6 ounces, 170 g	Corn kernels (2 ears, on the cob) roasted
I cup	4 ounces, 113 g	Jícama, peeled, 1/4 inch (.6 cm) dice
I		Serrano chile, seeded, minced
1/3 cup	2 ounces, 56 g	Black beans, cooked
I tablespoon	1/2 ounce, 14 ml	Lime juice
1/4 cup	2 ounces, 55 ml	Olive oil
to taste		Salt and black pepper

PROCEDURE

Combine all ingredients and let flavors develop 1 hour.

Tropical Fruit Salsa 4 SERVINGS

AMOUNT	MEASURE	INGREDIENT
1/2 cup	2 1/2 ounces, 70 g	Mango, 1/4 inch (.6 cm) dice
1/2 cup	3 ounces, 85 g	Orange sections
1/2 cup	3 ounces, 85 g	Pineapple, 1/4 inch (.6 cm) dice
1/2 cup	2 1/2 ounces, 70 g	Papaya, 1/4 inch (.6 cm) dice
1/2 cup	1 1/2 ounces, 42 g	Green seedless grapes, cut in half
1/4 cup	1 ounce, 28 g	Red bell pepper, 1/4 inch (.6 cm) dice
1 teaspoon	5 g	Jalapeño pepper, seeds removed, minced
1/4 cup	1 ounce, 28 g	Red onion, minced
1/4 cup	2 ounces, 58 ml	Rice wine vinegar
1 tablespoon	3 g	Cilantro, chopped
to taste		Salt and black pepper

PROCEDURE

1   Combine the mango, orange, pineapple, papaya, grapes, bell pepper, jalapeño, and red onion in a bowl and stir to mix.

2   Add the vinegar, cilantro, salt, and pepper and stir well. Adjust seasoning to taste and serve. (The salsa can be made up to 4 hours in advance and refrigerated in an airtight container.)

Corn Custard 4 SERVINGS

chef tip

To unmold the custard, make a small cut around the rim of the mold with a paring knife, hold the mold upside down with your fingers over the custard, and gently shake sideways until the custard releases.

AMOUNT	MEASURE	INGREDIENT
I cup	6 ounces, 170 g	Corn kernels (2 ears, on the cob)
2 tablespoons	I ounce, 28 g	Butter
¹/₄ cup	I ounce, 28 g	Carrot, minced
¹/₄ cup	I ounce, 28 g	Celery, minced
2 tablespoons	¹/₂ ounce, 14 g	Leek, ¹/₄ inch (.6 cm) dice
I		Garlic clove, minced
2		Eggs
2		Egg whites
³/₄ cup	6 ounces, 165 ml	Heavy cream
I tablespoon	3 g	Parsley, chopped
to taste		Salt and white pepper

PROCEDURE

1. Preheat the oven to 350°F (175°C).

2. Roast the ears of corn in hot oven for 30 minutes; remove kernels. Keep oven on.

3. Heat the butter over medium heat; add the carrot, celery, leek, and garlic; cook 5 minutes or until very soft. Cool.

4. Combine the vegetables with the corn, eggs, egg whites, cream, and parsley. Correct seasoning.

5. Spray 4-ounce molds with food release. Fill molds with custard three-quarters full and place in water bath.

6. Place parchment paper on top of molds so the custard does not brown, and bake for approximately 30 to 40 minutes or until a toothpick inserted in center comes out clean.

7. Take the molds out of the water bath. Let rest 5 minutes and unmold.

Key Lime Pie 8 SERVINGS

The Key lime is smaller than the more common Persian lime and is rounder, with a color more yellow than green. Outside of Florida and Mexico, where it is called *limon*, the Key lime is usually available only in Hispanic specialty markets.

Key lime pie became popular in the Florida Keys in the 1850s. The first Key lime pies were baked in a pastry crust and topped with a meringue, but now they are frequently baked in a graham cracker crust and served with a whipped cream topping. Key lime pie can also be served frozen, if desired. If true Key limes are not available, the juice from regular Persian limes will suffice, but the pie should be called a lime pie rather than a Key lime pie.

AMOUNT	MEASURE	INGREDIENT
For the Crust		
1 cup plus 1 tablespoon	5 ounces, 141 g	Graham cracker crumbs
1/4 cup	2 ounces, 56 g	Granulated sugar
1/4 cup	2 ounces, 56 g	Butter, melted
For the Filling		
2 cups	15 ounces, 470 ml	Sweetened condensed milk
6		Egg yolks
3/4 cup	6 ounces, 170 ml	Key lime juice
1 tablespoon	1/3 ounce, 10 g	Key lime zest
For the Topping		
1 cup	8 ounces, 235 ml	Heavy cream
1/2 cup	2 ounces, 56 g	Confectioners' sugar, sifted

PROCEDURE

1 Preheat the oven to 350°F (175°C).

2 Combine the graham cracker crumbs and sugar.

3 Add the melted butter and combine until the mixture resembles wet sand; press the mixture into a 9-inch (22.5 cm) pie pan.

4 Whisk the condensed milk with the egg yolks and blend in the lime juice and zest. Pour the mixture into the pan with the piecrust.

Key Lime Pie

5 Bake for approximately 15 minutes or until the filling is set; let the pie cool at room temperature for 1 hour. Be careful not to overbake the pie.

6 Prepare the topping by whipping the cream with the sugar, be careful not to overmix the cream.

7 Garnish pie with whipped cream.

Golden Gazpacho 4 SERVINGS

chef tip

Gazpacho began centuries ago as a poor people's food and consisted of nothing more than leftover bread, olive oil, vinegar, garlic, and water. Over the centuries, each region of Andalusia, Spain, developed its own distinctive version of gazpacho based on the same simple ingredients. The discovery of the New World introduced Spain to tomatoes and peppers, and later in the 19th century, Eugenia de Montijo, empress of France and Andalusian by birth, made the foods of her homeland fashionable throughout the French Empire. Gazpacho, traditionally being red or white, was one of those foods. Today there are as many varieties of gazpacho as there are towns in Andalusia, but the local chefs usually do not use cucumbers or onions in gazpacho. Some are like a chopped salad and others are made with almonds or lima beans or even sorbet of gazpacho.

AMOUNT	MEASURE	INGREDIENT
I cup	6 ounces, 170 g	Yellow beefsteak tomato, peeled, seeded, $^1/_4$ inch (.6 cm) dice
2 cups	8 ounces, 226 g	Yellow bell peppers, seeded, $^1/_4$ inch (.6 cm) dice
$^3/_4$ cup	4 ounces, 113 g	Papaya, peeled, seeded, $^1/_4$ inch (.6 cm) dice
2	I ounce, 28 g	Shallots, peeled, $^1/_4$ inch (.6 cm) dice
I cup	5 ounces, 140 g	Cucumber, peeled, seeded, $^1/_4$ inch (.6 cm) dice
2		Garlic cloves, $^1/_4$ inch (.6 cm) dice
2 tablespoons	I ounce, 28 ml	Tequila or water
2 slices	I$^1/_2$ ounces, 42 g	White bread, crusts removed
I tablespoon	$^1/_2$ ounce, 14 ml	Lime juice
I tablespoon	$^1/_2$ ounce, 14 ml	Sherry vinegar
2 tablespoons	I ounce, 28 ml	Olive oil
dash		Tabasco
to taste		Salt and black pepper

For the Garnish

$^1/_4$ cup	2 ounces, 55 ml	Sour cream
$^1/_4$ cup	I ounce, 28 g	Green bell pepper, $^1/_4$ inch (.6 cm) dice

PROCEDURE

1 Combine all the ingredients except the seasonings and garnish in a blender or food processor. Blend to desired consistency.

2 Correct seasoning and add Tabasco. Chill well.

3 Garnish with the sour cream and green bell pepper.

Puff Pastry Straws (Paillettes) 4 SERVINGS

These "little straws" are not dessert, but are one of the best known and best loved puff pastries. Traditionally served with clear soups, they are also an excellent cocktail pastry. Use only the best Parmesan cheese and Hungarian paprika (the word *Szeged* appears on the label) to complement the delicate flavor of the puff pastry.

AMOUNT	MEASURE	INGREDIENT
6 ounces	170 g	Puff pastry
1		Egg
pinch		Salt
$^1/_3$ cup	1 ounce, 28 g	Parmesan cheese, grated
1 teaspoon	2 g	Hungarian paprika

PROCEDURE

1   Preheat the oven to 400°F (205°C).

2   On a lightly floured surface, roll dough evenly to approximately an 8-inch (20 cm) square.

3   Beat the egg and salt together, then paint the surface of the dough.

4   Cover half the dough with an even layer of cheese, then paprika. Fold the other half of the dough over it and press to adhere the dough together. If the dough is soft or resistant, slide it onto a pan and chill briefly to firm.

5   Roll the dough back to an 8-inch (20 cm) square. Chill until firm.

6   Cut the chilled dough into $^1/_2$ x 8-inch (1.2 x 20 cm) strips. Twist the strips, one at a time, into corkscrew shapes: Position the strips at a 45-degree angle to left edge of the surface. Hold down the left end of the strip with the left hand. With the right hand, roll the right end of the strip until the strip is parallel to the edge of the surface, forming a corkscrew shape. Place on a paper-lined 10 x 15-inch (25 x 37 cm) pan, pressing the edges to the rim of the pan to prevent the straws from unraveling during baking.

7   Bake in the middle level of the oven for about 10 to 12 minutes, or until they are deep golden color. Immediately remove to a cutting board and trim off ends; cut the straws into 4- to 6-inch (10 to 15 cm) lengths. Cool.

Warm White Beans, Mesclun Salad, and Mango Chutney

4 SERVINGS

AMOUNT	MEASURE	INGREDIENT

For the Beans

AMOUNT	MEASURE	INGREDIENT
1 1/2 cups	10 1/2 ounces, 298 g	White beans, picked over, soaked overnight
1/4 cup	2 ounces, 55 ml	Olive oil
3		Garlic cloves, minced
1/2 cup	2 ounces, 56 g	Celery, 1/4 inch (.6 cm) dice
1/2 cup	2 ounces, 56 g	Onion, 1/4 inch (.6 cm) dice
1/2 cup	2 ounces, 56 g	Carrot, 1/4 inch (.6 cm) dice
2 cups	16 ounces, 470 ml	Chicken stock
1		Bay leaf
1/2 teaspoon	1 g	Ground cumin

For the Vinaigrette

AMOUNT	MEASURE	INGREDIENT
1/4 cup	2 ounces, 58 ml	Sherry vinegar
3/4 cup	6 ounces, 170 ml	Olive oil
2 tablespoons	1 ounce, 28 ml	Lemon juice
1/2 teaspoon	1 g	Dry mustard
to taste		Salt and black pepper
3 cups	4 1/2 ounces, 126 g	Mesclun (baby field greens) mix

PROCEDURE

1. Drain beans.

2. In the olive oil, sauté the vegetables for 3 minutes or until just soft.

3. Add the bay leaf and cumin, and sauté 1 minute.

4. Add the beans and stock, and simmer 30 minutes or until beans are tender. Add more liquid if necessary.

5. Combine all the vinaigrette ingredients; whisk to combine well.

6   Drain the beans if the liquid has not been absorbed, remove the bay leaf, and toss with all but ¹/₄ cup (2 ounces, 58 ml) of the vinaigrette.

7   Toss the mesclun mix with the remaining vinaigrette. Place the salad greens on plates with the warm beans. Garnish with Mango Chutney (page 171).

Warm White Beans, Mesclun Salad, and Mango Chutney

Mango Chutney 4 SERVINGS

AMOUNT	MEASURE	INGREDIENT
1/2 cup	4 ounces, 115 ml	Cider vinegar
2 tablespoons	1 ounce, 28 ml	Lime juice
1 tablespoon	1/3 ounce, 10 g	Honey
1 cup	6 ounces, 170 g	Mango, peeled, sliced
2 tablespoons	3/4 ounce, 20 g	Currants
2 tablespoons	3/4 ounce, 20 g	Raisins
2 tablespoons	1/2 ounces, 14 g	Red onion, minced
1/4 cup	1 ounce, 28 g	Green bell pepper, seeded, 1/4 inch (.6 cm) dice
2 tablespoons	2/3 ounce, 18 g	Almonds, slivered
1 teaspoon	5 g	Ginger, peeled, minced
1 teaspoon	2 g	Mustard seeds, crushed
1		Jalapeño pepper, minced

PROCEDURE

1 Combine all the ingredients and bring to a boil.

2 Reduce to a simmer, and cook 30 minutes.

3 Drain off the liquid and reduce by half.

4 Return the liquid to the chutney and stir to combine. Cool before serving.

Roasted Pork Loin Cuban Style 4 SERVINGS

AMOUNT	MEASURE	INGREDIENT
For the pork		
1/4 cup	2 ounces, 56 g	Garlic cloves, chopped
1 tablespoon	1/2 ounce, 14 g	Black pepper
1 tablespoon	1/2 ounce, 14 g	Ground cumin
1 teaspoon	5 g	Salt
1/8 teaspoon	1 g	Cayenne
2 pounds	907 g	Pork loin, boneless, preferably shoulder end
2 tablespoons	1 ounce, 28 ml	Vegetable oil
1 cup	8 ounces, 235 ml	Orange juice
For the sauce		
2 tablespoons	1 ounce, 28 ml	Vegetable oil
1/2 cup	2 ounces, 56 g	Onion, 1/4 inch (.6 cm) dice
1/2 cup	2 ounces, 56 g	Celery, 1/4 inch (.6 cm) dice
1/2 cup	2 ounces, 56 g	Green bell pepper, 1/4 inch (.6 cm) dice
1/3 cup	2 ounces, 56 g	Black beans, soaked overnight, drained
1 1/2 cups	12 ounces, 352 ml	Chicken stock
pinch		Cayenne
to taste		Salt and black pepper

PROCEDURE

1 Combine the garlic, pepper, cumin, salt, and cayenne. Rub the meat with the seasoning and marinate for at least 1 hour.

2 Preheat the oven to 375°F (190°C).

3 Heat the oil and sear the meat on all sides.

4 Remove the meat and deglaze the pan with the orange juice; reserve pan juice for sauce.

5 Roast the pork until it reaches 145°F to 160°F (60°C to 71°C) internal temperature. Let rest for at least 10 minutes before slicing.

6 While meat cooks, heat the oil for the sauce over medium heat. Add all the vegetables and cook 5 minutes or until soft.

7 Add the beans, and stock; bring it to a simmer. Simmer the sauce for about 45 to 60 minutes, until the beans are tender.

8 Add the reserved pan juice and season with salt and pepper.

9 Puree half of the sauce and combine with remaining beans; bring back to a simmer.

10 Season with a pinch of cayenne, salt, and pepper. Serve sauce with the sliced pork.

Mango and Jalapeño Mojo 4 SERVINGS

AMOUNT	MEASURE	INGREDIENT
1 cup	6 ounces, 170 g	Mango, peeled, ¹/₄ inch (.6 cm) dice
¹/₂ cup	4 ounces, 115 ml	Dry white wine
¹/₂ cup	4 ounces, 115 ml	Orange juice
1		Jalapeño pepper, seeded, minced
1 cup	1¹/₂ ounces, 42 g	Cilantro leaves, chopped

PROCEDURE

1　Combine half the mango, the white wine, and orange juice; puree.

2　Bring to a boil. Cool. Combine with remaining ingredients.

Spicy Orange Carrot Sticks 4 SERVINGS

AMOUNT	MEASURE	INGREDIENT
$^1/_2$ cup	4 ounces, 115 ml	Orange juice
2 tablespoons	1 ounce, 28 g	Granulated sugar
1 tablespoon	$^1/_2$ ounce, 14 g	Ginger, grated
3 cups	12 ounces, 340 g	Carrots, julienned
to taste		Salt and white pepper
2 teaspoons	2 g	Parsley, chopped

PROCEDURE

1 Combine the orange juice, sugar, ginger, and carrots.

2 Cover and cook over medium-high heat until the carrots are tender.

3 Season the carrots with salt, white pepper, and parsley.

Fried Plantain Chips 4 SERVINGS

AMOUNT	MEASURE	INGREDIENT
2		Green plantains
to taste		Coarse salt
as needed		Vegetable oil, for deep-frying

PROCEDURE

1. Using a paring knife, score the plantain skin enough to barely go into the flesh from one end to the other.

2. Deep-fry at 325°F (163°C) until the slit on the side opens significantly.

3. Remove from oil and allow to cool enough to handle, then remove the peel.

4. Raise temperature of oil to 375°F (190°C).

5. Slice the plantains on a mandolin or electric slicer $1/8$ inch (.3 cm) thick.

6. Fry the plantain chips for 2 to 3 minutes. Move them around in the fat for even cooking. Remove them to paper towels to drain. Season before serving.

Rice and Peas 4 SERVINGS

AMOUNT	MEASURE	INGREDIENT
1/2 cup	3 ounces, 85 g	Kidney beans, dried
1 1/2 cups	12 ounces, 352 ml	Coconut milk
1/2 cup	1 ounce, 28 g	Green onions, thinly sliced
1		Thyme sprig, chopped
1		Garlic clove, minced
1 1/4 cups	8 ounces, 226 g	Long-grain rice
1/2 teaspoon	3 g	Salt
1/2 teaspoon	3 g	Granulated sugar

PROCEDURE

1 Rinse the beans and cover with cold water. Soak overnight. Drain.

2 Combine the beans and coconut milk; simmer until beans are almost tender.

3 Add the green onions, thyme, garlic, rice, salt, and sugar.

4 Cook, covered, over medium heat for 15 minutes. Remove from heat and let stand, covered, for 5 to 10 minutes.

Shrimp with Roasted Garlic and Papaya 4 SERVINGS

AMOUNT	MEASURE	INGREDIENT
24 ounces	680 g	Shrimp (16–20 count)
1 head	2 ounces, 56 g	Garlic
1/4 cup	2 ounces, 58 ml	Vegetable oil
1/4 cup	1 ounce, 28 g	Celery, 1/4 inch (.6 cm) dice
1 cup	4 ounces, 113 g	Onion, 1/4 inch (.6 cm) dice
1 cup	8 ounces, 235 ml	Dry white wine
1		Bay leaf
1 cup	8 ounces, 237 ml	Fish stock
2 cups	8 ounces, 235 ml	Heavy cream
to taste		Salt and black pepper
1 1/2 cups	8 ounces, 226 g	Papaya
1 teaspoon	1 g	Basil, chopped
1 teaspoon	1 g	Thyme, chopped

PROCEDURE

1 Peel and devein the shrimp; refrigerate until needed.

2 Cut the top off the head of garlic and wrap the garlic in aluminum foil. Roast in a pre-heated 375°F (190°C) oven for approximately 30 to 45 minutes.

3 Heat the oil over medium heat.

4 Squeeze the cooked garlic pulp into the oil. Add the celery and onion. Cook 5 minutes or until the vegetables are soft.

5 Add the wine, bay leaf, and stock. Reduce the volume by half.

6 Add the cream and reduce the volume by half again, or to the nappé stage. Remove the bay leaf.

7 Add the shrimp and cook 2 to 3 minutes, until they are pink (do not overcook).

8 Correct seasoning.

9 Cut the papayas in half, remove the seeds, peel, and slice into long, thin strips; toss with the basil and thyme.

10 Spoon approximately ¹/₄ cup (2 ounces, 56 g) of the sauce into the center of each warm plate. Decoratively place the papaya strips around and on top of the sauce.

11 Top the papaya with 2 tablespoons (1 ounce, 30 ml) Avocado Salsa (below) and 6 cooked shrimp.

Avocado Salsa 4 SERVINGS

chef tip

Avocados in South Florida are often referred to as "alligator pears." The buttery-flavored avocado is rich in vitamin A and potassium. The red onions add a measure of sweetness to the tart salsa. Florida avocados typically have a higher water content than avocados from California, and a much milder flavor. If Florida avocados are not available, the California variety can easily be substituted. If cubanella peppers are not available, substitute 1 seeded and diced jalapeño pepper.

AMOUNT	MEASURE	INGREDIENT
1 cup	5¹/₂ ounces, 156 g	Avocado, peeled, seeded, ¹/₂ inch (1.2 cm) dice
1		Cubanella chile, minced
1 tablespoon	3 g	Cilantro leaves, chopped
1 cup	6 ounces, 170 g	Tomato, peeled, seeded, ¹/₄ inch (.6 cm) dice
¹/₂ teaspoon	1 g	Ground cumin
1 tablespoon	¹/₂ ounce, 14 ml	Lime juice
1 tablespoon	¹/₂ ounce, 15 g	Red onion, ¹/₄ inch (.6 cm) dice

PROCEDURE

Combine all ingredients and mix well; keep chunky.

Tropical Tuber Torta 4–6 SERVINGS

chef tip The sweet potatoes can be kept covered with a moist towel while layering the torta, but the yucca, boniato, and purple potatoes must be kept soaking. For a taller presentation, you can stack the section like checkers. Russet potatoes can be substituted for half the boniato or yucca.

AMOUNT	MEASURE	INGREDIENT
3 tablespoons	1 1/2 ounces, 44 ml	Vegetable oil, plus extra for brushing
I cup	4 ounces, 113 g	Red onion, thinly sliced
1/4 cup	2 ounces, 58 ml	Sherry vinegar
2 cups	10 ounces, 283 g	Peruvian purple potatoes, peeled, very thinly sliced
I cup	5 ounces, 141 g	Boniato, peeled, very thinly sliced
I cup	5 ounces, 141 g	Yuca, peeled, very thinly sliced
I cup	4 ounces, 11 g	Manchego cheese, finely grated
I cup	5 ounces, 141 g	Sweet potato, very thinly sliced
2 cups	16 ounces, 470 ml	Water
to taste		Salt and pepper

PROCEDURE

1. Preheat the oven to 350°F (175°C). Line a 9 x 13-inch (22 x 32 cm) baking pan with parchment paper.

2. Heat the oil; add the onion; season and cook over medium heat until caramelized, about 15 minutes.

3. Arrange the sliced potatoes in layers in a paper-lined baking pan. Season each layer, brush with oil, and spread a few onion pieces over each layer.

4. Do the same with the boniato, yuca, and sweet potatoes.

5. Add the cheese to the top layer and then top the cheese with one more layer of sweet potato.

6. Brush top with oil and season. Cover with parchment paper and then aluminum foil.

7. Place another pan on top of the torta and add water to gently compress the torta. Bake for 70 minutes. Remove and let cool for 10 minutes.

8. Remove foil and parchment covering, then cut into sections.

**New England
Boiled Dinner
with Horseradish
Sauce**

**Roasted Turkey
Roulade with
Cranberry
Sauce, Glazed
Turnips, Green
Beans with
Fried Onions,
and Mashed
Sweet
Potatoes**

Baked Boston
Scrod, Pureed
Potatoes, and
Summer Squash
Noodles

Braised Short
Ribs, Buttered
Homemade
Noodles, Red
Swiss Chard
and Spinach
Sauté

Roast Duck with Garlic and Honey, Orange Flavored Winter Root Vegetables, Roasted Potatoes and Pearl Onions

Scallops with Mushrooms and Asparagus

"Shaker-Style" Turkey Cutlet, Croquette Potatoes, Spaghetti Squash, and Green Beans

Watermelon and Watercress Salad with Shallot-Citrus Dressing

Pecan-Encrusted Catfish with Orange-Scented Sweet Potatoes and Succotash of Corn, Hominy, and Baby Lima Beans

Chicken with Tamarind Ginger Sauce, Stewed Pink Beans, Stuffed Chayote with Tomatoes, Mushrooms, and Cheese

Roasted Pork Loin, Cuban-Style, Fried Plantain Chips, and Spicy Orange Carrot Sticks

Golden Gazpacho with Puff Pastry Straws

Pan-Seared
Grouper, Corn
Custard, White
Rice, and
Tomatoes

Fried Fish in
Pearly Meal
with
Remoulade
Sauce

Braised Beef Daube with Cheese Grits, Glazed Carrots, and Sugar Snap Peas

Creole Jambalaya and Smothered Okra

Roast Chicken
with Wild Rice,
Walnuts, and
Dried Fruit
Stuffing, Winter
Vegetables with
Thyme

Pork
Medallions
with Blueberry
Sauce, Brussels
Sprouts with
Mushrooms,
Macaroni and
Cheese

Planked Whitefish with Green Onion Butter, Pickled Pearl Onions, Sautéed Green Beans, and Sunchoke Gratin

Caldo de Res

Grilled Apache-Style Pork Cutlets, Squash Salsa, and Tobacco Onions, Fingerlings with Parsley-Basil Dressing

Pumpkin Seed-Crusted Trout, Achiote Rice, Calabacitas con Maize

Chinese Chicken Salad

Sautéed Duck Breast with a Port Wine Reduction, Monterey Jack and Green Chile Polenta, Fried Fennel, and Creamed Spinach

San Francisco
Cioppino with
Rosemary
Focaccia

Mussels in Thai
Coconut Broth

Blackberry Barbecued Chicken, Cranberry Beans with Fresh Oregano, Walla Walla Onion Rings, and Green Beans

Sautéed Halibut with Warm Apple and Dried Cherry Compote, and Gai Lan (Chinese Broccoli) with Crispy Garlic

Hot-Smoked Apricot Salmon on Mushroom-Soba Noodle Salad

Roasted Lamb with Thyme-Merlot Sauce, Savory Bread Pudding, Glazed Carrots and Brussels Sprouts

Saimin with
Teriyaki Meat
Sticks

Macadamia
Nut–Crusted
Mahimahi with
Wasabi Cream
Sauce, and
Steamed
Japanese Rice

Louisiana's Cajun and Creole Cuisines

Louisiana has been described as a "cultural gumbo" in which each of the different ingredients is identifiable, yet all have blended, affecting each other. A complex blend of Native American, French, Spanish, German, English, African, and Italian influences creates a unique regional culture. These people have merged to become the Cajuns and Creoles—the source of Louisiana's culinary heritage. Cajun cooking, earthy and robust, has been described as "country cooking." It is based on food that was indigenous to the area and on one-pot meals that contain a variety of ingredients gathered from the "swamp-floor pantry." Creole cooking, like Cajun, depended heavily on whatever foods were available. But Creole food, unlike Cajun, began in New Orleans. Creole food, or "city food," was created by sharing cooking styles and is considered more sophisticated and complex than Cajun cooking. Though each cuisine represents its own style, the sharing and evolution continues, and Cajun and Creole cooking differences begin to blur. As these two regional cuisines become more difficult to separate, it is important to remember that food in Louisiana represents a celebration of life, a joy in living, and comes with the admonishment: *Laissez Les Bon Temps Rouler!* ("Let the Good Times Roll!").

Louisiana Known as "the Pelican State," Louisiana's state bird is the pelican. The pelican has been a symbol of Louisiana since the arrival of early European settlers, who were impressed with the pelican's generous and nurturing attitude toward their young. Louisiana is also known as the "Bayou State" for the many slow, sluggish, small streams that meander through the lowlands and marshes of the southern section of the state, and as the "Creole State" for the people of French and Spanish descent and the culture that they have preserved. The state crustacean is the crawfish, the state reptile is the alligator, and the state freshwater fish is the white perch (also called "sac-au-lait" or "white crappie"). The state insect is the honeybee, and the state drink is milk.

Major Influences on the State's Culture

No other state has a more varied or colorful past than Louisiana. The layers of history can be seen in the 18th-century French buildings of the Vieux Carre (New Orleans's French Quarter), with their splendid Spanish courtyards hidden just behind the gates. New Orleans began as a French settlement in 1718, became Spanish in 1762, then French again briefly just after 1800, and with the Louisiana Purchase in 1803, American.

EUROPEAN DISCOVERY AND SETTLEMENT

Before the age of European exploration, the region was inhabited by thousands of Native Americans. The largest tribes included the Caddo, the Natchez, the Chitimacha, and the Choctaw. They planted vegetables, hunted game, and fished along the east bank of the Mississippi River. The first Europeans to enter the area were from Spain. Among them were Hernando de Soto and his expedition that explored large parts of what is now the southern United States and came though Louisiana in 1542.

FRENCH RULE

The French established their first settlement in Natchitoches in 1686, but they found it difficult to attract settlers to this isolated part of the New World. King Louis XIV asked an organization of traders, called the Company of the West, to manage the colony. Headed by John Law, the Company tried several schemes to attract settlers, including attempts to lure fortune seekers by claiming Louisiana was a land filled with gold and silver. The French government encouraged prisoners and debtors to pay for their crimes by moving to the new colony. Nevertheless, not many people came to Louisiana until 1718, when Jean-Baptiste Le Moyne, Sieur de Bienville, established a port city, which he called New Orleans. Located just 110 miles upstream from the mouth of the Mississippi River, New Orleans later became the commercial center of the South and one of the country's most important international ports. The capital of the territory developed a strong character all its own. European settlers brought with them fine clothing and furnishings and established elegant traditions like banquets and balls.

SPANISH RULE

By 1762, France was deep in debt and at war with Britain over control of North America. No longer able to afford to develop the Louisiana territory, France offered it to Spain. For 40 years, Spain helped Louisiana to flourish and added its special flavor to its heritage. The territory's population boomed at this time. New arrivals from Europe joined the original French and Spanish settlers. These Europeans, called "Creoles," were generally wealthy and educated, and they brought with them a variety of celebrated European customs and traditions. Germans established towns and villages in the north-central region of the state. Scots, Irish, and British settlers arrived to settle in Louisiana's northeast. One of the most important groups to come was the Acadians, who established farms along the bayous west of New Orleans. Acadians were French settlers forced to leave Canada by the British during the Seven Years' War (1756–1763, also called the "French and Indian War"). Some returned to France or went to other colonies, but many chose to settle in southern Louisiana, where they became known as "Cajuns."

Slaves brought to work on Louisiana's expanding network of plantations made up the largest group of new residents. Many slaves were brought to the colony directly from the African regions, while others were taken from French islands in the Caribbean. By the beginning of the 1800s, more than 30,000 slaves would live in Louisiana, making up nearly half of its population.

BECOMING AMERICANS

In 1803, the French needed cash to finance another war with Britain. In a deal that would nearly double the size of the United States, President Thomas Jefferson bought the Louisiana Territory from the French for only $15 million. Just nine years later, in 1812, Louisiana became the 18th state to join the Union. Cotton, sugar, and rice were the three most valuable crops in the world during this time, and Louisiana's humid climate and rich soil were perfect for growing all three. More than 1,600 plantations were established. Steam-powered vessels found their way down the Mississippi River all the way from the East Coast to New Orleans. Goods produced throughout the United States could now travel by river to the Gulf of Mexico and from there, sail to international ports. By the mid-19th century, New Orleans was the largest city in the South, the third largest city in the nation, and one of the busiest ports in the world.

A Gumbo Society

CAJUN COUNTRY, ALSO KNOWN AS ACADIANA

The term *Cajun* describes both a geographical area and the people who live in or come from that region. Forcibly expelled by the British from their homes and farms in Canada during the second half of the 18th century, many Acadians made their way to southern Louisiana, where, over the generations, their descendants have formed the nucleus of Louisiana's Cajun life and culture. Originally farmers, trappers, and fisherman, the Cajuns had to rely on local resources, such as the fish, shellfish, and wild game. Native Americans taught them how to exploit the swamps, bayous, and surrounding forests. The Choctaws, Chitimacha, and Houmas showed them how to use ingredients such as corn, ground sassafras leaves or filé powder, and bay leaves. Wildlife, including alligator, crawfish, and turtles, were used by the Cajuns in their cooking. They depended on their black cast-iron pots. Because of the simple utilitarian kitchen of the traditional Cajun, one-pot meals were practical and common. This is reflected in their jambalaya, grillades, stews, étouffées, fricassées, soups, and gumbos. Because of the frugal nature needed to survive in the Bayou country, nothing was ever wasted by Cajuns, including all portions of butchered meats, stocks, and vegetables. The Cajun people are well known for their hospitality as well. In spite of the tragedy that befell them, they cook with a *joi de vive,* or love of life. They are also known for the term *lagniappe,* which refers to "something extra and not expected," like a few extra shrimp in the étouffée, or 13 cookies in a dozen (commonly known today as a "baker's dozen"). Cajun French, still spoken today, uses words and grammar derived from traditional French, English, Spanish, African, and Native American languages. Tucked away among the bayous and swamplands of the Atchafalaya Basin, this area is now considered one of the last great wilderness regions of the continental United States.

PLANTATION COUNTRY

Just west of New Orleans, winding along both sides of the Mississippi River, can be found flowing fields of sugarcane. Plantation agriculture flourished in Louisiana in the 18th century. These plantation owners influenced the area in many ways, particularly by teaching their slaves English rather than French. African Americans had a profound influence on the cooking style of the region. When they cooked, they combined ingredients such as rice, beans, and green leafy vegetables with traditional African ingredients such as okra, yams, onions, and garlic. They also favored a cooking technique called "slow roasting" and extended this idea of continuous cooking to traditional French roux.

Also, being closer to New Orleans and on major transportation routes, the Germans, Spanish, French, English, and Americans from along the Mississippi River were more cosmopolitan than people in the swamps and on the prairies to the west. A large number of Germans arrived during the Spanish period, settled upriver from New Orleans along the German coast, and provided most of the vegetable crops needed by New Orleans. The Germans also brought pigs, chicken, and cattle. Their extensive knowledge of all forms of *charcuterie* helped establish the *boucherie* and fine sausage making in South Louisiana. Escaping the lack of economic and social opportunities in Europe, the Italians came to the area as farmers, blacksmiths, and merchants. Famous for their own cooking skills, their influence on the cuisine can be seen in the pasta, red gravies, bread baking, garlic, eggplant, and artichoke dishes.

THE CROSSROADS

Central Louisiana became a meeting place for the many cultures of Louisiana. This is where the Native Americans thrived for centuries. All the tribes cultivated pumpkins, squash, and corn. They used wild berries, nuts, and persimmons in their cooking. Later, the French and the Spanish each ruled this region. Englishmen sought their fortunes here and American settlers flooded in after the Louisiana Purchase. Czech, Lebanese, Afro-Caribbean, Italian, and Syrian cultures contributed to the heritage of this region.

SPORTSMAN'S PARADISE

The forests and rolling hills of northern Louisiana were a hunter's paradise for Native Americans, French trappers, and American settlers of the early 1700s and 1800s. Today there is still opportunity for wild turkey, duck, partridge, and quail hunting. Catfish, both freshwater and pond raised, is abundant.

Food and Cultural Influences

GUMBO

Descended from the French bouillabaisse and renamed from the West African word for okra, *guingombo,* this type of hearty soup or stew is frequently served in the Louisiana region. There are as many recipes for gumbo as there are cooks. Over time, the dish evolved to include hot peppers, contributed by the Spanish settlers; okra, contributed by the Africans; and filé powder contributed by the Native Americans. Gumbo is the essence of cultural diversity. It blends and balances all the varied ethnic influences that have shaped present-day Louisiana cooking—the Spanish love of rice and spices, the Southern fondness for okra, the French technique of making roux, and the Caribbean art of combining seasonings. In New Orleans and southeastern Louisiana, seafood gumbo is made with shrimp and crabs, and tomatoes are added and cooked in the pot with the gumbo. In southwestern Louisiana, the favorite recipe includes chicken and andouille sausage gumbo thickened with only roux—no okra or tomatoes. Gumbo is traditionally served with or over rice.

THE MUFFULETTA

Many people think the only cultural and culinary heritage of New Orleans is French, Spanish, African, and Creole. When asked to name the quintessential sandwiches of New Orleans, many people will immediately reply "po'boy." But the muffuletta is as New Orleans as the popular po'boys and there's nothing Creole about it. This sandwich is pure Italian, and specifically Sicilian. New Orleans, in its population and its cuisine, owes much to Italy and especially to the Italians that have been coming since the 1880s.

The Italian contribution to local culture and cuisine has been considerable; in fact, Creole-Italian refers to one of the local subcuisines. It is said that the muffuletta sandwich was invented by Signor Lupo Salvadore, who opened the now-famous little Italian market called Central Grocery on Decatur Street in the French Quarter in 1906. He created the muffuletta sandwich for a favored customer. It is actually named for the baker of the round Italian bread on which the sandwich is served.

LOUISIANA'S GULF COAST

Louisiana's shores, marshes, bays, and bayous yield a variety of seafood. Blue crabs and oysters are harvested, and in the brackish waters where the Mississippi joins the Gulf of Mexico are some of the most fertile shrimping grounds in the country. Redfish, trout, flounder, and pompano are found farther out in the gulf. South Louisiana is the crawfish capital of the world, supporting a multimillion-dollar-a-year industry. Sometimes called "Louisiana lobster," the crawfish is much smaller and its color varies with the water in which it lives, as well as its variety. Although it is found in swamps and marshes throughout the state, the best wild populations occur in the overflow basins of the Atchafalaya, Red, and Pearl rivers. Crawfish farms have also been established where the crustaceans are cultivated for local use and for shipment to other states.

NEW ORLEANS

In 1718, Jean-Baptiste LeMoyne, Sieur de Bienville, chose a high spot along the Mississippi River to be the center of the French colony of Louisiana. It was strategically located to control traffic on the Mississippi. It was also a port that allowed immigrants to arrive from other countries. In the 18th century, the Spaniards governing New Orleans named all residents of European heritage *Criollo* (roughly translated from the Portuguese for "native to a region"). The name, which later became *Creole*, is claimed by different groups of people. The traditional New Orleans definition included those who could trace their lineage to aristocratic French or Spanish ancestry. They used the word to imply someone of refined cultural background with an appreciation for an elegant lifestyle. These people brought not only their wealth and education but also their chefs and cooks. With these chefs came the knowledge of the grand cuisines of France and other parts of Europe. Additional interpretations of Creole include former slaves who often took the same last name as their former owners and traced their lineage in the same fashion. Today, Creole cooking reflects the history of sharing and borrowing among the state's ethnic groups. In addition to the French, Spanish, and Americans, ethnic groups that included Haitians, Caribbeans, Italians, Germans, and Irish made significant contributions to the culture of the city.

Typical Cajun and Creole Dishes and Regional Foods

Alligator This large reptile, indigenous to the swamps, rivers, and marshes of Louisiana, is considered a Cajun specialty. High in protein while low in fat and cholesterol, it may be compared to chicken. The choicest cuts of alligator are the tail and jaw sections. Alligator meat needs to be trimmed of all fat and tendons before it is cooked to prevent it from becoming tough.

Bananas Foster A popular dessert prepared tableside and made famous at Brennan's Restaurant in New Orleans. Bananas are cooked in a mixture of butter, brown sugar, cinnamon, rum, and banana liqueur; it is served hot, right out of the pan, with a scoop of vanilla ice cream. The dish is named after Dick Foster, a political figure and friend of the Brennan family, and the restaurant claims to use over 35,000 pounds of bananas each year in the preparation of their classic dessert.

Beignet French for "fritter." Beignets are diamond-shaped, raised doughnuts without the hole in the middle. They are typically topped liberally with powdered sugar before serving.

Blackened Redfish A fish preparation invented and popularized by Chef Paul Prudhomme in 1979 in his New Orleans restaurant K-Paul. Chef Prudhomme prepares the fish by seasoning it with a custom blend of Cajun spices and cooking it at a super-hot temperature in a cast-iron skillet. Blackened redfish became so famous that it is now considered the icon of Cajun cooking, and at one time became so popular that redfish was placed on the endangered species list.

Boucherie A Cajun tradition and communal feast that centers around the slaughter of a pig. In the days before refrigeration, these gatherings were held in the fall or winter, when cooler temperatures allowed time to cure meats before they spoiled. Using "everything but the oink," the cooks prepared cracklings from the skin, headcheese from the brain, and lard from the fat. They used the entrails for sausage casings and made sausages such as boudin blanc, boudin rouge, andouille, and tasso. The organs were used to make a dish called "debris."

Bread Pudding Considered by many to be the apple pie of Louisiana, this dessert combines the influences of the French, with their bread, and the Germans, with their eggs and dairy products. A number of "authentic" regional recipes for bread pudding exist, but they all start with leftover French bread soaked in milk and eggs, then combined with ingredients such as nuts, raisins, nutmeg, and cinnamon, and baked in an oven. Whiskey sauce or caramel sauce is the traditional topping.

Brown Meunière Sauce A brown butter sauce, much like the French sauce beurre noisette. It is made by adding demi-glace sauce and cayenne pepper to brown butter, giving it a spicy flavor and a nutty aroma, used to top both meat and fish dishes.

Café au Lait Coffee made with the addition of ground chicory root and served with steamed milk. It became popular during the Civil War and remains a Louisiana specialty.

Calas A breakfast fritter like beignets, calas are fried balls of rice and dough that are eaten covered with powdered sugar. The word *calas* comes from one or more African languages meaning, "fried cake." African-American street vendors sold the fresh hot calas in the city's French Quarter, with cries of "*Calas, belles, calas tout chauds!*"

Cane Syrup The concentrated sap of the sugarcane plant, also referred to as "light molasses." Cane syrup is made by crushing sugarcane to extract the juice, treating to remove the impurities, and then boiling to concentrate it. The syrup is then processed to allow the cropping out of the sugar crystals. The technique is progressive so that the first syrup produced—molasses—can yield an additional crop of crystals, or brown sugar. The syrups derived from sugarcane vary in color from light brown to almost black and can be blended from different varieties of cane. Cane syrup is frequently substituted for maple syrup and molasses in Cajun and Creole preparations.

Chicory The root of a variety of Belgian endive that, when mature, is dried, roasted, and ground. When mixed with coffee beans and brewed, chicory imparts a bittersweet, somewhat nutty flavor to the coffee. Napoleon's troops first added chicory to coffee to stretch their dwindling supply of coffee beans, and the first French settlers continued this coffee-making tradition. Chicory is also added to warm milk and served after dinner to induce sleep. It is added to gravies, soups, and dark breads to add an element of richness and color.

Cracklings A Cajun specialty, typically prepared during a boucherie. Cracklings are small pieces of pork skin that are fried, seasoned, and eaten as a snack.

Crawfish A freshwater crustacean also known as a "mudbug," "crawdad," or "craw daddy." All the edible meat comes from the tail. They are available from December through May. Due to the small quantity of meat in the tail section, 7 pounds of crawfish yield 1 pound of meat. For a crawfish boil, a typical person will consume 4 to 5 pounds of whole crawfish. Crawfish are best cooked in boiling salted water flavored with spices and herbs.

Creole Cream Cheese A fresh white cheese, much like the French fromage blanc. Found only in Louisiana, the beneficial bacteria used to make Creole cream cheese are indigenous to the region and the results cannot be duplicated elsewhere. Creole cream cheese is eaten as a snack or served with any meal. Commonly eaten with sugar and strawberries, or plain—just seasoned with salt and pepper.

Creole Mustard A locally made mustard made from spicy dark mustard seeds that are marinated in vinegar before use. Creole mustard is quite pungent and is similar to horseradish. It is frequently used in remoulade sauce and served with ham and po'boy sandwiches.

Creole Tomato A locally grown tomato that has a very thin skin, a low acidity level, and a very high juice content. Known for its sweet aroma and characteristic taste, attributed to Louisiana's fertile soil and humid air. In season from June through August, it is rarely shipped outside of the region. Refrigeration diminishes its natural sweet flavor.

Crescent City Breakfast A breakfast of beignets and café au lait that may be enjoyed any hour of the day or night. Café du Monde in the French Quarter is one of the most well known establishments for this New Orleans tradition.

Dirty Rice Dirty rice gets its name from the ground livers and giblets that are added to the rice preparation and results in dark-colored rice. Dirty rice typically has diced celery, onions, and peppers (known as the "holy trinity") included in the recipe.

Eggs Hussard A brunch dish, inspired by eggs Benedict, created at Brennan's restaurant in New Orleans. Toasted English muffins are topped with sliced Canadian bacon, marchand de vin sauce, poached eggs, and cayenne-flavored hollandaise sauce. It is typically served with grilled tomatoes.

Etouffée A French word meaning "smothered" or "braised." A stew often of crawfish, crab, or shrimp slowly cooked in a thick sauce made with seafood stock, tomatoes, onions, celery, peppers, and seasonings. Etouffée is served over rice with hot pepper sauce.

Filé Powder A powder made from sassafras leaves that have been dried, ground, and passed through a sieve, it is a thickening agent discovered and shared by the Choctaw tribe of Native Americans. It is most commonly added just before serving to thicken gumbo.

Frog The bullfrog, also known as the "Creole frog," is the most frequently eaten. The legs are considered a delicacy and are broiled, fried, or sautéed.

Gumbo Z'herbs A Lenten dish, it was traditionally served on Good Friday and breaks all the rules of gumbo. It does not use okra or filé, and the roux is not prepared first. Legend has it that one would make as many friends as the number of different greens that were put in the gumbo. Seven greens meant seven new friends.

Gateau de Sirop A traditional spice cake that has been sweetened with cane syrup, topped with icing made from brown sugar, and sprinkled with pecans.

Grillade A thinly sliced piece of fresh pork or veal, pan-fried and slow-cooked with sliced onions, peppers, celery, and tomatoes. Stripped from the animal during a boucherie, the grillades were cooked in cast-iron pans over fires and served with grits or rice.

The Holy Trinity In Cajun and Creole country this refers to the mirepoix-style trio of vegetables that includes onions, green bell peppers, and celery. The proportions are determined by the dish that is being prepared.

Jambalaya The Spanish dish paella was the source for this rice dish. The Spanish immigrants adapted their recipe to local ingredients. Oysters and crawfish replace the clams and mussels, and andouille sausage replaces the ham. The dish was originally named *jambon a la yaya* after an African word for rice, *yaya*. Jambalaya has evolved into one of America's most popular rice dishes and is made with pork, chicken, and andouille sausage, or whatever products are available.

King Cake This cake is traditionally served during Mardi Gras celebration. It is a brioche ring filled with a mixture of nuts and topped with green, purple, and gold icing (the colors of Mardi Gras). A small prize is hidden inside the cake, and the person who finds the prize in his or her portion is expected to make a donation to charity. This tradition dates back to medieval Europe, where King cake was served on January 6 (Twelfth Night or King's Day) and had gold coins hidden inside. Today King cake is used to select the king and queen of the Mardi Gras celebration.

Mirliton A light green, pear-shaped vegetable also referred to as "chayote" in other regions of the United States. The mirliton came to Louisiana with settlers and slaves from the West Indies and is similar to squash. It is available from August through November. Though it can be prepared using a variety of cooking techniques, it is frequently stuffed with bread crumbs and seafood.

Mock Turtle Soup Because of the limited availability of turtle meat, this is a preparation for turtle soup made with a calf's head in lieu of turtle. Veal, duck, or beef may replace the calf's head.

Moussa A cornmeal mush frequently used as a substitute for rice. Gumbo was originally served over moussa before rice became plentiful.

Muffuletta A sandwich common in Louisiana that is made by slicing a round loaf of Italian bread horizontally and stuffing it with meats or seafood. It is dressed with a salad made from green and black olives and then the sandwich is sliced into quarters. These sandwiches were served in the early 1900s by Italian grocers who sold a lunch plate special with assorted meats, cheeses, and an olive salad with a Sicilian bread called a muffuletta. A busy worker split the bread and made a sandwich. This became so popular that the grocers started selling the sandwiches, wrapping them in the paper the bread came in. The label on the bread wrapper, Muffuletta, became the name of the sandwich.

Okra An oblong, tapered pod with ridged green skin. Okra seeds were brought to Louisiana by Congolese slaves in the early 1700s. The shortened name used by the slaves for this vegetable was *gombo*. When cooked, the white okra seed produces a glutinous substance that acts as a natural thickening agent. Okra may replace filé powder as the thickening agent in gumbo.

Pecan Praline Originally made in 17th-century France with almonds and called *amande rissolee dans de sucre,* this confection had one or two kinds of nuts coated with butter and caramelized sugar and left to harden into a candy. When the French arrived in Louisiana, they substituted the local pecans for the almonds called for in the recipe. They are typically served in the New Orleans area after dinner with a cup of coffee.

Po'Boy The most popular sandwich in Louisiana, it is similar to the hoagy, grinder, submarine, and hero sandwiches from other parts of the United States.

Rice Louisiana is America's third largest rice-producing state, behind California and Arkansas, and its population consumes more rice per capita than any other state. Southwestern Louisiana grows over 80 percent of the state's rice crop. Rice production began in earnest after the Civil War, with farmers switching from sugarcane because it required fewer farmhands. Because of their warm climate and long growing season, the rice fields can be harvested twice a year. The regional preference is for medium-grain white rice with a high gluten content. Others prefer long-grain or extra-long-grain rice.

> **Providence Rice** When rice first came to the Louisiana prairies, Cajun farmers planted small crops in places that couldn't be plowed, along coulees and ditches, bayous and ponds. They just threw rice into the standing waters. The reference to providence comes from the saying "it's up to the providence or the grace of God" to see the rice harvested.

Wild Pecan Rice or Popcorn Rice This long-grain rice is milled in such a way that most of the bran layer is left on. This rice is grown only in the parish (county) of New Iberia, Louisiana. It has nothing in common with wild rice, pecans, or popcorn, with its own distinctive taste and nutty aroma when cooked.

Red Beans and Rice Considered to have a Caribbean influence, red beans and rice is the traditional Monday meal in New Orleans. Monday was always wash day and the cook could put on a pot of beans to cook with the leftover ham bone from Sunday's dinner and then get on with her washing while the beans simmered. The bean is a red kidney bean and the ham bone is cracked to provide the marrow that gives the sauce its coating. It is such an important part of New Orleans culinary identity that Louis Armstrong used to close his letters with "Red beans and ricely yours."

Remoulade Sauce A mayonnaise-based sauce flavored with Creole mustard, finely diced vegetables, herbs, and spices that is commonly served with seafood. Each chef customizes his or her recipe with the choice of condiments and seasonings added to the sauce's mayonnaise base.

Roux A classic French thickening agent made by combining equal parts flour and butter and cooking it prior to use—the cooking process gradually colors the roux. There are four names that are generally associated with the varying shades of roux: It begins as a white roux, changes to a blond roux, then darkens to brown or dark roux depending on the temperature and time it takes to cook the flour. Any type of fat may be used, depending on the taste and purpose of the roux. In Creole cuisine, roux is typically cooked to the brown to dark states and used to thicken dishes like gumbos and stews. Animal fats, such as bacon or duck, are substituted for the butter for a lighter flavor. In Cajun cuisine, roux is usually made with vegetable oil or animal fat instead of butter and cooked to a dark caramel color. The dark roux used in Cajun and Creole cuisines helps provide richness and depth of flavor to the dishes.

Seafood Boil Crab, shrimp, or crawfish boils are common events in Louisiana and along the Mississippi Gulf Coast. The seafood is boiled in a deep pot. Bay leaves, allspice, cloves, mustard seed, coriander seeds, dill seeds, pepper, and other herbs and spices are tied in a cheesecloth sack and added to the pot. Seafood boils are typically held outdoors and the seafood is eaten on tabletops lined with newspapers. At the end of the meal, the newspapers, along with the shells and all, are rolled up and discarded.

Sugarcane Sugar was the first agricultural crop of any significance grown in Louisiana. A type of perennial grass that grows to 6 feet in height, sugarcane came to Louisiana in the mid-1700s from the West Indies. It is used primarily to make molasses, white and brown sugar, and cane syrup.

Sweet Potato The Louisiana yam is a variety of sweet potato discovered in the early 1700s by the Dutch explorer Antoine Simon le Page du Pratz, who represented France at the time. This sweet potato is not a true yam but has a soft sweet and moist flesh that differs from other sweet potatoes in the rest of the country, which are dry, mealy, and starchy. Slaves in the American South called the sweet potato *nyamis* because of its similarity to a vegetable of that name that they know from their homeland. Sweet potatoes adapt well to any cooking technique whether it is baking, frying, mashing, candying, grilling, or using them as an ingredient in desserts.

Tabasco Sauce A spicy hot sauce made from Tabasco peppers, vinegar, and salt, currently available in over 100 countries. New Orleans banker Edward McIlhenny formulated Tabasco sauce over 130 years ago. McIlhenny and his family lived in an area called Avery Island. This area was not an island but a massive salt dome just south of New Iberia. McIlhenny was given a gift of pepper seeds by a friend returning from a trip to Mexico. During the Civil War, the family was forced to abandon their home in Louisiana. Upon their return after the war, they found that everything was destroyed except the hearty pepper plants. In 1868, McIlhenny began to experiment with the fruits of the plants and eventually invented a sauce made by mashing the peppers with Avery Island salt, storing the mash in a crock for 30 days, and then adding French wine vinegar and storing for an additional 30 days. The resulting sauce was an immediate success. The name Tabasco is a Mexican term meaning "land where soil is humid." One small bottle of Tabasco contains 720 drops. Tabasco is best added to food after it is removed from heat.

Tasso A sausage of pork liberally seasoned with filé powder, garlic, and red pepper, and then cured and smoked for two to three days. Due to its heavy salt and smoke flavor, tasso is rarely eaten on its own but is used as a flavoring agent for a variety of preparations.

Turtle Until the middle of the 1990s, turtles were abundant in the Louisiana region and their meat was commonly sold at stalls in New Orleans's French Market. Due to a diminishing population, turtle meat is now available only through farms. Turtle was most frequently used to prepare soup, which was made as a clear broth, a cream soup, or thick like a stew. The fat from female turtles is considered a delicacy.

Menus and Recipes from Louisiana's Cajun and Creole Cuisines

MENU ONE

Chicken and Andouille Sausage Gumbo

Tomato and Haricot Vert Salad

Fried Fish in Pearly Meal with Remoulade Sauce

Crawfish Étouffée

Basic Boiled Rice

Smothered Okra

Bread Pudding with Whiskey Sauce

MENU TWO

Red Beans and Rice

Green Salad with Vinaigrette Dressing

Baked Cheese Grits

Braised Beef Daube with Cheese Grits, Glazed Carrots, and Sugar Snap Peas

Fried Oyster Po'Boy

Pecan Pralines

MENU THREE

New Orleans Shrimp Bisque

Roasted Eggplant and Oysters

Creole Jambalaya

Chicken Maquechoux

Braised Leeks with Hollandaise

OTHER RECIPES

Paneed Chicken with Fettuccine

Fried Stuffed Crawfish Heads

Muffuletta

Shrimp-Stuffed Mirlitons

Sautéed Chicken Livers Orleans

Chicken and Andouille Sausage Gumbo 4 SERVINGS

chef tip

Gumbo comes in many varieties, but every one reflects certain fundamental cooking techniques. First, most gumbos have a roux base that is cooked slowly to a rich brown, giving gumbo much of its characteristic thick texture and smoky taste. To prevent the roux from burning once it is done, add the cold vegetables all at once.

Filé powder, when used to thicken gumbo, should be added only after the gumbo is finished and removed from the heat. Once filé powder is stirred in, the soup cannot be reheated, as the filé will either turn stringy or solidify at the bottom of the pot. For the best results, let the gumbo stand in the pot for 5 minutes after adding the filé powder.

AMOUNT	MEASURE	INGREDIENT
For the Seasoning Mix		
¹/₂ teaspoon	3g	Salt
¹/₂ teaspoon	2 g	Black pepper
¹/₂ teaspoon	1 g	Cayenne
¹/₂ teaspoon	1 g	White pepper
¹/₂ teaspoon	1 g	Paprika
¹/₂ teaspoon	1 g	Onion powder
¹/₂ teaspoon	1 g	Garlic powder
For the Gumbo		
2 cups	16 ounces, 453 g	Chicken thigh meat, skin removed, 1-inch (2.5 cm) pieces
1 cup	4 ounces, 113 g	Onion, ¹/₄ inch (.6 cm) dice
1 cup	5 ounces, 141 g	Green bell pepper, ¹/₄ inch (.6 cm) dice
³/₄ cup	3 ounces, 85 g	Celery, ¹/₄ inch (.6 cm) dice
1¹/₄ cups	5¹/₂ ounces, 15 g	All-purpose flour
as needed	1¹/₂ cups, 352 ml	Vegetable oil
7 cups	56 ounces, 1.75 l	Chicken stock
1¹/₂ cups	8 ounces, 226 g	Andouille smoked sausage or any other pure smoked pork sausage such as Polish sausage (kielbasa) cut into ¹/₄-inch (.6 cm) cubes

1 teaspoon	5 g	Garlic, minced
to taste		Salt and black pepper

PROCEDURE

1   Combine the ingredients for the seasoning mixture. Divide in half.

2   Toss the chicken with half the seasoning mixture and set aside for 30 minutes.

3   Combine the onion, green pepper, and celery in a bowl and set aside.

4   Combine half the flour and the remaining seasoning mixture. Toss the chicken with the flour mixture until well coated.

5   Heat $1^1/_2$ inches (3.8 cm) oil in a heavy skillet until very hot, 390°F (199°C).

6   Fry the chicken until crust is brown on all sides and meat is cooked. Drain on paper towels.

7   Carefully pour the hot oil into a container, leaving as many of the browned particles in the pan as possible. Scrape the pan bottom to loosen any remaining particles.

8   Return $1/_4$ cup (2 ounces, 56 ml) hot oil to the pan over high heat. Gradually add the reserved flour. Cook, whisking constantly, until the flour is dark red-brown to black, 3 to 4 minutes, being careful not to scorch the roux.

9   Remove pan from heat and immediately add the vegetables, stirring constantly until the roux stops getting darker. Return to low heat and cook 5 minutes or until vegetables are soft, stirring constantly and scraping the pan bottom well.

10 In a separate pot, bring the stock to a boil, then reduce to a simmer.

11 Add the roux to the stock a little bit at a time, stirring until dissolved between each addition.

12 Bring to a boil. Reduce the heat to a simmer, and add the sausage and garlic. Simmer, uncovered, 30 minutes, stirring often as it begins to thicken.

13 Add the fried chicken and adjust the seasoning with salt and pepper.

14 To serve as a main course, mound a portion of cooked rice in the center of a soup bowl; ladle about $1^1/_4$ cups (10 ounces, 293 ml) gumbo around the rice. For an appetizer, place 1 heaping teaspoon (5 ml) of cooked rice in a cup and ladle about $3/_4$ cup (6 ounces, 178 ml) gumbo on top.

Tomato and Haricot Vert Salad 4 SERVINGS

AMOUNT	MEASURE	INGREDIENT
For the Dressing		
1 tablespoon	½ ounce, 15 g	Mayonnaise
1 teaspoon	5 g	Dijon mustard
2 tablespoons	1 ounce, 28 ml	Red wine vinegar
1 tablespoon	½ ounce, 14 ml	Lemon juice
1		Garlic clove, mashed with salt
½ cup	4 ounces, 115 ml	Olive oil
to taste		Salt and black pepper
For the Salad		
1 cup	4 ounces, 113 g	Fennel, stemmed, sliced paper-thin
1 cup	4 ounces, 113 g	Haricot vert, blanched
1½ cups	9 ounces, 255 g	Tomatoes, peeled, seeded, julienned
1 teaspoon	1 g	Chives, chopped
1 teaspoon	1 g	Basil, cut in chiffonade

PROCEDURE

1 Place the mayonnaise, mustard, vinegar, lemon juice, and garlic in a blender.

2 While the blender is running, slowly drizzle in the oil until the dressing is smooth and thick. Season with salt and pepper.

3 Toss salad ingredients with dressing and serve on a chilled plate.

Fried Fish in Pearly Meal with Remoulade Sauce 4 SERVINGS

chef tip

Yellow corn flour may be found in most gourmet shops. It may be sold as packaged, pre-seasoned seafood breading, such as Zatarain's Fish Fry. If unavailable in your area, use $^1/_3$ part cornstarch, $^1/_3$ part flour, and $^1/_3$ part yellow cornmeal as a substitute.

AMOUNT	MEASURE	INGREDIENT
4	16 ounces, 454 g, total	Whitefish fillets, (Speckled trout or freshwater bass, grouper, perch, brook trout)
I cup	8 ounces, 235 ml	Milk, cold for soaking
as needed		Vegetable oil, for deep-frying
I cup	4 ounces, 113 g	Yellow corn flour
I cup	6 ounces, 170 g	Yellow cornmeal
I $^1/_2$ teaspoons		Salt
$^1/_4$ teaspoon		Black pepper
pinch		Cayenne
I cup	2 ounces, 56 g	Romaine lettuce, coarsely chopped
I cup	8 ounces, 453 g	Remoulade Sauce (page 200)

PROCEDURE

1 Rinse the fillets; remove any bones or skin, and dry the fillets.

2 Cut the fish into strips measuring $^1/_2$ x $^1/_2$ x 2 inches (1.2 x 1.2 x 5 cm). Lay strips in a pan and add cold milk to just to cover fish. Soak 30 minutes.

3 Preheat the fryer to 375°F (190°C).

4 Combine the corn flour and cornmeal with the seasonings and mix well.

5 Drain fish. Dip in seasoned flour to coat evenly.

6 Fry fish until golden brown.

7 Serve with romaine lettuce and Remoulade Sauce.

Remoulade Sauce 4 SERVINGS

AMOUNT	MEASURE	INGREDIENT
4–5	3 1/2 ounces, 99 g	Green onions, coarsely chopped
1/2 cup	2 ounces, 56 g	Celery, coarsely chopped
2		Parsley sprigs, coarsely chopped
3 tablespoons	1 1/2 ounces, 45 g	Creole mustard
1 tablespoon	1/4 ounce, 7 g	Paprika
1 teaspoon	5 g	Salt
1/2 teaspoon	1 g	Black pepper
1/4 teaspoon	1 g	Cayenne
1/3 cup	3 ounces, 78 ml	White wine vinegar
1 1/2 tablespoons	3/4 ounce, 21 ml	Lemon juice
1 teaspoon	1 g	Basil, chopped
3/4 cup	6 ounces, 170 ml	Olive oil
1		Green onion, 1/4 inch (.6 cm) dice
2 tablespoons	1/2 ounce, 14 g	Celery, 1/4 inch (.6 cm) dice
1 tablespoon		Parsley, finely diced

PROCEDURE

1   In a food processor or blender, grind the green onions, celery, and parsley to a puree.

2   Combine the puree with the mustard, paprika, salt, pepper, and cayenne. Blend well.

3   Add the vinegar, lemon juice, and basil. Blend well.

4   Gradually add the olive oil, blending constantly to make an emulsion (mayonnaise).

5   Add the diced green onion, celery, and parsley and combine well. Refrigerate for at least 1 hour to combine flavors.

Crawfish Étouffée 4 SERVINGS

AMOUNT	MEASURE	INGREDIENT
6 tablespoons	3 ounces, 85 g	Butter
1/4 cup	1 ounce, 28 g	All-purpose flour
1 cup	4 ounces, 113 g	Onion, 1/2 inch (1.2 cm) dice
1/2 cup	2 1/2 ounces, 70 g	Green bell pepper, 1/2 inch (1.2 cm) dice
1/2 cup	2 ounces, 56 g	Celery, 1/2 inch (1.2 cm) dice
1 tablespoon	1/2 ounce, 15 g	Garlic, minced
1 1/2 cups	16 ounces, 453 g	Crawfish tails
6 tablespoons	3 ounces, 85 g	Crawfish fat, or butter
1 teaspoon	5 g	Salt
1/4 teaspoon	1 g	Black pepper
1/4 teaspoon	1 g	Cayenne pepper
1 teaspoon	5 ml	Lemon juice
1/3 cup	1 ounce, 28 g	Green onion tops, thinly sliced
1 tablespoon	3 g	Parsley, minced
1 cup	8 ounces, 235 ml	Fish stock or cold water

PROCEDURE

1 Melt the butter over low heat in a heavy pot.

2 Gradually add the flour and cook over low heat until a medium brown roux is formed.

3 Add the onion, green pepper, celery, and garlic. Cook, stirring, until the vegetables are tender, about 15 minutes.

4 Add the crawfish, crawfish fat, salt, pepper, cayenne, lemon juice, green onion, and parsley; mix well.

5 Add the fish stock or cold water. Bring to a boil, and simmer 5 to 8 minutes, stirring frequently. Set aside.

6 To serve, heat the étouffée slowly over low heat, thin with hot water if needed. Serve over boiled rice.

Basic Boiled Rice 4 SERVINGS

chef tip

Firm, fluffy, freshly prepared boiled rice is an essential accompaniment for gumbos, bean dishes, bisques, étouffées, and many other dishes.

AMOUNT	MEASURE	INGREDIENT
I cup	6¹/₂ ounces, 184 g	Long-grain rice
2 cups	16 ounces, 470 ml	Water, cold
I teaspoon	5 g	Salt
I teaspoon	5 g	Butter

PROCEDURE

1   Combine all the ingredients in a heavy 3-quart (3 l) saucepan with a tight-fitting cover and bring to a boil over high heat.

2   Stir once with a fork, then cover tightly and reduce the heat to very low. Cook, covered, for 15 minutes. Do not lift the cover during the cooking.

3   Remove pot from heat, let stand (covered) 5 to 10 minutes longer. Uncover, and fluff the rice gently with a fork.

Smothered Okra 4 SERVINGS

AMOUNT	MEASURE	INGREDIENT
2 tablespoons	1 ounce, 28 ml	Vegetable oil
1 cup	4 ounces, 113 g	Onion, thinly sliced
4 cups	13$^{1}/_{2}$ ounces, 382 g	Okra, whole, stems removed
$^{3}/_{4}$ cup	4 ounces, 113 g	Tomato, peeled, seeded, chopped
to taste		Salt and black pepper
$^{1}/_{8}$ teaspoon	1 g	Cayenne
$^{1}/_{8}$ teaspoon	1 g	Chili powder
$^{1}/_{8}$ teaspoon	1 g	Thyme (dried)

PROCEDURE

1   Heat the oil in a sauté pan. Add the onion and sauté over low heat until lightly brown.

2   Add the okra, tomato, and seasonings; cover and smother until the okra is tender. Smaller okra will take less time to cook than larger pods.

Bread Pudding with Whiskey Sauce 4 SERVINGS

chef tip This is the classic New Orleans bread pudding. Use half-and-half instead of milk, and an extra egg to make it even richer. You can add different fruits, nuts, and liqueurs, if desired.

AMOUNT	MEASURE	INGREDIENT
1 cup plus 6 tablespoons	11 ounces, 325 ml	Milk
2 cups (¹/₄ baguette)	2 ounces, 56 g	French bread, day-old, cut into 1¹/₂- to 2-inch (38 to 5 cm) cubes
1		Egg, beaten
¹/₃ cup	2¹/₂ ounces, 70 g	Granulated sugar
1¹/₂ teaspoons	7.5 ml	Vanilla extract
1 tablespoon	11 g	Raisins, soaked in Cointreau or Kirsch
1 teaspoon	2 g	Ground cinnamon
¹/₄ teaspoon	1 g	Grated nutmeg
2 tablespoons	1 ounce, 28 g	Dark brown sugar
1¹/₂ tablespoons	1¹/₂ ounces, 42 g	Unsalted butter, in small cubes

PROCEDURE

1　Soak the bread in 6 tablespoons (84 ml) of the milk for 1 hour.

2　Preheat oven to 300°F (149°C). Butter a 1-quart (32 ounce, 1 l) pan.

3　Beat the remaining milk, egg, sugar, and vanilla to combine well. Add the milk-soaked bread, then add the raisins and mix well.

4　Pour mixture into the prepared pan and sprinkle with cinnamon, nutmeg, and brown sugar. Top with butter cubes.

5　Bake for 1 hour, or until set. Allow to cool 30 minutes before cutting.

6　Serve with Whiskey Sauce (page 205).

Whiskey Sauce · 4 SERVINGS

chef tip For a nonalcoholic version, add a teaspoon of rum, or orange or vanilla extract.

AMOUNT	MEASURE	INGREDIENT
¹/₄ cup	2 ounces, 56 g	Unsalted butter
¹/₄ cup	I ounce, 28 g	Confectioners' sugar
I		Egg, beaten
¹/₄ cup	2 ounces, 56 ml	Bourbon

PROCEDURE

1 Melt the butter over low heat.

2 When hot, but not browned, add the sugar. Beat with whisk until thick and hot.

3 Remove pan from heat and whisk in the beaten egg. Beat until emulsified, about 2 minutes.

4 Whisk in the bourbon and serve warm.

Red Beans and Rice

Red Beans and Rice 4 SERVINGS

AMOUNT	MEASURE	INGREDIENT
2 cups	16 ounces, 453 g	Red kidney beans, soaked overnight
1 cup	4 ounces, 113 g	Onion, $^1/_4$ inch (.6 cm) dice
$^1/_4$ cup	$^1/_2$ ounce, 14 g	Green onion, chopped
$^1/_4$ cup	1$^1/_4$ ounces, 35 g	Green bell pepper, $^1/_4$ inch (.6 cm) dice
1 tablespoon	3 g	Parsley, minced
1 cup	6 ounces, 170 g	Ham, in 1-inch (2.5 cm) cubes
$^3/_4$ cup	6 ounces, 170 g	Bacon, in $^1/_2$-inch (1.2 cm) cubes
1	12 ounces, 340 g	Ham hock
$^1/_2$ tablespoon	3 g	Salt
$^1/_2$ teaspoon	1 g	Black pepper
$^1/_2$ tablespoon	8 g	Garlic, minced
pinch		Cayenne
pinch		Red pepper flakes
1		Bay leaf, broken into quarters
$^1/_4$ teaspoon	1 g	Thyme (dried)
pinch		Basil (dried)
1$^1/_4$ quarts	293 ml	Water or chicken or vegetable stock, cold

PROCEDURE

1   Drain the soaked beans. Combine with all the other ingredients and add just enough cold water to cover.

2   Bring to a boil over high heat. Reduce heat to a simmer and cook 2 to 3 hours or until beans are tender and a thick natural gravy has formed. Add 1 cup water toward the end of the cooking if the mixture appears too dry. During cooking, stir frequently and scrape down the sides and across the bottom to prevent scorching.

3   Remove the ham hock and cut meat into $^1/_2$-inch (1.2 cm) cubes; return to the beans.

4   Serve with rice.

Green Salad with Vinaigrette Dressing 4 SERVINGS

AMOUNT	MEASURE	INGREDIENT
For the Vinaigrette Dressing		
1/2 cup	4 ounces, 115 ml	Olive oil
2 tablespoons	1 ounce, 28 ml	White wine vinegar
2 teaspoons	10 ml	Lemon juice
1	5 g	Garlic clove, finely minced
1/4 teaspoon	2 g	Salt
1/8 teaspoon	1 g	Parsley, finely minced
to taste		Coarse salt and black pepper
For the Salad		
3 cups	4 1/2 ounces, 126 g	Boston lettuce, broken into large pieces, chilled
2 cups	4 ounces, 114 g	Romaine lettuce, cut into 1-inch (2.5 cm) squares, chilled
2 cups	4 ounces, 114 g	Red leaf lettuce, broken into large pieces, chilled
6		Leaves chicory greens, watercress, or Chinese cabbage, chilled
to taste		Salt and black pepper

PROCEDURE

1 Combine all ingredients for the dressing in a small bowl. Mix vigorously with a whisk for 1 minute, then cover the bowl with plastic wrap and let it stand at room temperature for 30 minutes to 1 hour.

2 When ready to serve, remove the chilled greens from the refrigerator, dry, and sprinkle with salt and pepper. Mix the dressing again and strain it, then mix again vigorously for about 1 minute before pouring it over the greens. Toss and divide evenly.

Baked Cheese Grits · 4 SERVINGS

AMOUNT	MEASURE	INGREDIENT
1 cup	6 ounces, 160 g	Hominy grits, quick-cooking
3 cups	24 ounces, 705 ml	Milk
1 teaspoon	5 g	Salt
2		Eggs, lightly beaten
1 cup	8 ounces, 235 ml	Water, hot
6	1 ounce, 28 g	Garlic cloves, chopped
6 tablespoons	3 ounces, 85 g	Butter
1 cup	4 ounces, 113 g	Cheddar cheese, grated
to taste		Salt and white pepper

PROCEDURE

1 Preheat the oven to 350°F (175°C).

2 Stir the grits into the milk and add the salt. Cook over medium heat, stirring often, so the mixture does not scorch, for 5 to 7 minutes or until thickened.

3 Remove from the heat and add the eggs. Then add the water, stirring vigorously.

4 Separately, sauté the garlic in the butter, then add to grits. Return the mixture to the heat and cook until thickened again.

5 Add the cheese and mix well. Season with salt and pepper.

6 Place in a baking pan and bake for 30 minutes.

7 Let rest 10 minutes before serving.

Braised Beef Daube 4–6 SERVINGS

chef tip

Daube is an ancient term for a meat stew with wine and spices, braised in a covered casserole.

AMOUNT	MEASURE	INGREDIENT
2 pounds	907 g	Beef knuckle, trimmed
to taste		Salt and black pepper
1/4 cup	2 ounces, 58 ml	Vegetable oil
1 cup	4 ounces, 113 g	Onion, 1/4 inch (.6 cm) dice
3	1/2 ounce, 14 g	Garlic cloves, 1/4 inch (.6 cm) dice
1 cup	4 ounces, 113 g	Celery, 1/4 inch (.6 cm) dice
1 cup	4 ounces, 113 g	Carrots, 1/4 inch (.6 cm) dice
1/2 cup	2 1/2 ounces, 70 g	Green bell pepper, 1/4 inch (.6 cm) dice
2/3 cup	4 ounces, 113 g	Tomato, peeled, seeded, 1/4 inch (.6 cm) dice
1/2 cup	4 ounces, 118 ml	Dry red wine
1 quart	32 ounces, 1 l	Beef stock
1		Sachet d'epice (3 sprigs parsley, 1 bay leaf, 6 peppercorns, 3 sprigs thyme, wrapped in cheesecloth and tied as a package)
2 tablespoons	6 g	Cornstarch mixed with 1 tablespoon (14 ml) water

PROCEDURE

1 Preheat the oven to 350°F (180°C).

2 Truss the beef and sear on all sides. Remove and season with salt and pepper.

3 In the same pan, over medium heat, add the oil, onion, garlic, and carrots. Caramelize the vegetables.

4 Add the celery, green pepper, and tomato. Cook 5 minutes.

5 Add the wine and scrape the pan well. Add the beef stock and bring to a simmer.

6 Combine the beef and vegetable stock mixture in a braising pan. Cover the pan with parchment, foil, and a lid. Braise for approximately 1 hour.

7 Add the sachet d'epice and turn the beef. Cook 1 hour longer, or until fork-tender.

8 Remove beef and discard the sachet d'epice. Keep the beef warm and moist.

9 Reduce the sauce, remove excess fat, and adjust seasoning. Stir the cornstarch slurry and add, stirring continuously until sauce has thickened.

10 Slice the beef and serve with the sauce.

Glazed Carrots 4 SERVINGS

AMOUNT	MEASURE	INGREDIENT
2 tablespoons	1 ounce, 28 g	Butter
3 cups	12 ounces, 340 g	Carrots, peeled, oblique cut
1 1/2 teaspoons	1/4 ounce, 7 g	Granulated sugar (optional)
1/2 cup	4 ounces, 115 ml	Chicken stock
to taste		Salt and black pepper

PROCEDURE

1 Heat a sauté pan and melt the butter. Add the carrots, sugar, chicken stock, and seasoning. Bring to a simmer and cook, covered, on low heat until the carrots are almost done.

2 Remove the cover and allow the liquid to reduce to a glaze. If carrots are done before glaze is formed, remove them with a slotted spoon, reduce the liquid, and return them to the pan to finish the process.

Sugar Snap Peas 4 SERVINGS

chef tip

Sugar snap peas are a cross between traditional English peas and snow peas. Some fresh sugar snap peas are available stringless, which means they are ready to use immediately after washing. Otherwise, snap off the end of each pea pod, pulling down the length of the pod to remove any tough strings.

AMOUNT	MEASURE	INGREDIENT
4 cups	9 ounces, 255 g	Sugar snap peas
2 tablespoons	1 ounce, 28 g	Butter
to taste		Salt and black pepper

PROCEDURE

1 Parboil the peas until almost tender in salt water. Drain and shock in ice water. Set aside.

2 Heat the butter in a sauté pan over medium heat. Add the peas and sauté until hot. Season with salt and pepper.

Fried Oyster Po'Boy 4 SERVINGS

AMOUNT	MEASURE	INGREDIENT
24		Oysters, shucked
to taste		Salt and black pepper
as needed		All-purpose flour
as needed		Egg wash
as needed		Bread crumbs
4		French bread, cut into 6-inch (15 cm) sections
2 cups	4 ounces, 113 g	Iceberg lettuce, shredded
2		Tomatoes, sliced (12 slices)
2		Lemons, cut in half, wrapped
as needed		Vegetable oil, for deep-frying
as desired		Remoulade Sauce (page 200)

PROCEDURE

1 Heat oil in a deep-fat fryer to 375°F (190°C).

2 Drain and dry the oysters. Season and dip them in the flour; shake off excess flour. Pass through egg wash, drain off excess egg wash, and coat in bread crumbs. Turn the oysters and pat until bread crumbs completely cover them.

3 Fry the oysters golden brown and crisp. Drain on paper towels.

4 Split the French breads lengthwise and warm or toast the halves.

5 Spread the insides with Remoulade Sauce.

6 Spread ¹/₂ cup (0.116 l) shredded lettuce over the Remoulade Sauce, then place 3 slices of tomato on each po'boy. Top tomatoes with 6 oysters and top half of bread.

7 Serve with half of a lemon.

Fried Oyster Po'Boy

Pecan Pralines 4 SERVINGS

AMOUNT	MEASURE	INGREDIENT
1 cup	7 ounces, 196 g	Brown sugar
1/2 cup	3 1/2 ounces, 98 g	Granulated sugar
1/4 teaspoon	2 g	Salt
1/2 cup	4 ounces, 115 ml	Heavy cream
1/4 teaspoon	1 g	Cream of tartar
1 cup	4 ounces, 112 g	Pecan pieces
2 tablespoons	1 ounce, 28 g	Butter
1/2 tablespoon	7 ml	Vanilla extract
pinch		Salt

PROCEDURE

1   Combine the sugars, salt, cream, and cream of tartar in a heavy pan. Stir over low heat until the sugar dissolves, wiping the crystals from the sides of the pan with a rubber spatula.

2   Over medium heat, cook for 15 minutes or until mixture reaches the softball stage, 234°F–240°F (112.5–115°C), on a candy thermometer.

3   Add the pecans. Cook, stirring constantly, for 2 minutes. Remove from heat.

4   Add the butter, vanilla, and salt.

5   Beat until the mixture looks creamy around edges of pan (this happens very quickly but if you need to speed the process, put saucepan in cold water while beating).

6   Drop the candy from a spoon onto waxed paper or baking parchment.

7   When cool, remove from the paper, or when the pralines cool and get firm, cut the waxed paper between each one and wrap individually.

New Orleans Shrimp Bisque 4 SERVINGS

chef tip

The basic reason for making a dark roux is for the distinctive taste and texture it lends to food. This roux taste and texture is characteristic of many dishes that Louisiana Cajuns make. Cooked roux is called "Cajun napalm"; it is extremely hot and sticks to your skin—be very careful to avoid splashing.

AMOUNT	MEASURE	INGREDIENT
For the Roux		
5 tablespoons	2¹/₂ ounces, 80 g	Bacon drippings or butter
I cup	4 ounces, 113 g	All-purpose flour
For the Bisque		
2 tablespoons	I ounce, 28 g	Butter
I cup	4 ounces, 113 g	Onion, ¹/₄ inch (.6 cm) dice
¹/₄ cup	I ounce, 28 g	Green onions, white parts only, thinly sliced
3 tablespoons	¹/₃ ounce, 9 g	Green onions, green tops, thinly sliced
2¹/₂ tablespoons	³/₄ ounce, 21 g	Celery, ¹/₄ inch (.6 cm) dice
2 tablespoons	6 g	Parsley, finely minced
I tablespoon	¹/₂ ounce, 15 g	Garlic, minced
I tablespoon	¹/₂ ounce, 15 g	Salt
¹/₄ teaspoon	I g	Black pepper
¹/₂ teaspoon	I g	Cayenne
2		Bay leaves, broken in half
I teaspoon	2 g	Thyme (dried)
¹/₂ teaspoon	I g	Dry mustard
¹/₂ teaspoon	I g	Basil leaves (dried)
4		Whole cloves
I cup	8 ounces, 226 g	Shrimp, peeled, chopped
2 cups	16 ounces, 2 l	Seafood stock or clam juice
I cup	8 ounces, 226 g	Shrimp, peeled, whole

PROCEDURE

1. Heat the bacon fat over low heat and gradually add the flour. Cook to a medium brown roux.

2   In a separate pan, melt the butter and slowly brown the onion and white parts of the green onions, about 15 minutes. The onions must be cooked before the roux is finished.

3   Add the cooked onions as soon as the roux obtains the desired color (color of rich peanut butter), then add the green onion tops, celery, parsley, garlic, and seasonings and herbs; mix thoroughly, cook 3 minutes.

4   Add the chopped shrimp. Gradually add the stock, stirring constantly to keep smooth. Bring the bisque to a boil, lower the heat, and simmer 30 minutes or more.

5   Add the whole shrimp and simmer 1 minute more.

6   Serve over boiled rice.

Roasted Eggplant and Oysters 4 SERVINGS

AMOUNT	MEASURE	INGREDIENT
2	2¹/₂ pounds, 680 g	Eggplants, firm
4 cups	16 ounces, 453 g	Onion, ¹/₂ inch (1.2 cm) dice
³/₄ cup	6 ounces, 170 g	Unsalted butter
I cup	8 ounces, 226 g	Bacon, ¹/₂ inch (1.2 cm) dice
¹/₂ cup plus 4 heaping teaspoons	1¹/₂ ounces, 42 g	Italian bread crumbs
I teaspoon	5 g	Salt
¹/₂ teaspoon	I g	Black pepper
1¹/₂ pints	24 ounces, 672 ml	Shucked oysters (about 2¹/₂ dozen medium-sized oysters), drained

PROCEDURE

1 Preheat the oven to 425°F (220°C).

2 Pierce the eggplants several times with a fork and place on a baking sheet.

3 Bake eggplants 30 minutes or until very tender. Test with a skewer to see if the center is done. Remove from oven and cool. Keep oven hot.

4 Sauté the onion in ¹/₄ cup (2 ounces, 56 g) of the butter until glazed, but not brown.

5 In another small skillet, fry the bacon until crisp. Drain on several layers of paper towels.

6 With a sharp knife, cut off the stem ends of the eggplants and peel them carefully. Discard the skin and place the pulp of the eggplants in a colander to drain. Chop into ³/₄-inch (1.9 cm) cubes and combine with the sautéed onion.

7 Crumble the bacon into the mixture, then add ¹/₂ cup (1¹/₄ ounces, 35 g) bread crumbs, the salt, pepper, and oysters.

8 Melt the remaining butter in a small saucepan.

9 Divide the eggplant pulp and oyster mixture into 4 equal portions and place in individual ramekins. Pour melted butter over each portion. Sprinkle each evenly with remaining bread crumbs.

10 Bake for 20 minutes, or until the mixture bubbles vigorously around the edges and the top is well browned.

Creole Jambalaya 4 SERVINGS

chef tip

One of the secrets of a great jambalaya is the way fat rendered from the chicken or sausage coats and seals the rice, helping it keep its texture during the long cooking process while absorbing the flavors that surround it. This cooking process is similar to the technique for making rice pilaf. Some jambalaya recipes call for the rice to be browned before adding the liquid. By using both dried and fresh herbs, intense and diverse flavors are imparted to the jambalaya.

When preparing jambalaya, cook the meats over medium heat, stirring constantly, until they are thoroughly browned. This process takes about 15 minutes. When the meats are browned, remove them from the pan and brown the vegetables in the same manner. Add the seasonings after the vegetables are browned and cook for 5 minutes more to build the flavors on top on one another.

AMOUNT	MEASURE	INGREDIENT
2 tablespoons	1 ounce, 28 g	Vegetable oil
1	3 pounds, 1.36 kg	Chicken fryer, cut into $^1/_8$ths, rinsed, dried
4 cups	16 ounces, 453 g	Onions, $^1/_2$ inch (1.2 cm) dice
$^2/_3$ cup	3 ounces, 85 g	Green bell pepper, $^1/_2$ inch (1.2 cm) dice
$^3/_4$ cup	2 ounces, 56 g	Green onion tops, thinly sliced
1 tablespoon	$^1/_2$ ounce, 15 g	Garlic, minced
2 tablespoons	6 g	Parsley, minced
$^3/_4$ cup	4 ounces, 113 g	Baked ham, $^1/_2$ inch (1.2 cm) dice
$1^1/_2$ cups	8 ounces, 226 g	Lean pork, in $^1/_2$-inch (1.2 cm) cubes
3 cups	16 ounces, 454 g	Smoked sausages, (Polish, French, garlic), $^1/_2$-inch (1.2 cm) slices
2 teaspoons	10 g	Salt
$^1/_2$ teaspoon	1 g	Black pepper
$^1/_4$ teaspoon	1 g	Cayenne
$^1/_2$ teaspoon	1 g	Chili powder
2		Bay leaves, crushed
$^1/_4$ teaspoon	1 g	Thyme (dried)
$^1/_8$ teaspoon	1 g	Ground cloves
$^1/_4$ teaspoon	1 g	Basil (dried)
$^1/_8$ teaspoon	1 g	Mace

| 1 1/2 cups | 9 3/4 ounces, 276 g | Long-grain rice |
| 3 cups | 24 ounces, 705 ml | Chicken stock |

PROCEDURE

1   Heat the oil over medium heat.

2   Brown the chicken, then remove.

3   Add the vegetables, parsley, ham, and pork. Cook over medium heat, stirring constantly, for about 10 minutes or until everything is brown.

4   Add the sausages and seasonings; continue to cook over low heat for 5 minutes, stirring occasionally and scraping pan bottom well.

5   Add the rice and increase the heat to medium; cook 5 minutes or until the rice is lightly browned, stirring and scraping the sides and bottom.

6   Return the chicken to the pot; add the stock. Mix well; bring to a boil.

7   Cover the pot and turn down to a simmer, or place in 350°F (180°C) oven. Cook 35 minutes, stirring occasionally.

8   Uncover the pot and cook 10 minutes. Raise the heat to medium to allow the rice to dry out, stirring very frequently.

9   Remove bay leaves and serve immediately.

Chicken Maquechoux 4 SERVINGS

AMOUNT	MEASURE	INGREDIENT
1/4 cup	2 ounces, 55 ml	Vegetable oil
1	3 pounds, 1.36 kg	Chicken fryer, cut in 1/8ths

For the Maquechoux

AMOUNT	MEASURE	INGREDIENT
5 1/4 cups	34 ounces, 978 g	Corn kernels, fresh, milk reserved
1/4 cup	2 ounces, 56 g	Unsalted butter
1 cup	4 ounces, 113 g	Onion, 1/2 inch (1.2 cm) dice
1/2 cup	2 1/2 ounces, 70 g	Green bell pepper, 1/2 inch (1.2 cm) dice
1/2 cup	2 1/2 ounces, 70 g	Red bell pepper, 1/2 inch (1.2 cm) dice
1/2 cup	2 ounces, 56 g	Celery, 1/2 inch (1.2 cm) dice
1 1/4 cups	8 ounces, 226 g	Tomatoes, peeled, seeded, 1/2 inch (1.2 cm) dice
1 teaspoon	5 g	Salt
1/2 teaspoon	1 g	Cayenne
1 teaspoon	2 g	Black pepper
2 tablespoons	1 ounce, 30 g	Granulated sugar
1/2 cup	4 ounces, 115 ml	Heavy cream
2 to 3 tablespoons	1 ounce, 28 ml	Milk

PROCEDURE

1 Heat the oil over medium heat.

2 Brown the chicken parts, turning frequently to brown evenly. Remove and drain fat from the pan.

3 Shuck the corn and remove all of the corn silk.

4 Hold each cob over a bowl and cut the kernels away in layers (don't cut whole kernels).

5 Scrape the knife along the cob to get all of the "milk" out of it.

6 Melt the butter over medium-high heat in the same pan used for the chicken.

7 Add the onion, bell peppers, celery, and tomatoes and sauté until the onion is transparent, about 10 minutes.

8 Stir in the salt and peppers.

9 Add the corn kernels and milk from the cobs, the sugar, and cream and stir well.

Reduce the heat to medium and cook until the corn is tender, 10 to 15 more minutes. Adjust seasonings.

10 Drain excess oil from chicken and return to corn mixture.

11 Reduce the heat to low. Cook until chicken is very tender, 30 minutes, stirring frequently. If mixture seems to be drying, add 2 to 3 tablespoons (1–1^1/$_2$ ounces, 30–45 ml) milk toward the end of the cooking period.

12 Serve hot in bowl.

Braised Leeks with Hollandaise 4 SERVINGS

AMOUNT	MEASURE	INGREDIENT
4		Leeks
1 cup	8 ounces, 235 ml	Beef stock
1 teaspoon	5 g	Salt
3 tablespoons	1^1/$_2$ ounces, 42 g	Butter
^{1}/$_4$ teaspoon	1 g	White pepper
^{1}/$_4$ teaspoon	1 g	Chervil (dried)
^{1}/$_4$ teaspoon	1 g	Basil (dried)

PROCEDURE

1 Cut off the top half of the leeks and discard the green leaves. Trim the stem ends and pull off the tough outer leaves. Cut the leeks into quarters lengthwise and wash thoroughly; drain.

2 Place leeks in parallel rows in proper cooking pan.

3 Combine stock and remaining ingredients. Bring to a boil and pour over leeks.

4 Cover loosely and simmer covered for 15 minutes or until leeks are tender.

5 Drain the leeks, and serve with Hollandaise Sauce (page 538).

Paneed Chicken with Fettuccine 4 SERVINGS

chef tip

This recipe has been adapted from the **Chef Paul Prudhomme's** *Louisian Kitchen* cookbook. *Paneed* is New Orleans terminology for pan-frying. **For the best pan-fried crust on meat or fish, the oil for frying should be just deep enough to come up the sides of the food but not to cover the top. This way the food is in contact with the pan bottom, which creates different levels of texture in the crust. It is essential that you do not overcrowd the pan.**

AMOUNT	MEASURE	INGREDIENT
For the Seasoning Mix		
¹/₄ cup	2 ounces, 56 g	Ketchup
3 tablespoons	1¹/₂ ounces, 42 g	Creole mustard
1 tablespoon	5 g	White pepper
1 teaspoon	2 g	Cayenne
2 teaspoons	3 g	Garlic powder
1 teaspoon	2 g	Paprika
¹/₂ teaspoon	2 g	Thyme (dried)
¹/₄ teaspoon	1 g	Sage (dried)
¹/₃ teaspoon	1 g	Basil (dried)
4		Eggs
4	5 ounces, 42 g, each	Chicken breasts, boned, skinned, flattened evenly
¹/₃ cup	1 ounce, 79 ml	Parmesan cheese, finely grated
For the Fettuccine		
2 cups	16 ounces, 470 ml	Heavy cream
¹/₂ teaspoon	1 g	Cayenne
¹/₂ cup	2¹/₄ ounces, 64 g	Parmesan cheese, finely grated
8 ounces	226 g	Fettuccine, fresh
2 cups	6 ounces, 168 g	Bread crumbs, fine, dry
as needed		Vegetable oil, for pan-frying

PROCEDURE

1   Combine the ingredients for the seasoning mix in a small bowl and mix well.

2   Combine the eggs and Parmesan cheese; beat well.

3   Spread an even layer of the seasoning mix over both sides of the chicken, then soak the chicken for 15 to 30 minutes in the egg mixture.

4   While chicken soaks, line a sheet pan with paper towels.

5   Combine the cream and cayenne, bring to a boil, lower the heat, and reduce cream by half, or until it coats the back of a spoon (nappé).

6   Remove cream from heat and gradually add the Parmesan, whipping until the cheese is melted; set aside.

7   Cook the fettuccine in boiling water until al dente. Drain and cool; set aside.

8   In a large skillet, heat about $1/4$ inch (.6 cm) of oil to at least 350°F (175°C).

9   Drain the excess egg mixture from the chicken, then dredge chicken pieces in the bread crumbs; press to obtain an even coating of crumbs, then shake off the excess.

10 Pan-fry in hot oil until golden brown; drain well on paper towels.

11 Reheat cream sauce, adding additional cream if necessary to achieve correct consistency.

12 Add the fettuccine and toss until thoroughly coated and hot.

13 Serve 1 portion of fettuccine with 1 serving of chicken.

Fresh Fettuccine 4 SERVINGS

AMOUNT	MEASURE	INGREDIENT
1¹/₄ cups	6 ounces, 170 g	All-purpose flour
¹/₂ cup	2 ounces, 56 g	Semolina flour
1		Egg
1 tablespoon	¹/₂ ounce, 14 ml	Vegetable oil
to taste		Salt
4 tablespoons	2 ounces, 56 g	Butter

PROCEDURE

1 Place the flours in a mixing bowl with a dough hook.

2 Combine the egg, oil, and salt. Beat together.

3 Add the egg mixture to the dry ingredients while mixing on low, until well incorporated.

4 Wrap the dough and refrigerate for 30 minutes.

5 Roll the dough through the pasta machine several times. Start at a thick setting and work down to the thinnest setting. Dust with flour as needed.

6 Cut the dough into ¹/₄-inch (.6 cm)-wide noodles and let them dry.

7 Cook the noodles in a large quantity of salted water until al dente; drain.

Fried Stuffed Crawfish Heads 4 SERVINGS

chef tip

Stuffed crawfish heads are crawfish shells filled with sautéed chopped crawfish meat, vegetables, and bread. Don't try to eat the shells—even good frying won't make them edible.

AMOUNT	MEASURE	INGREDIENT
For the Stuffing		
3 tablespoons	1 1/2 ounces, 42 g	Butter
1 cup	4 ounces, 113 g	Onion, 1/4 inch (.6 cm) dice
1/2 cup	2 1/2 ounces, 70 g	Green bell pepper, 1/4 inch (.6 cm) dice
1/4 cup	1 ounce, 28 g	Celery, 1/4 inch (.6 cm) dice
1/3 cup	1 1/2 ounces, 42 g	Green onions, 1/4 inch (.6 cm) dice
2 tablespoons	6 g	Parsley, finely minced
3/4 teaspoon	4 g	Salt
1/4 teaspoon	1 g	Black pepper
1/8 teaspoon	1 g	Cayenne
1/8 teaspoon	1 g	Thyme (dried)
1/8 teaspoon	1 g	Ground allspice
12 ounces	340 g	Crawfish meat, chopped
1/2 cup	1 ounce, 28 g	Bread crumbs, fresh, white, crusts trimmed off
For the Crawfish		
2		Eggs
2 tablespoons	1 ounce, 28 ml	Water
1 cup	4.4 ounces, 124 g	All-purpose flour
1 teaspoon	5 g	Salt
1/2 teaspoon	1 g	Black pepper
24		Crawfish shells, cleaned
as needed		Vegetable oil, for deep-frying

PROCEDURE

Melt butter over low heat. Add the vegetables and parsley. Sauté until soft and just beginning to brown.

2   Add the seasoning and blend. Add the chopped crawfish meat. Then add the soaked bread and toss to combine. Cook over very low heat, stirring constantly, for 8 to 10 minutes.

3   Remove from the heat. Set aside.

4   Combine the eggs and water; beat together.

5   Combine the flour and seasonings.

6   Fill crawfish shells with stuffing.

7   Dip the stuffed heads in beaten egg and dampen all over.

8   Roll in the seasoned flour to coat evenly. Let dry.

9   Heat oil to 375°F (190°C).

10   Fry stuffed heads until deep golden brown. Drain on paper towels.

11   Serve hot.

Muffuletta 4 SERVINGS

AMOUNT	MEASURE	INGREDIENT
For the Olive Salad		
1/2 cup	2 ounces, 56 g	Large pimento-stuffed green olives, slightly crushed, well drained
1/4 cup	I ounce, 28 g	Pickled cauliflower, drained, sliced
1/2 teaspoon	2 g	Capers, drained
1/4 cup	I ounce, 28 g	Celery, thinly sliced diagonally
2 tablespoons	1/2 ounce, 28 g	Carrot, peeled, thinly sliced diagonally
pinch		Celery seeds
pinch		Oregano (dried)
I		Garlic clove, minced
to taste		Black pepper
1/4 cup	I ounce, 28 g	Pepperoncini, drained, left whole
1/4 cup	I ounce, 28 g	Greek black olives, chopped
1/4 cup	I ounce, 28 g	Cocktail onions, drained, chopped
For the sandwich		
I		Round loaf Italian bread (6 inch)
2 ounces	56 g	Mortadella, thinly sliced
2 ounces	56 g	Ham, thinly sliced
2 ounces	56 g	Hard Genoa salami, thinly sliced
2 ounces	56 g	Mozzarella cheese, sliced
2 ounces	56 g	Provolone cheese, sliced
as needed		Olive oil

PROCEDURE

1 Combine all ingredients for salad and cover with oil. Refrigerate at least 24 hours.

2 Split bread horizontally.

3 Spread each half with equal parts olive salad and oil from salad.

4 Place meats and cheeses evenly on bottom half and cover with top half of bread.

5 Cut into quarters.

Shrimp-Stuffed Mirliton　4 SERVINGS

chef tip One of New Orleans's favorite vegetables, mirliton, also called "vegetable pear" or "chayote squash," grows wild in Louisiana. Mirlitons have a very mild flavor.

AMOUNT	MEASURE	INGREDIENT
4		Small mirlitons, sliced lengthwise
¹/₂ cup	4 ounces, 113 g	Bacon, lean, ¹/₂ inch (1.2 cm) dice
1¹/₂ cups	6 ounces, 170 g	Onions, ¹/₂ inch (1.2 cm) dice
¹/₂ cup	2¹/₂ ounces, 71 g	Green bell pepper, ¹/₂ inch (1.2 cm) dice
¹/₄ cup	1 ounce, 28 g	Celery, ¹/₂ inch (1.2 cm) dice
1 tablespoon	¹/₂ ounce, 15 g	Garlic, minced
2 cups	12 ounces, 340 g	Tomatoes, peeled, seeded, medium dice
¹/₄ cup	1 ounce, 28 g	Green onions, chopped
1¹/₂ teaspoons	7 g	Salt
¹/₂ teaspoon	1 g	Black pepper
³/₄ teaspoon	1 g	Thyme (dried)
2		Bay leaves, crushed
3 tablespoons	9 g	Parsley, minced
¹/₈ teaspoon	1 g	Cayenne
2 cups	16 ounces, 453 g	Shrimp, peeled, deveined, in ¹/₂-inch (1.2 cm) pieces
¹/₂ cup	¹/₂ ounce, 15 g	Bread crumbs, white, fresh, crusts removed

PROCEDURE

1 Boil the mirlitons in lightly salted water until pulp is tender enough to scoop from shells.

2 Drain and cool under tap water to room temperature.

3 Scoop out pulp but leave shells intact about ¹/₃ inch (.8 cm) thick.

4 Chop pulp and set aside.

5 Sauté the bacon until almost crisp.

6 Preheat the oven to 375°F (190°C).

7 Add the onions, green pepper, celery, garlic, tomatoes, green onions, and mirliton pulp. Cook for 8 minutes, or until vegetables just begin to turn soft.

8   Add the salt, pepper, thyme, bay leaves, parsley, and cayenne. Blend well.

9   Add the shrimp and cook until just pink.

10 Add the bread crumbs and blend well.

11 Fill the reserved mirliton shells with the shrimp mixture to a raised, rounded shape.

12 Bake stuffed mirlitons for 20 to 30 minutes, or until the tops are nicely browned.

Sautéed Chicken Livers Orleans   4 SERVINGS

AMOUNT	MEASURE	INGREDIENT
$^1/_4$ cup	2 ounces, 56 g	Butter
I tablespoon	$^1/_2$ ounce, 15 g	Onion, $^1/_4$ inch (.6 cm) dice
I tablespoon	$^1/_2$ ounce, 15 g	Celery, $^1/_4$ inch (.6 cm) dice
2 tablespoons	I ounce, 30 g	Green onion, $^1/_4$ inch (.6 cm) dice
I $^1/_2$ tablespoons	$^3/_4$ ounce, 21 g	Garlic, minced
36 (2 cups)	16 ounces, 454 g	Chicken livers
I teaspoon	I g	Thyme leaves
I teaspoon	I g	Basil, chopped
$^1/_4$ cup	2 ounces, 55 ml	Brandy
I cup	8 ounces, 235 ml	Demi-glace, veal
to taste		Salt and pepper
2 tablespoons	6 g	Parsley, finely chopped

PROCEDURE

1   Heat a sauté pan over medium heat; melt butter.

2   Add the onion, celery, and green onion; cook for 3 minutes or until onions are transparent.

3   Add the garlic, cook 1 minute.

4   Add the chicken livers; brown on all sides.

5   Add the thyme and basil. Add the brandy and cook 1 minute.

6   Add the demi-glace; bring to a boil.

7   Remove from the heat and correct seasoning with salt and pepper.

8   Add the parsley. Serve warm with toast points or pasta.

The Cuisine of the Central Plains

Known as the land of milk and grain, the **Central Plains** are the breadbasket and main source of food crops for the United States. The region includes the corn belt and the wheat belt, and has a long history during which cattle "kingdoms" reigned. Expertise in dairy farming has resulted in innovative and extensive cheese making. Meats, game, and poultry are staples of the **Central Plains**, and the lakes, streams, and rivers of the region supply many varieties of freshwater fish. The cultural diversity of the residents of the **Central Plains** has added a wealth of culinary knowledge and variety to what we know today as American regional cuisine.

Illinois Known as "The Prairie State," Illinois's rich black soil makes it one of the leading agriculture states in the nation. Farms take up more than 80 percent of the state's total land mass. Corn is Illinois's chief crop, though the state also produces large amounts of soybeans, oats, wheat, and livestock.

Indiana "The Hoosier State," also known as the "Crossroads of America." Corn and soybeans are grown in every county.

Iowa "The Hawkeye State" raises one-fifth of the nation's corn and one-quarter of its pork.

Kansas "The Sunflower State" is the nation's leader in wheat production. Beef is the state's most valuable farm product.

Michigan "The Wolverine State," Michigan is so named because early fur traders were often looking for wolverine fur. Heavily forested, the state is prime land for foraging for the highly prized morel mushrooms in spring.

Minnesota "The Gopher State," where wheat remains a main crop, is a leader in the production of corn, wild rice, dairy goods, and livestock.

Missouri "The Show Me State," where farm products from throughout the Great Plains were processed in Missouri for shipment east, and the stockyards of Kansas City were famous for many years.

Nebraska "The Cornhusker State," where ranching is the most important agricultural industry. Corn is the biggest crop. Nebraska produces about 10 percent of the country's corn.

North Dakota "The Flickertail State." Wheat is the most important crop, and much of North Dakota's wheat goes to making pasta. More waterfowl, like ducks and geese, breed in North Dakota than in any other state.

Ohio "The Buckeye State" where the rich soil makes Ohio part of the fertile farmland of the corn belt.

South Dakota "The Mount Rushmore State" produces some of the nation's leading amounts of rye, wheat, and corn. Ranches raise beef cattle and sheep.

Wisconsin "The Badger State," also known as the "Dairy State," is world famous for its cheese. With over 1 million milk cows, Wisconsin produces more cheese and milk than any other state.

History

The first Europeans to travel through the Central Plains were the French fur traders, known as "mountain men," in the 1600s. Although they were not settlers, they did establish outposts in the region. These outposts were significant because only there could the mountain men obtain food and supplies. Typically, the foods available in the outposts were those from the local area. Relatively few changes occurred in the Central Plains over the next century and a half.

In 1803, President Thomas Jefferson purchased the Louisiana Territory from France for $15 million. This event, known as the Louisiana Purchase, included 800,000 square miles of territory west of the Mississippi River to the Rocky Mountains and north to Canada. The United States had little geographic knowledge of the West at the time of the purchase, so President Jefferson selected Meriwether Lewis and William Clark to explore the northern reaches of the new purchase and then to proceed to the Pacific Ocean. Lewis and Clark traveled up the Missouri River from St. Louis, crossed the Rocky Mountains, and descended the Columbia River on the West Coast. They gathered a vast amount of geographic and scientific information and established diplomatic and trade relations with some Native American tribes. They were later followed by Zebulon Pike and Stephen Long, both of whom explored the central Great Plains area. At that time, the dry, flat, prairie land of the Central Plains offered little to farmers who were used to working on land with plentiful rainfall and having available trees to build houses.

In 1849, gold was discovered in California, and the Oregon and Santa Fe trails opened, signaling the start of the land rush. A few European immigrants and people from other parts of America began to settle in the Great Plains to farm, ranch, build towns, and work on the railroads.

The Homestead Act of 1862 encouraged agricultural expansion. The act offered 160 acres virtually free to any citizen willing to develop the land. Lawmakers hoped that the Homestead Act would lead to agricultural development in the western states. Farming families settled on the millions of acres traveled over by those who had migrated to more inviting places on the Pacific Coast. These hardy families farmed the plains with new techniques and equipment developed after the Civil War. The federal government, in an effort to contribute to the development of these new farming methods, conducted research in the newly created Department of Agriculture and endowed agricultural colleges. These universities are today many of the Big Ten schools, including Ohio State, Michigan State, and Iowa State. To produce crops in an area that had little rainfall, farmers on the Great Plains used new methods of dry farming and irrigated land close to streams. And while the prairies were covered with wild grasses and wildflowers, it was difficult to farm. These grasses had roots deep in the soil, and plows had a hard time cutting through the tangled roots; farmers struggled just to prepare a few acres of land for planting. In 1838, John Deere, a blacksmith living in Illinois, invented a new steel plow that made it easier to turn the soil. These farmers benefited greatly from the industrial revolution, and inventions and innovations in farm machinery have allowed them to continue to cultivate the land and grow more crops.

Immigration and Migration

THE SCANDINAVIAN INFLUENCE

Between 1820 and 1914, over 2 million Scandinavians immigrated to America. Norwegians were the first to arrive, and they began to work along the East Coast as loggers, fishermen, and farmers. Soon, many moved inland, where they found the weather and lands of the Midwest and Central Plains similar to Norway. Around 1840, the Norwegians settled in the area of the upper Mississippi Valley—specifically, the region that today makes up much of Minnesota and Wisconsin. Following the Norwegians were many immigrants from Sweden and Denmark, who also settled in the Central Plains. As this westward migration took place, the Mississippi River quickly became a dividing line between the "civilized" East and the "untamed" West. The Central Plains, with the Mississippi River running through the middle, lured new residents with hopes of agricultural wealth and great prosperity.

These immigrants from northern Europe who settled throughout the Central Plains first learned how to harvest corn and wild rice from the Native Americans. Native Americans taught them techniques for hunting the abundant wild game of the region, including pheasant, quail, grouse, wild turkey, deer, and buffalo. The settlers also learned how to fish in the many rivers and lakes, which contain walleye, yellow perch, trout, and pike, and are home to many varieties of duck, geese, and other waterfowl. Most important, the vast lands were well suited for farming and for grazing livestock. Rustic stews, breads, and the root vegetables that were the traditional foods of Scandinavians became dietary staples. The Scandinavians brought to the area many other food traditions from the Old Country, such as cheese and sausage making, and smoking fish and meat.

THE EASTERN EUROPEAN INFLUENCE

As western migration continued, people from Eastern Europe began to settle in the Central Plains, which also reminded them of their homelands. Germans, Poles, and Austrians settled in Illinois and Iowa as well as Minnesota and Wisconsin. They farmed the land and raised dairy cattle as their primary source of income. Wisconsin became a popular destination of German and Swedish immigrants. Cheese production began in Wisconsin in the 1830s, and Cheddar cheese was made in the English tradition while other cheeses from the Old Country, such as brie, ricotta, Limburger, mozzarella, feta, and gouda, were made as well. Two of the three cheeses invented in America—brick and Colby—were first produced in the 1870s. Today, there are over 200 cheese-making plants in Wisconsin alone. Wisconsin is also the number-one dairy state in the country, producing milk, butter, and excellent domestic cheese.

Germans and Bohemians who emigrated to the region brought the art of brewing and their love of beer. The extensive prairies and farmlands of the Central Plains were perfect for growing wheat, oats, barley, rye, and corn, which are the grains used to produce beer. The region's major trade areas of St. Louis, Milwaukee, Chicago, Cincinnati, St. Paul, and Kansas City became homes to America's first breweries. By the end of the 19th century, thousands of breweries had sprung up and began to produce unique beers. The great beer industry went into decline during Prohibition, which began in 1920; by 1933, when Prohibition ended, only 400 of the original breweries were able to reopen for business. Although many of the original brewers no longer operate in Milwaukee, residents still enjoy the traditions and culture that beer brewing left behind.

German immigrants also brought their expertise in sausage making. Not only were they experts in sausage production, they were inventive as well. The German farmers of the Central Plains regions originated sausage varieties such as knackwurst, bratwurst, liverwurst, Mettwurst, and Thuringer, which are still popular products today. They also built smokehouses to smoke hams, bacon, and fish from the region's lakes and rivers.

THE EFFECT OF THE RAILROADS

The growth of railroads encouraged westward expansion more than any other single development. By the mid-1800s, railroads had connected the East with the West, and the Central Plains became a major hub. Railroads were also responsible for the growth of ranching. After the Civil War there was growing demand for beef in the eastern and northern cities. Railroads provided the means of linking supply with demand. Cattle were herded northward out of Texas along the Chisholm and Great Western trails to towns on the Great Plains. There they were loaded into specially built rail cars and carried to slaughterhouses in Kansas City, Chicago, and other urban centers.

By the late 1800s, cattle drives were no longer necessary. As Native American tribes were defeated, cattle ranching spread into the Great Plains states of Kansas, Nebraska,

Corn and Wheat

Corn is the foundation on which ancient civilizations, such as the Maya and the Aztec, were built. Throughout the 19th century, the size of the corn crop increased as the settlers moved into the western territories. In the mid-1800s, a new hybrid, called "Reid's Yellow Dent," began to be widely cultivated in the Midwest. By 1882, people were referring to the corn-producing states of the Midwest as the "Corn Belt." Over 85 percent of all corn grown is called "dent corn," or "field corn," and is used primarily to feed animals and live-stock, making it an important American commodity. From 1877 through 1920, American horticulturists developed many new hybrids that became standard on the country's farms. In 1950, Dr. J. R. Laughnam of the University of Illinois discovered some very sweet strains of corn. In the 1960s, Dr. A. M. Rhodes, also at the University of Illinois, developed an even sweeter corn. Mature sweet corn is eaten fresh, boiled and buttered. It is found frozen and canned. Corn is also used to make products such as ethanol, corn syrup, and corn oil.

Wheat is a grain that was brought to America by the European colonists. It is a grass whose seed belongs to the cereal grains group, and it contains gluten, the basic structure for forming doughs for breads, rolls, and other baked goods. Due to difficulties in cultivation, wheat was not a major crop until the end of the 19th century, when Turkey Red Winter Wheat began to grow well in the Central Plains. The growth and development of wheat crops in the Central Plains are attributed to Mennonite farmers, originally from the

and North and South Dakota. New breeds of cattle that could withstand the harsh conditions could now be fattened on plains grasses and shipped east with relative ease. Ranching became a big business and many of the largest ranches were owned by corporations funded by millions of dollars in stock sold in the East, Britain, and Europe.

One of the original forces behind westward expansion—farmers looking for better land—was also important in the development of the plains states. The railroads provided a way to transport harvested crops to markets. Men like Adolphus Swift and George A. Hormel developed methods of keeping food refrigerated in railcars so that quality and sanitary conditions could be maintained during the long trip.

Ukraine, who, with land provided by the Santa Fe Railroad in 1875, began farming along the rail lines in Kansas. Six classes of wheat are grown in the United States, and Kansas produces three of them:

HARD RED WINTER (98 PERCENT) High in protein, with strong gluten. Used for yeast breads and rolls.

SOFT RED WINTER (1 PERCENT) Used for flat breads, cakes, pastries, and crackers.

HARD WHITE (1 PERCENT) Used for yeast breads, hard rolls, tortillas, and noodles.

The three main parts of the wheat kernel are the endosperm, bran, and germ:

ENDOSPERM Constituting about 83 percent of the total kernel mass, this is the source of white flour. Enriched flour products contained added quantities of riboflavin, niacin, thiamin, and iron.

BRAN About 14 percent of the kernel, this part is included in whole wheat flour. Bran is the outer coat and is an excellent source of fiber.

GERM About 2.5 percent of the kernel, this is the embryo or sprouting section of the seed. It is usually separated because it contains the fat that limits the keeping quality of flours.

CHICAGO, A CITY OF DIVERSITY

Chicago's stockyards emerged in the late 1800s. With them came a huge migration of newly freed slaves from the South, as well as Irish, Italian, and Polish immigrants seeking new opportunities in the fastest growing city of the Central Plains. Small ethnic communities sprang up, providing a great deal of ethnic and cultural diversity. Even though the stockyards are no longer there, ethnic neighborhoods still exist in Chicago. Hispanic, Swedish, Asian, Jewish, Pakistani, Indian, and Arab cultures, to name a few, are vital communities making up Chicago's rich cultural diversity. Small enclaves of Russians, African Americans, Italians, Greeks, and Poles contribute to the cuisine found in Chicago today and have allowed Chicago to grow into one of America's great food cities.

Some of the greatest chefs in the world are in Chicago, including Charlie Trotter, Rick Bayless, and Michael Foley. These famous chefs and their restaurants have helped support today's market farmers, who grow and sell crops only for urban markets and restaurants featuring high-quality ingredients. The farmers follow the principle of "farm to table," indicating that their products are usually less than a day off the vine or out of the ground when sold. These people are committed to respecting the region's culture and demand to keep its food sources strong and healthy.

Typical Central Plains Ingredients and Dishes

Bigos A rich and heartily flavored Polish hunter's stew made from fresh pork, bacon, kielbasa sausage, mushrooms, and sauerkraut. The traditional recipe requires three days for preparation.

Black Walnut the Black walnut is about the same size as the English walnut, but with an oily nutmeat that has an earthy, pungent taste. Grown in Missouri, black walnuts are used more as a cooking ingredient than as a snack nut. These nuts are becoming hard to find and very expensive, owing to the harvesting of the trees for hardwood.

Cheese

Brick Cheese One of the three cheeses invented in America this smooth, cow's milk cheese was created in 1877 by John Jossi of Wisconsin. It is formed into bricks that weigh about 5 pounds each, have small holes, and are aged about three months.

Cheddar Cheese The most popular cheese in America. Wisconsin devotes about half its annual cheese production to the Cheddar variety. Cheddar comes in two colors and many flavors. (Americans west of the Mississippi River seem to prefer their Cheddar an orange color, made by adding annato seed extract to the milk during production, while Americans east of the Mississippi prefer cheddar white, or uncolored. The flavors are identical. Flavor variations of Cheddar cheese are based on how long the cheese is aged. Mild Cheddar is aged fewer than four months; aging between four and ten months creates a medium sharp flavor; and more than ten months results in a sharp flavor. The color of the wax found on the Cheddar indicates its age—clear wax for mild cheddar, red wax for medium-sharp, and black wax for sharp.)

Colby Cheese A granular cheese made by the Steinwand family in the town of Colby, Wisconsin. This is also one of the three cheeses invented in America. (Monterey Jack cheese, discussed in the chapter on California Cuisine, is the third cheese invented in America.) The FDA standards require that it contain not less than 50 percent milk fat.

Maytag Blue Cheese A blue-veined, tangy, smooth-textured cheese first made by the Maytag family in cooperation with Iowa State University. Containing the milk from Holstein cows, this cheese is aged for six months—nearly twice the time for traditional blue cheese. This is the first artisan cheese in America.

Processed Cheese The most commonly consumed cheese product in America, it is made by melting various kinds of cheeses with emulsifiers, acids, and flavorings. The cheese is then colored and shaped in a mold that resembles a block of cheese. The most common processed cheese is called American cheese and was invented by James L. Kraft in the early 1900s. It is available sliced prior to packaging and as individually wrapped slices.

Fish

Muskellunge Also referred to as "muskie," this is the largest of the pike fish and the state fish of Wisconsin. Known to grow as large as 70 pounds, it has very sharp teeth and is a vicious fighter, making it a favorite among anglers.

Pike There are six species, many of which are found in rivers and lakes. The largest of the pike is the muskie, and the most common is the great northern pike, usually weighing between 4 and 10 pounds.

Smelt First introduced into the Great Lakes in 1906, the freshwater smelt resembles a very small salmon and is a member of the salmon family. About 7 to 8 inches long, smelt have a fatty, rich mild flavor. They are typically either deep-fried or pan-fried.

Walleye Also known as "walleye pike," it is actually a perch. This mild-tasting fish with a delicate flesh is also called "yellow pike" or "blue pike."

Whitefish Considered to be one of the best freshwater fishes in the United States; the meat is fatty, snow white, and flaky. It is a member of the salmon and trout family and is found in the frigid waters of the Great Lakes. Though often poached for a cold presentation, it is also found smoked. The roe of the female is considered as desirable as shad roe.

Yellow Perch A river and lake fish known for its especially sweet-tasting flesh; not readily available owing to a recent ban imposed to protect the species from extinction.

Fish Boil A social event at which various kinds of fish are boiled in a huge kettle of water over an outdoor fire. Various whitefish, potatoes, and onions are added to water that has been heavily salted. Just before serving, kerosene is thrown onto the fire, allowing the kettle to boil over and remove the impurities from the broth. Door County, Wisconsin, is famous for this annual Scandinavian feast.

Game Birds Quail, pheasant, partridge, and turkey are found throughout the Central Plains.

Holupka A Russian term for stuffed cabbage rolls.

Honey A major product of the Central Plains, primarily North and South Dakota, which process over 60 million pounds of honey each year. The most popular types of honey are clover and blossom, which are light in color and mildly sweet in flavor. Wildflower honey is much darker than and not as sweet as clover honey. Wildflower honey is excellent for cooking, as it provides dishes a distinct flavor without adding extra sweetness.

Jerusalem Artichoke This bulb of the perennial sunflower plant is also referred to as a "sunchoke." It is usually chopped up raw and used in salad, or may be boiled or steamed.

Juniper Berries Common among German and Scandinavia settlers, these are used as a seasoning in sauerkraut or in marinades for game and pork. It is also the flavoring in gin.

Kielbasa A Polish type of cured sausage with garlic flavoring, usually cooked by boiling or grilling.

Lefse A flat bread of Norwegian origin made by the farm women of western Minnesota. The dough, made from potatoes, is rolled extremely thin with a special rolling pin called a "lefse roller." The bread is cooked on a griddle and served with butter and cinnamon sugar.

Lutefisk A Scandinavian style of prepared fresh cod. To prepare lutefisk, cod fillets are soaked in a lye solution made with the ashes of birch wood. The cod is then air-dried. This method of preserving fish may be primitive, but fish preserved in this manner can remain unspoiled for years in regions with cold climates. To serve, it is softened by simmering in salted water for about ten minutes, and served with a white sauce and potatoes on the side.

Morel A tan to black mushroom with a cone-shaped, umbrella-capped stem that grows primarily in the deep wooded forests of Michigan. Morels are found growing beneath oak, elm, and ash trees. Their growing patterns are inconsistent and unpredictable, making them scarce as well as expensive. The fresh morel season lasts just a few short weeks from April to May.

Oblaten The first course of the traditional meatless Polish meal served on Christmas Eve. Also referred to as the "holy wafer," this thin bread is elaborately stamped prior to baking.

Paczki A filled doughnut of Polish heritage, usually served during Lent. Laczki are traditionally filled with raspberry preserves but may also be made with a variety of fruit fillings.

Persimmon Also known as a "date plum," this Native American fruit grows in southern Indiana, Illinois, and Missouri. About the size of a golf ball, the persimmon has a vibrant orange color with a deep green crown. If not fully ripe, it has an astringent flavor. Most often used for persimmon pudding; it is also used for jams, jellies, and preserves.

Pirogi A filled dumpling of Eastern European heritage. The flour dough of traditional pirogi may be filled with ground, seasoned pork, sauerkraut, and farmer or cottage cheese, or may be filled with sweet fruit, such as cherries or apples. Pirogis are typically fried in bacon fat or oil.

Popcorn From the variety called "flint corn," popcorn is harvested after it has matured and dried on the stalk. The small hard kernels contain only a small amount of soft starch and a moisture content of about 13.5 percent. The outside, elastic layer resists the buildup of steam until the temperature reaches abound 400°F. The kernel expands and the endosperm violently ruptures. Orville Redenbacher became the world's largest grower of hybrid popcorn after buying an agricultural business in 1952. In 1965, after years of cross-breeding, he finally developed a yellow corn that popped twice as big as others and left very few unpopped kernels.

Rullepolse A type of cured, spiced, and pressed beef flank made by the Danish descendants of Elk Horn, Iowa.

Sausage The Central Plains are considered the home of sausage in the United States. Illinois produces and butchers the most hogs, and the Danish, Bavarian, and Scandinavian immigrants have had significant influence on the style of sausage making. Other German and Polish sausages include Sheboygan bratwurst, Usingers Thuringer sausage, Polish sausage, knackwurst, beerwurst, and liverwurst.

Sorghum A canelike grass plant, originally from Africa, that grows well in the Central Plains. A sweet, dark syrup is extracted from the plant and is used in a fashion similar to molasses or honey. The use of sorghum as a sweetener dates back to the days of the pioneers.

Sunflower A perennial plant that dates as far back as 3000 B.C. It was a major crop in the Central Plains for Native Americans as well as for the European settlers in the region.

Sunflower seeds grown for oil are solid black in color. Sunflower seeds grown for eating are striped. A perennial sunflower variety also produces a bulb that is used as a vegetable, known as Jerusalem artichoke.

Tart Cherry Grown primarily on the shores of northern Michigan from the variety known as "Montmorency cherry." These cherries are light and clear and sometimes called "transparent cherries" or "pie cherries." Very tart and sour, they are sweetened with sugar to make excellent pies, cobblers, and preserves.

Waterfowl A large number of ducks and geese migrate south for the winter from Canada. Hunting is popular and these birds continue to be a large part of the diet for the residents of the Central Plains.

Wild Rice Not a true rice, but the grain of a tall aquatic grass grown predominately in Minnesota and Wisconsin. This is the only cereal grain indigenous to North America.

Menus and Recipes from the Cuisine of the Central Plains

MENU ONE

Wisconsin Cheddar and Beer Soup

Beet and Apple Salad with Horseradish Vinaigrette

Planked Whitefish with Green Onion Butter

Mashed Celeriac and Potatoes

Pickled Pearl Onions

Sautéed Green Beans and Cherry Tomatoes

Brownie Pudding Cake

MENU TWO

Barley Beef Soup

Kansas City Barbecued Ribs

Steak Fries

Cannellini Beans with Tomatoes and Basil

Roast Chicken with Wild Rice, Walnuts, and Dried Fruit Stuffing

Winter Vegetables with Thyme and Broccoli Florets

MENU THREE

Corn and Wild Rice Cakes and Morel Mushrooms with Spinach

Garden Lettuce, Watercress, and Escarole with Goat Cheese and Sun-Dried Tomatoes

Pork Medallions with Blueberry Sauce

Brussels Spouts with Mushrooms

Macaroni and Cheese

Sour Cream Coffee Cake

OTHER RECIPES

Bratwurst (Farmer Style) with German Potato Salad

Chicago Deep-Dish Pizza

Pioneer Buffalo Stew

Pan-Seared Steak with Maytag Blue Cheese Butter

Sunchoke Gratin

Wisconsin Cheese and Beer Soup 4 SERVINGS

chef tip

When adding cheese to hot liquid, make sure the liquid is between 140°F (60°C) and 185°F (85°C). If the temperature of the liquid is too hot, the cheese will not melt, but curdle. Wisconsin cheese and beer soup is traditionally served with a warm soft pretzel.

AMOUNT	MEASURE	INGREDIENT
1/2 cup	4 ounces, 113 g	Unsalted butter
1/2 cup	2 ounces, 56 g	Onion, 1/4 inch (.6 cm) dice
1/4 cup	1 ounce, 28 g	Celery, 1/4 inch (.6 cm) dice
1/4 cup	1 ounce, 28 g	Red bell pepper, 1/4 inch (.6 cm) dice
1/2 cup	2 ounces, 56 g	All-purpose flour
1 teaspoon	2 g	Dry mustard
1/8 teaspoon	1 g	Paprika
1/2 teaspoon	1 g	Ground thyme
2 tablespoons	1 ounce, 28 ml	Worcestershire sauce
1 1/2 cups	12 ounces, 352 ml	Beer
2 cups	16 ounces, 470 ml	Chicken stock
2 cups	16 ounces, 470 ml	Milk
1 1/3 cups	8 ounces, 226 g	Kielbasa sausage, 1/4 inch (.6 cm) dice
to taste		Salt and white pepper
2 cups	8 ounces, 226 g	Wisconsin sharp Cheddar cheese, grated
1/2 cup	1 ounce, 28 g	Green onions, thinly sliced

PROCEDURE

1   Heat the butter over medium heat; add the onion, celery, and red bell pepper, and cook 4 minutes or until the onion is translucent.

2   Add the flour; whisk in to make a roux. Add the seasonings and cook 3 minutes.

3   Add the beer and stock; stir vigorously to dissolve the roux, then simmer for 30 minutes.

4   Heat the milk separately and add to the soup.

5   Sauté and render the fat out of the sausage. Remove, drain on paper towels, then add sausage to the soup. Simmer for an additional 5 minutes.

6   Remove from the heat and stir in the grated cheese until smooth.

7   Season with salt and pepper.

8   Garnish with the green onions when serving.

Beet and Apple Salad with Horseradish Vinaigrette 4 SERVINGS

AMOUNT	MEASURE	INGREDIENT
For the Horseradish Vinaigrette		
1 tablespoon	1 ounce, 28 g	Mustard, brown or grainy
2 tablespoons	1 ounce, 28 g	Prepared horseradish
1/4 cup	2 ounces, 55 ml	Raspberry vinegar
3/4 cup	6 ounces, 170 ml	Olive oil
to taste		Salt and black pepper
For the Salad		
1 pound	453 g	Beets, mixed red and golden, if available
1/4 cup	1 ounce, 28 g	Green onions, white parts only, minced
1 tablespoon	3 g	Chives, minced
2 tablespoons	6 g	Flat-leaf parsley, chopped
2		Apples, sweet or tart, julienned
1/2 cup	2 ounces, 56 g	Celery hearts, sliced 1/4 inch (.6 cm) thick
1 teaspoon	5 ml	Lemon juice
3 cups	6 ounces, 170 g	Escarole leaves or mixture of escarole, curly endive, romaine hearts, and radicchio, cleaned, washed, dried

PROCEDURE

1 Preheat the oven to 400°F (205°C).

2 In a food processor, combine all the ingredients for the vinaigrette except the oil. Slowly add the oil until emulsified. Adjust the seasoning with salt and pepper.

3 Leaving the roots and 1 inch (2.5 cm) of stem on the beets, rinse them. Bake with 1/4 inch (.6 cm) water, covered, 25 to 40 minutes or until beets can be easily pierced with a knife. Cool.

4 When the beets are cool enough to handle, peel and julienne.

5 Toss the beets with 2 tablespoons (1 ounce, 30 ml) vinaigrette and half the green onions.

6   Combine the chives, parsley, and apples with the celery and remaining green onions. Toss with 2 tablespoons (1 ounce, 30 ml) vinaigrette.

7   Dress the escarole leaves and dress with remaining vinaigrette.

8   Place the escarole leaves on a chilled plate. Place a serving of beets on top of the escarole, with the celery and apples scattered over and around.

Beet and Apple Salad with Horseradish Vinaigrette

Planked Whitefish with Green Onion Butter 4 SERVINGS

chef tip

Planking is a method of cooking fish that the settlers of the region learned from the Native Americans. A whole fish is tied to a large piece of driftwood and placed vertically next to a fire, where it cooks slowly until done. Today, planking is accomplished by placing a fish fillet on a soaked plank of wood—usually cedar, which gives off a tasty and unique flavor. The fillet is then cooked, plank and all, on a grill over a fire or even by baking in an oven.

The cedar planks used in this preparation are easy to find at a local building supply store. Cedar roof shingles are usually smooth on one side and the perfect shape for a fish fillet of this size. Be sure to purchase the untreated variety, as some shingles come with a chemical fire retardant that leaves an unpleasant aftertaste on the fish. The shingles are inexpensive. It is recommended, for sanitary reasons, that they not be reused. The whitefish called for in this **Central Plains** recipe can be walleye, pike, or yellow perch. However, the procedure yields excellent results with any type of round fish or large flatfish, such as halibut or turbot. Small flatfish, like sole and flounder, should be avoided, as they are too delicate and tend to absorb too much flavor from the wooden planks.

AMOUNT	MEASURE	INGREDIENT
4		Untreated cedar wood planks or shingles, 4 x 6 x $^1/_2$ inch (10 x 15 x 1.2 cm)
$^1/_2$ cup	4 ounces, 115 ml	Butter, softened
1		Egg yolk
2 tablespoons	1 ounce, 28 ml	Lemon juice
1 tablespoon	1 ounce, 28 g	Dijon mustard
$^1/_4$ cup	1 ounce, 28 g	Bread crumbs
$^1/_4$ cup	1$^1/_2$ ounces, 42 g	Green onions, chopped
2 tablespoons	6 g	Parsley, chopped
1		Garlic clove, smashed
$^1/_4$ cup	2 ounces, 55 ml	Vegetable oil
4	5 ounces, 141 g each	Whitefish fillets, skinned and boned
to taste		Salt and black pepper

PROCEDURE

1 Soak the cedar planks in water for at least a few hours before proceeding.

2 Mix the butter, egg yolk, lemon juice, mustard, bread crumbs, green onions, parsley, and garlic in a food processor. Pulse for 1 minute to combine into a paste. Roll the paste into a cylinder about 1 inch (2.5 cm) thick, and wrap in plastic wrap. Refrigerate until firm.

3 Preheat the oven to 425°F (220°C).

4 Remove the planks from water, dry, brush with the oil, and place in the oven on a baking sheet for 5 minutes to begin to season the wood.

5 Brush the fish with oil and season with salt and pepper.

6 Remove the paste from the refrigerator and cut into $1/4$-inch (.6 cm)-thick slices. Place 1 to 2 slices on each fillet.

7 Place the fish on the hot plank and return to the oven. Bake the fillets for 8 to 10 minutes (or until opaque and flaky), until the butter has melted into a brown crust.

8 Remove and serve immediately.

Mashed Celeriac and Potatoes   4 SERVINGS

AMOUNT	MEASURE	INGREDIENT
2 cups	10 ounces, 280 g	Celeriac, peeled, 1-inch (2.5 cm) cubes
2 cups	10 ounces, 280 g	All-purpose potatoes, quartered
3	$^1/_2$ ounce, 15 g	Garlic cloves, peeled, quartered
to taste		Salt and white pepper
pinch		Grated nutmeg
2 tablespoons	1 ounce, 28 g	Butter

PROCEDURE

1   Combine the celeriac, potatoes, garlic, and salt with water to cover.

2   Bring to a boil. Reduce heat to medium and simmer for 30 minutes or until tender.

3   Drain the vegetables, reserving the liquid.

4   Force the vegetables through a ricer or food mill or mash with a potato masher.

5   Season with salt, pepper, and nutmeg. Add enough of the cooking liquid to soften the consistency (like mashed potatoes) and return the mixture to a pan over low heat, stirring until heated through.

6   Add the butter and serve hot.

Pickled Pearl Onions   4 SERVINGS

AMOUNT	MEASURE	INGREDIENT
4 cups	20 ounces, 567 g	Pearl onions
1 tablespoon	6 g	Mustard seeds
1 tablespoon	6 g	Celery seeds
1 piece	1 inch, 2.5 cm	Fresh horseradish
1 cup	8 ounces, 235 ml	Cider vinegar
3 tablespoons	2 ounces, 42 ml	Honey
2		Hot chiles, fresh or dried

PROCEDURE

1 Bring a large pot of water to a boil, add the onions, and cook 2 minutes. (This will make them easier to peel.)

2 Drain in a colander and rinse under cold water. Trim away the onion tops and hairs at the stem end, leave the base of the stem end intact, then peel.

3 Combine the mustard seeds, celery seeds, horseradish, and vinegar. Bring to a boil, then simmer for 15 minutes.

4 Add the honey and chili pepper. Remove the horseradish and simmer for another 10 minutes.

5 Add the onions and cook until tender, about 10 minutes.

6 Remove the onions and continue cooking the liquid until reduced by half.

7 Pour liquid over onions.

Sautéed Green Beans and Cherry Tomatoes   4 SERVINGS

AMOUNT	MEASURE	INGREDIENT
4 cups	16 ounces, 453 g	Green beans, trimmed
2 tablespoons	1 ounce, 28 g	Unsalted butter
1		Shallot, minced
1		Garlic clove, minced
1 teaspoon	5 ml	Lemon juice
1 tablespoon	$^1/_2$ ounce, 14 ml	Dry white wine
1 cup	5 ounces, 141 g	Cherry tomatoes, halved
1 tablespoon	3 g	Tarragon, chopped
to taste		Salt and black pepper

PROCEDURE

1 Trim the stems from the beans; cook in boiling salted water for approximately 6 to 8 minutes, until tender. Shock the beans in ice water and drain. Chill until needed.

2 Heat the butter; add the shallot and garlic, and cook 2 minutes. Add the lemon juice and wine, and cook 1 minute more or until almost dry.

3 Add the beans; season and cook 2 minutes.

4 Add the cherry tomatoes and tarragon. Cook 2 minutes or just long enough to heat tomatoes.

5 Season with salt and pepper. Serve immediately.

Brownie Pudding Cake 4 SERVINGS

AMOUNT	MEASURE	INGREDIENT
I cup	4 ounces, 113 g	All-purpose flour
²/₃ cup	3 ounces, 85 g	Cocoa powder (unsweetened)
³/₄ teaspoon	3 g	Baking powder
³/₄ teaspoon	4 g	Salt
I cup	7 ounces, 198 g	Sugar, granulated
6 tablespoons	3 ounces, 84 g	Unsalted butter, melted, cooled
¹/₂ cup	4 ounces, 115 ml	Heavy cream
2		Eggs
I teaspoon	5 ml	Vanilla extract
I ¹/₃ cups	II ounces, 305 ml	Boiling water
³/₄ cup	6 ounces, 170 g	Light brown sugar, packed

PROCEDURE

I Preheat the oven to 350°F (175°C).

2 Sift together the flour, ¹/₃ cup (1¹/₂ ounces, 42 g) cocoa powder, baking powder, and salt; set aside.

3 In a mixer, using the paddle attachment, mix the granulated sugar, butter, cream, eggs, and vanilla.

4 Add the flour mixture and beat on low speed until just combined, about 30 seconds.

5 Spread in an ungreased 8-inch (20 cm) square baking pan; set aside.

6 Whisk together the remaining ¹/₃ cup (1¹/₂ ounces, 42 g) cocoa powder, the boiling water, and brown sugar; pour over batter.

7 Bake about 35 minutes or until a wooden skewer tests clean.

8 Serve warm.

Beef Barley Soup 4 SERVINGS

AMOUNT	MEASURE	INGREDIENT
2 tablespoons	1 ounce, 28 ml	Vegetable oil
6 ounces	170 g	Beef, boneless, lean, 1/4 inch (.6 cm) dice
3/4 cup	3 ounces, 85 g	Carrots, peeled, 1/4 inch (.6 cm) dice
3/4 cup	3 ounces, 85 g	Celery, 1/4 inch (.6 cm) dice
3/4 cup	3 ounces, 85 g	Onion, 1/4 inch (.6 cm) dice
1		Garlic clove, minced
1 cup	4 ounces, 113 g	Pearl barley
2 tablespoons	1 ounce, 28 g	Tomato paste
1/8 teaspoon	1 g	Thyme leaves (dried)
3 cups	24 ounces, 705 ml	Chicken stock
1 tablespoon	1/2 ounce, 14 ml	Worcestershire sauce
1/2		Bay leaf
to taste		Salt and white pepper
1 teaspoon	1 g	Chives, chopped

PROCEDURE

1   Heat the oil over medium heat and cook the meat until it is well browned.

2   Turn down the heat, add the vegetables, and cook 5 minutes.

3   Add the barley and coat with oil. Add the tomato paste and cook 1 minute.

4   Add the herbs, stock, Worcestershire sauce, and bay leaf. Bring to a simmer. Simmer 30 minutes, until barley is tender. Skim fat as needed.

5   Remove bay leaf. Correct seasoning. Garnish with chopped chives.

Kansas City Barbecued Ribs with Steak Fries

Kansas City Barbecued Ribs   4 SERVINGS

chef tip

If a smoky flavor is not desired, the ribs can be cooked in a combination oven at 275°F (135°C) or a traditional oven at 325°F (162.8°C). Numerous varieties of baby back ribs are available on the market. Some of the region's most notable ribs come from the pork-producing states of Kansas, Missouri, Iowa, and Illinois. To be classified as baby back ribs, the entire rack of ribs should not exceed $1^3/4$ pounds. Larger racks are simply called back ribs.

AMOUNT	MEASURE	INGREDIENT
4 pounds	2 kilos	Baby back ribs, peeled

For the Seasoning Mix

AMOUNT	MEASURE	INGREDIENT
$1/2$ cup	$3^1/2$ ounces, 70 g	Granulated sugar
$1/4$ cup	1 ounce, 28 g	Paprika
2 tablespoons	1 ounce, 28 g	Kosher salt
2 tablespoons	1 ounce, 28 g	Celery salt
$1^1/2$ tablespoons	$3/4$ ounce, 21 g	Onion powder
$1^1/2$ tablespoons	$3/4$ ounce, 21 g	Chili powder
1 teaspoon	2 g	Ground cumin
1 tablespoon	$1/4$ ounce, 7 g	Black pepper
1 teaspoon	2 g	Dry mustard
$1/4$ teaspoon	1 g	Cayenne

For the Sauce

AMOUNT	MEASURE	INGREDIENT
$1/2$ cup	4 ounces, 113 g	Light brown sugar
$1/2$ teaspoon	1 g	Chili powder
$1/2$ teaspoon	1 g	Dry mustard
$1/2$ teaspoon	1 g	Ground ginger
$1/8$ teaspoon	1 g	Ground allspice
$1/8$ teaspoon	1 g	Paprika
$1/8$ teaspoon	1 g	Mace
$1/8$ teaspoon	1 g	Black pepper
$1/2$ cup	4 ounces, 115 ml	Cider vinegar
$1/3$ cup	4 ounces, 78 ml	Molasses
1 teaspoon	5 ml	Liquid Smoke

2 cups	16 ounces, 470 ml	Ketchup
1/4 cup	2 ounces, 55 ml	Water
as needed		Wood chips for smoking

PROCEDURE

1   Remove the thin, transparent skin from the back side of the rib racks. This is easily done by scraping the corner of the bone on the small side of the rack on the backside. Lift the skin and pull. The skin should separate from the rack in 1 piece.

2   Combine all ingredients for the seasoning mix.

3   Rub the ribs liberally with seasoning mix.

4   Cover and refrigerate for at least 24 hours or until needed.

5   Prepare the sauce by placing all the ingredients in a small saucepot. Bring to a boil, stirring constantly, turn the heat down to a simmer, and simmer for 1 hour.

6   Prepare a smoker with soaked wood chips.

7   Coat the ribs liberally with the barbecue sauce.

8   Place the rib racks in the smoker. Smoke for 2 hours at 250°F (122°C), basting every hour with the extra barbecue sauce.

9   Reheat the remaining sauce when serving.

Steak Fries 4 SERVINGS

AMOUNT	MEASURE	INGREDIENT
2	12 ounces, 340 g, each	Russet potatoes
to taste		Coarse salt and black pepper
as needed		Vegetable oil, for deep-frying

PROCEDURE

1 Peel and wash the potatoes. Cut lengthwise into 8 wedges.

2 Parboil the potatoes in boiling salted water for 3 to 5 minutes. Drain, cool, and dry. Set aside until needed.

3 Fry the potatoes in a 350°F (175°C) fryer in 2 steps. First, let the potatoes get soft and form a skin. Remove them from the oil. Let the temperature of the oil recuperate. Second, shake the basket, place the potatoes back into the hot oil, and let the potatoes get golden brown and crisp.

4 Drain the potatoes on paper towels and season with salt and pepper.

Cannellini Beans with Tomatoes and Basil 4 SERVINGS

AMOUNT	MEASURE	INGREDIENT
I cup	7 ounces, 198 g	Cannellini beans, dried, sorted, soaked overnight
I		Bay leaf
2		Thyme, marjoram, sage, and parsley sprigs
$^1/_2$ cup	3 ounces, 84 g	Red onion, $^1/_2$ inch (1.2 cm) dice
$^1/_2$ teaspoon	3 ml	Champagne vinegar
2 tablespoons	I ounce, 28 ml	Red wine vinegar
2 teaspoons	$^1/_3$ ounce, 10 g	Zest from 2 lemons
2		Garlic cloves, minced
to taste		Salt and black pepper
$^1/_3$ cup	3 ounces, 78 ml	Olive oil
I$^1/_2$ cups	9 ounces, 352 ml	Tomatoes, peeled, seeded, $^1/_2$ inch (1.2 cm) dice
$^1/_4$ cup	$^1/_2$ ounce, 14 g	Basil, chopped

PROCEDURE

1 Drain and rinse the beans. Cover generously with cold water. Add the bay leaf and herb sprigs.

2 Bring to a boil, reduce to a simmer, and cook 20 to 25 minutes or until tender and begin to open.

3 Blanch the onion in boiling water for 15 seconds. Remove and toss with the Champagne vinegar.

4 Combine the red wine vinegar, lemon zest, garlic, $^3/_4$ teaspoon (4 g) salt, and $^1/_4$ teaspoon (1 g) pepper; whisk in the oil.

5 Drain the beans and toss immediately with the vinaigrette. The hot beans will soak up the flavors. Let cool.

6 Add the tomatoes, onion, and basil to beans. Marinate for 1 to 2 hours.

7 Correct seasoning and serve at room temperature.

Cannellini Beans with Tomatoes and Basil

Roast Chicken with Wild Rice, Walnut, and Dried Fruit Stuffing 4 TO 6 SERVINGS

AMOUNT	MEASURE	INGREDIENT
$^1/_2$ cup	4 ounces, 113 g	Unsalted butter
1 cup	4 ounces, 113 g	Leeks, halved lengthwise, cleaned, thinly sliced
2 cups	8 ounces, 226 g	Onions, $^1/_2$ inch (1.2 cm) dice
$^3/_4$ cup	3 ounces, 85 g	Celery, $^1/_2$ inch (1.2 cm) dice
1 cup	$6^1/_2$ ounces, 184 g	Wild rice
3 cups	24 ounces, 705 ml	Apple cider
2 cups	16 ounces, 470 ml	Chicken stock
$^1/_2$ cup	4 ounces, 115 ml	Applejack brandy
$^1/_2$ cup	2 ounces, 56 g	Green apple, peeled, cored, and $^1/_2$ inch (1.2 cm) dice
$^1/_4$ cup	1 ounce, 28 g	Dried cherries, diced
$^1/_4$ cup	1 ounce, 28 g	Dried apples, diced
1 cup	4 ounces, 113 g	Walnuts, toasted, chopped
4 tablespoons	$^1/_2$ ounce, 12 g	Rosemary, chopped
2 tablespoons	$^1/_4$ ounce, 6 g	Thyme, chopped
to taste		Salt and pepper
1	6 pounds, 2.72 kg	Roasting chicken

PROCEDURE

1 Preheat the oven to 325°F (163°C).

2 Melt half the butter over medium heat.

3 Add the leeks, onions, and celery; sauté until tender, about 6 minutes.

4 Add the wild rice and sauté for 2 minutes.

5 Add 1 cup (8 ounces, 237 ml) apple cider, the chicken stock, and Applejack. Bring to a boil, cover, and reduce to a simmer. Cook 30 minutes or until tender.

6 Add the fresh apple and dried fruit. Cover and cook 15 minutes more or until rice is tender.

7 Stir in the nuts and half the rosemary and the thyme. Correct the seasonings and cool stuffing completely.

8 Combine the remaining butter and rosemary. Set aside.

9 Season the chicken on all sides. Loosen the skin from the breasts and spread the rosemary butter over the breast meat under the skin. Stuff chickens with rice mixture; do not pack too tightly.

10 Set the chicken on a rack in a shallow pan. Roast, basting with remaining apple cider, until juices run clear, about 2 hours.

11 Let stand 10 minutes before serving. Serve with pan drippings and rice stuffing.

Winter Vegetables with Thyme 4 SERVINGS

AMOUNT	MEASURE	INGREDIENT
2 cups	9 ounces, 255 g	Turnips, peeled, ¹/₄-inch (.6 cm) slices
2 cups	9 ounces, 255 g	Rutabagas, peeled, ¹/₄-inch (.6 cm) slices
I cup	4 ounces, 113 g	Broccoli stalks, peeled, julienned
I cup	4 ounces, 113 g	Carrots, peeled, julienned
to taste		Salt
¹/₄ cup	2 ounces, 56 g	Unsalted butter
I teaspoon	I g	Parsley, chopped
I teaspoon	I g	Thyme leaves
to taste		Black pepper

PROCEDURE

1   Taste the vegetables to determine if any seem tougher than others, which means they will need longer to cook. Bring water to a boil and add salt.

2   Cook the vegetables, starting with the toughest first, until just tender, a minute or so. Drain and set aside.

3   Heat the butter with the parsley and thyme.

4   Add the vegetables and cook gently to evaporate the water; don't fry the vegetables.

5   Adjust seasoning and serve hot.

Broccoli Florets 4 SERVINGS

AMOUNT	MEASURE	INGREDIENT
2 cups	5 ounces, 141 g	Broccoli florets
2 tablespoons	1 ounce, 28 g	Unsalted butter
to taste		Salt and white pepper

PROCEDURE

1 Trim the broccoli florets.

2 Heat water to a boil, add salt and parboil the broccoli until just before tender. Shock in ice water and drain.

3 Heat the butter, add the broccoli, and toss to coat. Cook until hot; correct seasoning.

Corn and Wild Rice Cakes

Corn and Wild Rice Cakes 4 SERVINGS

AMOUNT	MEASURE	INGREDIENT
1 1/2 teaspoons	8 g	Butter
3/4 cup	3 ounces, 85 g	Leeks, cleaned, white part only, very thinly sliced
1	5 g	Garlic clove, minced
1/2 cup	2 1/2 ounces, 70 g	Corn kernels, fresh or frozen
1 cup	7 ounces, 198 g	Wild rice, cooked
1		Egg, lightly beaten
1/4 cup	2 ounces, 55 ml	Heavy cream
1 tablespoon	3 g	Parsley, chopped
1 tablespoon	3 g	Chives, chopped
1/4 teaspoon	1 g	Black pepper
1/2 teaspoon	1 g	Salt
1/4 cup	1 ounce, 28 g	All-purpose flour
as needed		Vegetable oil

PROCEDURE

1   Heat the butter over medium heat. Cook the leeks and garlic until leeks are soft.

2   Combine the leeks, garlic, and corn with the wild rice.

3   Mix the egg and cream together until blended. Mix in the chopped herbs, pepper, and salt.

4   Combine the wild rice with the egg-cream mixture. Stir in the flour until rice can be formed into cakes. You may need to add more or less flour.

5   Form cakes using 1/3 cup (2 3/4 ounces, 85 ml) measuring cup. Let chill 30 minutes.

6   Sauté cakes in oil until lightly browned, about 3 minutes per side.

Morel Mushrooms with Spinach 4 SERVINGS

chef tip

If fresh morel mushrooms are unavailable or too expensive, dried morels can be substituted. The dried mushrooms need to be reconstituted prior to using. Boil a small pot of water, add the dried mushrooms, cover, and remove from the heat. Steep the mushrooms 4 to 5 minutes and remove from the hot water. Generally, the mushrooms expand to 5 times their dried weight, so to get 10 ounces (283 g) of reconstituted mushrooms, use just 2 ounces (57 g) of dried. The water that the mushrooms steep in is flavorful and can be used in a variety of soups and sauces. In addition, dried forest mushroom mix is available at a very reasonable cost.

AMOUNT	MEASURE	INGREDIENT
6 cups	12 ounces, 340 g	Spinach, young, washed, stalks removed
to taste		Salt
1 cup	4 ounces, 113 g (2 ounces dried)	Morel mushrooms, fresh, washed, large ones may be cut in half
6 tablespoons	3 ounces, 84 g	Unsalted butter
1/4 cup	2 ounces, 55 ml	Heavy cream
to taste		Salt and pepper
to taste		Grated nutmeg

PROCEDURE

1   Blanch the spinach in boiling salted water for 1 minute; drain. Refresh in ice water, drain again. Gently squeeze to remove excess water.

2   Trim away bases of fresh morels (keep to make stock). Brush and lightly wash and rinse them to make sure they are completely clean and free of grit. (If using dried mushrooms, soak them in warm water for at least 30 minutes. Drain the water and pat the mushrooms dry.)

3   Melt 1/4 cup (2 ounces, 55 ml) butter, add mushrooms, and heat through.

4   Add the spinach, cook on high heat, and stir. If too much liquid, drain excess.

5   Add the cream, bring to boil, and reduce by half.

6   Correct seasoning and stir in remaining butter.

Garden Lettuce, Watercress, and Escarole with Goat Cheese and Sun-Dried Tomatoes 4 SERVINGS

AMOUNT	MEASURE	INGREDIENT

For the Balsamic Vinaigrette

AMOUNT	MEASURE	INGREDIENT
$^1/_4$ cup	2 ounces, 55 ml	Balsamic vinegar
I tablespoon	$^1/_2$ ounce, 15 g	Garlic, minced
$^1/_2$ teaspoon	3 g	Salt
$^1/_2$ teaspoon	I g	Black pepper
$^3/_4$ cup	6 ounces, 170 ml	Olive oil
2 cups	4 ounces, 133 g	Escarole, tender inner leaves
3 cups	6 ounces, 170 l	Mixed baby greens
I		Watercress bunch
I tablespoon	$^1/_3$ ounce, 9 g	Sunflower seeds, toasted
2		Sun-dried tomatoes packed in oil, drained, thinly sliced
	I ounce, 28 g	Goat cheese, creamy mild (chèvre or Montrachet)
to taste		Black pepper

PROCEDURE

1 Combine ingredients for vinaigrette.

2 Tear large leaves of escarole into pieces. Wash greens and dry in a spinner.

3 Toss the lettuce, escarole, watercress, sunflower seeds, and sun-dried tomatoes with the vinaigrette.

4 Crumble the cheese onto the salad and toss again.

5 Sprinkle with black pepper. Serve.

Pork Medallions with Blueberry Sauce 4 SERVINGS

AMOUNT	MEASURE	INGREDIENT
1 tablespoon	$^1/_2$ ounce, 14 g	Butter
$^1/_4$ cup	2 ounces, 56 g	Onion, $^1/_2$ inch (1.2 cm) dice
$^1/_8$ cup	1 ounce, 28 g	Celery, $^1/_2$ inch (1.2 cm) dice
$^1/_8$ cup	1 ounce, 28 g	Carrot, $^1/_2$ inch (1.2 cm) dice
2 cups	16 ounces, 473 ml	Brown stock
1$^1/_2$ cups	8 ounces, 141 g	Blueberries, fresh or frozen
$^1/_4$ cup	2 ounces, 56 g	Butter, cubed
to taste		Salt and white pepper
8	total 16 ounces, 453 g	Pork medallions, 2-ounce portions
as needed		Flour
as needed		Butter
$^1/_4$ cup	2 ounces, 55 ml	Vegetable oil

PROCEDURE

1 Preheat the oven to 350°F (175°C).

2 Heat 1 tablespoon ($^1/_2$ ounce, 14 g) butter and add onion, celery, and carrot. Cook until vegetables are caramelized, 10 to 15 minutes.

3 Add the stock and blueberries; simmer 30 minutes or until reduced by half. Strain. Press out liquid from solids and discard solids. Set aside sauce.

4 Season and dust the pork medallions in flour. Heat oil in pan and sauté to desired doneness, about 2 to 3 minutes per side.

5 Reheat sauce and whisk in the butter cubes. Serve sauce with pork.

Brussels Sprouts with Mushrooms 4 SERVINGS

AMOUNT	MEASURE	INGREDIENT
2 cups	7 ounces, 198 g	Brussels sprouts, trimmed
2 tablespoons	I ounce, 28 g	Bacon, $^1/_4$ inch (.6 cm) dice
2 tablespoons	I ounce, 28 g	Unsalted butter
I		Garlic clove, minced
$^1/_4$ cup	I ounce, 28 g	Onion, $^1/_4$ inch (.6 cm) dice
I $^1/_4$ cups	3 ounces, 85 g	White mushrooms, $^1/_4$-inch (.6 cm) slices
to taste		Salt and white pepper

PROCEDURE

1. Trim the bottoms of the Brussels sprouts and score an X into the bottom of each with a paring knife.

2. Cook Brussels sprouts in boiling salted water until tender in the center. Shock sprouts in an ice-water bath and reserve.

3. Cook the bacon over medium heat to render fat, then cook until crisp.

4. Add the butter, garlic, and onion. Cook 5 minutes or until onion is soft.

5. Add the mushrooms and cook 5 minutes more, or until mushrooms are cooked.

6. Cut Brussels sprouts in half and add to mushrooms.

7. Cook until Brussels sprouts are hot. Correct seasoning.

Macaroni and Cheese 4 SERVINGS

AMOUNT	MEASURE	INGREDIENT
2 cups	8 ounces, 226 g	Elbow macaroni
1/4 cup	2 ounces, 56 g	Butter, softened
dash		Tabasco
1 1/2 cups	12 ounces, 352 ml	Evaporated milk, warm
2		Eggs, beaten
1 teaspoon	2 g	Dry mustard, dissolved in a little water
4 cups	16 ounces, 453 g	Cheddar cheese (sharp)
to taste		Salt and white pepper

PROCEDURE

1 Preheat the oven to 350°F (175°C).

2 Cook the macaroni in boiling salted water until just barely tender.

3 Drain and toss with the butter.

4 Mix Tabasco with 1 cup (8 ounces, 235 ml) milk. Add the eggs, mustard, and 12 ounces (340 g) of cheese. Combine well and check seasoning. Mix in macaroni.

5 Transfer to a baking pan and set in oven. Every 5 minutes, stir in some of the reserved cheese, adding more evaporated milk as necessary to keep the mixture moist and smooth. When you have incorporated all the cheese, the mixture should be creamy, about 20 minutes.

Sour Cream Coffee Cake 6–8 SERVINGS

AMOUNT	MEASURE	INGREDIENT
1½ cups	12 ounces, 352 ml	Sour cream
1 cup	7 ounces, 198 g	Granulated sugar
1		Egg
½ cup	2 ounces, 56 g	Dried cranberries
½ cup	2 ounces, 56 g	Dried cherries, chopped
½ cup	2 ounces, 56 g	Dried apples, chopped
2 cups	9 ounces, 255 g	All-purpose flour
2 teaspoons	8 g	Baking powder
½ teaspoon	3 g	Salt
1 cup	4 ounces, 113 g	Walnuts, black or regular, chopped
½ cup	4 ounces, 113 g	Light brown sugar, packed
1 teaspoon	2 g	Ground cinnamon
¼ cup	2 ounces, 56 g	Unsalted butter

Sour Cream Coffee Cake

PROCEDURE

1 Preheat the oven to 350°F (175°C). Grease a 9-inch (22 cm) springform pan.

2 Combine the sour cream, granulated sugar, and egg.

3 Stir in the cranberries, cherries, and apples.

4 In separate bowl, combine the flour, baking powder, and salt.

5 Add the flour mixture to the sour cream mixture and stir thoroughly.

6 Scrape into prepared pan. Smooth surface and sprinkle evenly with the walnuts, brown sugar, and cinnamon. Dot with butter.

7 Bake for 1 hour or until a wooden skewer tests clean.

8 Let cool 10 minutes before unmolding.

Bratwurst (Farmer Style) 4 SERVINGS

chef tip

One important point: Don't ever boil bratwurst! You may see recipes that call for parboiling or boiling. Boiling will cause the casings to burst. Instead, always simmer. Bratwurst can also be pan-fried. Nevertheless, at a Wisconsin "brat fry," the bratwurst are cooked on a grate over charcoal, usually on a kettle grill. Bratwurst is made from pork and veal typically in a 60 percent pork to 40 percent veal ratio. Authentic bratwurst is a fresh sausage, which must be cooked thoroughly before eating.

AMOUNT	MEASURE	INGREDIENT
19 ounces	550 g	Lean boneless pork butt, in 1-inch (2.5 cm) cubes
13 ounces	367 g	Veal, in 1-inch (2.5 cm) cubes
2 teaspoons	$^1/_3$ ounce, 10 g	Pickling salt
1 teaspoon	5 g	Onion salt
1 teaspoon	2 g	White pepper
1 teaspoon	2 g	Ground marjoram
1 teaspoon	1 g	Parsley, chopped
$^1/_2$ teaspoon	1 g	Grated nutmeg
$^1/_2$ teaspoon	1 g	Celery seed
$^1/_4$ teaspoon	.5 g	Ground ginger
$^1/_4$ teaspoon	.25 g	Ground mace
$^1/_4$ teaspoon	1 g	Ground cardamom (optional)
	4 ounces, 112 g	Crushed ice
as needed		Pork or sheep casing
2 tablespoons	$^1/_2$ ounce, 14 g	Onion, chopped

PROCEDURE

1 Grind meat through a $^3/_{16}$-inch (.4 cm) plate of a meat grinder.

2 Combine all the ingredients except the onion, ice, and casings. Mix well. Chill in freezer for 30 minutes.

3 Chill all the grinder parts.

4 Mix meat again and grind through the $^1/_4$-inch (.6 cm) plate with onion.

Bratwurst (Farmer Style)

5   Place ground meat into a food processor and add crushed ice while blending, 30 to 60 seconds.

6   Stuff mixture into casings and air-dry for 30 minutes or until dry to the touch.

7   To cook, simmer in beer or water for 20 minutes; drain. Or grill bratwurst, until browned, about 10 minutes.

German Potato Salad 4 SERVINGS

AMOUNT	MEASURE	INGREDIENT
For the Vinaigrette		
2 tablespoons	I ounce, 28 g	Bacon, $^1/_4$ inch (.6 cm) dice
$^1/_4$ cup	I ounce, 28 g	Shallots, $^1/_4$ inch (.6 cm) dice
2 tablespoons	I ounce, 28 ml	Sherry vinegar
$^1/_4$ cup	2 ounces, 55 ml	Olive oil
$^1/_2$ cup	4 ounces, 115 ml	Chicken stock
to taste		Salt and black pepper
4 cups	20 ounces, 567 g	Red Bliss potatoes
I tablespoon	3 g	Chives, finely sliced

PROCEDURE

1   Render the bacon over medium heat; do not crisp.

2   Add the shallots and cook 3 minutes.

3   Deglaze with the sherry vinegar, add the chicken stock, and stir in the olive oil. Bring to a boil, then remove from the heat. Season with salt and pepper. Keep hot

4   Wash the potatoes, cover with cold salted water, and bring to a simmer. Simmer until tender. Drain and dry. When you can handle them, slice into $^1/_8$-inch (.3 cm)-thick slices with the skin on.

5   Pour the hot bacon vinaigrette over the sliced potatoes; combine.

6   Serve at room temperature; garnish each serving with the chives.

Chicago Deep-Dish Pizza 4 SERVINGS

AMOUNT	MEASURE	INGREDIENT
For the Dough		
1 1/2 teaspoons	5 g	Active dry yeast
6 tablespoons	3 ounces, 84 ml	Water, warm (110°F, 42°C)
6 tablespoons	3 ounces, 84 ml	Milk
pinch		Granulated sugar
2 tablespoons	1 ounce, 20 ml	Olive oil
1 tablespoon	1/2 ounce, 15 g	Cornmeal, fine-grind
1/2 teaspoon	3 g	Salt
3 tablespoons	24 g	Whole-wheat flour
1 3/4 cups	7 ounces, 198 g	All-purpose flour
For the Tomato Sauce		
2 tablespoons	1 ounce, 20 ml	Olive oil
1 cup	4 ounces, 113 g	Onion, 1/4 inch (.6 cm) dice
1		Garlic clove, minced
3 cups	18 ounces, 510 g	Tomatoes, peeled, seeded, chopped
1/4 cup	2 ounces, 56 g	Tomato puree
1/8 teaspoon	1/4 g	Basil (dried)
1/8 teaspoon	1/4 g	Oregano (dried)
to taste		Salt and black pepper
1 cup	4 ounces, 113 g	Italian sausage, sliced
3 cups	12 ounces, 340 g	Mozzarella cheese, shredded
1/2 cup	2 ounces, 56 g	Red bell pepper, cored, seeded, thinly sliced
1/3 cup	1 ounce, 28 g	Parmesan cheese, grated

PROCEDURE

1 Dissolve the yeast in the warm water and set aside in a warm place for 3 to 4 minutes.

2 Combine the milk, olive oil, and cornmeal. Add the yeast mixture. Add the salt and whole-wheat flour; mix well.

3 Gradually add the white flour and work to a soft, workable dough.

4   Turn out onto a lightly floured surface and knead for 5 minutes. Put the dough in an oiled bowl and turn to coat the surface with oil. Cover the bowl and let the dough rise in a warm place until doubled in bulk, about 35 to 45 minutes.

5   Punch down the dough and allow to rise until double again, about 30 minutes.

6   Heat the oil, add the onion and garlic, and cook 3 minutes.

7   Stir in the diced tomatoes, puree, basil, oregano, salt, and pepper; simmer for 30 minutes, until thick.

8   Preheat the oven to 450°F (225°C). Lightly oil a 9-inch (22 cm) round baking pan that is 1^1/$_2$ inches (3.8 cm) deep.

9   Roll the dough into a 12-inch (30 cm) circle and fit it into the pan. The dough should just cover the bottom and sides of the pan, with no overhang. Prick dough all over with a fork.

10 Cook the sausage and cool. Slice into ^{1}/$_2$-inch (1.2 cm)-thick slices.

11 Spread half the mozzarella over the dough. Spread the tomato sauce over the cheese, covering completely. Spread the sausage and red peppers over the tomato sauce. Top with remaining mozzarella and the Parmesan cheese.

12 Bake 25 minutes, or until the cheese and crust are golden and the filling is bubbly. Remove from oven and allow to sit for 5 minutes before cutting.

Pan-Seared Steak with Maytag Blue Cheese Butter 4 SERVINGS

AMOUNT	MEASURE	INGREDIENT
For the Blue Cheese Butter		
1	2 ounces, 56 g	Garlic head
3		Shallots, peeled
1 cup	8 ounces, 226 g	Unsalted butter
³/₄ cup	3 ounces, 85 g	Maytag Blue Cheese
to taste		Black pepper
2 teaspoons	2 g	Parsley, chopped
2 tablespoons	1 ounce, 28 ml	Dry red wine
¹/₂ cup	¹/₂ ounce, 15 g	Bread crumbs, fresh
For the Steak		
4	6 ounces, 170 g, each	Top loin steaks
to taste		Salt and black pepper
as needed		Vegetable oil

PROCEDURE

1 Preheat the oven to 375°F (190°C).

2 Cut the top off the garlic head and wrap in foil with the shallots. Roast for 30 to 45 minutes. Remove and, while still warm, squeeze garlic pulp out of roasted head.

3 Chop garlic and shallots to make a paste. Cool.

4 Combine the butter and cheese in a mixer with paddle or in a food processor. Add the roasted garlic and shallots and blend 1 minute. Add the remaining butter ingredients and combine well.

5 Place the butter on plastic wrap or parchment paper and roll up into a cylinder. Refrigerate until firm.

6 Season the steaks and sear in hot oil until brown on both sides; cook to desired doneness.

7 Place each steak on a hot plate and top with some blue cheese butter. Brown the butter on top of the steaks under the broiler or salamander for approximately 30 seconds.

Pioneer Buffalo Stew 4 SERVINGS

AMOUNT	MEASURE	INGREDIENT
16 ounces	453 g	Buffalo stew meat, 1-inch (2.5 cm) cubes
as needed		Flour, for dusting
2 tablespoons	1 ounce, 28 ml	Vegetable oil
2 tablespoons	1 ounce, 28 g	Bacon, $^1/_2$ inch (1.2 cm) dice
1 cup	4 ounces, 113 g	Onion, $^1/_2$ inch (1.2 cm) dice
1		Garlic clove, minced
$^1/_4$ cup	1 ounce, 28 g	All-purpose flour
$^1/_2$ tablespoon	$^1/_4$ ounce, 7 g	Tomato paste
$^3/_4$ cup	6 ounces, 170 ml	Beer (lager)
4 cups	32 ounces, 1 l	Brown stock
1		Bay leaf
$^1/_2$ teaspoon	1 g	Thyme (dried)
$^1/_2$ teaspoon	1 g	Oregano (dried)
to taste		Salt and black pepper
1 cup	4 ounces, 85 g	Carrots, $^3/_4$-inch (1.9 cm) cubes
$^1/_2$ cup	2 ounces, 56 g	Celery, $^3/_4$-inch (1.9 cm) dice
1 cup	4 ounces, 85 g	Turnip, $^3/_4$-inch (1.9 cm) cubes
1 cup	5 ounces, 141 g	Red potatoes, $^3/_4$-inch (1.9 cm) cubes
1 tablespoon	3 g	Parsley, chopped

PROCEDURE

1 Lightly dust the stew meat with flour.

2 Heat the oil over medium-high heat and sear the meat on all sides. Remove and set aside. (This step has to be done in batches.)

3 Remove any excess oil. Add the bacon, onion, and garlic; caramelize.

4 Add the tomato paste and cook 2 to 3 minutes until it is caramelized.

5 Add the flour and stir in thoroughly.

6 Deglaze with beer and add the stock. Stir vigorously to dissolve the flour, then add the herbs and seasoning. Bring to a simmer.

7   Add the meat and stew for approximately 30 to 40 minutes.

8   Add the vegetable and potatoes. Bring back to a simmer and cook until the meat and vegetables are tender.

9   Remove bay leaf. Taste and adjust seasoning. Serve in bowls and garnish with parsley.

Sunchoke Gratin · 4 SERVINGS

AMOUNT	MEASURE	INGREDIENT
4 cups	16 ounces, 453 g	Sunchokes, peeled, $^1/_4$-inch (.6 cm) slices
1 tablespoon	$^1/_2$ ounce, 14 ml	Vegetable oil
$^1/_2$ cup	2 ounces, 56 g	Onion, $^1/_4$ inch (.6 cm) dice
1		Garlic clove, minced
1		Thyme sprig, chopped
1 cup	8 ounces, 235 ml	Heavy cream
$^1/_4$ cup	1 ounce, 28 g	Cornstarch
to taste		Salt and white pepper
2 tablespoons	1 ounce, 28 g	Unsalted butter
2 tablespoons	$^1/_2$ ounce, 14 g	Bread crumbs, dry
$^1/_3$ cup	1 ounce, 28 g	Parmesan cheese, finely grated
pinch		Paprika

PROCEDURE

1 Parboil the sunchokes in a pot of salted water for 5 minutes. Shock the sunchokes in an ice-water bath, drain, and reserve.

2 Preheat the oven to 400°F (205°C).

3 Heat the oil over medium heat. Add the sunchokes, onion, garlic, and thyme and cook approximately 2 minutes.

4 Reserve 2 tablespoons (1 ounce, 28 g) of the heavy cream; add the remainder to the vegetables and bring to a simmer.

5 Mix the cornstarch with the reserved cream to make a slurry and add to the simmering liquid; simmer over low heat for 3 minutes. Season with salt and white pepper.

6 Place in a buttered casserole or soufflé dish.

7 Mix the bread crumbs and cheese together, then sprinkle over top. Sprinkle with paprika.

8 Bake for about 20 minutes or until set.

9 Let the sunchoke gratin rest for 10 minutes before serving.

Texas and Tex-Mex Cuisine

Big as Texas. A state that is as large as all of New England, New York, Pennsylvania, Ohio, and Illinois combined, Texas has served under six flags and reflects a culture that includes cowboys, rodeos, and ten-gallon hats. It is a region that bred a cuisine described as the only food that is truly native to the United States. A cooking style that merges the Texas and Mexican cultures, Tex-Mex cooking was originally regarded as a poor man's Mexican food based on corn, pinto beans, tomatoes, and chiles. It was developed by people working with primitive kitchens and limited ingredients, and owes its appeal to the inventiveness of its creators, who were able to make their foods interesting by combining the same ingredients in different ways. Today it has become sophisticated while still adhering to many south-of-the-border traditions. Additionally, Longhorn cattle, cowboys, chuckwagon cooking, and Lone Star chili come to mind. The beef and chilis we associate with the cuisine of Texas are remnants of the state's Spanish and Mexican heritages. From the famous "bowl of red"—Texas chili—to tacos, fajitas, and salsa, these flavorful introductions influence the eating habits of not only Texans but also of all other Americans.

Texas The "Lone Star State" nickname comes from the symbolism of the star on the 1836 flag, which signified that Texas was an independent republic, and was a reminder of the state's struggle for independence from Mexico. "Friendship" is the state motto. The state tree is the pecan, and the state fruit is the Texas red grapefruit. The state vegetable is the Texas 1015 sweet onion, the state native pepper is the chiltepin, and the state pepper is the jalepeño chile. The state plant is the prickly pear cactus, and chili was proclaimed the state dish by the Texas Legislature in 1977. Rodeo is the official sport of Texas.

Major Influences On the State's Culture

In 1519, Spain was the first European nation to claim what is now Texas. The Spanish came to Texas in search of a shorter route to the Far East and with hopes of finding treasure while they "civilized" and Christianized the natives. They built their first settlement in Texas: Ysleta Mission in present El Paso, established in 1681. Gradually expanding from Mexico, the Spanish built other missions, forts, and civil settlements for nearly 150 years, until Mexico threw off European rule and became independent in 1821. During that time, those who came to this land survived on game that included buffalo, venison, hogs, and the native wild cattle. They learned to raise gourds, squash, sweet potatoes, and corn. Other small grains such as oats and rye had been imported, while the settlers grew most of the other foods that they consumed.

Planning to expand its base from French Louisiana, France planted its flag in eastern Texas near the Gulf Coast. But the first colony, called Fort St. Louis, was not successful owing to natural and political disasters that included disease, famine, and hostile Indians.

For more than a decade after Mexico became independent, hardy pioneers from the Hispanic south and the Anglo north flowed into Texas, a frontier for both groups. But conflicting social and political attitudes alienated the two cultures. Texans revolted, and they won their independence on April 21, 1836. Those who had come and survived continued to depend on wild game and corn, though many brought familiar breeds of cattle, hogs, sheep, and poultry with them.

During nearly ten years of independence, the Texas republic endured epidemics, financial crises, and continued volatile clashes with Mexico. But it was during this period that unique aspects of the Texas heritage developed. Texas became the birthplace of the American cowboy; the Texas Rangers were the first to use Sam Colt's remarkable six-shooters; and Sam Houston became an American ideal of rugged individualism. In contrast to the Wild West, the eastern coast of Texas had become highly settled, with seaports and plantations. The leading port of Galveston reflected European and Southern influences in its culture and cuisine, and staples such as salt, coffee, sugar, and wheat flour were brought from New Orleans to Galveston.

In 1845, Texas became the 28th state to join the United States of America. But 16 years after Texas joined the Union, the American Civil War erupted. Ignoring the advice of Governor Sam Houston to establish a neutral republic, Texas cast its lot with the doomed Southerners, reaping devastation and economic collapse as did all Confederate states. But two events fixed Texas and Texans as somehow different in the nation's eyes. First, Texas troops on Texas soil won the final battle of the Civil War, not knowing the South had surrendered a month earlier. Second, returning Texans found a population explosion of wild Longhorns, sparking the great trail drives that became one of America's legends.

Pushing aside the defeat and bitter reconstruction after the Civil War, the offspring of Texas pioneers marshaled their strengths to secure a future based on determined self-reliance. One of the first successes was the famous Texas Longhorn, providing beef for a growing nation. Newly turned topsoil on vast farm acreage yielded bountiful crops. The 20th century dawned with the discovery of fabulous sources—gushers roaring at a place called Spindletop near Beaumont in East Texas. By the mid-20th century, modern Texas industries were developing in a climate of advanced technology. Today, Texas horizons continue to expand, reaching up to the limitless reaches of outer space.

The People . . . Texans by Choice

DEEP EAST TEXAS

Two distinct economic classes settled in the piney woods of what is known as Deep East Texas. People from Alabama, Georgia, Mississippi, and Louisiana included plantation owners, who brought the tradition of fine foods and Southern hospitality to their Texas plantations. They also brought Cajun and Creole cookery from nearby Louisiana. Shrimp, oysters, crabs, and fish from the Gulf of Mexico were widely available and used in spicy seafood Creoles, gumbos, and jambalayas. Rice crops were grown in the low marshy coastal plains near the Gulf of Mexico. But those who worked on the plantations and in the rice fields were less fortunate, and their meals continued to be limited to wild berries, fruits, edible weeds, wild duck, dove, quail, and other game. While the inland pines continue to supply a giant lumbering industry and almost all of the state's huge rice crop comes from East Texas, today the real wealth of East Texas is from its immense, rich oil fields and the heavy industry that crowds the Gulf Coast.

CENTRAL TEXAS

Stephen F. Austin settled in central Texas with more than 300 of his loyal followers. Large land grants were available, and Germans wrote home of the opportunities that made Texas seem like an earthly paradise. A steady stream of immigrants left northwestern Germany and established what is known as the "German Belt," which stretched in broad but fragmented clusters across the south-central part of the state. Large numbers of Czechs and Poles joined this immigration as well. These people brought their skills at preparing the foods of their homeland, but they adapted them to the ingredients they found available. Their specialties included sausage making and meat smoking. Indeed, the German method of meat smoking is considered a major force in the origin of Texas barbecue, which comes from this region, and some feel the German treatment of veal à la Wiener schnitzel is the predecessor of the Texas favorite—chicken-fried steak.

WEST TEXAS

Texas ranches were established to raise beef cattle on land granted to Mexican families by the king of Spain. The well-known Texas Longhorns, descendants of the wild cattle left by the Spanish in the 16th century, were popular because they could withstand the extreme weather of the deserts of West Texas. Until the discovery of oil in West Texas, cattle production was the biggest industry in the state. Although the Longhorns were well suited to the region, their meat was not considered the most tender or flavorful. Today, beef is still the primary meat of the region; however, the ranchers prefer to raise Hereford, Brahma, and Angus cattle. Other meats are now being raised in West Texas, including bison, ostrich, emu, axis venison, and antelope.

THE GULF COAST

The Gulf's coastal areas were first settled by Native Americans and fiercely protected by the Karankawas (rumors that they practiced cannibalism slowed ventures into this region). Galveston was where Cabeza de Vaca, the first European to set foot on Texas soil, landed in 1528, and where pirate chieftan Jean Laffite ruled. Many of the immigrants who settled the rest of Texas and the Southwest entered through this port. Today, on the Gulf

Chuck Wagon Cooking

The legendary time of the trail drives lasted only about 20 years, from the end of the Civil War to the mid-1880s. In that period, around 10 million cattle were herded from Texas to rail heads in Kansas and Missouri. Many of these cattle went as far as Wyoming, to Chicago, and even into Canada. In the early days of the great trail drives, the cowhand had to make do with what he could carry with him. Texas rancher Charles Goodnight is given credit for the efficient design of the chuckwagon. Using a surplus military wagon, he added a chuck box and tailgate that served as a workstation. This chuck box had shelves and drawers to hold what the cook would need to prepare meals for the day, including a coffee grinder and other cooking utensils to provide hot meals for the dozen or more cowboys and the trail boss. The most essential cooking tool was the cast-iron Dutch oven. This heavy stew pot rested above the coals on three stubby legs. It had a tight-fitting lid with a raised rim. The cook would then pile more hot coals onto the lid. The ability to heat from both above and below allowed for roasting and braising, as well for baking the cowboys' favorite camp bread—the buttermilk biscuit. A large water barrel was attached to the side of the wagon, along with tool boxes, hooks, and brackets. *Chuck* was the cowboy word for "food" and cooking was usually done over an open fire. The chuckwagon cook was called a "cookie" or "coosie," from the Spanish word *cocinero* (male cook). Favorite meals included grilled steaks, smoked brisket, and biscuits. Mexican music and Mexican food quickly became part of the cowboy culture. Cowboys learned to play the guitar and compose ballads in English that mimicked the sentiments of Spanish love songs. Mexican cowboys introduced their favorite foods—chili, beans, and tortillas—to chuckwagon cooking.

Coast, seafood is as much a part of Texas cuisine as are chili and chicken-fried steak. More than 100 million pounds of shrimp, oysters, blue crabs, and finfish, including redfish, red snapper, pompano, flounder, and speckled trout, are harvested annually from the Gulf of Mexico. Natural and manmade oyster reefs are found along the Texas coastline. The American commercial oyster thrives in the bays and estuaries behind barrier islands separating the Texas mainland from the Gulf of Mexico. Here, fresh water and saltwater combine to create the environment oysters need to flourish. Several types of shrimp are caught along the coastline, each named for its color, which is determined by its diet. The two most popular are white shrimp and brown shrimp.

SOUTH TEXAS

South Texas was originally cleared by farmers from the Midwest who were attracted by the subtropical climate and long growing season, allowing them to produce two crops in one year on the same land. They planted vegetables, reaping the first agricultural bonanza from valley soil. The Rio Grande Valley produces more than 40 crops—primarily cotton, grain sorghum, sugarcane, fruits, and vegetables. Today, the major food crops grown include cabbage, onions, carrots, peppers, broccoli, citrus fruits, and cantaloupes and honeydew melons. The onion is Texas's top produce crop, one of more than 45 types of produce grown in Texas, the nation's third largest producer of fruits and vegetables. The famous 1015 onion, developed at Texas A&M University specifically for Rio Grande Valley growing conditions, is so sweet and mild it has been voted the sweetest tasting onion in a national competition, and it is tearless. It is named 1015 for the day it is planted—October 15.

The food of the settlers in this South Texas region was based primarily on the cuisine of Mexico and Spain. Tacos, guacamole, enchiladas, burritos, and tortillas became staples. Those, along with fajitas with spicy salsas and fresh flour tortillas, were the start of the first true American regional cuisine.

Typical Tex-Mex Dishes and Regional Foods

Anticucho A Tex-Mex shish kebab usually made with sirloin chunks marinated with jalapeño and tomato, then skewered and grilled over a mesquite wood fire.

Arroz Spanish for "rice," the staple of Tex-Mex cooking. Texmati rice is a brand name for a crossbreed of white, long-grain, and the aromatic basmati rice. It is known for its delicious nutty taste and when cooking, it smells like popcorn.

Barbacoa In Spanish, *barbacoa* means "food cooked over or adjacent to an open fire." In Tex-Mex cooking, it is a Mexican-style shredded beef made from the cow's head. Barbacoa is typically served with pico de gallo and freshly made corn or flour tortillas.

Boracho A cooking term indicating the inclusion of beer in a recipe—for example, in *frijoles borachos,* which means "beans cooked with beer."

Burrito A large flour tortilla filled with any number of ingredients that could include meat, beans, or vegetables. The burrito is formed by tucking the ends of the tortilla inside as it is rolled to seal in the filling. They are usually eaten with condiments such as salsa, lettuce, tomato, cheese, and guacamole.

Cabrito Spanish for "goat." Like cattle and sheep, goats are a major source of revenue on many Texas ranches, but they also run wild throughout parts of the state. Grilled or barbecued, split or butchered, goat is a feature for large gatherings or feasts. Older goat is used for milk and cheese products.

Caldo de Res A Spanish beef soup with vegetables, often served with corn on the cob that has been cut into thick slices.

Cheeses

Queso Spanish for "cheese." In Tex-Mex cooking, Cheddar is the most frequently used cheese. One of the most distinct differences between Tex-Mex and American Southwest foods is the choice of cheese. In American Southwest cuisine, fresh goat cheese, or queso fresca, is used for traditional dishes. In Tex-Mex cooking, Cheddar and Monterey Jack are the cheeses used.

Queso Blanco Spanish for "white cheese." Queso blanco is the Mexican cheese Monterey Jack was named after. It became popular as an economical product that could be made with little equipment and even when only a small amount of milk was available.

Chicken-Fried Steak An original Texas recipe made with tenderized round steak or cubed steak coated with egg and flour and pan-fried. Local Texans usually refer to chicken-fried steak by the abbreviation CFS. Chicken-fried steak is traditionally served covered with a white cream gravy and with side dishes of mashed potatoes, green beans, and biscuits.

Chiles Chiles are considered the premier seasoning in Tex-Mex cooking. Over 7,000 varieties have been identified. The chile (of the genus Capsicum) is a member of the nightshade family, which also includes tomatoes and potatoes. The word *capsicum* is a from the Greek word *kapto,* meaning "to bite"—a reference to the chile's intense heat and pungent, biting flavor. This heat source, capsaisin, spreads unevenly throughout the inside of the pod and is concentrated in the ribs of the pod. The seeds are not sources of heat, but because of their proximity to the ribs, the seeds do occasionally absorb capsaicin through the preparation of the pepper. Aztecs called the peppers *chilli* or *chiltepin.* In 1912, a chemist named Wilbur Scoville measured the heat index of chiles by diluting ground chili in water until the heat dissipated. The result was Scoville units, measured in increments of 100. Scoville units go from 1 to 16 million, the latter of which was Scoville's rating of pure capsaicin, the chemical responsible for the chile's potent heat. A more modern version used by many chile writers is called Scoville Scale, with a rating of 0 to 10. Bell peppers rate a 0 because they contain no capsaicinoid. The Habanero rates highest with a 10 on the heat scale. A few of the more popular chiles include:

Anaheim, or Green Chile These mild green chiles (also called Big Jim or Colorado peppers) are among the most common varieties of chiles (rated 1 or 2 on the heat scale) and are best when roasted and peeled.

Poblano Chile A dark green chile that tapers down to a point and is 4 to 6 inches long. This chile is most often used for chile rellenos. It's relatively mild, about 3 or 4 on the heat scale. It is also known in its dried form as ancho chile.

Jalapeño Chile Named after the region of Jalapa, this is the most popular and well known chile in North America. A fairly spicy, small chile that turns from green to red as it matures, as with most chiles, the heat comes mainly from the seeds. The jalapeño is placed at about 5 on the heat scale.

Serrano Chile Literally meaning "highland" or "mountain," it is a small, fresh, hot chile measuring about $1^1/_2$ inches long. As it matures, it turns from dark green to red, then to yellow. Usually the smaller a serrano chile is in size, the hotter it is. It is placed at about 6 on the heat scale. The serrano chile is usually used when making pico de gallo.

Cayenne Pepper Almost always sold in its dried state, this chile is very popular as a powder. It registers about an 8 on the heat scale. Cayenne is used extensively in Cajun and Creole cooking.

Habanero Chile Closely related to the Caribbean Scotch Bonnet, this is the hottest chile known to man. Marble shaped and registering 10 on the heat scale, it comes in a variety of colors, including green, yellow, orange, and red.

The process of drying chiles concentrates their natural sugars and intensifies their flavors. Tex-Mex cooking professionals generally choose to blend their own chili powder by grinding a special mix of dried chiles in a coffee grinder. This technique is used to bring an exact flavor to a given recipe by carefully balancing the different flavors of various chiles. Select dried chiles that are clean and not discolored; they should not be faded, dusty, or broken. Freshly dried chiles will be relatively soft and supple, with a distinct aroma. The more popular dried chiles include:

Ancho Chile A ripe poblano chile that has been dried. This is the most commonly used dried chile in Tex-Mex cooking. It has an earthy, smoky flavor and is the basis for commercial chili powders and ranks 3 on the heat scale.

Cascabel Chile About $1^1/_2$ inches in diameter and shaped like an acorn. Cascabel chiles have a distinctive flavor and are dark orange to red in color. The seeds of the cascabel chile rattle in the pod, which explains the literal translation of its name, "jingle bell." Also known as the "rattler", it is about a 4 or 5 on the heat scale.

Chíltepin Chile Considered tiny, dried red-orange bullets of fiery heat, they are the Texas state native chile and are rated 9 on the heat scale.

Chipotle Chile A smoked and dried jalapeño. Chipotle chiles are brick red in color and available fresh as well as canned. They are moderately hot but possess a distinct, complex flavor with no equivalent substitute. The heat of chipotle chiles is placed at about 2 on the heat scale.

Pasilla Chile A dried chilaca, this chile's name means "little raisin." Long, dark, and wrinkled, this is an essential ingredient in many moles. It is about 3 or 4 on the heat scale, with smoky, dried fruit overtones.

Gebhardt's Chili Powder A popular brand of chili powder from San Antonio, Texas. Gebhardt's chili powder features ground dried chiles enhanced with herbs and spices.

Use caution in handling and storing chile peppers. When using fresh or dried chiles, wear gloves to protect your hands because the oils in the peppers can cause severe burns. Don't touch your face or eyes. If chiles come in contact with your bare hands, wash your hands thoroughly with soapy water. When grinding dried chiles, beware of the chile dust in the air, which will irritate eyes and throats.

Chile Relleno *Relleno* is Spanish for "stuffed." Authentic Tex-Mex chiles rellenos are fresh, large poblano chiles stuffed with cheese and dipped in egg batter. They are then pan-fried in oil and served with refried beans and rice.

Chili The official state dish of Texas, chili is a Tex-Mex adaptation of an American Southwest dish of meat (usually beef or pork) that is slowly simmered in a sauce made from dried chiles and spices. In Tex-Mex cooking, beans are never included. San Antonio is credited with being the birthplace of today's Texas chili. Back then, the market area was a central point for cattle drives, the army, missionaries, and railroad men. Women of the mission would prepare large kettles of traditional stews or chili and bring them to the plaza to feed the hungry crowds. These ladies were known as "chili queens" and this practice lasted until the early 1940s—until sanitation laws forced them out of business.

Chimichanga A burrito that has been deep-fried.

Chorizo A spicy Mexican sausage made with pork and seasonings. Mexican chorizo is made with fresh pork, while Spanish chorizo calls for smoked pork. The casing is usually removed before cooking.

Churro A light, crisp pastry dough made from cornmeal and sugar. The dough is piped out of a pastry bag into strips and deep-fried until golden brown. Churros are served sprinkled with cinnamon sugar.

Cilantro A highly aromatic herb related to parsley; it is used extensively in Tex-Mex cooking. Cilantro is also referred to as "Chinese parsley." The leaves of the herb are usually finely chopped and used as a condiment or as an ingredient in Tex-Mex recipes. The stems can be chopped and used in soups, beans, or anything that is simmered. The seeds of the plant are known as "coriander." When the seeds have been dried and ground to a fine, powdery consistency, the spice is referred to as "cumin" or "comino."

Colache A Tex-Mex version of ratatouille, using the procedure of respecting each vegetable's individual cooking time.

Enchilada A corn tortilla rolled with a filling made from cheese, beans, chicken, pork, or beef. Enchiladas are typically smothered with a thin, red, chile sauce, referred to as enchilada sauce, topped with Cheddar cheese, and baked in an oven until the cheese is completely melted.

Escabeche A method of pickling that is frequently used to prepare fish or vegetables. Escabeche is typically served as an appetizer, light entrée, or side dish. It is best served at room temperature after resting under refrigeration overnight. The resting process allows the flavor of the vegetables to fully develop.

Fajita An original Tex-Mex recipe made by grilling marinated skirt steak, then slicing it and serving it with smoked strips of green chiles and tortillas. Fajitas originated along the Rio Grande on the Texas-Mexico border and were typically eaten by cattle wranglers. The skirt steak (the diaphragm muscle of the steer) is the usual cut of meat used for fajitas. Skirt steaks were originally the discards given to the cowboys after cattle were slaughtered. Dramatic, but not authentic, the presentation of fajitas with sizzling bell peppers and onions on a hot, cast-iron plate is an adaptation created to market the menu item.

Flauta A white or yellow corn tortilla stuffed with beef, chicken, or pork. Flautas are rolled and pan- or deep-fried until crisp. They are usually about $^3/_4$ inch in diameter and served two or three to a plate. Flautas may be topped with cheese, sour cream, and guacamole.

Flan A Tex-Mex dessert similar to French crême caramel. Flan is made either as a pie and cut into slices or in individual cups.

Frijoles Spanish for "beans." After corn, beans are historically the most important ingredient in the Tex-Mex pantry. The pinto (from the word "painted," owing the brownish pink streaks on the beige bean) is the most used bean in this country.

Guacamole An avocado mixture made from the fruit's flesh. Guacamole is usually blended with lemon or lime juice, diced onion, and chopped cilantro. It is used as a side dish or condiment in numerous Tex-Mex dishes.

Jícama A crisp, crunchy root vegetable with a thick brown skin that must be removed prior to use. The flavor of jícama is similar to a mild apple crossed with a potato—this makes it excellent for use in salads and salsas. Some use it in place of water chestnuts. Unlike apples, the flesh of jícama does not turn brown after it is peeled. In Mexico, it is eaten thinly sliced, with a squeeze of lime and a dusting of cayenne.

Mole Derived from the Aztec word *molli,* meaning a "concoction," "stew," or "sauce." Mole is a complex dish woven together with dried chiles, nuts, seeds, vegetables, spices, and chocolate. Each local area has its own version of mole, from Texas to Arizona to Mexico. The most frequently seen are green mole, made with tomatillos, and red mole, made with pumpkin seeds. Mole is typically made as a sauce and used to braise meat and poultry items.

Nachos Made with tostadas (a "toasted chip") and the addition of toppings such as beans, meats, or cheese. They may also be served with guacamole and sour cream.

Nopales The whole paddles or pads of the prickly pear cactus. Nopalitos are cactus pads that have been peeled and cut into julienne. They are available in cans and jars. Some say that cactus pads have a flavor similar to green bell peppers. Others say nopales taste more like green beans. They are commonly used as an ingredient in salads. Nopalitos should be rinsed several times under cold water before using.

Pico de Gallo The literal translation is "beak of the rooster." Pico de gallo is an uncooked salsa made from tomatoes, onions, serrano chiles, and cilantro, all cut into a very small dice (as if pecked by a rooster).

Ranchero A Tex-Mex cooking term referring to the addition of tomatoes, bell peppers, and garlic in a recipe. Ranchero is usually used to describe a cooked salsa or a cooking technique, as in frijoles rancheros.

Refried Beans A well-known recipe frequently served in the Tex-Mex region. Refried beans are commonly referred to as "refritos" and are usually made from pinto beans. The Spanish word *refritos* means "well fried" but is frequently misinterpreted as refried or twice fried. Typically, pinto beans are cooked and drained, and then mashed with hot lard or bacon fat, seasonings, and sometimes chiles. Despite their name, refried beans are fried only once.

Ruby Red Grapefruit An important crop produced in Texas is the red grapefruit, which began as a mutation of the pink grapefruit tree. Today, all red grapefruits are descendants of the Ruby Red first grown in Mission, Texas, in the 1920s. The Ruby Red grapefruit was the first grapefruit to be granted a U.S. patent. During the 1970s, several important mutations found on the Ruby trees produced fruit even redder than the 1929 Ruby Red grapefruit. Dr. Richard Hensz—of Texas A&M University—spent many years in the laboratory working to produce the reddest grapefruit through mutations caused by ionizing radiation. In 1970, the Star Ruby variety was released, making it the first commercial grapefruit produced by artificial means. Red grapefruit contains high levels of a chemical called lycopene that studies have shown seems to prevent some cancers.

Salsa The Spanish word for "sauce." In Tex-Mex cooking, it refers to a relish or condiment, a mixture of chopped vegetables, fruits (usually tomatoes), and seasonings that may be cooked or uncooked, is usually not pureed, and is served as an accompaniment to a dish. Salsa that is blended finely in a food processor is usually called "picante sauce." Owing to an increased awareness of nutritional issues, salsas have risen in popularity because they are low in cholesterol, fat, and calories. Salsa has recently replaced tomato ketchup as the best-selling condiment in North America.

Salsa Verde Made from the tomatillo, a small, green Mexican fruit of the tomato family. Tomatillos are covered with a brown husk. They are used mainly in making fresh and cooked salsas. The tomatillos are simmered and then blended in a food processor with spices.

Taco A folded, grilled, or deep-fried corn tortilla typically filled with meat such as pork, beef, chicken, and more recently duck or fish. Tacos are usually topped with lettuce, tomatoes, and cheese and served with pico de gallo.

Tamale A traditional Tex-Mex recipe whose name is derived from the ancient Aztec word *tamalli.* Tamales are made from masa dough and typically are filled with shredded pork or beef. They are usually 5 or 6 inches long and about 1 inch thick. The tamale is wrapped in a soaked corn husk, steamed, and topped with red chili. Tamales are a Hispanic holiday tradition throughout Texas and are always served at Christmas and New Year.

Tortilla Spanish for "little cakes," which the conquistadors thought the Native American recipe resembled. Before the European colonists introduced wheat flour to the region, tortillas were made exclusively from the corn grown by the Native Americans and were the staple food. In Tex-Mex cooking, tortillas are a thin round made of either corn flour or wheat flour. Once the dough (called "masa") is made, the tortillas are formed in a tortilla press or hand-shaped by patting the dough. Tortillas are then cooked quickly on a hot skillet or griddle called a "coma." They are eaten either by themselves or with other Tex-Mex dishes. Corn tortillas are usually about 6 inches in diameter—much smaller than their flour counterparts, which can be as large as 24 inches around. Tortillas are also used to wrap a variety of Tex-Mex foods, such as beans, meats, and vegetables, and eaten like a taco.

Menus and Recipes from Texas and Tex-Mex Cuisine

MENU ONE

LBJ Pedernales River Chili

Jalapeño Cornbread

Crab Quesadillas with Green Chile Chutney

Lone Star Chicken-Fried Steak with Cream Gravy

Mashed Potatoes

Black-Eyed Peas

Mexican Wedding Cookies

MENU TWO

Caldo de Res

Pork Flautas

Guacamole

Pico de Gallo

Tex-Mex Plate

Shrimp Tacos with Green Chile Sauce

Cheese Enchiladas

Arroz a la Mexicana

Refried Beans

Flan

MENU THREE

Grilled Quesadillas

Tortilla Soup

Starburst Grapefruit Salad

Frijoles a la Charra

Tex-Mex Fajitas

OTHER RECIPES

Mole de Pollo

Braggin' Rights Brisket

Homemade Tamales

LBJ Pedernales River Chili 4 SERVINGS

AMOUNT	MEASURE	INGREDIENT
1 tablespoon	¹/₂ ounce, 14	Vegetable oil
1¹/₂ pounds	680 g	Beef chuck, in ¹/₂-inch (1.2 cm) cubes
2 cups	8 ounces, 226 g	Onions, ¹/₄ inch (.6 cm) dice
2	10 g	Garlic cloves, minced
¹/₂ teaspoon	1 g	Oregano (dried)
1 teaspoon	2 g	Ground cumin
1 tablespoon	¹/₄ ounce, 7 g	Chili powder
3 cups	18 ounces, 705 ml	Tomatoes, peeled, seeded, ¹/₄ inch (.6 cm) dice
1 cup	8 ounces, 235 ml	Beef stock, hot
to taste		Salt and black pepper

PROCEDURE

1 Heat the oil and brown the meat. (This step must be done in small batches.) Remove meat and set aside.

2 Add the onions and garlic, and cook 4 minutes or until vegetables begin to brown.

3 Add the spices and cook 2 minutes. Return the meat.

4 Add the tomatoes and stock; bring to a boil, then reduce to a simmer. Simmer 1 hour. Skim fat as it cooks out, adjust seasoning, and add more water if necessary.

Jalapeño Cornbread 4 SERVINGS

AMOUNT	MEASURE	INGREDIENT
3/4 cup	4 ounces, 113 g	Cornmeal
1 cup	5 ounces, 141 g	All-purpose flour
1 tablespoon	1/2 ounce, 15 g	Granulated sugar
1 tablespoon	1/2 ounce, 15 g	Baking powder
1/2 teaspoon	2 g	Salt
1 cup	8 ounces, 226 g	Cream-style corn
1 cup	4 ounces, 113 g	Cheddar cheese, shredded
1/2 cup	4 ounces, 113 g	Sour cream
2		Eggs, beaten
1/3 cup	2 ounces, 56 g	Poblano chile, roasted, peeled, seeded, 1/4 inch (.6 cm) dice
1		Jalapeño chile, seeded, minced

PROCEDURE

1 Preheat the oven to 400°F (205°C). Grease an 8-inch (20 cm) pan.

2 Combine the cornmeal, flour, sugar, baking powder, and salt.

3 Add the remaining ingredients and blend well. Do not overmix.

4 Pour into pan and bake 30 to 40 minutes or until it pulls away from the sides and the top is slightly brown.

Crab Quesadillas 4 SERVINGS

chef tip

These tortillas are made with masa harina, unlike the packaged tortillas that are found on store shelves.

AMOUNT	MEASURE	INGREDIENT
1 tablespoon	1/2 ounce, 15 g	Shortening or lard
1 cup	5 ounces, 141 g	Masa harina
1 tablespoon	7 g	All-purpose flour
1/2 cup	4 ounces, 115 ml	Chicken stock
1/4 teaspoon	2 g	Salt

For the Filling

AMOUNT	MEASURE	INGREDIENT
2 tablespoons	1 ounce, 28 ml	Vegetable oil
3/4 cup	3 ounces, 85 g	Onion, 1/4 inch (.6 cm) dice
1/2 cup	3 ounces, 85 g	Tomato, peeled, seeded, 1/4 inch (.6 cm) dice
1		chile, seeded, finely dice
8 ounces	226 g	Crab meat (claw or body)
several leaves		Epazote, chopped (optional)
to taste		Salt and black pepper
about 2 cups		Vegetable oil, for frying

PROCEDURE

1 Mix the lard, flour, and masa harina well.

2 Add the stock (may need a little more) and salt. Knead until the dough is pliable and leaves the sides of the bowl fairly clean.

3 Cover and let the dough rest about 1 hour.

4 Heat the 2 tablespoons (1 ounce, 30 ml) oil and add the onion, tomato, and jalapeño. Cook until mixture is soft and begins to dry out.

5 Fold in crab meat and epazote. Correct seasoning. Set aside.

6 Press out tortillas. If rolling out tortillas between sheets of waxed paper, it is fairly easy to peel the paper off one side, fill the tortilla, and use the other sheet of paper to help fold the tortilla dough around the filling.

7   Add 1 tablespoon stuffing to the middle of each tortilla. Fold in half and press edges together to seal. Repeat until all stuffing is used.

8   Heat the frying oil to 375°F (190°C).

9   Fry the quesadillas, turning once or twice, until golden. Transfer to paper towels to drain, then serve immediately.

green Chile Chutney 4 SERVINGS

AMOUNT	MEASURE	INGREDIENT
	16 ounces, 453 g	Anaheim chiles or New Mexico green chiles, roasted, peeled, 1/2 inch (1.2 cm) dice
2		Jalapeño chiles, roasted, peeled, seeded, 1/4 inch (.6 cm) dice
1 cup	7 ounces, 198 g	Granulated sugar
1 1/2 teaspoons		Mexican oregano, ground, toasted
1 ounce	28 g	Slivered almonds
2 tablespoons	1 ounce, 28 ml	Lime juice
6 tablespoons	3 ounces, 84 ml	Cider vinegar
1 teaspoon	5 g	Salt
1 tablespoon	3 g	Cilantro, chopped

PROCEDURE

1 Combine all ingredients except cilantro.

2 Bring to a boil and reduce heat to a simmer. Simmer 15 to 20 minutes.

3 Allow to cool, add cilantro, then serve cold.

Lone Star Chicken-Fried Steak with Cream Gravy 4 SERVINGS

chef tip

Chicken-fried steak is traditionally served with "the works"—white cream gravy, mashed potatoes, fresh corn or green beans, and biscuits. In Texas, it is considered "great" if the portion size is large enough to hang over the plate.

AMOUNT	MEASURE	INGREDIENT
2		Eggs
$^1/_2$ cup	4 ounces, 115 ml	Milk
1 cup	4 ounces, 113 g	All-purpose flour
1 teaspoon	5 g	Salt
$^1/_4$ teaspoon	1 g	Black pepper
4	5 ounces, 140 g each	Beef round steak, trimmed, and tenderized $^1/_2$ to $^1/_4$ inch (1.2–.6 cm) thick
as needed		Vegetable oil, for frying

PROCEDURE

1 Combine the eggs and milk, beat well.

2 Separately combine the flour, salt, and pepper.

3 Dip the steaks into the egg mixture, then into the seasoned flour.

4 Pan-fry steaks in hot oil until browned on both sides.

5 Drain on paper towels.

Lone Star Chicken-Fried Steak with Cream Gravy

Cream Gravy 4 SERVINGS

AMOUNT	MEASURE	INGREDIENT
2 tablespoons	1 ounce, 28 ml	Fat with drippings, from frying steaks
2 tablespoons	$^1/_2$ ounce, 15 g	All-purpose flour
2 cups	16 ounces, 470 ml	Milk, warmed
to taste		Salt and black pepper

PROCEDURE

1 Place the drippings in pan over medium-high heat. When hot, stir in the flour.

2 Remove from the heat and whisk in the warm milk.

3 Return to the heat and whisk until thickened and smooth. Cook 5 to 10 minutes.

4 Season with salt and pepper. Don't skimp on the pepper.

Black-Eyed Peas 4 SERVINGS

AMOUNT	MEASURE	INGREDIENT
1 cup	6 ounces, 170 g	Black-eyed peas (dried)
$^1/_4$ cup	2 ounces, 56 g	Bacon, $^1/_2$ inch (1.2 cm) dice
$^1/_2$ cup	2 ounces, 56 g	Onion, $^1/_2$ inch (1.2 cm) dice
1		Garlic clove, minced
1$^1/_4$ cups	10 ounces, 28 ml	Water, more if needed
1		Thyme sprig
2 ounces	56 g	Salt pork
to taste		Salt and black pepper

PROCEDURE

1 Soak the black-eyed peas overnight in water. Drain.

2 Over medium heat, render the bacon until almost crisp.

3 Add the onion and garlic, and cook about 4 minutes, or until the onion is soft.

4   Add the black-eyed peas, water, thyme, salt pork, and seasoning.

5   Bring to a boil. Reduce to a simmer, and cook 45 to 60 minutes, or until the black-eyed peas are tender.

6   Remove salt pork and serve.

Mashed Potatoes   4 SERVINGS

chef tip

Mashed potatoes can be made by either baking or boiling the potatoes. When boiling, do not cut the potatoes too small, as they will become waterlogged and prevent the finished mashed potatoes from being light and fluffy, which is the desired texture for this starch. A ricer is a culinary tool frequently used to mash potatoes.

AMOUNT	MEASURE	INGREDIENT
5 cups	1 1/2 pounds, 680 g	Russet potatoes, peeled, quartered
1/2 teaspoon		Salt
2/3 cup	5 ounces, 156 ml	Heavy cream, warmed
1/4 cup	2 ounces, 56 ml	Butter, softened
to taste		Salt

PROCEDURE

1   Cover the potatoes with cold water, add salt, bring to a boil, and simmer until tender, approximately 25 minutes.

2   Drain the potatoes and return to the pot. Cook over low heat for approximately 3 minutes to allow them to dry.

3   Mash, grind, or rice the potatoes.

4   Blend in the butter and cream (adjust the consistency as desired with warm cream or milk).

5   Season to taste with salt.

Mexican Wedding Cookies
YIELDS ABOUT 4 DOZEN COOKIES

AMOUNT	MEASURE	INGREDIENT
1 cup	8 ounces, 226 g	Unsalted butter, softened
1/2 cup	2 ounces, 56 g	Confectioners' sugar, sifted
1 tablespoon	15 ml	Vanilla extract
2 1/4 cups	10 ounces, 283 g	All-purpose flour
1/2 tablespoon	1/4 ounce, 8 g	Salt
3/4 cup	3 ounces, 85 g	Pecans, finely chopped
as needed		Confectioners' sugar, to roll the cookies in

PROCEDURE

1 Cream the butter and sugar, and then add vanilla.

2 Sift the flour and salt together and stir in by hand.

3 Add pecans; stir to combine.

4 Chill the dough for 1 hour.

5 Preheat the oven to 400°F (205°C).

6 Roll the dough into 1-inch (2.5 cm) balls. Place on an ungreased cookie sheet.

7 Bake until set, but do not brown, approximately 15 minutes.

8 While still warm, roll in additional sugar.

9 Cool, roll in sugar again, and serve.

Caldo de Res 4 SERVINGS

chef tip

This Mexican beef soup is garnished with slices of corn still on the cob for an authentic presentation.

AMOUNT	MEASURE	INGREDIENT
I piece	16 ounces, 453 g	Beef shank or chuck
3	9 ounces, 255 g	Red-skin new potatoes
2	10 ounces, 283 g	Carrots, peeled, whole
I	6 ounces, 170 g	Onion, peeled, whole
2 quarts	2 l	Water, cold
I		Corn on the cob, cleaned, in 1-inch (2.5 cm) slices
$^1/_2$ teaspoon	I g	Thyme
I		Bay leaf
I		Parsley sprig
I cup	8 ounces, 226 g	Green cabbage, 1 inch (2.5 cm) dice
$^1/_2$ cup	2 ounces, 56 g	Zucchini squash, 1-inch (2.5 cm) cubes
to taste		Salt and black pepper
I tablespoon	$^1/_2$ ounce, 14 g	Lime juice
2 tablespoons	6 g	Cilantro, chopped

PROCEDURE

1 Wash and rinse meat and all whole vegetables. Place in a large pot with the cold water.

2 Add the corn, cabbage, thyme, bay leaf, parsley, salt, and pepper.

3 Bring to a simmer over low heat; simmer until all ingredients are cooked and tender. As ingredients become tender, remove them from the pot.

4 Let vegetables cool, and cut into 1-inch (2.5 cm) cubes or bite-size pieces.

5 Strain the stock and reduce until very flavorful.

6 Remove the fat and cartilage from the beef. Dice the meat into $^1/_2$-inch (1.2 cm) pieces.

7 Return the diced meat and chopped vegetables to the broth and bring to a simmer.

8 Add the zucchini and correct the seasoning. Remove bay leaf.

9 Add the lime juice and cilantro just before serving.

Pork Flautas 4 SERVINGS

AMOUNT	MEASURE	INGREDIENT
as needed		Vegetable oil
3¹/₂ cups	18 ounces, 510 g	Pork Deshebrada (below)
12		6-inch (15.2 cm) corn tortillas
2 cups	4 ounces, 113 g	Iceberg lettuce, shredded
¹/₄ cup	2 ounces, 55 ml	Sour cream

PROCEDURE

1   Heat a sauté pan with ¹/₂ inch (1.2 cm) of oil until hot but not smoking.

2   Place some Deshebrada pork in a strip on one side of each tortilla. Roll up the tortillas as tight as possible, using toothpicks to help secure them, if needed.

3   Fry the flautas a few at a time in the oil until crisp, 1 to 2 minutes. Drain on paper towels and keep warm.

4   To serve, arrange flautas on shredded lettuce and top with Guacamole (page 310) and sour cream.

Pork Deshebrada 4 SERVINGS

AMOUNT	MEASURE	INGREDIENT
For the Red Chile Puree		
9	3 ounces, 85 g	New Mexico red chiles (dried)
2 cups	16 ounces, 470 ml	Water
1 cup	4 ounces, 113 g	Onion, in chunks
2		Garlic cloves
	5–6 pounds, 2.26–2.72 k	Pork shoulder roast, bone-in
1¹/₂ cups	6 ounces, 170 g	Onions, thinly sliced
		Garlic cloves, finely chopped
2 teaspoons	2 g	Oregano (dried)

2 teaspoons	2 g	Ground cumin, preferably from toasted seeds
2 teaspoons	2 g	Salt
I quart	32 ounces, I I	Chicken stock
to taste		Salt and black pepper

PROCEDURE

1. Toast the chiles in a 300°F (149°C) oven for 4 minutes or until they smell toasted. Cool slightly.

2. Discard stems and seeds. Combine chiles, water, onion, and garlic in a saucepan. Simmer until soft, about 30 minutes.

3. Remove from heat and cool slightly.

4. In blender or food processor, blend until smooth. Rub the puree through a fine strainer and discard residue. Set aside

5. Preheat the oven to 375°F (190°C).

6. Lay the pork, fat side up, in a braising pan.

7. Combine $^3/_4$ cup (6 ounces, 170 ml) red chile puree and stock.

8. Top pork with onion, garlic, oregano, cumin, and salt.

9. Add chile liquid and bring to a simmer. Cover and braise pork for up to 4 hours or until fork-tender. (You may also cut the meat into smaller pieces to shorten cooking time.)

10. Cool pork in braising liquid. Transfer to a cutting board, trim fat, and remove bone.

11. Shred meat by using the tines of 2 forks, one held in each hand. Shred the meat in a downward, pulling motion.

12. Strain and degrease broth. If holding the meat, use broth to moisten.

Guacamole 4 SERVINGS

chef tip

Guacamole should be mixed by hand. Use a fork to blend the ingredients until the mixture has a chunky consistency. Do not use a blender or food processor, as the consistency will be too thin. For a more distinctive appearance, split the avocado, remove the seed, and with a paring knife, cut through the flesh, making ¹/₄-inch (.6 cm) slices both vertically and horizontally down to the skin. Using a tablespoon, scoop the sliced flesh out of the skin. The result is a small dice that can then be mixed gently with the other ingredients.

Guacamole naturally oxidizes and turns brown if stored overnight. To reuse the guacamole, carefully skim the oxidized portion away and discard. Do not mix it in. To prevent oxidation, a little lemon juice can be spread over the top of the guacamole before storing.

AMOUNT	MEASURE	INGREDIENT
2	12 ounces, 340 g	Avocados, ripe
¹/₂ cup	2 ounces, 56 g	Red onion, ¹/₄ inch (.6 cm) dice
1		Jalapeño chile, seeded, deribbed, minced
¹/₄ cup	¹/₂ ounce, 15 g	Cilantro leaves
¹/₂ cup	3 ounces, 85 g	Tomato, peeled, seeded, ¹/₄ inch (.6 cm) dice
2 tablespoons	1 ounce, 28 ml	Lemon juice
¹/₂ teaspoon	3 g	Salt
¹/₈ teaspoon	1 g	White pepper
1 tablespoon	¹/₂ ounce, 15 ml	Lime juice

PROCEDURE

1 Peel and pit the avocados.

2 Place the avocado pulp in a bowl and mash to a chunky texture.

3 Add the remaining ingredients and mix thoroughly. Season to taste.

Pico de gallo 4 SERVINGS

AMOUNT	MEASURE	INGREDIENT
1 tablespoon	1/2 ounce, 15 ml	Olive oil
1		Garlic clove, minced
1 cup	4 ounces, 113 g	Onion, 1/4 inch (.6 cm) dice
1		Serrano pepper, minced
1 1/2 tablespoons	5 g	Cilantro, minced
1 cup	6 ounces, 170 g	Tomato, peeled, seeded, 1/4 inch (.6 cm) dice
1 tablespoon	1/2 ounce, 15 ml	Lime juice
to taste		Salt and black pepper

PROCEDURE

1. Heat the oil over medium heat. Add the garlic, onion, chile, and cilantro. Toss and remove from heat. Let cool.

2. Combine onion mixture with remaining ingredients and correct seasoning. Serve warm or at room temperature.

Shrimp Tacos

Shrimp Tacos 4 SERVINGS

AMOUNT	MEASURE	INGREDIENT
For the Green Chile Sauce		
16 ounces	453 g	Tomatillos (about 8) husked
2 tablespoons	1 ounce, 30 g	Shallots, chopped
2		Garlic cloves, chopped
1 cup	4 ounces, 112 g	Poblano or Anaheim chiles, roasted, peeled, chopped
1/4 cup	1/2 ounce, 15 g	Cilantro, chopped
1		Jalapeño chile, seeded, chopped
1 tablespoon	1/2 ounce, 15 ml	Lime juice
as needed		Water
to taste		Salt
1/4 cup	2 ounces, 55 ml	Vegetable oil
For the Tacos		
8		Corn tortillas, prepared
1 cup	4 ounces, 113 g	Onion, 1/4 inch (.6 cm) dice
1/2 cup	2 ounces, 56 g	Green bell pepper, julienned
1/2 cup	2 ounces, 56 g	Red bell pepper, julienned
1		Garlic clove, minced
1		Serrano chile, finely diced
16	16 ounces, 454 g	Shrimp, peeled, cleaned (16–20 count)
2 cups	4 ounces, 113 g	Iceberg lettuce, shredded

PROCEDURE

1 Blanch half the tomatillos in boiling water for 1 minute. Cool quickly.

2 Puree with remaining sauce ingredients in a blender. Add water to achieve the desired consistency. Adjust seasoning. Set aside.

3 Heat the oil to 375°F (190°C) and fry the tortillas. While tortillas are still pliable, fold one half over the other—not too tightly as there should be an opening of about 2 inches (5 cm) between the halves at the top. Turn as the tortillas become crisp to make sure they are done on both sides and at the fold in the bottom. (It may be necessary to insert tongs in the middle to keep them from closing up. The result should be a crisp, U-shaped cup.)

4 Drain on paper towels, and keep warm.

5 Reheat the oil and add the onion, peppers, garlic, and chile. Cook until limp but not soft.

6 Add the shrimp and cook until firm, approximately 2 minutes.

7 Place the mixture in the tortillas.

8 Top with warm sauce and fill with lettuce.

Cheese Enchiladas 4 SERVINGS

 *chef tip*

This chili gravy is essential for enchiladas, tamales, and a host of other Tex-Mex dishes. The taste of chili gravy explains Tex-Mex cuisine more eloquently than words ever will. The thick brown gravy with Mexican spices is neither Mexican nor American. It wasn't created in the homes of Texas Mexicans, either. It was invented in old-fashioned Mexican restaurants that catered to Anglo tastes. But what's amazing about it today is the way it illustrates how our tastes have changed.

AMOUNT	MEASURE	INGREDIENT
For the Chile Gravy		
2 tablespoons	I ounce, 28 g	Lard or butter
$^1/_2$ cup	2 ounces, 56 g	Onion, $^1/_4$ inch (.6 cm) dice
I		Garlic clove, minced
$^1/_4$ cup	I ounce, 28 g	All-purpose flour
2 tablespoons	I ounce, 28 g	Chili powder
I teaspoon	2 g	Ground cumin
$^1/_8$ teaspoon		Oregano (dried)
2 cups	16 ounces, 470 ml	Beef stock
to taste		Salt and black pepper
For the Enchiladas		
8		Corn tortillas
$^1/_4$ cup	2 ounces, 55 ml	Vegetable oil
$^1/_2$ cup	2 ounces, 56 g	Onion, $^1/_4$ inch (.6 cm) dice
2 cups	8 ounces, 226 g	Longhorn cheese, grated

PROCEDURE

1   Melt the lard over medium heat. Sauté the onion and garlic until the onion is softened but not browned, 3 minutes.

2   Stir in the flour, chili powder, cumin, and oregano. Cook for 2 minutes while stirring.

3   Add the beef stock, a little at a time, stirring well. Simmer, uncovered, for 30 minutes, until mixture is reduced and thickened.

4   Adjust thickness and seasoning. Set aside.

5   Preheat the oven to 400°F (205°C). Heat the oil in a deep-fat fryer to 350°F (175°C).

6   Pick up a tortilla with tongs and place it into the hot oil for about 15 seconds. This first step is to soften the tortilla.

7   Remove the tortilla from the oil, letting the excess oil drip back. Dip the tortilla into the chili gravy, coating both sides.

8   Place the now-coated tortilla in the pan, put a handful of onion and cheese on one edge of the tortilla, and roll it up. Place the rolled tortilla seam side down in one end of a lightly greased pan.

9   Repeat the process with the remaining tortillas. The pan should be full.

10 Pour the remaining chili gravy on top of the enchiladas.

11 Sprinkle the enchiladas generously with the remaining grated cheese.

12 Bake for about 10 minutes, until the cheese is bubbly. Serve immediately.

Arroz a la Mexicana 4 SERVINGS

AMOUNT	MEASURE	INGREDIENT
2 tablespoons	1 ounce, 28 ml	Vegetable oil
1/2 cup	2 ounces, 56 g	Onion, 1/4 inch (.6 cm) dice
1		Garlic clove, minced
1 cup	7 ounces, 198 g	Long-grain rice, washed twice
1/2 cup	2 ounces, 56 g	Carrot, 1/4 inch (.6 cm) dice
1 cup	6 ounces, 170 g	Tomato, peeled, seeded, 1/4 inch (.6 cm) dice
2 cups	16 ounces, 470 ml	Chicken stock
to taste		Salt and black pepper

PROCEDURE

1 Heat the oil over high heat. Add the rice and sauté, stirring frequently, until it begins to brown.

2 Stir in the onion and garlic. Cook, stirring constantly, until the rice is nicely browned and has a nutty aroma.

3 Add the carrot, tomato, stock, and seasoning. Bring to a simmer, cover, reduce the heat, and simmer for approximately 20 minutes.

4 Remove cover and cook 5 minutes longer. Fluff the rice with a fork and serve.

Refried Beans 4 SERVINGS

chef tip

The bacon fat in this recipe can be replaced with a simple vegetable oil if a more nutritionally sound dish is desired. In the American Southwest, authentic refried beans call for smoking-hot lard to be poured over the cooked, mashed pinto beans and stirred in, thus the name refried beans. Owing to the unusually high cholesterol content of lard, we use a small amount of bacon fat and refry the beans from the bottom as opposed to the traditional procedure. A cast-iron frying pan yields the best results, however, a nonstick pan will also work.

AMOUNT	MEASURE	INGREDIENT
1 cup	8 ounces, 226 g	Pinto beans, dried
1 1/2 quarts	1.5 l	Chicken stock
2 ounces	56 g	Bacon, 1/4 inch (.6 cm) dice
1/2 cup	2 ounces, 56 g	Onion, 1/4 inch (.6 cm) dice
1		Garlic clove, minced
to taste		Salt and black pepper
1 cup	4 ounces, 112 ml	Queso fresco, grated

PROCEDURE

1 Wash and soak the beans overnight.

2 Drain the beans and add the stock. Bring to a simmer, turn down the heat, and simmer for approximately 1 1/2 hours, or until tender.

3 Render the bacon over medium heat, until almost crisp. Add the onion and garlic and cook 4 minutes.

4 Add the beans. Using the back of a large wooden spoon or a potato masher, mash the beans into the bottom of the pan, stirring frequently so they do not stick. When the beans are broken up but still have visible pieces, simmer for a few minutes.

5 Season with salt and pepper, and serve with grated cheese.

Flan 4 SERVINGS

chef tip

The process of tempering is done in this recipe to prevent the eggs from cooking or scrambling when placed in the scalded milk. To temper the eggs, stir approximately 4 to 6 fluid ounces of the scalded milk into the beaten eggs to warm them gradually, then stir the egg mixture into the remaining scalded milk.

AMOUNT	MEASURE	INGREDIENT
³/₄ cup	6 ounces, 169 g	Granulated sugar
I tablespoon	¹/₂ ounce, 14 ml	Water
¹/₂ teaspoon		Lemon juice
I¹/₂ cups	12 ounces, 352 ml	Milk
4		Eggs
¹/₂ cup	4 ounces, 115 ml	Condensed milk
I tablespoon	14 ml	Vanilla extract

PROCEDURE

1   Combine ¹/₄ cup (2 ounces, 56 g) sugar, the water, and a few drops of fresh lemon juice in a pan. Over moderate heat, caramelize the sugar, cooking to golden brown. Do not overcook.

2   Pour the sugar into 4 ramekins. Set aside.

3   Preheat the oven to 325°F (163°C). Heat water for a hot-water bath.

4   Heat the milk in a nonreactive pan to just before a simmer and remove from the heat.

5   Combine the eggs, remaining sugar, condensed milk, and vanilla and pour in some hot milk to temper the eggs. Pour in the remainder of the milk and strain.

6   Pour the custard into the ramekins and pour hot water halfway up the side of the molds after the pan is in the oven. Bake until set, about 30 minutes. Test by inserting the blade of a knife into the center of the custard, taking care not to pierce the bottom of the flan. If the blade comes out clean, then it is cooked.

7   Remove from heat and cool completely before unmolding. Do not cool in refrigerator. (With the tip of a paring knife, go around the top where the custard is baked onto the ramekin, turn the ramekin upside down onto a dessert plate, and shake the ramekin sideways to release the custard.

Grilled Quesadillas 4 SERVINGS

AMOUNT	MEASURE	INGREDIENT
4		Flour tortillas, 8 inches (20 cm) in diameter
2 cups	8 ounces, 226 g	Mexican cheese (Oaxaca, Chihuahua, or asadero) or whole milk mozzarella, thinly sliced or shredded
2 tablespoons	1 ounce, 28 g	Poblano chile, roasted, peeled, $1/4$ inch (.6 cm) dice
2 tablespoons	6 g	Cilantro leaves, chopped
2 tablespoons	1 ounce, 28 ml	Butter, melted

PROCEDURE

1 Soften the tortillas by heating a nonstick skillet over medium-high heat for about 3 minutes. Put tortillas in a skillet one by one, turning each once until soft.

2 Prepare a grill.

3 Place some cheese on half of each tortilla, leaving a 1-inch (2.5 cm) border.

4 Top with chile and cilantro, and fold over.

5 Brush both sides liberally with melted butter. Place on grill. When marked, turn over and continue to cook until cheese melts.

6 Serve with Pico de Gallo (page 311) and Guacamole (page 310).

Tortilla Soup 4 SERVINGS

chef tip

This soup was originally created in order to use leftover tortillas.

AMOUNT	MEASURE	INGREDIENT
1 cup	4 ounces, 113 g	Onion, quartered
2 cups	12 ounces, 340 g	Plum tomatoes, quartered
1/4 cup	2 ounces, 55 ml	Vegetable oil
1		Corn tortilla, cut into short strips
2		Garlic cloves, minced
1/2		Ancho chile, stemmed, seeded, toasted, finely chopped
1/2		Bay leaf
1 teaspoon	2 g	Ground cumin
3 cups	24 ounces, 705 ml	Chicken stock
1/4 cup	2 ounces, 56 g	Tomato sauce
to taste		Salt and black pepper
2 cups	8 ounces, 226 g	Chicken meat, cooked, julienned
1 cup	4 ounces, 113 g	Cheddar or Monterey Jack cheese, shredded
1 cup	4 ounces, 113 g	Avocado, peeled, pitted, cubed
1 cup	4 ounces, 112 g	Corn tortilla, fried strips

PROCEDURE

1 Rub the onion and tomatoes with the oil and grill on all sides until well charred, 15 to 20 minutes. You may also do this on a sheet pan under the broiler.

2 Put the tomatoes and onion in a blender or processor and blend until smooth. Set aside.

3 Heat the remaining oil. Add the tortilla, garlic, and chile and sauté for 3 to 4 minutes.

4 Add the bay leaf, cumin, and stock; bring to a boil.

5 Stir in the tomato mixture and the tomato sauce. Simmer for 30 minutes.

6 Season and strain through a coarse strainer. Taste and adjust seasoning.

7 Heat the soup and serve. Garnish with the chicken, cheese, avocado, and crisp tortilla strips.

Tortilla Soup

Starburst Grapefruit Salad · 4 SERVINGS

AMOUNT	MEASURE	INGREDIENT
2	26 ounces, 737 g, total	Texas Ruby Red grapefruits, peeled, sectioned
1 1/2 cups	8 ounces, 226 g	Strawberries, stemmed, cut in half
2 tablespoonns	1 ounce, 28 ml	Sherry vinegar
1/2 tablespoon	1/4 ounce, 8 g	Granulated sugar
1 tablespoon	1/2 ounce, 15 g	Shallot, finely diced
1/4 teaspoon	2 g	Salt
1/4 cup	2 ounces, 55 ml	Vegetable oil
1/2 teaspoon	1 g	Poppy seeds
1/2 teaspoon	3 g	Grapefruit zest
4 cups	8 ounces, 226 g	Spinach, cleaned in bite-size pieces

PROCEDURE

1 Peel and section the grapefruits over a bowl, reserving the juice and sections for the salad and dressing.

2 Combine the grapefruit sections and strawberries in a bowl. Toss gently and reserve until needed.

3 In a blender, combine the vinegar, sugar, shallot, reserved grapefruit juice, and salt. Process until smooth.

4 Slowly drizzle the oil through the hole in the lid while the blender is running and process until the dressing has thickened.

5 Remove from the blender and stir in the poppy seeds and grapefruit zest.

6 Toss the grapefruit and strawberries with the poppy-seed dressing.

7 Arrange spinach on chilled plates. Place the grapefruit sections and strawberries on top. Serve immediately.

Starburst Grapefruit Salad

Frijoles a la Charra 4 SERVINGS

chef tip

For a little variety, add 4 ounces (120 g) each medium-diced carrots and celery. To prepare frijoles borrachos, substitute beef stock for chicken stock. To prepare frijoles fronterizos, substitute 8 ounces (240 g) chorizo sausage for the pork and bacon called for in the recipe.

AMOUNT	MEASURE	INGREDIENT
1 1/4 cups	8 ounces, 226 g	Pinto beans (dried)
1 quart	32 ounces, 1 l	Chicken stock
1/3 cup	2 ounces, 56 g	Boneless pork butt, 1/2 inch (1.2 cm) dice
1/4 cup	2 ounces, 56 g	Bacon, 1/4 inch (.6 cm) dice
1 cup	4 ounces, 113 g	Onion, 1/4 inch (.6 cm) dice
2		Garlic cloves, minced
1/3 cup	2 ounces, 55 ml	Poblano chile, charred, peeled, 1/4 inch (.6 cm) dice
1 cup	6 ounces, 170 g	Tomato, peeled, seeded, 1/4 inch (.6 cm) dice
1/2 teaspoon	3 g	Salt
1/4 teaspoon	1 g	Oregano (dried)
1/4 teaspoon		Ground cumin
1/2 cup	1 ounce, 28 g	Cilantro, chopped

PROCEDURE

1 Wash and soak the pinto beans overnight. Drain.

2 Combine the beans, stock, and pork. Simmer for 1 hour.

3 Sauté the bacon in a sauté pan; remove when crisp and reserve.

4 To bacon fat, add the onion, garlic, and poblano; cook 2 minutes.

5 Add the tomato and cook 2 minutes.

6 Add the tomato mixture to the beans. Add seasonings and herbs and simmer 30 minutes longer.

7 Adjust the seasoning, stir in the cilantro, and garnish with bacon.

Tex-Mex Fajitas 4 SERVINGS

Texans would love to be able to lay claim to having originated fajitas, but the honor goes to the south-of-the-border *vaqueros* who learned to make good use of a tough and membranous cut of beef known as "skirt steak."

Before fajitas became popular throughout the United States, skirt steak was a cheap cut of meat scorned by all but the most dedicated beefeaters. The Mexican term for grilled skirt steak is *arracheras*, and its American counterpart is fajitas. Therefore, the term "chicken fajitas" is not truly possible. But these days, the word fajita has come to describe just about anything cooked and eaten, rolled up, in a flour tortilla. The only true fajitas, however, are made from skirt steak.

Fajitas start with the marinade. Marinades for beef fajitas rely on acid ingredients like lime juice not just for flavor but also to tenderize the meat. So that the marinade will have time to work, beef fajitas should be marinated several hours or up to 24 hours. The skirt steak is the traditional cut used and was reserved primarily for the chief cowboy. Other cuts of beef can be substituted, such as flank steak or sirloin, but the skirt is by far the most tender, flavorful, and authentic.

You might be wondering where the cast-iron griddle with the sizzling bell peppers and onions are in their recipe. While such a serving method may be dramatic, it is an affectation developed mainly by chain restaurants and is not a part of authentic Tex-Mex fajitas.

AMOUNT	MEASURE	INGREDIENT
Marinade I		
1/3 cup	2 1/2 ounces, 78 ml	Lime juice
1/4 cup	2 ounces, 55 ml	Tequila
I teaspoon	I g	Oregano (dried), crushed (preferably Mexican oregano)
2		Garlic cloves, crushed
I tablespoon	3 g	Cilantro, minced
2 teaspoons	4 g	Ground cumin
I teaspoon	2 g	Black pepper
Marinade II		
I cup	8 ounces, 235 m	Light soy sauce
1/4 cup	2 ounces, 156 g	Brown sugar, packed

1 teaspoon	2 g	Garlic powder
1 teaspoon	2 g	Onion powder
2 tablespoons	1 ounce, 28 ml	Lemon juice
1 teaspoon	5 g	Ground ginger

For the Fajitas

1 pound	453 g	Skirt steak
8		Flour tortillas, 8 inches (20 cm), warmed

PROCEDURE

1   For Marinade I, combine all ingredients and mix well. Refrigerate overnight, or up to 24 hours. For Marinade II, combine soy sauce, brown sugar, garlic, onion powder, lemon juice, and ginger. Mix well and let stand refrigerated overnight.

2   Marinate the steak in either marinade for 2 hours at room temperature, or overnight in the refrigerator. Remove from the marinade and dry with paper towels.

3   Preheat the grill until hot.

4   Sear the outside of the meat, then cook until medium-rare—it should take 3 to 4 minutes a side if the meat is $3/4$ inch (1.9 cm) thick or less. Brush meat with marinade 2 or 3 times while cooking

5   Transfer the meat to a cutting board. Let sit 5 minutes.

6   Cut the meat into thin strips.

7   Serve meat strips with warm, soft flour tortillas and Pico de Gallo (page 311) and Guacamole (page 310).

Mole de Pollo 4 SERVINGS

AMOUNT	MEASURE	INGREDIENT
2 tablespoons	1 ounce, 28 ml	Vegetable oil
1	3 pounds, 1.36 kg	Chicken, cut into 8 pieces
2	3 ounces, 85 g	Ancho chiles
2	3 ounces, 85 g	Cascabel chiles
2 cups	16 ounces, 470	Chicken stock
2 cups	8 ounces, 226 g	Onion, 1/2 inch (1.2 cm) dice
3		Garlic cloves, minced
2		Cilantro sprigs
1 cup	6 ounces, 170 g	Tomato, peeled, seeded, 1/2 inch (1.2 cm) dice
1/4 cup	1 ounce, 28 g	Almonds, sliced
1/8 teaspoon		Ground cloves
1/8 teaspoon		Ground cinnamon
1/4 teaspoon		Ground cumin
1/2 tablespoon	1/2 ounce, 15 g	Lard or shortening
4 tablespoons	1 ounce, 28 g	Chocolate, unsweetened, crushed
to taste		Salt and white pepper
4 tablespoons	1 ounce, 28 g	Sesame seeds, toasted

PROCEDURE

1. Heat the oil over medium heat and brown chicken pieces on all sides. Remove chicken and reserve.

2. Rehydrate the dried chiles by simmering them in a small, covered pot of water for 10 minutes. Remove the chiles from the water and cool. Remove skins, stems, and seeds.

3. Place chiles, 1 cup (8 ounces, 235 ml) of stock, onion, garlic, cilantro, tomato, almonds, and spices in a blender and puree.

4. Heat the lard in a pan. Add the puree and simmer over low heat, for 5 minutes.

5. Add the remaining stock. Add the chocolate. Stir to incorporate.

6. Add the dark pieces of chicken and simmer until almost cooked, about 15 minutes.

Mole de Pollo

7   Add the breast meat and continue to cook for an additional 15 minutes, or until all pieces of chicken are cooked. Correct seasoning.

8   Serve sauce over the chicken. Garnish with toasted sesame seeds.

Braggin' Rights Brisket 8 OUNCES

chef tip

Hardwoods such as hickory, pecan, or oak are very slow burning and are the best hardwoods for slow smoking. Mesquite, although very aromatic and great for grilling, burns too hot to be used for barbeque and leaves an oily taste to the meat. Notwithstanding, mesquite is still commonly used in West Texas. True Texas barbeque takes place in a long, narrow pit. A fire is built at one end and several inches or more separate the meat from it. The meat is cooked slowly at a very low temperature for up to 6 hours, during which time sauce is liberally applied from time to time.

AMOUNT	MEASURE	INGREDIENT
4 pounds	1.8 kg	Beef brisket, untrimmed
2 teaspoons	4 g	Black pepper
I teaspoon	2 g	Cayenne
I teaspoon	2 g	Onion salt
¹/₂ teaspoon	I g	Dry mustard
as needed		Hickory, pecan, or mesquite chips, soaked
2 tablespoons	12 g	Salt

PROCEDURE

1 Season the brisket with the peppers, onion salt, and mustard.

2 Organize your smoker as indicated in the illustrations.

3 Sear the brisket on the grill (or in a roasting pan over very high heat for 5 minutes on each side). Brown both sides thoroughly.

4 Place the brisket into the smoker and smoke for 1 hour.

5 Sprinkle with the salt and smoke for an additional 1 hour.

6 Preheat the oven to 300°F (149°C).

7 Cover brisket with foil and bake until it becomes fork-tender.

lid

product to be smoked

rack

drip tray

hardwood chips

smoke roasting pan

8   Remove roast from the oven and let rest for 25 minutes, covered loosely with aluminum foil. (Reserve the rendered fat from the brisket to use in the preparation of the barbeque sauce.)

9   Pull the meat apart to create a shredded effect or slice the brisket across the grain. Serve on hot plates and top with barbeque sauce.

Barbeque Sauce   1 QUART

Hot pepper sauce comes in hundreds of varieties, flavors, and levels of heat. Tabasco is one of the most popular hot pepper sauces available in America. Feel free to experiment until you find the hot sauce that yields the ideal flavor for your special barbeque sauce recipe.

AMOUNT	MEASURE	INGREDIENT
$1/2$ cup	4 ounces, 115 ml	Rendered fat from barbequed meat
$1/3$ cup	$1 1/2$ ounces, 43g	Onion, small dice
$1 1/2$ cups	12 ounces, 352 ml	Ketchup
$1/2$ cup	4 ounces, 115 ml	Worcestershire sauce
$1/2$ cup	4 ounces, 115 ml	Lemon juice
$1/3$ cup	$2 1/2$ ounces, 71g	Brown sugar
6 tablespoons	3 ounces, 84 ml	Water
to taste		Hot pepper sauce

PROCEDURE

1   Heat the rendered fat in a small saucepot. Add the onion and sauté until translucent, 3 minutes.

2   Add the ketchup, Worcestershire sauce, and lemon juice. Lower the heat and stir in the brown sugar and water. Simmer for 15 minutes.

3   Season to taste with hot pepper sauce.

Homemade Tamales 18 TAMALES

chef tip

The shredded beef and pork can also be prepared by simmering the meats in water until fork-tender. A chicken filling can be made by boiling chicken with seasonings such as cumin, chili powder, garlic, and salt; once cooked, the chicken meat should be removed from the bones and shredded. Simply substituting refried beans for the shredded meat can make bean tamales. A thin slice of jalapeño or a strip of fried bacon can be added to the beans for extra flavor, if desired.

Making genuine, homemade Tex-Mex-style tamales is a three-day process: one day to prepare the meat filling, a second day to prepare and roll the tamales, and a third day to steam and serve the tamales. However, a number of techniques are used today to speed this process. One method we recommend, if time is of the essence, is to substitute coarse-ground pork and/or beef for the roast meats used in the filling. The ground meat can be quickly cooked, seasoned, and cooled. Then the seasoned ground meat can be used to fill the tamales without the lengthy resting period needed to make the traditional shredded-meat filling.

AMOUNT	MEASURE	INGREDIENT
12 ounces	340 g	Pork butt roast
6 ounces	170 g	Beef chuck roast or bottom round
	1 ounce, 28 g	Ancho chiles
1 tablespoon	$^1/_2$ ounce, 15 g	Garlic, minced
1 cup	8 ounces, 226 g	Lard
1 tablespoon	$^1/_4$ ounce, 7 g	Ground cumin
1 teaspoon	$^1/_8$ ounce, 3 g	Black pepper
$^1/_2$ teaspoon	1 g	Oregano (dried)
to taste		Salt
18		Cornhusks
1$^1/_2$ pounds	680 g	Masa (or $^3/_4$ pound, 340 g masa harina, reconstituted)
1 tablespoon	$^1/_4$ ounce, 7 g	Chili powder
1 tablespoon	$^1/_4$ ounce, 7 g	Paprika
3 tablespoons	$^3/_4$ ounce, 21 g	Garlic powder

PROCEDURE—DAY 1

1 Preheat the oven to 300°F (149°C).

2   Place the pork and beef in a roasting pan, cover, and roast for approximately 4 hours, or until the meats are fork-tender.

3   Remove the meats from the heat and pull or shred the meat. Set aside.

4   Remove the stems from the ancho chiles and split open the pods along one side. Rinse the chiles under cold running water. Rinse the seeds from the chiles and discard them. Place the chiles in a pot of water, cover, and simmer for 15 minutes.

5   Remove the chiles from the water and scrape the pulp from the skin. Discard the skin. Chop the pulp and reserve both the pulp and liquid until needed.

6   Sauté the garlic in 2 tablespoons (1 ounce, 30 ml) of the lard.

7   Combine the cooked meat, sautéed garlic, chile pulp, cumin, pepper, and oregano. Season with salt. Cover and refrigerate overnight to allow the flavors to develop and permeate the meats.

PROCEDURE—DAY 2

1   Soak the cornhusks in water for at least 2 hours. Separate them one by one and stack them ready for use.

2   Prepare the dough by combining the masa or reconstituted masa harina with the remaining lard, chili powder, paprika, and garlic powder. Adjust the consistency of the dough as needed with the reserved liquid used to simmer the ancho chiles.

3   Combine this mixture with your hands until it is thoroughly mixed. The more air that is incorporated into the masa dough, the better, as it will result in moist and fluffy tamales. It is impossible to overmix this dough.

4   Place an unbroken cornhusk on a tray or work surface in front of you with the small end away from you.

5   Using a spatula or masa spreader, spread approximately 1 to 2 tablespoons ($^{1}/_{2}$–1 ounce, 14–30 ml) of the masa dough on the cornhusk in such a way that it covers the lower two-thirds and right 4 inches (10.2 cm) of the husk. The masa should be spread thick enough so that you cannot see through to the husk.

6   Place the desired amount of meat filling in the middle of the masa. (The amount of meat filled into the tamales is a matter of personal preference.) Seal each tamale by rolling it over, starting from the right side where the masa and meat are. The unspread side covers the outside of the tamale and holds it together.

7   Fold the unfilled end at the top over to the middle. Tie the tamale, if necessary, with thin strips torn from a soaked cornhusk. Cover the tamales, and store overnight in the refrigerator.

PROCEDURE—DAY 3

1   Set up a steamer in a large saucepot with an elevated bottom and tight-fitting lid. Add water to the saucepot until it reaches just under the elevated bottom. Place the tamales on the elevated bottom, standing them shoulder to shoulder with the open ends facing up. Cover the saucepot and steam for about 1 hour or until the masa peels away from the shuck.

2   Check the water level in the saucepot from time to time and add additional water as needed in order to keep the pot from boiling dry.

3   Let the tamales rest for 10 to 15 minutes before serving. This will allow them to become firm.

4   Remove the tamales from their cornhusks. Fold the cornhusks and place one on each hot serving plate. Place 2 to 3 tamales, depending on size, on top of the husks.

The Cuisine of the Southwest and the Rocky Mountain Region

Several different groups, each with its own proud history and traditions, have contributed to the Southwest's distinct character. The Native Americans in the area that is now the states of New Mexico and Arizona have had more success maintaining their languages, religions, and traditions than American Indians in other parts of the United States. The Hispanics of the region are proud of their long history. Many of their families were granted land by the Spanish Crown long before the United States existed. Although they have had to adapt to many changes over the centuries, their pride in their heritage is unwavering.

In the Rocky Mountain states—Colorado, Idaho, Montana, Utah, and Wyoming—the miners, cowboys, and frontier families that ventured into this once harsh and remote land had a courage and self-reliance that is reflected in the independent streak of their sons and daughters.

Arizona "The Grand Canyon State," where the apache, or Arizona trout is the state fish, the state reptile is the ridge-nosed rattlesnake, the state neckware is the bolo tie, and the state flower is the saguaro cactus blossom.

Colorado "The Centennial State," where the state animal is the Rocky Mountain bighorn sheep, the state fish is the green cutthroat trout, and the state folk dance is the square dance.

Idaho "The Gem State," known for the state fruit, which is the huckleberry; the state vegetable is the potato, and the state fish is the cutthroat trout.

Montana "The Treasure State," also known as "Big Sky Country" and the "Mountain State," has the state fish as the blackspotted cutthroat trout and the state animal as the grizzly bear.

New Mexico Considered the "Land of Enchantment," New Mexico has chiles and pinto beans as the state vegetables, the piñon pine as the state tree, the Rio Grande cutthroat trout as the state fish, and the roadrunner as the state bird. The state cookie is the bizcochito and the New Mexico state question is: "Red or green?" (as in the state's most famous vegetable, chile). The answer? Both!

Utah "The Beehive State," where the state fruit includes both sweet and tart cherries, the state vegetable is the Spanish sweet onion, the state historic vegetable is the sugar beet, the state animal is the Rocky Mountain elk, and the state cooking pot is the Dutch oven.

Wyoming "The Evergreen State," also known as the "Cowboy State," "Big Wyoming," and the "Equality State," where bison is the state mammal, cutthroat trout is the state fish, and the state sport is the rodeo.

The Development of Southwestern Cuisine

When the Spanish first came to the Southwest, they found 98 Native American settlements, called "pueblos," along the Rio Grande. The Spanish were amazed to discover that the Native Americans had already developed an irrigation system capable of bringing enough water to the desert fields to sustain a variety of local crops, primarily consisting of corn, squash, and beans.

The tribes that have most significantly influenced the cuisine of this area include the Navajo, Pima, Hopi, Pueblo, and Zuni. Typically, food for the Native Americans meant much more than simple sustenance; it had religious and cultural implications as well.

The Pima tribe is known to have lived in this region since the fourth century, when they established a highly effective irrigation system that brought water to their fields in the desert. The Pima were descendants of the ancient Hohokam tribe and were known for their expertise in growing beans—so great that they were also referred to as the Papago, or "bean people."

The Navajo tribe migrated from arctic regions in the 13th century. Originally, the Navajo were nomadic hunters and gatherers, but after arriving in the region, they adapted to some of the agrarian ways of the Pueblo tribes already living in the area. When the Europeans arrived in the region and brought with them sheep, cattle, and horses, the Navajo learned to be herders as well as farmers.

The Hopi tribe is considered to have made the most significant contributions to cooking. The Hopi, descendants of the ancient Anasazi tribe, cultivated many varieties of squash, beans, and corn. They learned to cook in beehive-shaped ovens, called *hornos,* made of adobe clay, and frequently used cooking vessels made of fired pottery ornately decorated with geometric patterns to boil foods.

THE SPANIARDS ARRIVE

The first Europeans to venture into this region were the Spanish. In 1540, Coronado led an expedition north from Mexico in search of the Seven Cities of Cibola, where the streets were allegedly paved with gold. Finding only mud huts and hostile Indians, Coronado returned home to Mexico, discouraged and disgraced. In the following decades, the Spaniards returned and solidified their control over the area.

The introduction of meats other than wild game is attributed to the Spanish, who brought livestock with them. Capitán General Juan de Onate first introduced sheep to the region in 1598, and by the 1880s, millions of sheep, cattle, and hogs were being raised, many of which were shipped to other regions of the United States. The Spanish also grew crops and introduced wheat flour to the Native Americans. Wheat became so popular that it was planted all over the region, and by the 16th century, it was more common in the American West than in Spain. Eventually, flour tortillas became as popular as corn tortillas, the original staple bread of the region. They also introduced peaches, apricots, and apples. As they had in other areas of the country, especially in Texas, the Spanish introduced many varieties of chiles that were integrated into the cuisine.

THE NATIVE AMERICANS AND THE "THREE SISTERS OF FOOD"

The "three sisters"—corn, beans, and squash—are the New World foods indigenous to the Southwest and Rocky Mountains. These foods supported the Native Americans and early European settlers of the region. The crops were easy to dry and store for long periods and, when eaten together, provided a complete source of protein. The farming techniques are also designed to be harmonious. When all three crops are planted together, the tall stalks of corn provide the vertical structure to which the bean plants cling, and the squash vines help provide shade and control weeds by forming a groundcover.

The Native American Indians believed that corn was given to them by the corn maiden as a life-giving grain. It is the food that has the most cultural significance for them. Corn in the region comes in six colors: red, white, blue, black, yellow, and variegated—which many Native American tribes associate with the six directions of the compass. The Zuni tribe believed that if dried corn kernels were scattered in the path of the Spanish conquistadors, they would be protected from the invaders. The Hopi tribe used each of the six colors of corn for distinctly different purposes, many religious in nature. Native Americans learned to use wood ash while cooking cornbread, and discovered that wood ash could be used as a seasoning and leavening agent.

Another of the three sisters foods is beans. Native Americans used wild beans in their diets almost 7,000 years ago. Beans, when combined and eaten with grains, seeds, or nuts, provide all the amino acids needed to create complete proteins. The Europeans, until the 15th century, were familiar with only a few varieties of beans, such as fava and broad beans, but were introduced to a large variety of New World beans by the Native Americans of the Southwest. The most common beans utilized today in the American Southwest are the pinto bean and its smaller relative, the pinquito. However, a number of ancient varieties, called "heirloom beans," are experiencing a resurgence in the United States.

The last member of the food triad is squash. Summer squash such as zucchini, yellow squash, and numerous varieties of Indian squash are all grown in the Southwest. This culturally important food staple is often referred to by its Spanish name, *calabacitas*.

By the 19th century, many tribes raised a variety of fruits including peaches, figs, and apricots. Most of this fruit was dried for winter use.

Indians used a variety of implements—such as stone mortars—to grind or pulverize their foods. They shelled or hulled seeds and ground meat to tenderize it. They soaked corn in water mixed with wood ashes (forming lye) to turn the corn into hominy. Both fish and meat were pulverized and then mixed with berries and fat to form a nutrient-rich, easy-to-carry food source. If it contained meat, this mixture was known as pemmican and was stored in a buffalo-skin bag.

THE MEXICAN INFLUENCE

The spiciness and high seasoning of many traditional dishes are similar to those used in the Mexican states of Chihuahua and Sonora—typically, not simple but rich and complex. Flavors derived from different chiles, herbs, and seasonings are generally used to attain the characteristics of American Southwest cuisine.

Major Influences in the Rocky Mountain States

The most significant influence in the region was the rapid settlement of the American West in the mid-1800s, before the transcontinental railroad was built. Prospectors and others heading to the gold rush of California traveled two main routes: the Oregon Trail and the Santa Fe Trail.

The northern route, the Oregon Trail, began in Missouri, crossed the Rocky Mountains into Utah, and veered north through Idaho and into Oregon, while the Santa Fe Trail took a more southerly route through Colorado into New Mexico. The first known group to follow the Oregon Trail, left Independence, Missouri, in 1842 and, over the next two decades, hundreds of thousands of settlers left their homes to follow the quest for gold. The Mormons, however, followed the Oregon Trail for religious freedom. The Mormons left Illinois in the winter of 1846 to move their church to the west. They veered south once in the Great Basin of Utah, and by the end of 1847, some 5,000 pioneers had settled in the Salt Lake Valley.

In the 1820s, Mexico finalized its independence from Spain, and the Santa Fe Trail from Missouri to New Mexico opened. This caused the city of Santa Fe to become a trading hub for the region. During the Civil War, Congress passed the Homestead Act of 1862, offering 160 acres of land free to any citizen or intended citizen who was head of the household. From 1862 to 1900, up to 600,000 families took advantage of the government's offer.

The "Three Sisters" of Food

Corn is one of the sacred plants of the Southwest; it has been cultivated by the Hopis for over 2,000 years. This grain must be planted deliberately, as corn plants cannot naturally sow their own seed. Every part of the corn was used, including the husks, which were used as the wrapping for tamales; the cornmeal dough, called "masa," was used to fill tamales and to prepare corn tortillas. Blue corn is culturally and religiously the single most important corn variety grown by the Native Americans of the Southwest. Used extensively by the Hopi, Navajo, and Pueblo tribes, the blue color occurs naturally in Indian corn. Dishes made with blue corn have a flavor that is both rich and earthy. The distinctive flavor is attributed to the drying of the kernels over a piñon wood fire. Blue corn can be used in most Southwest dishes that call for yellow corn; however, it is softer and less starchy than other Indian corns. Owing to its tendency to crumble, blue corn may need to be blended with a little wheat flour before use.

Heirloom beans are any of the ancient wild and cultivated beans indigenous to the Southwest and once eaten by Native Americans. Heirloom beans have recently been revived in the region and are grown by specialty farmers who support and subscribe to the techniques of preservation agriculture. They include:

ANASAZI BEAN Also known as "New Mexico cave beans," this bean was cultivated by the earliest Native Americans and may be the forerunner of the pinto bean. A purple, red, and white bean, it cooks in about two-thirds of the time of an ordinary pinto bean and has less of the specific carbohydrate that causes gastric distress. From the Navajo word that means "ancient ones," the Anasazi bean is trademarked by Adobe Mills, a privately owned company.

APPALOOSA BEAN Named after the spotted horse, this bean is black and white or red and white. These beans are quick to cook and are frequently used in place of pinto beans.

In the late 1880s, railroad companies laid their tracks across the Southwest, bringing with them improved commerce and access to new markets. Thousands of settlers from the East began to arrive in masses. The beef industry boomed, creating vast cattle kingdoms on the southeastern plains, and by the 1900s, the settlers who had brought modern tools and farming techniques had transformed over five million acres of land into fertile farms.

BOLLITO BEAN Smaller than the pinto, it has a better flavor and is beige in color. This bean takes a little longer to cook than pintos and is usually boiled.

JACOB'S CATTLE BEAN Originating in Germany, this bean is similar to appaloosa beans but is white and maroon in color. They are fairly sweet in flavor and may be referred to as "trout beans" or "Dalmation beans."

PINTO BEAN The most widely used bean is this country. A variation of the kidney bean, it is a pinkish beige color and slightly streaked.

TEPARY BEAN This earthy-flavored bean was domesticated by prehistoric Native Indians and was of particular ceremonial importance to the Zuni. The tepary is rarely cultivated because it can harbor a mold spore that is deadly to other varieties of bean. They are variegated in color and come in a number of sizes and shapes.

Squashes are native to the Southwest and were cultivated by a number of Southwestern Indian tribes. As one of the "three sisters" of the Southwest, squash was of ceremonial importance. It was eaten in all stages of development and was sun-dried for winter consumption. The Spanish settlers introduced new varieties to the region that included:

ACORN SQUASH A sweet winter squash that is dark green on the outside with orange flesh. Often baked whole.

BUTTERNUT Tan, creamy, and sweet, it is shaped like a bowling pin.

CHAYOTE Also known as a vegetable pear, it is pale green to cream in color, with smooth skin and a flavor similar to zucchini.

PUMPKIN Familiar orange-colored squash. The seeds may be dried and salted, ground, and used as an ingredient for regional sauces.

HUBBARD SQUASH Oversized with yellow flesh and gray outside.

TURBAN A multicolored squash rich in flavor, much like pumpkin or butternut squash.

THE PIONEERS

The areas first tracked by trappers, prospectors, and trailblazers began to attract farmers and families and other pioneers by the 1840s. The Oregon Trail—nothing more than two wagon ruts—was blazed in 1841; by the mid-1840s, a trickle of pioneers had made that long walk west. Their daily sustenance included sourdough breads, quick breads, salt pork preparations, wild game and fish, and what could be foraged from the forests, mountain valleys, and plains. Their "prairie schooners," or covered wagons, were piled high with flour, beans, bacon, dried fruit, coffee, salt, and vinegar. Their cooking styles were similar to that of the cowboys who ate chuckwagon cooking in Texas.

In the late 1800s and early 1900s, German-Russian immigrants came to homestead and farm. They found that the San Luis Valley in Colorado did not have to depend on rivers for its water supply. The valley has artesian wells that do not need pumps to bring the water to the surface. This enabled the valley to be turned into an important agricultural area, where a variety of vegetables, especially potatoes, are grown.

The Basque people who emigrated from southwestern France and northern Spain came to the West as sheepherders who worked on the ranches of Idaho, Nevada, and Wyoming. In many remote areas, thriving communities of Basque descendants developed. Hearty stews of beef, chicken, and lamb flavored with onions, garlic tomatoes, bell peppers, and herbs best describe the Basque contribution to the cooking of the region. The largest Basque community in existence today, outside of Europe, is in Boise, Idaho. The Basque restaurants found in America today are known for their family-style service and many courses of hearty food, served on long communal tables.

Much of the wild game enjoyed for its own sake today in the Rocky Mountains was first eaten out of necessity; today, game is considered a delicacy. Fowl, venison, boar, and bison thrive in the mountains of the region. But today, the game animals served in restaurants are not considered true wild game. Because the U.S. Department of Agriculture does not inspect wild game, the meat served in commercial food-service operations is raised in closely controlled environments and developed specifically for the industry by game farms and ranches. Considered to be low in fat, game available to the public is increasingly popular.

Typical Southwestern and Rocky Mountain Ingredients and Dishes

Achiote The seed of the tropical annatto tree. Also referred to as "annatto seeds," achiote is used commercially as a natural orange coloring agent for butter and cheese. Achiote is also a useful ingredient when sautéing, as it imparts a vibrant yellow-orange tint to proteins. The seeds are available dried or crushed and can be used to flavor oil. Achiote oil can be drizzled over meat or shellfish for both color and subtle flavoring and can be added to salad dressings as a flavoring ingredient.

Agua Fresca Originating in Mexico, a fresh fruit drink made from pureed fruit, sugar, and sparkling water. The fruits most commonly used are tamarind, watermelon, banana, strawberry, and mango.

Almendrado An almond-flavored dessert made from beaten egg white bound with gelatin and usually served with a creamy custard sauce. The gelatin is frequently tinted with colors to resemble the Mexican flag.

Atole An ancient soup made from ground dried corn or masa harina. Sometimes made with blue corn, atole may be thinned and sweetened and used as a beverage. It can also be found as a fermented beverage.

Buffaloberry Used primarily to make jams and jellies, this wild berry, orange or red in color, is somewhat bitter in flavor. Found throughout the mountains and plains, it ripens in early to late fall. If picked just after a frost, the buffaloberry is sweet enough to use in pies.

Buñuelo A pastry similar to a fried tortilla, usually served with a scoop of ice cream and a sprinkle of cinnamon sugar. They are a holiday season tradition in Mexico, but in the American Southwest they are more frequently eaten as a snack.

Capirotad A Southwestern bread pudding made with cheese and caramel sauce. Though it is a traditional dish in the region during Lent, it is frequently found on restaurant menus throughout the year.

Chico A dried kernel of corn, sometimes referred to as "parched corn." Chicos are steamed and added to soups and stews.

Chokecherry A small, orange-purple fruit that is a member of the plum family. It is common throughout the Rocky Mountains and is quite hardy and extremely resistant to changes in the weather. The name chokecherry describes its taste—very astringent—which makes it well suited for jams, jellies, and syrups. They can be eaten from the vine when they are at their peak of ripeness; however, their leaves and pits are poisonous.

Cold Flour A parched corn that was pounded into a coarse meal similar to polenta, mixed with sugar and cinnamon, and eaten as a cereal. This was an important provision of the chuckwagons that traveled west along the Oregon Trail.

Colorado Lamb World renowned for its excellent flavor, low fat content, and large eye in the rack. Lamb is one of the largest agricultural products of the Rocky Mountains.

Cutthroat Trout A variety of freshwater trout with distinctive markings on its neck.

Dandelion A wild leafy plant with a bright yellow flower harvested by the Native American Indians. The leaves are usually blanched and served in salad. Dandelions should be eaten before they flower, after which they are bitter. Dandelion roots are used as a vegetable in Japanese cooking.

Empanada A small, half-moon-shaped pastry stuffed with meat, fish, or cheese. Empanadas are served hot as an hors d'oeuvre or appetizer.

Epazote A wild herb with jagged, serrated edges with a strong flavor reminiscent of kerosene. The young, small leaves are best and can be used like greens in soups or stews. It is frequently used in cooked beans of all types to reduce their gaseousness. It is also known as "ambrosia," "lamb's quarters," "wormseed," "stinkweed," and "pigweed."

Fried Green Jerky A traditional dish of the Pueblo tribe made from dried beef that is softened, fried with onions and chiles in lard, and simmered with fresh chopped tomatoes.

Game Meats

Buffalo Also called "bison," a member of the Bovidae family and believed to be a descendant of wild cattle. There were over 40 million buffalo in the mid-1800s; however, the population shrank to less than 1,000 by 1900. Today there are over 150,000, as the buffalo population is strictly controlled and monitored. Buffalo is once again being raised for consumption and has become popular owing to its rich, sweet taste and low fat content compared to beef. Buffalo should be cooked a lower temperature and a shorter time than beef.

Elk A very large relative of the deer. The meat is very dark and coarsely grained, without significant marbling. Smoked elk's tongue is considered a delicacy by many in the Rocky Mountains.

Venison A generic term for any variety of deer meat. One of the most popular varieties of game, venison needs to be hung and marinated before cooking, unless the animal is very young. There are over 40 recognized species of deer. The most common venison served in the United States today is cervenna, derived from farm-raised Scottish red deer. The best venison comes from the buck, which is about two years old. The most popular cut is the haunch or leg. Whitetailed deer is considered the most tender and flavorful, without the gamier taste associated with other varieties of venison.

Wild Boar Boar meat is a deeper red than port, and is somewhat less fatty. The meat of the young boar is tender, but older animals have considerably tougher meat with a gamier taste.

Horchata A sweet beverage made from milk, ground raw rice, and almonds and flavored with cinnamon. It is garnished with toasted pumpkin seeds (pepitas) and is said to counteract the effects of eating very hot chiles, leaving only the essence of the flavor.

Huitalacoche Also referred to as "acuitlacoche," this is a fungus that grows on corn. The fungus is used in fairly large pieces as an ingredient in many Southwestern dishes and is prepared similarly to mushrooms.

Indian Flat Bread Also referred to as "Navajo fry bread," this all-purpose flat bread is made with corn flour by the Native Americans of the Four Corners region.

Jerky Cured and salted, air- or oven-dried strips of beef or bison.

Limon A Mexican lime of the same variety as the Key lime. It is small, round, with a yellowish skin. True limons are usually found in the region's specialty markets.

Mexican Hot Chocolate Invented by the Aztecs, this drink is derived from the beans of the cocao plant and could be drunk only by priests and important rulers for ceremonial purposes. Today, Mexican hot chocolate is a common breakfast drink and is used as a substitute for coffee and tea.

Mexican Oregano A form of wild marjoram, it is similar in flavor to the oregano plant of the Mediterranean, but with a much stronger flavor.

Montana Whitefish This whitefish from Flathead Lake in Montana, weighs up to 9 pounds. It is known for its mild, pleasant-tasting flesh and excellent golden roe. The introduction of the whitefish in Flathead Lake was an accident. In an attempt to lure salmon, shrimp were seeded into the lake. Instead of the salmon, the whitefish came to the lake and thrived.

Nixtamal Kernels of corn partially processed with slaked lime and similar to hominy, the ground kernels are mixed with seasonings to make a dough, like masa, to make tamales. Nixtamal is also used whole in soups and stews. It can be used as a substitute for posole. It is found packaged in the refrigerated sections of Southwest markets.

Palisade Peach Indigenous to the western slopes of Colorado near the city of Grand Junction, palisade peaches are world renowned for their sweet flavor and firm texture.

Panocha This rustic dessert is a pudding originally made before sugar was available and when honey was scarce. The settlers discovered that moistened wheat kernels left in a warm place would convert to a form of sugar. This wheat could be ground and would provide sweetness to a recipe. Today, flour made from sprouted grain is still available and used to make panocha.

Pepita The Spanish name for a pumpkin seed or squash seed of any variety. They are typically dried and roasted and eaten as a snack, used as a garnish for salads, or ground and used as a flavoring agent for regional sauces.

Piki Bread A traditional unleavened bread made by the Hopi tribe with blue corn. It has many thin, papery layers and is cooked on heated piki stones. These stones have been seasoned with bone marrow or cooked sheep's brains and serve the same function as a cast-iron skillet or wok.

Pine Nuts Also known as "piñon nuts," they are harvested from the cones of pine trees growing at high altitudes in the Rock Mountains and the Southwest. Considered to be the largest uncultivated crop in North America, pine nuts can be roasted or ground to add a distinctive flavor to any dish.

Posole A dried form of nixtamal, used like masa harina for making tamales and tortillas. Posole also refers to a traditional Southwestern soup or stew that uses this type of corn. Posole is available in four colors—blue, red, yellow, and white. Posole is a convenient and safe way to store corn for long periods, but it needs to be reconstituted with water prior to use. Nixtamal or hominy can be substituted for posole.

Potatoes One of the most famous foods in the Rocky Mountains is the potato. Over 100 varieties are farmed, mostly in Idaho and Colorado. In fact, Idaho Potato is now a registered trademark. Idaho Potatoes are usually grown in volcanic soil and irrigated with fresh mountain runoff water. Russet potatoes from Idaho are the most popular and common potato variety and are used primarily as baking potatoes and for the production of french fries. Colorado, while also producing Russets, is known more for its specialty potatoes that come in a variety of colors, sizes, and flavors. They include:

> *Alaskan Sweetheart Potato* This variety of potato is slightly pink in color, with a red skin. Good for baking and boiling, it is also an excellent choice for a colorful potato salad.

> *Baby All-Blue Potato* These potatoes are small, thin, and long. Also known as "fingerling potatoes," they have a bluish-lavender flesh and are best cooked whole by steaming, roasting, or boiling.

> *Ozette Potato* A yellow-skinned and yellow-fleshed fingerling potato best cooked by roasting or baking.

> *Purple Peruvian Potato* A fingerling potato, originating in South America, with a deep

purple color. The purple Peruvian potatoes have an extremely earthy flavor and are excellent either boiled or baked.

Red Bliss Potato Also known as a Cherry Red potato, it is white fleshed, with a deep red skin and a creamy, buttery taste.

Red Sangre Potato These medium potatoes are named after the Sangre de Cristo Mountain Range in the southern part of Colorado. They are white fleshed, with a red skin, and are excellent for both baking and boiling.

Russet Potato This is the most popular potato in America. It is raised primarily in Idaho, where the volcanic soil and mountain runoff provide excellent growing conditions. Though not very attractive, they are large and oblong, with a slightly rough skin. Their low moisture content makes them perfect for making light and fluffy baked potatoes. Their low sugar content makes them suitable for french fries. (Americans eat more than 4.5 billion pounds of french fries annually.)

Yellow Fin or Yukon Gold Potato A yellow-skinned and yellow-fleshed potato developed in Finland, marketed in America by Michigan farmer Jim Huston, and now grown in the San Luis Valley of Colorado. These potatoes have a creamy texture and a butter flavor suitable for any potato preparation.

Rainbow Trout This native American trout is considered one of the world's best game fishes. Rainbow trout are easily identified by the broad reddish band, or "rainbow," that runs along the side of the fish from head to tail. This freshwater fish begins life in the rivers of Idaho. The young fish travel many hundreds of miles to the Pacific Ocean through a network of streams and rivers to live there for approximately four years. The trout return to their spawning grounds through the same rivers and streams. Modern trout farms now raise these fish for the commercial market.

Rocky Mountain Oysters A culinary tradition of the Old West, Rocky Mountain oysters are the testicles of a sheep or young bull, roasted whole in a pan. Eating Rocky Mountain oysters was a ritual test of manhood for the cowboys of the Old West. Today, they are usually coated, breaded, then pan- or deep-fried and served with a spicy dipping sauce.

Sangria A red wine and fresh fruit beverage first made by the Spanish priests, who introduced wine grapes to New Mexico. It is considered an excellent accompaniment to the spicy fare of the region. Tequila may be added.

Sopaipilla A rectangle of wheat flour dough, deep-fried and served as a savory bread. It may also be filled with honey, sprinkled with powdered sugar, and served as a dessert.

Squash Blossoms The flowers of almost any squash can be sautéed as a vegetable, deep-fried, added to soups and quesadillas, or used as a garnish. The blossom of the zucchini is most frequently seen. Squash blossoms need to be used immediately, as their quality quickly deteriorates.

Teswin A Native American punch made from dried corn and finely ground roasted wheat. It is often flavored with anise, cloves, and cinnamon.

Tunas The fruit of the prickly pear cactus with an orange or red flesh and a sweet, yet tart flavor. In Europe, this cactus is referred to as a Barbary fig. Tunas needs to be trimmed of its spines and outer skin before use. The cactus fruit is used in dessert preparations and as an ingredient in salads.

Cross-Referenced Typical Ingredients and Dishes

The following ingredients are used in both Tex-Mex and Southwestern/Rocky Mountain cooking. See "Texas and Tex-Mex Cuisine" for the following:

Chiles

Cilantro

Jícama

Masa, Masa Harina

Mole

Nopales

Queso Fresco

Salsa

Tamale

Tomatillo

Tortilla

Menus and Recipes from the Cuisine of the Southwest and the Rocky Mountain Region

MENU ONE

Tortilla Chips, Salsa Fresca, and Tomatillo Salsa

Poblano and Potato Soup with Tortilla Strips

Marinated Grilled Quail on Spinach Salad

Pumpkin Seed–Crusted Trout

Calabacitas con Maize

Annatto Rice and Queso Fresco

Tres Leches Cake

MENU TWO

Grilled Vegetable Gazpacho

Spicy Pork Empanadas with Marinated Dried Bean Salad Colorado

Lamb Shoulder with Cilantro Pesto and Jalapeño Preserves

Broccoli with Candied Pecans

Fingerlings with Parsley-Basil Dressing

Lemon Chess Pie

MENU THREE

Navajo Fry Bread

Porrusalad-Leek Soup

Chiles Rellenos with Roasted Tomato Salsa

Jícama Salad

Grilled Apache-Style Pork Cutlets, Squash Salsa, and Tobacco Onions

Sopaipillas

OTHER RECIPES

Smoked-Roasted Acorn Squash

Venison Steaks with Dried Wild Mushrooms

Tortilla Chips 4 SERVINGS

AMOUNT	MEASURE	INGREDIENT
12		Corn tortillas, 8 inches (20 cm)
to taste		Salt

PROCEDURE

1 Preheat a deep-fryer to 350°F (175°C).

2 Cut the corn tortillas into quarters and fry until crisp.

3 Remove and drain on paper towels. Season with salt.

Tomatillo Salsa 4 SERVINGS

AMOUNT	MEASURE	INGREDIENT
1 1/2 cups	8 ounces, 226 g	Tomatillos
1 1/2 tablespoons	3/4 ounce, 21 g	Red onion, 1/8 inch (.3 cm) dice
1/2		Serrano chile, minced
1 tablespoon	1/2 ounce, 15 ml	Lime juice
1/4 cup	1/2 ounce, 15 g	Cilantro, roughly chopped, packed
1 tablespoon	1/2 ounce, 15 ml	Vegetable oil
pinch		Granulated sugar

PROCEDURE

1 Husk the tomatillos and wash under very hot water.

2 Cool, and then puree.

3 Add the red onion, chile, lime juice, cilantro, and oil. Add a pinch of sugar if the tomatillos are too sour.

Tortilla Chips, Salsa Fresca, and Tomatilla Salsa

Salsa Fresca 4 SERVINGS

AMOUNT	MEASURE	INGREDIENT
1¹/₄ cups	8 ounces, 226 g	Tomatoes, peeled, seeded, ¹/₈ inch (.3 cm) dice
1 cup	4 ounces, 113 g	Onion, ¹/₈ inch (.3 cm) dice
1		Garlic clove, minced
1		Serrano chile, seeded, minced
¹/₄ cup	¹/₂ ounce, 15 g	Cilantro leaves, packed, finely chopped
to taste		Salt and black pepper
1 tablespoon	¹/₂ ounce, 14 ml	Lime juice

PROCEDURE

Combine all the ingredients in a stainless steel bowl. Correct seasoning with salt, pepper, and lime juice.

Poblano and Potato Soup 4 SERVINGS

AMOUNT	MEASURE	INGREDIENT
2 tablespoons	1 ounce, 28 ml	Vegetable oil
1 cup	4 ounces, 113 g	Onion, $^1/_2$ inch (1.2 cm) dice
$^1/_2$ cup	2 ounces, 56 g	Carrot, $^1/_2$ inch (1.2 cm) dice
$^1/_2$ cup	2 ounces, 56 g	Celery, $^1/_2$ inch (1.2 cm) dice
3	6 ounces, 170 g	Poblano chiles, roasted, peeled, seeded, $^1/_2$ inch (1.2 cm) dice
2 cups	10 ounces, 280 g	Russet potato, $^1/_2$ inch (1.2 cm) dice
1 quart	1 l	Chicken stock
$^3/_4$ cup	6 ounces, 170 ml	Heavy cream, warmed
1 tablespoon		Cilantro leaves
to taste		Salt and white pepper
		Tortilla strips, fried
$^1/_4$ cup as needed	1 ounce, 28g	Queso fresco or white cheese, grated

PROCEDURE

1 Heat the oil in a saucepan over medium heat. Add the onion, carrot, and celery, and cook 5 minutes.

2 Add the chiles, potato, and stock. Simmer for 30 minutes.

3 Puree the soup. Bring back to a simmer.

4 Adjust the thickness (using additional stock) and season with salt and pepper.

5 Add the cream and cilantro just before serving. Garnish the soup with fried tortilla strips and grated cheese.

Marinated Grilled Quail on Spinach Salad 4 SERVINGS

AMOUNT	MEASURE	INGREDIENT
For the Vinaigrette		
2 tablespoons	1 ounce, 20 ml	Olive oil
1/4 cup	2 ounces, 55 ml	Vegetable oil
1/4 cup	1 ounce, 56 g	Shallots, fine chopped
1 tablespoon	3 g	Parsley, chopped
2 tablespoons	1 ounce, 29 ml	Balsamic vinegar
to taste		Salt and black pepper
For the Salad		
2 cups	4 ounces, 113 g	Spinach, cut in chiffonade
1/2 cup	2 ounces, 56 g	Red bell pepper, roasted, peeled, seeded, julienned
1/2 cup	2 ounces, 56 g	Yellow bell pepper, roasted, peeled, seeded, julienned
1/2 cup	2 ounces, 56 g	Green bell pepper, roasted, peeled, seeded, julienned
3/4 cup	4 ounces, 113 g	Tomato, peeled, seeded, julienned
8		Bamboo skewers, soaked in water for 30 minutes
4		Quails, split at the back

PROCEDURE

1 Combine all ingredients for dressing in a blender and process until smooth. Correct seasoning.

2 Place each quail on 2 skewers in a straight line to hold its shape.

3 Liberally brush the quails with half of the dressing and allow to marinate, refrigerated, for 1 hour.

4 Prepare the grill.

5 Grill the quail for 3 to 5 minutes on each side or until the quail are completely cooked. Be careful not to burn or overcook the quail.

6   Toss the salad ingredients with all but 2 tablespoons (1 ounce, 28 ml) of the remaining vinaigrette.

7   Place the salad in the center of the plate. Remove the skewers from each quail and place on top of the salad.

8   Drizzle the remaining vinaigrette over the quail.

Pumpkin Seed–Crusted Trout   4 SERVINGS

AMOUNT	MEASURE	INGREDIENT
³/₄ cup	4 ounces, 113 g	Pumpkin seeds, green, hulled, crushed
¹/₄ cup	1¹/₂ ounces, 42 g	Cornmeal
¹/₂ cup	2 ounces, 56 g	All-purpose flour
2		Eggs, beaten with a pinch of salt and a little water for egg wash
4	5 ounces, 140 g each	Trout fillets with skin, all bones removed
to taste		Salt and black pepper
2 tablespoons	1 ounce, 28 ml	Vegetable oil
¹/₂ cup	4 ounces, 113 g	Butter
1 tablespoon	3 g	Flat-leaf parsley, finely chopped
1 tablespoon	¹/₂ ounce, 15 ml	Lime juice

PROCEDURE

1   Heat the oil over medium-high heat to 350°F (175°C).

2   Combine the pumpkin seeds and cornmeal.

3   Season the trout with salt and black pepper. Dredge flesh side in flour, shaking off excess. Then dip flesh side in egg, letting excess drip off.

4   Coat fillets with cornmeal mixture.

5   Add trout seed side down to pan and cook until golden, 2 to 3 minutes.

6   Turn fillets and cook until just done, 1 minute. Transfer to heated platter and keep warm.

7   Heat the butter until it starts to foam and just begins to brown. Add the parsley and lime juice. Spoon over trout fillets.

Calabacitas con Maize 4 SERVINGS

AMOUNT	MEASURE	INGREDIENT
2 tablespoons	1 ounce, 28 g	Unsalted butter
1/2 cup	2 ounces, 56 g	Onion, 1/4 inch (.6 cm) dice
1		Garlic clove, minced
2 1/2 cups	10 ounces, 284 g	Zucchini squash, 1/2 inch (1.2 cm) dice
1/2 cup	2 ounces, 56 g	Corn kernels
1		Serrano chile, seeded, diced small
1/8 teaspoon		Oregano (dried)
to taste		Salt and black pepper
1/2 cup	3 ounces, 85 g	Tomato, peeled, seeded, diced

PROCEDURE

1 Melt the butter over medium-high heat.

2 Add the onion and garlic, and cook until the onion is translucent.

3 Add the zucchini, corn, and chile. Cover, lower the heat, and cook for 3 to 5 minutes or until the vegetables are tender.

4 Season with oregano, salt, and pepper.

5 Just before serving, add the tomato and toss until thoroughly heated.

Annatto Rice and Queso Fresco   4 SERVINGS

AMOUNT	MEASURE	INGREDIENT
1 cup	7 ounces, 198 g	Long-grain rice
1/4 cup	2 ounces, 55 ml	Vegetable oil
1/2 cup	2 ounces, 56 g	Onion, 1/4 inch (.6 cm) dice
1		Garlic clove, minced
1/4 cup	1 ounce, 28 g	Carrot, 1/4 inch (.6 cm) dice
1/4 cup	1 ounce, 28 g	Celery, 1/4 inch (.6 cm) dice
1 tablespoon	1/4 ounce, 7 g	Annatto powder
1 1/2 cups	12 ounces, 352 ml	Chicken stock
to taste		Salt and black pepper
1 cup	4 ounces, 113 g	Queso fresco, grated
2 tablespoons	1/4 ounce, 7 g	Cilantro, chopped

PROCEDURE

1 Rinse the rice in cold water and drain.

2 Heat the oil over medium heat. Cook the onion, garlic, carrot, and celery for 2 minutes, stirring occasionally.

3 Add the rice and annatto powder and stir for 3 minutes, until the rice is well coated with the oil.

4 Add the stock and season with salt and pepper. Bring to a boil, reduce the heat, and simmer for 20 minutes.

5 Remove from the heat and let stand, covered, for 5 minutes.

6 Add the cheese and cilantro, and stir into the rice with a fork.

Tres Leches Cake   4–6 SERVINGS

AMOUNT	MEASURE	INGREDIENT
1 1/2 cups	6 ounces, 170 g	All-purpose flour
1 teaspoon	4 g	Baking powder
1/2 cup	4 ounces, 113 g	Unsalted butter
2 cups	14 ounces, 396 g	Granulated sugar
5		Eggs
1 1/2 teaspoons		Vanilla extract
1 cup	8 ounces, 235 ml	Milk
2/3 cup	7 ounces, 156 ml	Sweetened condensed milk
2/3 cup	6 ounces, 156 ml	Evaporated milk
1/3 cup	2 2/3 ounces, 78 ml	Liqueur, Frangelico, Brandy, or Chambord, (optional)
1 1/2 cups	12 ounces, 352 ml	Heavy cream

PROCEDURE

1 Preheat the oven to 350°F (175°C). Grease and flour a 9 x 13-inch (22 x 32 cm) baking pan.

2 Sift the flour and baking powder together and set aside.

3 Cream the butter and half the sugar together until fluffy.

4 Add the eggs and half the vanilla. Beat well.

5 Add the flour mixture to the butter mixture in 3 stages, mixing well until blended.

6 Pour batter into prepared pan and bake for 30 minutes. When cake has finished baking, pierce it in 8 or 10 places with a fork or skewer, and let it cool.

7 Combine the milk, condensed milk, evaporated milk, and liqueur and pour over the top of the cooled cake.

8 Refrigerate for at least 2 hours before serving.

9 When ready to serve, combine the cream and the remaining vanilla and sugar, whipping until thick. Spread over top of cake. (Because of the milk in the cake, it is very important that you keep the cake refrigerated until ready to serve.) Serve chilled.

Grilled Vegetable Gazpacho　4 SERVINGS

AMOUNT	MEASURE	INGREDIENT
$^1/_2$ cup	2 ounces, 56 g	Red onion, $^1/_2$-inch (1.2 cm) slices
$^1/_2$ cup	2 ounces, 56 g	Zucchini, $^1/_2$-inch (1.2 cm) slices
1 tablespoon	$^1/_2$ ounce, 14 ml	Olive oil
1 cup	5 ounces, 141 g	Green bell pepper, roasted, peeled, seeded, $^1/_4$ inch (.6 cm) dice
2 cups	12 ounces, 340 g	Tomato, peeled, seeded, $^1/_4$ inch (.6 cm) dice
1 cup	4 ounces, 113 g	Cucumber, peeled, seeded, $^1/_4$ inch (.6 cm) dice
2	10 g	Garlic cloves, minced
$^1/_2$ cup	$^1/_2$ ounce, 15 g	Bread crumbs
1 tablespoon	$^1/_2$ ounce, 14 ml	Red wine vinegar
$1^1/_2$ cups	12 ounces, 336 ml	Tomato juice or V8 juice
1 tablespoon	3 g	Cilantro, chopped
2 tablespoons	1 ounce, 28 ml	Olive oil
to taste		Salt and black pepper
as needed		Chicken stock

For the Garnish

as needed		Corn tortillas, julienned, fried
as needed		Green onions, sliced on the bias

PROCEDURE

1　Brush the onion and zucchini slices with olive oil and cook on a preheated grill until tender. Watch the vegetables carefully to prevent burning.

2　Place the grilled onion and zucchini and the roasted pepper into a food processor and pulse to a coarse puree. Do not overprocess, as the vegetables will become too thin and lose their natural juices and flavor.

3　Mix the tomato, cucumber, and garlic with the processed vegetables in a stainless steel bowl.

4   Add the bread crumbs, vinegar, tomato or V8 juice, cilantro, and olive oil. Season with salt and black pepper. Chill thoroughly. Correct consistency with chicken stock or juice.

5   Carefully ladle the gazpacho into well-chilled soup cups or plates. Garnish each portion by placing a small pile of fried tortilla strips on the surface of the soup. Sprinkle the sliced green onions on top of the tortilla strips.

Spicy Pork Empanadas with Jicama Salad

Spicy Pork Empanadas 4 SERVINGS

AMOUNT	MEASURE	INGREDIENT
For the Dough		
1/4 cup	2 ounces, 56 g	Butter, softened
1/4 cup	2 ounces, 56 g	Cream cheese, softened
3/4 cup	3 ounces, 85 g	All-purpose flour
1/4 teaspoon	1 g	Baking powder
1 tablespoon	1/2 ounce, 14 ml	Water, cold
1/2 tablespoon	1/4 ounce, 7 ml	Vegetable oil
dash		Cider vinegar
to taste		Salt and black pepper
For the Filling		
1/4 cup	2 ounces, 55 ml	Vegetable oil
1/2 cup	4 ounces, 113 g	Ground pork
1/4 cup	1 ounce, 28 g	Onion, 1/4 inch (.6 cm) dice
1		Garlic clove, minced
1		Serrano chile, seeded, finely diced
1/3 cup	2 ounces, 56 g	Tomato, peeled, seeded, 1/4 inch (.6 cm) dice
1 tablespoon	3 g	Cilantro, chopped
to taste		Salt and black pepper
as needed		Vegetable oil, for frying

PROCEDURE

1   Combine butter and cream cheese. Sift flour and baking powder together.

2   Combine cream cheese mixture with flour, water, and vinegar. With generously floured hands, work the dough until you have a smooth, resilient dough, 3 to 4 minutes. Set aside.

3   Heat the oil over medium heat. Add the pork, onion, and garlic and cook, stirring constantly, for about 5 minutes.

4   Add the chile, tomato, and seasonings and simmer over low heat for about 10 minutes. Taste and adjust seasoning, if necessary. Cool the mixture before making the empanadas.

5   Roll out the dough to ¹/₈ inch (.3 cm) thickness and cut out 3-inch (7.6 cm) circles. Place a heaping tablespoon of filling in the centers, fold over, and seal the edges of the empanadas. Cover with plastic so they will not dry out. Refrigerate the empanadas until service time.

6   Heat the oil in a deep-fryer to 350°F (175°C).

7   Fry the empanadas until golden brown.

Marinated Dried Bean Salad Colorado 4 SERVINGS

AMOUNT	MEASURE	INGREDIENT
	1 ounce, 28 g	Red beans (dried)
	1 ounce, 28 g	Lentils
	1 ounce, 28 g	Pinto beans (dried)
	1 ounce, 28 g	Anasazi beans (dried)
1/2 cup	2 ounces, 56 g	Onion, 1/2 inch (1.2 cm) dice
1		Jalapeño, seeded, diced
1 cup	4 ounces, 113 g	Green bell pepper, roasted, 1/2 inch (1.2 cm) dice

For the Vinaigrette

AMOUNT	MEASURE	INGREDIENT
1 tablespoon	3 g	Sage leaves, cut in chiffonade
2		Garlic cloves, minced
3 tablespoons	1 1/2 ounces, 42 ml	Cider vinegar
6 tablespoons	3 ounces, 84 ml	Olive oil
to taste		Salt and black pepper

For the Salad

AMOUNT	MEASURE	INGREDIENT
2 cups	8 ounces, 226 g	Tomatoes, peeled, thinly sliced (20 slices)
2 1/2 cups	5 ounces, 141 g	Leaf lettuce
1/2 cup	2 ounces, 56 g	Green onions, sliced
2 tablespoons	1 ounce, 55 ml	Heavy cream
1 teaspoon	5 ml	Cider vinegar
to taste		Salt and black pepper

PROCEDURE

1. Presoak each type of bean individually overnight.
2. Cook the beans individually in salted water until tender. Drain and cool, reserving the liquid from the red beans.
3. Roast, peel, seed, and dice the jalapeño and green pepper.
4. Whisk together the vinaigrette ingredients.

Marinated Dried Bean Salad Colorado

5   Toss together the cooked beans, chiles, pepper, onions, and dressing. Let the mixture marinate.

6   Clean, dry, and trim the lettuce and green onions. Chop green onions finely.

7   Combine the cream, vinegar, green onion, and salt and black pepper in a bowl.

8   Toss the lettuce in the cream mixture, divide by 4 onto salad plates, and shingle 5 slices of tomato from rim to rim down the center of each plate. Season the tomatoes lightly with salt and pepper.

9   Serve about $^1/_2$ cup (4 ounces, 115 ml) of the marinated bean salad with the greens.

Lamb Shoulder, with Red Chile Marinade and Cilantro Pesto
4 SERVINGS

AMOUNT	MEASURE	INGREDIENT
1	3 pounds, 1.36 kg	Lamb shoulder, boned, butterflied, formed to a rough rectangle shape

For the Red Chile Marinade

1		Ancho chile, stemmed, seeded, halved
1		Pasilla chile, stemmed, seeded, halved
1/2 tablespoon	1/4 ounce, 7 g	Chipotle chile puree (puree chile with adobo sauce, canned product)
1/2 tablespoon	5 g	Cumin seeds, toasted, ground
1 tablespoon	1/2 ounce, 14 g	Vegetable oil

For the Cilantro Pesto

1 cup	2 ounces, 56 g	Cilantro, leaves, no stems
1		Garlic clove, chopped
1 tablespoon	6 g	Pumpkin seeds
1 tablespoon	1/2 ounce, 14 ml	Lime juice
1 teaspoon	5 g	Salt
1/4 teaspoon	1 g	Black pepper
1/4 cup	2 ounces, 55 ml	Olive oil

PROCEDURE

1 Preheat the oven to 350°F (175°C).

2 Heat a pan and add cumin seeds. Toast over medium-high heat, shaking the pan constantly until the seeds are fragrant, about 15 seconds. Grind the seeds in a coffee grinder or with a mortar and pestle.

3 Set the ancho and pasilla chiles in a small pan. Place the pan in the oven until chile pieces develop a sheen—no more than 30 seconds. Cut chiles into pieces small enough to grind in a coffee grinder. Grind to a powder and mix with chipotle puree and oil. Set aside.

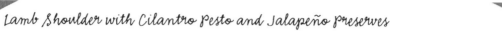

Lamb Shoulder with Cilantro Pesto and Jalapeño Preserves

4   Place the cilantro, garlic, pumpkin seeds, lime juice, salt, and pepper into a blender. Blend until the cilantro is minced. With the blender running slowly add oil so the pesto emulsifies. Set aside.

5   Pound the lamb shoulder to a $^1/_2$-inch (1.2 cm) thickness.

6   Spread two-thirds of the cilantro pesto in a thin layer over the meat, leaving at least a 1-inch (2.5 cm) border. Reserve the remaining pesto for serving.

7   Season and roll the lamb into a tight cylinder and truss. Rub the roast on all sides with the chile marinade; let it set out at room temperature for 1 hour.

8   Preheat the oven to 450°F (225°C).

9   Roast the lamb for 15 minutes. Reduce the heat to 350°F (175°C) and cook to medium, 135°F (57°C).

10   Let the roast rest at room temperature for 10 to 15 minutes, then slice diagonally, about $^1/_4$ inch (.6 cm) thick. Serve with the remaining cilantro pesto and jalapeño preserves.

Jalapeño Preserves 4 SERVINGS

AMOUNT	MEASURE	INGREDIENT
1 cup	6 ounces, 170 g	Red bell pepper, finely chopped
1		Jalapeño chile, seeded, finely chopped
$^1/_2$ cup	3$^1/_2$ ounces, 100 g	Granulated sugar
$^1/_4$ cup	2 ounces, 55 ml	Red wine vinegar
1 tablespoon	$^1/_4$ ounce, 7 g	Fruit pectin, dry

PROCEDURE

1   In a nonreactive pan, combine the red pepper, jalapeño, sugar, and vinegar. Bring to a boil, then turn down the heat and simmer for 20 minutes, stirring periodically.

2   Remove the pan from the heat and add the fruit pectin. Return to heat and bring back to a simmer. Remove the pan from the heat and let it cool to room temperature. The jelly will be on the thin side until it chills.

Broccoli with Candied Pecans 4 SERVINGS

AMOUNT	MEASURE	INGREDIENT
3 cups	9 ounces, 255 g	Broccoli florets

For the Candied Pecans

AMOUNT	MEASURE	INGREDIENT
2 tablespoons	1 ounce, 28 g	Unsalted butter
2 tablespoons	1 ounce, 28 g	Brown sugar
1 tablespoon	$^1/_2$ ounce, 15 ml	Water
$^1/_8$ teaspoon		Cayenne
1 cup	4 ounces, 113 g	Pecans, large pieces
2 tablespoons	1 ounce, 28 g	Butter
to taste		Salt and pepper

PROCEDURE

1. Parboil the broccoli florets in saltwater until tender. Remove, shock in ice water, drain, and set aside.

2. Heat the butter over medium heat; add the brown sugar, water, and cayenne.

3. Bring to a boil, add and toast the pecans; toss with the spicy sugar mixture until well coated. Place the pecans on parchment paper and cool. Chop to medium pieces.

4. Heat the butter in a saucepan. Add the broccoli and cook until hot. Season with salt and pepper. Serve, sprinkled with the spicy pecans.

Fingerlings with Parsley-Basil Dressing 4 SERVINGS

AMOUNT	MEASURE	INGREDIENT
3 cups	16 ounces, 453 g	Fingerlings, or other new potatoes
1/4 cup	2 ounces, 55 ml	Olive oil
1		Garlic clove, coarsely chopped
2 tablespoons	6 g	Parsley leaves, chopped
2 tablespoons	6 g	Basil leaves, chopped
2 tablespoons	1 ounce, 28 ml	Lemon juice
to taste		Salt and black pepper

PROCEDURE

1   Preheat the oven to 350°F (175°C).

2   Wash, drain, and dry the potatoes.

3   Combine the potatoes and olive oil in a roasting pan. Roast the potatoes in the oven for 1 hour.

4   When the potatoes are tender, remove from the oven and drain any excess oil.

5   Toss the potatoes with the garlic, herbs, and lemon juice. Season and serve immediately.

Lemon Chess Pie ONE 9-INCH (22 CM) PIE

chef tip It is important that all ingredients for the pie be at room temperature. Otherwise, blending may be difficult, and the cold ingredients, especially buttermilk or lemon juice, will cause the butter to resolidify and separate from the mixture.

AMOUNT	MEASURE	INGREDIENT
4		Eggs, at room temperature
1¹/₂ cups	11 ounces, 311 g	Granulated sugar
1 tablespoon	¹/₄ ounce, 7 g	White cornmeal
1 tablespoon	¹/₄ ounce, 7 g	All-purpose flour
¹/₂ teaspoon	3 g	Salt
5 tablespoons	2¹/₂ ounces, 70 g	Butter, melted, cooled to room temperature
¹/₂ cup	4 ounces, 115 ml	Buttermilk
5 tablespoons	2¹/₂ ounces, 70 ml	Lemon juice
1 tablespoon	10 g	Lemon zest
¹/₂ teaspoon	2.5 ml	Vanilla extract
1		Unbaked 9-inch (22 cm) pie crust
		Whipped cream (optional)

PROCEDURE

1   Preheat the oven to 350°F (175°C).

2   Whisk the eggs to blend.

3   Add each of the ingredients through vanilla in order, completely incorporating one before adding the next.

4   Pour the filling into the piecrust and bake in the middle of the oven for 30 to 40 minutes, until the pie is golden brown on top and almost set. The center of the pie should remain slightly loose; it will set as it cools.

5   Cool completely before cutting.

Navajo Fry Bread 4 SERVINGS

chef tip

When the Spanish came to America, they brought wheat, giving the native cooks an alternative to cornmeal. Navajo fry bread, also known as Indian fry bread, is ubiquitous at powwows and feast days. It can be sweet and savory and forms the base for the Indian taco, another dish often seen at festivals and gatherings.

AMOUNT	MEASURE	INGREDIENT
I cup	4 ounces, 113 g	All-purpose flour
¹/₂ teaspoon		Baking powder
¹/₄ teaspoon		Salt
2 tablespoons plus I teaspoon	1¹/₄ ounces, 33 ml	Milk

PROCEDURE

1　Combine the flour, baking powder, and salt in a mixing bowl.

2　Stir in the milk and work into a dough. Knead the dough until it is smooth and elastic. Form the dough into egg-size balls; cover and set aside for 15 minutes.

3　Heat a deep-fryer to 375°F (190°C).

4　Roll the dough into 8-inch (20 cm) circles and prick all over with a fork.

5　Fry each round in the hot oil for 2 minutes on each side. Drain on paper towels and serve.

Porrusalda—Leek Soup 4 SERVINGS

AMOUNT	MEASURE	INGREDIENT
1/4 cup	2 ounces, 55 ml	Olive oil
2 cups	8 ounces, 226 g	Leeks, white and light green parts, cleaned, sliced
1/2 cup	4 ounces, 113 g	Pork sausage
3 cups	15 ounces, 425 g	Red Bliss potatoes, peeled, 1/4 inch (.6 cm) dice
2		Thyme sprigs
1/4 teaspoon		White pepper
2 teaspoons	10 g	Salt
1		Garlic clove, minced
1 tablespoon	1/4 ounce, 7 g	Flour
2 cups	16 ounces, 470 ml	Chicken stock
2		Bay leaves
2 tablespoons	6 g	Parsley

PROCEDURE

1 Heat the oil over medium-high heat.

2 Add the leeks and sausage, and cook until lightly browned. Add the potatoes, seasonings, and flour. Toss together until the flour is incorporated.

3 Add the chicken stock, and stir until all ingredients are well combined. Bring to a simmer. Add bay leaves and simmer for 1 hour.

4 Remove bay leaves; stir in parsley just before serving.

Chiles Rellenos with Roasted Tomato Salsa

Chiles Rellenos 4 SERVINGS

AMOUNT	MEASURE	INGREDIENT
4		Poblano chiles

For the Filling

AMOUNT	MEASURE	INGREDIENT
2 tablespoons	I ounce, 28 ml	Vegetable oil
1/2 cup	2 ounces, 56 g	Onion, 1/4 inch (.6 cm) dice
I		Garlic clove, minced
2 cups	8 ounces, 226 g	Corn kernels
1/8 teaspoon		Oregano (dried)
1/4 cup	2 ounces, 55 ml	Sour cream
I cup	4 ounces, 113 g	Queso fresco or white farmer cheese, grated
to taste		Salt and white pepper

For the Batter

AMOUNT	MEASURE	INGREDIENT
3		Eggs, separated
2 tablespoons	I ounce, 14 ml	Water, cold
1/4 cup	I ounce, 28 g	All-purpose flour
2 teaspoons	1/4 ounce, 7g	Baking powder
1 1/2 teaspoons	1/4 ounce, 7 g	Salt

PROCEDURE

1 Roast, peel, and split the chiles on one side only. Cut out the seed pod but leave on the stem; let cool.

2 Heat the oil, add the onion and garlic, and cook until soft but not brown.

3 Add the corn and salt, then cover the pan and cook until corn is tender (if corn is dry, you may have to add some water). Add the oregano and adjust the seasoning. Set aside to cool.

4 Blend in the sour cream and cheese; season.

5 Stuff the chiles with the cheese mixture. Reshape and chill for 30 minutes.

6 Beat the egg yolks and water until foamy. Add the flour, baking powder, and salt.

7 Whip the egg whites to soft peaks; fold the egg whites into the egg yolks.

8   Heat the oil in a deep-fryer to 350°F (175°C).

9   Dip the stuffed chiles in flour and then in the batter, and fry them until golden brown on one side. Turn over and fry until golden brown on the other side. Drain on paper towels.

Roasted Tomato Salsa 4 SERVINGS

AMOUNT	MEASURE	INGREDIENT
1¹/₄ cups	8 ounces, 226 g	Tomatoes, cored, quartered
1		Jalapeño chile, seeded, quartered
1	6 ounces, 170 g	Onion, quartered
2		Garlic cloves
pinch		Ground cumin
2 tablespoons	1 ounce, 55 ml	Vegetable oil
to taste		Salt and black pepper
as needed		Chicken stock (optional)

PROCEDURE

1   Preheat the oven to 450°F (225°C).

2   Toss the ingredients together, place on a sheet pan, and roast for 15 to 20 minutes, until vegetables begin to brown and char. (It is important that they char; the flavor comes from the browning and charring of the vegetables.)

3   Puree, then thin, if needed, with chicken stock. Check seasoning.

Jícama Salad 4 SERVINGS

AMOUNT	MEASURE	INGREDIENT
2 cups	10 ounces, 284 g	Jícama, julienned
¹/₂ cup	2 ounces, 56 g	Red bell pepper, julienned
¹/₄ cup	1 ounce, 28 g	Yellow bell pepper, julienned
1 cup	4 ounces, 113 g	Cucumber, European, peeled, julienned
¹/₄ cup	2 ounces, 55 ml	Olive oil
2 tablespoons	1 ounce, 28 ml	Lime juice
¹/₂ tablespoon		Parsley, finely chopped
to taste		Salt and white pepper

PROCEDURE

1   Combine vegetables with olive oil in a bowl.

2   Season with lime juice, parsley, salt, and pepper. Refrigerate until ready to serve.

Grilled Apache-Style Pork Cutlets 4 SERVINGS

AMOUNT	MEASURE	INGREDIENT
For the Cumin Spice Mix		
2		Garlic cloves, minced
I teaspoon	2 g	Chili powder
1/2 teaspoon	I g	Paprika
I teaspoon	2 g	Ground cumin
1/4 teaspoon		Cayenne
I teaspoon	5 g	Salt
8	3 ounces, 85 g each	Pork cutlets
as needed		Vegetable oil

PROCEDURE

1 Combine all the ingredients for spice mix and mash to a smooth paste.

2 Rub pork with spice mix and let marinate for 15 to 20 minutes.

3 Preheat the grill.

4 Brush pork with oil, then grill.

Squash Salsa 4 SERVINGS

AMOUNT	MEASURE	INGREDIENT
1/2 cup	2 ounces, 56 g	Red onion, minced
1/2 cup	2 ounces, 56 g	Zucchini, 1/8 inch (.3 cm) dice
1/2 cup	2 ounces, 56 g	Yellow summer squash, 1/8 inch (.3 cm) dice
1/4 cup	I ounce, 28 g	Carrot, 1/8 inch (.3 cm) dice
1/2 cup	3 ounces, 85 g	Tomatillos, husked, 1/8 inch (.3 cm) dice
I cup	6 ounces, 170 g	Tomato, peeled, seeded, 1/8 inch (.3 cm) dice
I		Garlic clove, minced

I		Serrano chile, minced
I tablespoon	3 g	Marjoram, chopped
4 teaspoons	³/₄ ounce, 21 ml	Olive oil
I tablespoon	¹/₂ ounce, 15 ml	Sherry vinegar
to taste		Sugar
to taste		Salt

PROCEDURE

1 Rinse the onion under very hot water and drain.

2 Combine onion with remaining ingredients.

3 Correct seasoning. Add more chile for extra heat, if desired. Let sit for at least 1 hour at room temperature before serving.

Tobacco Onions 4 SERVINGS

AMOUNT	MEASURE	INGREDIENT
I small	10 ounces, 283 g	Red onion
I small	10 ounces, 283 g	Yellow onion
I cup	4 ounces, 113 g	All-purpose flour
I tablespoon	¹/₄ ounce, 7 g	Salt and black pepper
I tablespoon	¹/₄ ounce, 7 g	Paprika
¹/₂ teaspoon	I g	Cayenne
¹/₂ teaspoon	I g	Chili powder

PROCEDURE

1 Slice the onions very thinly into rings.

2 Combine the flour and seasonings in a large bowl. Add the onion rings and toss until they are well coated with flour and dry.

3 Heat the oil in a deep-fat fryer to 350°F (175°C).

4 Fry the onions quickly, in small batches, until golden brown.

5 Remove and drain on paper towels. Serve immediately.

Sopaipillas 4 SERVINGS

AMOUNT	MEASURE	INGREDIENT
1/2 teaspoon	3 g	Salt
10 tablespoons	5 ounces, 140 ml	Water, warm
2 cups	8 ounces, 226 g	All-purpose flour
1 teaspoon	4 g	Baking powder
2 teaspoons	10 g	Granulated sugar
2 tablespoons	1 ounce, 28 g	Shortening
as needed		Oil or shortening, for frying
as needed		Confectioners' sugar
as needed		~~Honey~~ Agave!

PROCEDURE

1   Dissolve the salt in the water.

2   Combine the flour, baking powder, and sugar. Cut in the shortening until mixture resembles very fine bread crumbs. Add the salted water to the flour and mix the dough until it comes cleanly away from the sides of the bowl.

3   Turn the dough onto a lightly floured surface and knead and pull it out for 5 minutes. Divide dough into small balls approximately 1 1/4 inches (3.1 cm) in diameter. Cover and set aside for 20 minutes.

4   Heat oil or shortening to 375°F (190°C).

5   Roll the dough balls to a 1/8-inch (.3 cm) thickness on a lightly floured board. The balls should roll into 5- to 5 1/2-inch (12.7–13.9 cm) circles—they will not necessarily be evenly shaped. (Sopaipillas can be cut into any shape.) The dough should be thin, but not transparent.

6   Cut the circles into 4 triangular pieces and immediately, while the dough is still damp, put into the hot oil.

7   Fry until golden on both sides, turning once. (If shortening is sufficiently hot, the sopaipillas will puff and become hollow shortly after being placed in the shortening.) Drain sopaipillas on absorbent towels.

8   Sprinkle with sugar and drizzle with honey when serving.

Smoked-Roasted Acorn Squash 4 SERVINGS

AMOUNT	MEASURE	INGREDIENT
1		Acorn squash
1/4 cup	2 ounces, 56 g	Butter, melted
2 tablespoons	1 ounce, 28 ml	Sherry wine
2 tablespoons	1 ounce, 28 g	Brown sugar
to taste		Salt and black pepper

PROCEDURE

1 Cut the acorn squash into quarters and remove the seeds.

2 Place the squash into a stovetop smoker and smoke for 10 minutes. Remove and place on aluminum foil.

3 Preheat the oven to 350 °F (175°C).

4 Mix the butter, sherry, and sugar. Brush the glaze on the squash and season with salt and pepper. Wrap with foil. Bake the squash until tender. Baste periodically with reserved butter and sugar mixture.

Venison Steaks with Dried Wild Mushrooms 4 SERVINGS

AMOUNT	MEASURE	INGREDIENT
	I ounce, 28 g	Dried cèpes or chanterelles
6 tablespoons	3 ounces, 84 g	Unsalted butter
2 tablespoons	I ounce, 28 ml	Vegetable oil
4	5 ounces, 142 g each	Venison steaks, cut from the leg
2 tablespoons	I ounce, 20 g	Shallots, minced
¹/₄ cup	2 ounces, 55 ml	Dry red wine
I cup	8 ounces, 235 ml	Demi-glaze
to taste		Salt and black pepper

PROCEDURE

1. Cover the mushrooms with warm water and let stand for 30 minutes. Remove and cut or chop, depending on the mushroom. Decant the mushroom soaking liquid, so none of the dirt or other particles are left at the bottom of the soaking bowl. Reserve liquid for sauce.

2. Heat 2 tablespoons (28 ml) butter and all of the oil over medium heat. Cook the steaks to desired doneness. Remove steaks and drain the fat.

3. To the same pan, add 2 tablespoons (28 ml) butter and the shallots. Cook for 3 minutes.

4. Add the wine and reduce until almost dry. Add the mushroom liquid and reduce by half.

5. Add the demi-glaze and mushrooms; reduce to nappé (coat the back of a spoon). Finish with remaining butter and correct seasoning.

6. Serve 2 tablespoons sauce with venison steaks.

The Cuisine of California

Compared to the United States as a whole, California has a relatively young cuisine, the foundation of which is innovation. The third largest state in America and with the largest population, it has a wide variety of microclimates and geography, making it well suited for growing and raising foods of all kinds. Agriculture is the core of the state's economy and California produces more crops than any other state. Home to the largest irrigation systems built in America, farmers even in the most remote deserts have the opportunity to raise and harvest valuable crops.

California cuisine takes advantage of the region's abundant natural resources. With the wide variety of fresh produce and vast grazing land for livestock, obtaining fresh, local, seasonal ingredients is easy. The inclination toward a healthy lifestyle has also encouraged the development of California cuisine. Foods grown and harvested naturally, prepared simply, and without preservatives and fats, along with the constant flood of aspiring chefs bringing their culinary heritage, have assured California has its share of creativity with regard to food and food-related products. Chefs today recognize they have a commitment to the environment, to their community, and to using their talents to continue to lead the nation in fresh, new ideas that change the culinary landscape.

California "The Golden State," California's history and development has been intertwined with gold in one form or another. The state flower is the golden poppy, the state tree is the California redwood, and the state animal is the grizzly bear. The state bird is the California quail, and the state fish is the golden trout. The state motto is "Eureka"—the Greek word meaning "I have found it."

History

The earliest residents of California were Native Americans. There were hundreds of small groups, speaking more than 100 languages, with no central government, but they existed in relative peace and isolation. Mountain tribes lived in small villages and ate deer and other small game. Coastal tribes harvested fish and shellfish from the sea. Their diets also included fruit and nuts. Acorns were an important food for almost all of California's native population. After drying the acorns, and leaching out the tannin, the acorns were ground into flour to make dough that was cooked on hot rocks or made into a mush.

EUROPEAN CONTACT

The first settlers to arrive in California were the Spanish. Many were Roman Catholic missionaries who traveled to California to "civilize" and convert the natives to Christianity. Franciscan friar Junipero Serra established the first mission at San Diego in 1769, and eventually 21 California missions stretched from San Diego to Sonoma. The food in the missions reflected the Mexican and Spanish influences in the area. They grew crops such as wheat and corn and raised livestock, including cattle and pigs. The missionaries taught the Native American tribes about farming and other trades.

Along with the missionaries, a group of people known as "Californios"—Spanish-speaking people from Mexico or Spain—settled in California. These were powerful and often wealthy families who held vast territories under Spanish land grants and raised tens of thousands of cattle. They established sprawling ranchos, or cattle ranches, along the California coast. Most of the rancheros sold cattle hides and tallow, or animal fat used to make candles and soap. Some made wine and grew citrus fruits, which were exported.

They lived and entertained in grand style. Beef was the main staple of their diet. The fortunes of the Californios changed after the Mexican-American War of 1846 to 1848. Mexico lost the war and, in 1848, ceded California to the United States. Though they lost their land, the Californio legacy remains. The citrus and wine trade continue to be two of California's largest industries, and the names of many California cities—including San Francisco, San Jose, Monterey, Los Angeles, and San Diego—are reminders of the Spanish-speaking people who first settled them.

THE CALIFORNIA GOLD RUSH

In 1848, shiny particles were found near a sawmill owned by German-speaking Swiss immigrant John Sutter. The particles were gold, and it was not long before more gold was found by other workers at Sutter's mill and news of the chance discovery began to spread. When the news reached San Francisco, virtually the whole town flocked to the Sacramento Valley to pan for gold. As gold fever traveled eastward, overland migration to California rose from 400 people in 1848 to over 44,000 by 1849. By the end of 1849, California's population exceeded 100,000. The rest of the world caught gold fever as well. Among the so-called "forty-niners"—the prospectors who came to California in 1849— were people from Asia, South America, and Europe. The discovery of gold revolutionized California's economy. Gold financed the development of farming, manufacturing, shipping, and banking. Because of its location, San Francisco became the supply center of the region. Ships linked California markets to the expanding markets of the rest of the United States.

THE TRANSCONTINENTAL RAILROAD

Even after the gold rush, California remained the fastest growing state in the nation. Entrepreneurs Charles Crocker, Mark Hopkins, Collis Huntington, and Leland Stanford—known as the "Big Four"—joined together to build the western railroad link to overcome California's geographic isolation from the East Coast. Their crews laid over a thousand miles of track to join the eastern and western railroad lines.

When they needed workers to lay the track, they hired primarily Chinese immigrants. By 1869, when the railroad was finished, 10,000 Chinese workers had helped to build it. After completing the job, the Chinese turned to the agriculture, mining, and manufacturing industries for work. They lived in their own neighborhoods, establishing large Chinatowns in San Francisco, Los Angeles, and other cities.

HOLLYWOOD

In the early years of the 20th century, moviemakers found their homes and fortunes in California. Southern California made outdoor filming possible during the winter months, and striking landscapes soon turned it into the glamour capital of the world. Catering to the movie studios and its stars, restaurants such as the Cocoanut Grove, the Brown Derby, and Chasen's opened and quickly learned to provide high-quality food with excellent service, setting the trend for today's modern California cuisine restaurants.

The Geography and Microclimates

When discussing any great area of agriculture, it is helpful to organize it into regions reflecting climate, geography, and culture. The coastline of California stretches 1,264 miles from the Oregon border in the north to Mexico in the south. More than half of California's population resides in the coastal region. Most live in the major cities that developed around harbors at San Francisco Bay, San Diego Bay, and the Los Angeles Basin. The San Francisco Bay, one of the finest natural harbors in the world, covers about 450 square miles and is famous for its ocean breezes and the fog that rolls in from the sea. It became the gateway for newcomers heading to the states' interior in the nineteenth and twentieth centuries. The completion of the Santa Fe Railroad in 1885 spurred population growth, as did the establishment of major army and navy bases during World War I. The Los Angeles Basin is the largest lowland area in California, and with construction of a huge breakwater along the harbors of San Pedro and Long Beach, this bustling port overtook New York City in 1994 as America's premier gateway for foreign trade.

Mountains cover most of California. The mountains guard the rich agricultural valleys from the intense heat of the desert to the east and shield the coastal valleys from the Pacific Ocean and its winds to the west.

The Central Valley lies between the coastal ranges and the Sierra Nevada. With the rich soil washed down from the surrounding mountains, this is the most productive agricultural area in California. This valley is actually two valleys in one, with the San Joaquin Valley in the south and the Sacramento Valley in the north. The climate in the San Joaquin and Sacramento valleys supports an expansive array of fruits and vegetables. After the gold rush in 1849, European settlers established vast wheat farms on the valleys' fertile soils. The great Central Valley Project, constructed in the mid-20th century, established a series of dams, reservoirs, and canals and guaranteed sufficient water for the diversification of crops. The improvements in irrigation enabled the valleys to produce tomatoes, potatoes, alfalfa, sugar beets, olives, almonds, walnuts, peaches, pears, apricots, and dozens of other fruits and vegetables.

Much of the eastern half of Southern California is a large desert triangle. Among the deserts of California are the Mojave and Colorado, as well as the notorious Death Valley. The Mojave is the largest desert in California, and Death Valley, a deep trough that is measured as the lowest point below sea level in the Western Hemisphere, was named by a group of gold seekers who struggled through the region in 1849. The Colorado Desert stretches over 4,000 miles in Southern California and includes the Coachella and Imperial valleys. In 1849, California visionary Oliver Wozencraft became convinced that these two valleys could be irrigated and turned into thriving farmland. He had a creative irrigation plan, which, over the subsequent years, was modified into a chain of levees that brought water to the valleys from the Colorado River. Many settlers moved to the valleys as farming was made easier and more profitable by the constant sunshine, inexpensive water supply, and rich soil. The settlers found that in this desert area of California, they could raise crops, harvest them, and sell them in the market before their competitors in the north. The nation's only commercial date palm grove grows in this desert oasis, and today the desert is known as Palm Springs and is a place of fashionable boutiques, exclusive resorts, and magnificent and opulent living.

Major Influences and Innovations

INNOVATION IN FOOD

The largest of California's agricultural industries is dairy farming, which today produces over $3 billion worth of dairy products each year. The cheese industry of California, working with the milk of cows, goats, and sheep, is an example of the state's diversity. Small local artisans make prize-winning, hand-crafted, high-quality cheeses that compete well with their older, more established European counterparts. At the other end of the spectrum are high-tech cheese factories that produce hundreds of millions of pounds of cheese each year. Monterey Jack, one of the three cheeses invented in America, is from California.

Agricultural innovation in California began with a horticulturist named Luther Burbank, who moved to Southern California from New England in the late 1800s. During a lifetime devoted to plant breeding, Luther Burbank developed more than 800 strains and varieties of plants, including 113 varieties of plums and prunes, 10 varieties of berries, 50 varieties of lilies, and the Freestone peach. In 1871, he developed the Burbank potato, which was introduced in Ireland to help combat the blight epidemic. He sold the rights to the potato and used the proceeds to travel to Santa Rosa, California. In Santa Rosa, he established a nursery garden, greenhouse, and experimental farms that have become famous throughout the world. At any one time, he maintained as many as 3,000 experiments involving millions of plants. In his work on plums, he tested about 30,000 new varieties. From this original research, California scientists began to develop new varieties of produce carefully selected for resistance to disease, bugs, and extreme weather conditions, as well as for characteristics of size, color, flavor, and shelf life. Although a significant amount of controversy surrounds these selectively bred fruits and vegetables, especially now that some are being genetically modified, one thing is for certain: The technological advances started by Burbank in California allowed the state's produce industry to supply not only America but also the world.

MODERN CALIFORNIA CUISINE

Culinary professionals credit Alice Waters for her role in the development of California cuisine. While studying in France, Waters experienced a cuisine based on using premier ingredients grown by local farmers. She returned to America and opened her own restaurant, Chez Panisse, in Berkeley, in 1971, and partnered with local growers from Northern California. She used a single fixed-price menu that changed daily. This menu format allowed her to focus on serving not only the highest-quality products but also only when ingredients were in season, understanding that the dish is only as good as its components. As other restaurants began to adopt her philosophy, many artisan producers found opportunities to specialize in and market certain products, such as baby vegetables, varietal tomatoes, and other market-fresh produce. Chez Panisse is still considered one of the best restaurants in the United States.

About ten years later, Austrian-born chef Wolfgang Puck, the chef at Ma Maison in Los Angeles, a popular hangout for Hollywood celebrities, became one of America's first celebrity chefs. In 1982, Puck opened his own restaurant in Los Angeles, called Spago, and became known for his designer pizzas and specialty pasta dishes. He brought a lighter style of cooking to California cuisine and added an entertaining and energetic atmosphere emphasizing an "open kitchen" where guests could watch the chefs prepare their food.

Recently, fusion cuisine has become a popular innovation originating in California.

California Grapes

Father Junipero Serra is credited with planting the first grape vines at the San Diego Mission shortly after its founding. The early Spanish missionaries were the first to produce wine in California from local Mission grapes. However, it was not until after the 1849 gold rush that the wine industry took root. A Frenchman living in California, Jean-Louis Vignes, recognized the value of the soil and the climate, but he felt that the wines would improve if the European grape varieties grown in France could be transplanted to California. Between the plentiful sunshine and the cooling effects of the fog that rolls in from the Pacific Ocean, California's climate was similar to the climate that vines were used to in Europe. Later, Hungarian Agoston Haraszthy took note of Vignes's success in growing French grapes. He established the first California winery, Buena Vista, in 1857. In 1861, he traveled to Europe to buy cuttings and brought over 100,000 vine cuttings representing over 300 varieties of grapes. He planted them in Sonoma Country and became known as the father of California's wine industry. Wine making in California prospered until 1916, when the vines were almost wiped out by a vine-killing root louse called phylloxera. Added to that were the 14 "dry" years during the era of Prohibition, from December 1917 until February 1933. Most of California's 713 pre-Prohibition wineries closed their doors, but a few wineries stayed in business by making legally sanctioned sacramental and medicinal wines. Others survived by shipping grapes cross-country by rail to home wine-making markets. A provision of the Volstad Act allowed families to make 200 gallons annually for home consumption. Many of them also purchased "wine bricks," "wine loaves," or grape concentrate to make their wine. Vintners produced and sold concentrate with a creative label that read, "Warning: Do not add water to this product as it is likely to ferment." Public opinion eventually turned against Prohibition and the act was repealed in 1933. The California wine-making industry recovered by the 1940s; however, the existing grape-growing and wine-making techniques produced many low- to average-quality wines. After experimentation throughout the 1950s, 1960s, and 1970s, wine making in California began to reach its maturity, now yielding high-quality wines that can compete with many older, more established European wines.

Using a creative mix of flavors, techniques, and ingredients of more than one region or international cuisine, California chefs began creating dishes that both represent and serve the diverse people and cultures in the state today.

California society has been shaped by many different kinds of people. From the Native Americans, to Spanish aristocrats, to gold hunters, railroad tycoons, and movie moguls, each group has left its imprint on the state. And immigration to California continues as Mexican, Japanese, Southeast Asian, Italian, French, northern European, Middle Eastern, Spanish, and Greek people contribute to the multicultural blend that keeps California cuisine fresh, imaginative, and exciting.

Typical California Ingredients and Dishes

Abalone The meat from a large mollusk that lives off the coast of California. There are eight species that inhabit the Pacific waters: red (the largest, and most important commercial abalone), green, black, flat (small in size and most prized), white (found in depths up to 150 feet and commercially included with the pink abalone), and the three least common species—threaded, pink, and pinto. All varieties offer meat that is extremely sweet and tasty, but it is usually tough and rubbery and requires tenderizing with a mallet prior to cooking. Their colorful, ear-shaped shells are sometimes referred to as "mother-of-pearl." Today, the abalone industry is highly regulated, as the mollusks continue to be the favorite food of sea otters and are scarce.

Anaheim Chile Also referred to as the "California green chile," this 6- to 8-inch chile is bright green with mild to moderate heat. When this chile is grown in New Mexico, it is referred to as a "New Mexico green chile." It was popularized by Emilio Ortega, a California rancher who opened the first chile cannery near Anaheim in 1900.

Artichoke A member of the thistle group of the sunflower family with a large, globular flower head. It is grown predominately in California in the town of Castroville. The Green Globe artichoke is most common to the area. Artichoke hearts have an especially appealing flavor and texture. Artichokes are served hot or cold, as an appetizer or a main dish, and as an ingredient in other dishes such as pasta sauces, vegetable dishes, and in soups and stews.

Asparagus Over 70 percent of all asparagus served in America is produced in the southern half of California's Great Central Valley. Asparagus is a member of the lily family, and the varieties include white, green, and a new breed of purple, Purple Passion.

Avocado Dating back to almost 8,000 B.C., the avocado originated in Mexico and was considered an aphrodisiac by the Aztecs. Avocados were first introduced to California in 1848. Today, California produces 95 percent of the nation's crop. A single California avocado tree can produce up to 60 pounds of fresh fruit each year, approximately 120 individual avocados. The most popular varieties are the Hass and the Fuerte, which are known for their sweet, slightly nutty flavor.

Calamari Italian for "squid." Squid is found all along the California coast. It can be cooked by sautéing, frying, steaming, poaching, or broiling. Large squid are usually stuffed and braised. Squid has an ink sac in the head containing a dark black liquid that can be used (but only if the squid is extremely fresh) in sauces or as a flavoring and coloring agent for fresh pasta. Squid and octopus belong to the same family, but squid have ten arms and a long, cigar-shaped body with fins at the end; octopuses have eight arms and a stubbier body.

California Roll A form of sushi made with avocados, crab meat, cucumbers, and other ingredients wrapped in vinegared rice.

Cioppino A fish stew cooked with tomatoes, wine, and spices. This stew is associated with the Italian fishermen who came to the San Francisco Bay area in the late 1800s.

Cheese As the largest farming state in the United States, dairy farms and dairies processing the milk of cows, goats, and sheep can be found all over the state.

> *Dry Jack* A type of cheese discovered by mistake in the early 1900s by a cheese wholesaler who apparently left some in storage too long. The aged Jack cheese had hardened and developed a sweet, nutty flavor. During World War I, the supply of Romano and Parmesan cheeses previously imported to America became sporadic and inconsistent. Dry Jack, with a texture and flavor similar to the dried Italian cheese, became popular as a substitute. It is now produced as a California artisan-style cheese.

> *Feta Cheese* A salty, crumbly white cheese made in the style of Greek goat's milk cheese. American varieties are often made from cow's milk. After the curds are formed, the cheese is pickled in a brine solution.

> *Goat Cheese* Called chèvre in France, goat cheese has become a signature ingredient in California cuisine. It is typically an intensely flavored cheese.

> *Monterey Jack* One of the three cheeses invented in the United States (along with Colby and brick, from the Central Plains region). A mild white, semisoft cheese that originated in Monterey, California, much like the cheeses produced in the early mis-

sions. It was named after David Jacks, a dairy farmer who made the cheese just after California's gold rush years.

Chop Suey An American invention created by the cooks who fed the Chinese immigrants working to construct the Western Pacific Railroad in the mid-1800s. Considered to be "a little of this and that" from the Mandarin words *tsa tsui,* the widely varying ingredients usually include bamboo shoots, water chestnuts, bean sprouts, celery, soy sauce, and chicken or pork. Americanized Chinese dishes such as this and chow mein continue to be served in Chinese restaurants to American customers.

Citron A citrus fruit that looks like a large, lumpy lemon. Another common variety grown in California is mostly as an ornamental, called the Fingered citron or Buddha's Hand, that has formed by a half dozen or more long twisting fingers growing outward from the stem end. Only the rind is used, much like lemon rind. Citron rind is most frequently candied and often used in baking.

Cobb Salad A chopped salad made with avocado, lettuce, celery, tomato, bacon, chicken, chives, hard-boiled egg, watercress, and Roquefort cheese. Originally created at the Brown Derby Restaurant in Los Angeles in 1934, it is now commonly used to describe many types of chopped salads.

Date The name is from the Greek word for "finger," after the shape of the fruit. Date palm trees require at least ten years from the time the tree is planted to the time fruit can be picked. The only places in the Western Hemisphere where dates are commercially grown are the Yuma Valley in Arizona and the Coachella Valley in California, where the climate is similar to that of the Middle East and North Africa. The best dates are picked soft, and then frozen to maintain the enzymes in the fruit that produce the natural sugar powder that forms on the skin. Lower-quality dates are allowed to cure on the tree and then are softened by steaming, which destroys the enzymes.

Figs Planted at the Spanish missions, the Mission (or Black Mission) fig has purple-black skin. Other varieties include the Brown Turkey fig, which is amber in color and milder than the Mission fig. The most commonly grown fig in California is the Calimyrna, a greenish yellow to golden colored fig more frequently seen as whole dried figs.

French Dip The house specialty of Phillippe's, a Los Angeles restaurant dating back to 1908. The sandwich calls for thinly sliced beef, pork, or lamb served hot on a French bread roll and dipped in warm pan juices.

Garlic A major crop from Gilroy, California, located in the San Joaquin Valley. Over 90 percent of all garlic consumed in the United States is grown here. Garlic is native to Central Asia; Japanese immigrants started garlic farming in the area in the 1920s.

Green Goddess Dressing A mayonnaise-based salad dressing made with anchovies, tarragon, chives, and parsley, invented by the chef at the Palace Hotel in San Francisco. Green Goddess dressing was created in 1921 in honor of George Arliss, a guest of the hotel, who was starring in the play *The Green Goddess,* being performed in the city.

Guacamole A dip made from the mashed pulp of avocados mixed with herbs, seasonings, and sometimes tomatoes and onions. In California, recipes for guacamole are passed down from generation to generation and guarded as stringently as chili recipes in Texas and gumbo recipes in New Orleans. Guacamole can be smooth or chunky, mild or spicy.

Kiwi This round green fruit with black seeds and fuzzy brown skin was known as the Chinese gooseberry and originated in China. Today, 95 percent of the U.S. crop is grown in California, primarily in the San Joaquin Valley.

Olive California has four main varieties—Mission, originally planted by the Franciscan missionaries; Manzanillo, which account for most of the acreage; and Sevillano and Ascolano, which produce the larger sizes. Approximately 75 percent of ripe olives consumed in the United States come from California. Over 90 percent of the California crop is processed as black ripe olives. The remaining olives are processed into various specialty styles or crushed for olive oil.

Oranges After Florida, California produces the most oranges of any state. The most common varieties include:

Blood Orange Called blood oranges because of a pigment that gives the flesh a deep red color reminiscent of blood. With the most interesting and complex flavor of any orange, the fruit's degree of red color in the flesh and peel varies according to variety, growing area, and degree of maturity. Brought to the United States by Spanish and Italian immigrants, the Ruby Blood and Moro varieties are raised in California.

Navel Orange This variety arrived in California from Brazil in 1873. Called "navel" because of a secondary fruit at the end of the main fruit that causes a belly-button look. They are known for their large size, sweet taste, seedless flesh, and ease of peeling.

Valencia Orange The most important of the juice oranges, this variety comes originally from Spain and is grown in large quantities in Southern California. Valencia oranges are large, thin skinned, and very juicy, with excellent flavor and few seeds.

Pacific Sole A common flatfish found in the waters off the California coast. Several varieties of Pacific sole are available, including the English or lemon sole, rex sole, California Dover sole, rock sole, and petrale or brill sole. All of the varieties have a white, sweet-tasting flesh with a lean, fine texture. The rex and the petrale sole are two of the most sought after fish in the region. They are frequently sautéed and served with a light sauce.

Pummelo Two varieties of this grapefruit-like fruit were developed in California. The Chandler pummelo is large and round, with yellow skin and pink flesh. The Reinkin variety is larger and pear shaped, with white flesh.

Raisin A sweet, dried grape. California produces the most raisins of any region of the world, mostly of the Thompson Seedless variety. It is suggested that the raisin was created by accident when a heat wave dried a farmer's grapes on the vine before he could pick them. The grape industry devotes almost 2 million tons of grapes each year to the production of raisins.

Sand Dab A miniature relative of the flounder that is common in the waters off the California coast. They are small flatfish between 8 and 10 ounces and both eyes, brown in color and mottled with orange or black spots or blotches, are found on the same side of the fish. This fish has a sweet flesh with a fine texture and is usually pan- or deep-fried.

Sashimi Very fresh, top-quality, carefully handled fish, eaten raw.

Sea Urchin Spiky "hedgehogs of the sea" have become fashionable first-course menu items. The roe is the only edible part of the sea urchin and is considered a great delicacy.

Smoothie A health drink that dates back to the 1970s, typically found in juice bars. Recipes for smoothies vary; however, the essential ingredients include whole fruit, fruit juice, and yogurt, which are blended together and served in tall glasses.

Sourdough Bread A uniquely flavored bread originally made in the San Francisco Bay area beginning in 1849 by French baker Louis Boudin. Boudin's bread had a chewy texture, crisp crust, and signature sour flavor. Popular among the prospectors during the California gold rush, it is still considered a San Francisco signature.

Sourdough Starter A fermented leavener made from a paste of flour and water, activated by yeast and used to make sourdough bread. Sourdough starter was so valuable to miners and prospectors who depended on it to survive the wilderness that they carried it in a pouch hung from their necks. They became known as "sourdoughs" themselves.

Sourdough starter is usually used over and over again. Each time a batch of sourdough bread is made, a portion of the dough is reserved, then mixed with water and a little salt, which maintains the starter. It is later added to the next batch of dough in order to make it rise. The process is repeated over and over again.

Sushi A bite-size Japanese rice and fish preparation popularized in the United States by Californians. Two main varieties of sushi are popular: maki and niguri. Sushi maki is made with sweet, sticky rice that is rolled in seaweed with raw, cooked, or smoked fish or shellfish, or vegetables, and cut into bite-size pieces. Niguri sushi has pieces of raw fish or seafood decoratively placed on top of an oblong log of sweet, sticky rice. Sushi needs to be served freshly made from the highest quality fish or seafood available. It is typically served with soy sauce, pickled ginger slices, and wasabi, a Japanese green horseradish.

Table Grape About one-third of the fruit and nut revenues of California come from table grapes. The Thompson Seedless grape, which is native to Iran, took its name in the United States from an Englishman named William Thompson, who planted the grapes in the Sacramento Valley in the 1860s. Today, table grapes are extensively grown from the Mexican border to many parts of the San Joaquin Valley, with over 500,000 acres of land devoted to the crop. Among the many popular table grape varieties are Ribier, Flame, Emperor, Red Globe, and Calmeria.

Wine Grape Approximately 20 varieties of grape are used today by California wine makers, planted on more than 350,000 acres of land, primarily near the north and central coasts. The most commonly grown grape varieties for the production of white wines are the Chardonnay, French Colombard, Chenin Blanc, and Sauvignon Blanc grapes. For the production of red wines, the most common grape varieties used are the Zinfandel, Cabernet Sauvignon, Merlot, and Barbera grapes.

Menus and Recipes from California Cuisine

MENU ONE

Chilled Avocado and Cucumber Soup

Warm Scallop Salad with Tomato, Mint, and Lime Dressing

Sautéed Duck Breast with a Port Wine Reduction

Monterey Jack and Green Chile Polenta

Fried Fennel

Creamed Spinach

MENU TWO

Cream of Garlic Soup

Warm Baked Goat Cheese with Baby Greens

Calamari, Artichoke, and Penne Pasta, Monterey-Style

Raspberry Chicken

Swiss Chard with Golden Raisins

Rice with Red Peppers and Pine Nuts

Strawberry Shortcake with Cornmeal Biscuit

MENU THREE

Dilled Carrot Soup

Caesar Salad

Hangtown Fry

San Francisco Cioppino

Kiwifruit and Grape Rice Pudding

OTHER RECIPES

Chèvre (Goat Cheese) and Pistachio Wrapped in Filo

Chinese Chicken Salad

Asparagus with Toasted Hazelnuts

Garden Pasta Salad

Oven-Roasted Potatoes

Rosemary Focaccia

Steamed Asian Vegetables

Stuffed Pork with Apples or Pears and Prunes

Chilled Avocado and Cucumber Soup 4 SERVINGS

chef tip If the surface of the soup oxidizes or turns brown after being chilled, simply skim off and discard the discolored surface before serving.

AMOUNT	MEASURE	INGREDIENT
1/2 cup	4 ounces, 115 ml	Heavy cream
1 1/4 cups	8 ounces, 226 g	Avocado, peeled, seeded, 1/4 inch (.6 cm) dice
1 cup	6 ounces, 170 g	Cucumber, peeled, seeded, 1/4 inch (.6 cm) dice
1 tablespoon	1/2 ounce, 14 ml	Lime juice
1 cup	8 ounces, 224 ml	Chicken or vegetable stock
1 cup	8 ounces, 224 ml	Yogurt (plain)
1		Garlic clove, minced
1/2 cup	4 ounces, 115 ml	Sour cream
1 tablespoon	3 g	Dill, coarsely chopped
1 tablespoon	3 g	Parsley, coarsely chopped
to taste		Salt and white pepper
1/2 cup	4 ounces, 115 ml	Milk, more if needed

For the Garnish

1/4 cup	2 ounces, 55 ml	Sour cream
1/2 cup	1/2 ounce, 14 g	Green onions, thinly sliced

PROCEDURE

1 Set aside 2 tablespoons (1 ounce, 28 g) each of the avocado and cucumber for garnish. Place remainder and the ingredients, except the milk, in a blender or food processor and blend until smooth.

2 Add the milk a little at a time and blend until the desired consistency of soup is attained.

3 Pour the soup into a stainless-steel container. Place a piece of plastic wrap on the surface of the soup to prevent discoloration. Chill the soup, under refrigeration at 40°F (4°C) or below until thoroughly chilled.

4 When ready to serve, carefully ladle the soup into chilled soup bowls or onto plates, and garnish each portion with the reserved avocado, cucumber, a dollop of sour cream, and the green onions.

Warm Scallop Salad with Tomato, Mint, and Lime Dressing   4 SERVINGS

AMOUNT	MEASURE	INGREDIENT
For the Dressing		
6 tablespoons	3 ounces, 84 ml	Olive oil
1 1/2 tablespoons	3/4 ounce, 21 g	Shallot, minced
1 1/2 tablespoons	3/4 ounce, 21 ml	Lime juice
1/2 teaspoon	3 g	Salt
1/2 teaspoon	1 g	Black pepper
1 1/2 cups	9 ounces, 255 g	Tomatoes, peeled, seeded, 1/4 inch (.6 cm) dice
1 1/2 tablespoons	5 g	Mint, finely chopped
For the Salad		
	12 ounces, 340 g	Scallops (bay or sea), well drained and patted dry
2 tablespoons	1 ounce, 28 ml	Olive oil
1/2 cup	2 ounces, 56 g	Jícama, peeled and julienned
2		Watercress bunches, large stems removed

PROCEDURE

1 Heat the olive oil. Sauté the shallots until soft, but do not brown.

2 Add the lime juice, salt, and pepper; remove from heat. Combine with remaining dressing ingredients.

3 If using sea scallops, remove the small white muscle. If scallops are 1 inch (2.5 cm) in diameter or larger, cut the scallop in half, lengthwise, before using.

4 Heat the olive oil. Add the scallops and sauté over medium-high heat, turning often. They should be just cooked, slightly translucent in the middle. Remove from heat.

5 Pour half of the dressing over the warm scallops in the pan. Correct seasoning and keep warm.

6 Divide the watercress evenly among plates. Place the scallops with dressing in the center of the watercress.

7 Sprinkle the jícama over the salad. Spoon additional dressing onto the plate.

Sautéed Duck Breast with a Port Wine Reduction 4 SERVINGS

AMOUNT	MEASURE	INGREDIENT
4	6 ounces, 170 g each	Duck breasts, boneless, skin on
to taste		Salt and white pepper

For the Sauce

AMOUNT	MEASURE	INGREDIENT
2 tablespoons	1 ounce, 28 g	Shallots, finely diced
1 cup	8 ounces, 235 ml	Port wine
³/₄ cup	6 ounces, 170 ml	Brown stock
2 tablespoons	1 ounce, 28 g	Butter

PROCEDURE

1 Remove any excess fat and score the duck breast in a crosshatch pattern with a sharp knife. Season with salt and white pepper and place skin side down in a heavy-bottomed sauté pan. Without turning the breasts, cook them over low heat, rendering the fat from their skin, until the skin is golden brown and crisp, approximately 15 minutes.

2 Turn the duck breast, and cook to medium rare.

3 Remove the duck breast from pan and allow to rest in a warm place for 10 minutes.

4 Pour off excess fat from pan. Add the shallots and sauté until translucent.

5 Deglaze the pan with the wine and reduce the volume of liquid by half over medium-high heat.

6 Add the brown stock. Continue to reduce until the sauce has a glaze consistency (will coat the back of a spoon).

7 Add the butter and whisk in. Adjust the seasoning.

8 Slice the duck breasts. Arrange on warm plates and serve with sauce.

Monterey Jack and Green Chile Polenta 4 SERVINGS

AMOUNT	MEASURE	INGREDIENT
10 tablespoons	5 ounces, 140 ml	Chicken stock
10 tablespoons	5 ounces, 140 ml	Milk
2 tablespoons	1 ounce, 28 g	Butter
1 teaspoon	5 g	Granulated sugar
1/2 teaspoon	3 g	Salt
1/2 cup	3 ounces, 90 g	Polenta
1/2 cup	2 ounces, 56 g	Monterey Jack cheese, grated
1		Poblano chile, roasted, peeled, seeded, 1/4 inch (.6 cm) dice
to taste		Salt and white pepper

PROCEDURE

1　Bring the chicken stock to a boil. Reduce to a simmer and stir in the milk, butter, sugar, and salt.

2　Slowly add the polenta in a thin stream, whisking constantly. Lower the heat and continue stirring for about 10 to 20 minutes, or until the mixture starts to thicken.

3　Stir in the cheese and chile. Continue to stir while cooking over low heat until the mixture is thick and easily falls away from the sides of the pan.

4　Season with salt and white pepper.

Fried Fennel 4 SERVINGS

AMOUNT	MEASURE	INGREDIENT
4	3 ounces, 84 g each	Fennel bulbs, $^1/_4$-inch (.6 cm) slices
as needed		All-purpose flour, for dusting
to taste		Salt

For the Tempura Batter

2		Eggs
2 cups	16 ounces, 470 ml	Water, ice cold
2 cups	8 ounces, 226 g	All-purpose flour, sifted
to taste		Coarse salt
as needed		Vegetable oil, for deep-frying

PROCEDURE

1 Combine the eggs and water; whisk, blending in flour and salt; stir in lightly (do not beat). Refrigerate for 30 minutes.

2 Dust the fennel with the flour. Shake off the excess flour.

3 Heat the oil in a deep-fryer to 350°F (175°C).

4 Dip the fennel in the batter, shake off excess, and fry until golden brown.

5 Drain on paper towels. Season lightly with salt. Serve hot.

Creamed Spinach 4 SERVINGS

AMOUNT	MEASURE	INGREDIENT
8 cups	16 ounces, 452 g	Spinach, washed, tough stems removed
2 tablespoons	1 ounce, 28 g	Unsalted butter
1/2 cup	2 ounces, 56 g	Shallots, 1/4 inch (.6 cm) dice
1 teaspoon		Garlic, minced
1/2 cup	4 ounces, 115 ml	Heavy cream
1/2 teaspoon	3 g	Salt
1/2 teaspoon	1 g	Black pepper
1/4 teaspoon		Grated nutmeg

PROCEDURE

1 Blanch the spinach in boiling salted water for 1 minute. Drain. Run under cold water and press to remove as much water as possible.

2 Chop the spinach and set aside.

3 Melt the butter over medium-high heat. Add the shallots and garlic; cook for 3 minutes.

4 Add the spinach and toss to combine. Cook until the liquid is released (drain liquid if there is excess).

5 Add the cream, salt, pepper, and nutmeg. Reduce by half, about 4 to 5 minutes. Serve immediately.

Cream of Garlic Soup 4 SERVINGS

Gilroy, a small town in central California, is the self-proclaimed garlic capital of the world. Typically, in California cuisine, the use of roux as a thickening agent is unpopular. In this recipe, the potatoes pureed into the soup act as the thickening agent.

Chive flowers make a great garnish for this soup. They can be used in addition to the minced chives or as a replacement.

AMOUNT	MEASURE	INGREDIENT
1 tablespoon	$^1/_2$ ounce, 14 ml	Vegetable oil
$^1/_2$ cup	2 ounces, 56 g	Onion, $^1/_4$ inch (.6 cm) dice
$^2/_3$ cup	2 ounces, 56 g	Leek, white part only, cleaned, $^1/_4$ inch (.6 cm) dice
1$^1/_2$ cups	8 ounces, 226 g	Russet potatoes, peeled, $^1/_2$ inch (1.2 cm) dice
$^1/_3$ cup	2 ounces, 56 g	Garlic cloves, roughly chopped
1 quart	1 l	Chicken stock
$^1/_2$ cup	4 ounces, 115 ml	Heavy cream
to taste		Salt and white pepper
1 tablespoon		Chives, finely minced

PROCEDURE

1 Heat the oil and cook the onion and leek over medium-high heat until the onion is tender and translucent, 3 minutes.

2 Add the potatoes, garlic, and stock. Bring to a boil, then reduce the heat to a simmer. Simmer the soup until the potatoes and garlic are tender and thoroughly cooked.

3 Puree the mixture in a food processor or blender.

4 Return to the heat and add the cream. Correct the seasoning and reheat the soup, but do not bring to a boil.

5 Garnish with chives.

Warm Baked Goat Cheese with Baby Greens 4 SERVINGS

AMOUNT	MEASURE	INGREDIENT
I cup	8 ounces, 226 g	Chèvre (goat cheese)
1/4 cup	2 ounces, 55 ml	Olive oil
4		Thyme sprigs
1/2 cup	2 ounces, 56 g	Bread crumbs, dry
1/4 cup	I ounce, 28 g	Walnuts, finely chopped

For the Vinaigrette

AMOUNT	MEASURE	INGREDIENT
1/4 cup	2 ounces, 55 ml	Red wine vinegar
I teaspoon	5 g	Dijon mustard
1/4 cup	2 ounces, 55 ml	Walnut oil
1/4 cup	2 ounces, 55 ml	Olive oil
to taste		Salt and black pepper
as needed		Butter, clarified, or olive oil
4 cups	8 ounces, 226 g	Baby greens
2 tablespoons	6 g	Chives, chopped

PROCEDURE

1 Shape the goat cheese into eight (1-ounce, 28 g) patties.

2 Marinate the patties in the olive oil and thyme. Refrigerate for 2 hours.

3 Combine the bread crumbs and walnuts. Roll the patties in this mixture. Place them on a sheet pan with parchment paper and refrigerate for 30 minutes.

4 Combine vinegar and mustard and slowly whisk in the oils until creamy. Correct the seasoning and set aside.

5 Pan-fry the goat cheese in the clarified butter until golden brown and hot.

6 Toss the baby greens in the vinaigrette and divide evenly among chilled plates. Place 2 goat-cheese patties on top of each plate of greens, and garnish with chives.

Calamari, Artichoke, and Penne Pasta—Monterey Style 4 SERVINGS

AMOUNT	MEASURE	INGREDIENT
4 1/2 cups	12 ounces, 340 g	Penne pasta (dried)
1/4 cup	2 ounces, 56 g	Olive oil
1 tablespoon	3 g	Parsley, chopped
1/2 tablespoon	2 g	Cilantro leaves, chopped
1/2 tablespoon	2 g	Basil, chopped
1/2 tablespoon	2 g	Thyme, chopped
1/8 teaspoon		Red pepper flakes (dried)
	1 ounce, 28 g	Anchovy fillets
2		Garlic cloves, minced
1 cup	6 ounces, 170 g	Tomato, peeled, seeded, 1/4 inch (.6 cm) dice
1 tablespoon	1/2 ounce, 15 g	Capers, drained
1/2 cup	3 ounces, 85 g	Calamata olives, pitted, coarsely chopped
3 cups	1 1/2 pounds, 681 g	Baby artichokes, cut into wedges, heart removed, cooked
2 cups	12 ounces, 340 g	Calamari rings and tentacles, cleaned
1/2 cup	1 1/2 ounces, 42 g	Parmesan cheese, shaved
to taste		Salt and black pepper

PROCEDURE

1 Cook the pasta in boiling salted water until al dente.

2 Cool the pasta slightly under cold running water. Drain well and toss with 1 table-spoon (15 ml) olive oil to prevent the pasta from sticking together.

3 Toss the pasta with the chopped herbs and season with the red pepper flakes. Set aside.

4 Combine the anchovies and garlic. Mash thoroughly until a paste forms.

5 Heat the remaining olive oil over medium heat. Add the anchovy-garlic mixture. Add the tomato, capers, and olives. Stir and place over medium heat until the mixture comes to a boil. Reduce the heat to low and simmer, uncovered, stirring occasionally, until the sauce thickens to the desired consistency.

6   Add the artichokes and calamari. Continue cooking for 30 to 60 seconds or until calamari is cooked.

7   Return the penne to the calamari and reheat.

8   Divide the pasta onto 4 warm serving plates or bowls, taking care to distribute the artichoke hearts and calamari evenly among the portions. Garnish each portion with shaved Parmesan cheese and a sprinkling of salt and pepper.

Raspberry Chicken 4 SERVINGS

AMOUNT	MEASURE	INGREDIENT
4	4–6 ounces each	Chicken breasts, boneless, skinless
as needed		All-purpose flour, for dusting
2 tablespoons	1 ounce, 28 g	Unsalted butter
1/2 cup	2 ounces, 56 g	Onion, 1/4 inch (.6 cm) dice
1/4 cup	2 ounces, 55 ml	Raspberry vinegar
1/4 cup	2 ounces, 55 ml	Chicken stock
1/4 cup	2 ounces, 55 ml	Heavy cream
1/3 cup	2 ounces, 56 g	Tomato, peeled, seeded, 1/4 inch (.6 cm) dice
1 pint	6 ounces, 170 g	Raspberries, cleaned

PROCEDURE

1 Flatten the chicken breasts so they are even.

2 Heat the butter in a sauté pan over medium heat.

3 Dry, season, and dust the chicken breasts in flour. Shake off the excess flour.

4 Sauté the chicken in butter. Turn and cook until they are light golden brown. Remove the chicken breasts from the pan and set aside.

5 Lower the heat and add the onion. Cook until onion is caramelized, about 5 minutes.

6 Add the vinegar. Raise the heat and cook, stirring occasionally, until the vinegar is reduced to a syrupy consistency.

7 Whisk in the stock, cream, and tomato. Simmer for 2 minutes.

8 Return the chicken to the pan and simmer gently in the sauce until they are just done. Do not overcook.

9 Remove the chicken with a slotted spoon and add fresh raspberries to the sauce. Cook over low heat for 1 minute. Do not stir in the berries with a spoon; merely swirl them in the sauce by shaking the pan.

10 Serve chicken with the sauce and a few whole raspberries.

Swiss Chard with Golden Raisins 4 SERVINGS

AMOUNT	MEASURE	INGREDIENT
2 tablespoons	³/₄ ounce, 21 g	Golden raisins
3 cups	16 ounces, 453 g	Swiss chard, red or white, rinsed
2 tablespoons	1 ounce, 28 g	Unsalted butter
4	1 ounce, 28 g	Shallots, ¹/₄ inch (.6 cm) dice
1		Garlic clove, minced
1 teaspoon	5 ml	Rice wine vinegar
to taste		Salt and black pepper

PROCEDURE

1 Soak the raisins in hot water for 15 minutes. Drain and set aside.

2 Separate chard leaves from ribs. Chop the red or white ribs into ¹/₄-inch (.6 cm) pieces. Immerse the ribs in a small pan of boiling water and boil 2 minutes. Drain and set aside.

3 Melt the butter over medium heat. Sauté shallots and garlic about 2 minutes.

4 Add chard leaves and sauté. Cover the pan and steam 3 to 5 minutes over low heat. Mix in cooked ribs. Add vinegar and raisins. Correct seasoning.

5 Serve immediately.

Rice with Red Peppers and Pine Nuts 4 SERVINGS

AMOUNT	MEASURE	INGREDIENT
3 tablespoons	1 ounce, 28 g	Pine nuts
2 cups	16 ounces, 470 ml	Chicken stock
1 cup	7 ounces, 198 g	Long-grain white rice
1/2 teaspoon	3 g	Salt
1/8 teaspoon		White pepper
2 tablespoons	1 ounce, 28 g	Unsalted butter
2 tablespoons	1 ounce, 28 ml	Vegetable oil
1 cup	4 ounces, 113 g	Onion, 1/4 inch (.6 cm) dice
1/2 cup	2 ounces, 56 g	Red bell pepper, 1/2 inch (1.2 cm) dice
1/2 cup	2 ounces, 56 g	Celery, 1/2 inch (1.2 cm) dice
2 tablespoons	8 g	Parsley, finely chopped

PROCEDURE

1 Preheat the oven to 350°F (175°C). Toast the pine nuts for 3 to 4 minutes or until lightly browned.

2 Bring the stock to a boil over high heat.

3 Add the rice, salt, and pepper; stir. Lower the heat, cover, and simmer 20 minutes.

4 Heat the butter and oil over medium heat. Add the onion and sauté, stirring, until soft.

5 Add the red pepper and celery. Sauté 3 to 5 minutes. The vegetables should be slightly crisp.

6 When the rice is cooked, add the vegetables, pine nuts, and parsley. Toss to combine and correct seasoning.

Strawberry Shortcake with Cornmeal Biscuits

Strawberry Shortcake with Cornmeal Biscuits 4 SERVINGS

AMOUNT	MEASURE	INGREDIENT

For the Biscuits

AMOUNT	MEASURE	INGREDIENT
3 cups	12 ounces, 340 g	All-purpose flour
3/4 cup	4 ounces, 113 g	Yellow cornmeal, fine grind
1 tablespoon	1/2 ounce, 15 g	Baking powder
1 tablespoon	1/2 ounce, 15 g	Granulated sugar
1/2 teaspoon	3 g	Salt
2 tablespoons	1 ounce, 28 ml	Butter, chilled, in 1/2-inch (1.2 cm) cubes
1 1/2 cups	12 ounces, 352 ml	Heavy cream

For the Berries

AMOUNT	MEASURE	INGREDIENT
3 cups	18 ounces, 510 g	Strawberries, washed, hulled, sliced
1/4 cup	2 ounces, 56 g	Granulated sugar
1 teaspoon or to taste	5 ml	Lemon juice
1 cup	8 ounces, 235 ml	Heavy cream
1/4 teaspoon	2 ml	Vanilla extract

PROCEDURE

1. Preheat the oven to 425°F (220°C).

2. Combine the flour, cornmeal, baking powder, sugar, and salt. Mix in butter until the mixture has the appearance of coarse meal.

3. Add the cream; stir until a moist dough forms. Knead by hand until the dough is moist and manageable. Place on a floured work table and knead gently for 1 minute.

4. Roll dough into a rectangle approximately 6 x 9 inches (15 x 22.5 cm) and 3/4 inch (1.9 cm) thick. Cut dough into uniform biscuits and place on lined baking sheet.

5. Bake for approximately 20 minutes, or until the buiscuits have risen and are lightly brown in color. Let cool slightly.

6. Combine strawberries and 3 tablespoons (42 ml) of the sugar. Let stand for 15 minutes at room temperature.

7. Crush half the strawberries, adding a little lemon juice; set aside.

8   Combine the cream, remaining sugar, and vanilla. Whip to soft peaks.

9   Split each biscuit in half horizontally and place the bottom piece of each biscuit on a chilled plate.

10   Spoon the berry mixture onto the biscuit bottoms in equal portions. Top with a large dollop of whipped cream. Cover with the top portions of the biscuit, spoon some berry liquid on top, and serve.

Dilled Carrot Soup 4 SERVINGS

AMOUNT	MEASURE	INGREDIENT
2 tablespoons	1 ounce, 28 g	Butter
1 cup	4 ounces, 113 g	Leeks, white part only, thinly sliced
4 cups	16 ounces, 453 g	Carrots, peeled, $^1/_4$ inch (.6 cm) dice
4 cups	16 ounces, 453 g	Russet potatoes, peeled, $^1/_4$ inch (.6 cm) dice
1 quart	1 l	Chicken stock
1$^1/_2$ teaspoons		Thyme, finely chopped
1		Bay leaf
1$^1/_2$ cups	12 ounces, 352 ml	Half-and-half, warm
$^1/_4$ teaspoon	2 g	Grated nutmeg
2 tablespoons	1 ounce, 28 ml	Lemon juice
to taste		Salt and white pepper
dash		Tabasco
2 tablespoons	6 g	Dill, chopped

PROCEDURE

1 Heat the butter. Sauté the leeks, stirring occasionally, until soft.

2 Add the carrots and potatoes. Sauté for 5 minutes.

3 Add the stock and bring to a simmer. Add the thyme and bay leaf and simmer for 20 to 30 minutes, or until carrots and potatoes are tender. Remove bay leaf.

4 Puree vegetables and liquid in a blender. Add remaining ingredients. Correct seasoning and bring back to almost a boil.

5 Serve hot, garnished with dill.

Caesar Salad 4 SERVINGS

chef tip

Caesar salad is considered the benchmark of salads that can be prepared table-side. A wooden bowl is selected to extract the greatest amount of oil from the garlic and anchovies. It allows for a great marriage of flavors once the dressing is completed. In a typical Caesar salad bowl, no more than three portions should be made at once.

Grinding the black pepper directly onto the bare place is recommended so you can see how much pepper has been ground. Regular olive oil is recommended for maximum flavor. Extra-virgin olive oil is more expensive, has an overpowering flavor, and is slightly more acidic.

Caesar Cardini conceived this salad in 1924 at his restaurant in Tijuana, Mexico, just across the border from California. Owing to Prohibition in America, restaurants in Tijuana were popular with Hollywood stars. One evening, a group of actors entered his restaurant near closing time, and the kitchen was out of most items, including fish, chicken, and meat. Romaine lettuce, oil and vinegar, lemon, garlic, mustard, cheese, and croutons were available. In order to satisfy this Hollywood group, Caesar gathered what he had, brought it to the dining room, and assembled his new creation in front of his guests. They raved about it, and the rest is history. Shortly afterward, the International Society of Epicures in Paris named Caesar salad the greatest recipe originating from the New World in 50 years.

AMOUNT	MEASURE	INGREDIENT
For the Croutons		
¹/₄ cup	2 ounces, 55 ml	Olive oil
1		Garlic clove, crushed
2 cups	6 ounces, 170 g	Sourdough bread, crusts removed, in ¹/₂-inch (1.2 cm) cubes
For the Dressing		
1		Garlic clove, minced
2 tablespoons	1 ounce, 28 ml	Lemon juice
2 teaspoons	14 ml	Anchovy paste
¹/₄ teaspoon		Black pepper
1		Egg

Caesar Salad

| $^1/_2$ cup | 4 ounces, 115 ml | Olive oil |
| to taste | | Salt |

For the Salad

| 8 cups | 16 ounces, 454 g | Romaine lettuce, dark outer leaves removed, torn into bite-size pieces |
| $^1/_2$ cup | $1^1/_2$ ounces, 42 g | Parmesan cheese, freshly grated |

PROCEDURE

1 Heat the oil over medium heat and add the garlic. Sauté 1 minute and discard garlic.

2 Increase the heat to high and add the bread cubes, turning frequently so that they brown evenly on all sides and are crisp and golden. Add more oil if necessary to keep from burning. Drain on paper towels. Reserve.

3 Combine the minced garlic, lemon juice, anchovy paste, salt, and pepper. Whisk to blend.

4 Immerse the egg in a small pan of boiling water and cook for exactly 1 minute. Remove the egg and crack it into the bowl with other ingredients. Whisk to combine.

5 Add the oil in a steady stream and whisk until smooth.

6 Combine the lettuce, Parmesan cheese, croutons, and dressing. Toss and taste for seasoning.

7 Place on individual plates. Serve immediately.

Hangtown Fry 4 SERVINGS

chef tip

Hangtown was a town in California noted for the many public hangings held there during the California gold rush days. The dish was created when a successful miner brought a sack of gold to the local restaurant and asked for the most expensive meal in the house. The chef suggested oysters and eggs, two very high-priced items at the time. Bacon was added at the miner's request. The town has since been renamed Placerville.

AMOUNT	MEASURE	INGREDIENT
$^1/_2$ cup	4 ounces, 113 g	Bacon strips, $^1/_2$ inch (1.2 cm) dice
$^1/_2$ cup	2 ounces, 56 g	Ham, julienned
4		Eggs
$^1/_4$ cup	2 ounces, 55 ml	Heavy cream
2 tablespoons	1 ounce, 28 ml	Water
1 tablespoon	3 g	Parsley, chopped
$^1/_2$ cup	$1^1/_2$ ounces, 42 g	Parmesan cheese, freshly grated
to taste		Salt and white pepper
8		Oysters
$^1/_4$ cup	1 ounce, 28 g	All-purpose flour
1		Egg, beaten with a little water
$^1/_2$ cup	2 ounces, 56 g	Bread crumbs, dry
to taste		Salt and white pepper

PROCEDURE

1 Preheat broiler. Cook the bacon over medium heat until crisp. Drain on a paper towel, crumble, and set aside.

2 Fry the ham pieces in the bacon fat. Drain on a paper towel and set aside. Remove all but 2 tablespoons fat.

3 In a bowl, combine the eggs, cream, water, parsley, and cheese; season to taste.

4 Dip the oysters in the flour, beaten egg, and bread crumbs. Fry in the bacon fat for 1 minute on both sides. Stir in bacon and ham.

5 Pour the egg mixture over the oysters and let them cook over low heat, without stirring, until the eggs begin to set, 8 to 10 minutes.

6 Place the skillet under the broiler and lightly brown the top. Serve immediately.

San Francisco Cioppino 4 SERVINGS

Cioppino is typically served with San Francisco sourdough bread or fresh-baked focaccia. Freshly made garlic croutons dipped in fresh minced herbs are also a frequent garnish. The fish and shellfish listed in this recipe are our choices. Feel free to substitute different varieties of seasonal fresh fish and shellfish to suit your taste and preferences.

Cioppino is a famous seafood recipe that originated in the **North Beach** area of San Francisco. Cioppino is basically a **West Coast** version of French bouillabaisse. The dish typically uses a tomato-based broth to stew a variety of local fish and seafood. Dungeness crab is often the featured protein in cioppino. This souplike fish stew is generally served as an entree.

AMOUNT	MEASURE	INGREDIENT
For the Sauce		
1 tablespoon	$^1/_2$ ounce, 14 ml	Vegetable oil
1 cup	4 ounces, 113 g	Onion, $^1/_2$ inch (1.2 cm) dice
$^1/_2$ cup	2 ounces, 56 g	Leek, $^1/_2$ inch (1.2 cm) dice
$^1/_2$ cup	2 ounces, 56 g	Green bell pepper, $^1/_2$ inch (1.2 cm) dice
1 tablespoon	$^1/_2$ ounce, 15 g	Garlic, minced
$^1/_2$ cup	2 ounces, 56 g	Celery, $^1/_2$ inch (1.2 cm) dice
$^1/_2$ cup	2 ounces, 56 g	Carrot, $^1/_4$ inch (.6 cm) dice
1 cup	6 ounces, 170 g	Plum tomato, peeled, seeded, $^1/_4$ inch (.6 cm) dice
1 tablespoon	$^1/_2$ ounce, 15 g	Tomato paste
2 cups	16 ounces, 470 ml	Fish fumet or clam juice
$^1/_2$ cup	4 ounces, 115 ml	Red wine
1 tablespoon	$^1/_2$ ounce, 14 ml	Lemon juice
1		Bay leaf
1 teaspoon	1 g	Oregano, chopped
1 teaspoon	1 g	Basil, chopped
to taste		Salt and black pepper

For the Cioppino

8		Mussels, scrubbed and debearded
8		Littleneck or cherrystone clams, scrubbed
2 cups	16 ounces, 470 ml	Water
	16 ounces, 453 g	Fish, any lean, firm white flesh, cut into serving-size pieces
	16 ounces, 453 g	Shrimp (16–20 count), peeled and deveined
4		Sea scallops
1 tablespoon	1/2 ounce, 15 ml	Hot sauce
2 tablespoons	6 g	Parsley, finely chopped

PROCEDURE

1 Heat the oil and cook the onion, leek, green pepper, garlic, celery, and carrot until tender, about 3 minutes.

2 Add the tomato and cook 3 minutes. Add the tomato paste, fish fumet, wine, lemon juice, and bay leaf. Simmer 30 minutes. Remove the bay leaf.

3 Add the fresh herbs and correct seasoning. Set aside.

4 Clean and steam the mussels and clams in the water until the shells open. Save the cooking liquid and strain it through cheesecloth. Add the cooking liquid to the sauce.

5 Add the fish and simmer 3 minutes. Add the shrimp and scallops and simmer 2 minutes.

6 Add the hot sauce and return the mussels and clams to the pot; heat 1 minute.

7 Divide the fish and shellfish evenly into warmed soup bowls. Ladle the sauce over the seafood and sprinkle with parsley.

Kiwifruit and Grape Rice Pudding 4 SERVINGS

chef tip

Originally from China, the kiwi was cultivated at the turn of the century in New Zealand and brought to California in the 1930s. Kiwis are grown all over the world on vines; however, California has the greatest kiwi production in the United States.

AMOUNT	MEASURE	INGREDIENT
3 cups	24 ounces, 705 ml	Milk
1/4 cup plus 1 tablespoon	1 3/4 ounces, 49 g	Granulated sugar
1/4 teaspoon		Salt
1/2 cup	3 ounces, 85 g	Rice
2		Kiwis, peeled, sliced, quartered
1/2 cup	1 1/2 ounces, 42 g	Seedless red grapes, halved
1 tablespoon	1/2 ounce, 14 g	Unsalted butter
1/8 teaspoon		Ground cinnamon
2		Kiwi, peeled, sliced, for garnish

PROCEDURE

1 Combine the milk, 1/4 cup (1 3/4 ounces, 46 g) sugar, and salt. Heat until small bubbles form around the edge of the pan.

2 Stir in the rice. Cover and cook over low heat for 35 to 45 minutes or until the rice is tender and most of the milk is absorbed. Stir occasionally.

3 Stir in the kiwi quarters, grapes, and butter.

4 Combine remaining sugar with the cinnamon. Sprinkle each serving with cinnamon sugar and garnish with sliced kiwi fruit. Serve warm.

Chèvre (Goat Cheese) and Pistachio Wrapped in Filo 4 SERVINGS

AMOUNT	MEASURE	INGREDIENT
³/₄ cup	3 ounces, 85 g	Pistachio nuts, chopped to the consistency of cornmeal
¹/₄ cup	2 ounces, 56 g	Chèvre (goat cheese)
2 tablespoons	I ounce, 28 g	Ricotta cheese
I teaspoon	I g	Thyme, chopped
I teaspoon	I g	Basil, chopped
¹/₂ teaspoon	.5 g	Tarragon, chopped
¹/₂ teaspoon	.5 g	Dill, chopped
I teaspoon	I g	Chives, chopped
I		Garlic clove, minced
to taste		Salt and white pepper
4 sheets		Filo dough
as needed		Butter, melted

PROCEDURE

1 Preheat the oven to 375°F (190°C).

2 Combine the nuts, cheeses, herbs, and garlic. Season with salt and pepper.

3 Lay out a sheet of filo dough and brush with melted butter. Lay another sheet of filo dough on top of the first sheet. Repeat with other two sheets. Cut each double sheet into four 3-inch (7.6 cm)-wide strips.

4 Place 1 tablespoon (¹/₂ ounce, 15 ml) of filling at one end of the strip, then fold the dough over diagonally from one side to the other, all the way down the strip. Continue this procedure with all 8 strips.

5 Transfer the triangles to a baking sheet that has been lined with parchment paper. Brush the goat cheese triangles with melted butter and bake until golden brown.

Chinese Chicken Salad 4 SERVINGS

AMOUNT	MEASURE	INGREDIENT
For the Chicken		
2 cups	16 ounces, 470 ml	Chicken stock
¹/₂ tablespoon	8 g	Ginger, peeled, minced
¹/₂ tablespoon	8 g	Garlic, minced
16 ounces	453 g	Chicken breasts, boneless, skinless
For the Dressing		
¹/₄ cup	2 ounces, 55 ml	Red wine vinegar
¹/₄ cup	2 ounces, 55 ml	Soy sauce
2 tablespoons	1 ounce, 28 ml	Orange juice
1 tablespoon	¹/₂ ounce, 14 ml	Lemon juice
¹/₂ tablespoon	8 g	Ginger, peeled, minced
¹/₂ tablespoon	8 g	Garlic, minced
¹/₂ teaspoon	2 ml	Hot sauce (Tabasco)
1 tablespoon	¹/₂ ounce, 14 ml	Sesame oil
¹/₂ cup	4 ounces, 115 ml	Vegetable oil
For the Salad		
¹/₂ cup	1¹/₂ ounces, 42 g	Napa cabbage, cut into very thin strips
¹/₂ cup	1¹/₂ ounces, 42 g	Red cabbage, cut into very thin strips
2¹/₂ cups	3 ounces, 85 g	Baby field greens, cleaned
¹/₂ cup	1 ounce, 28 g	Green onions, ¹/₄-inch (.6 cm) bias cut
¹/₂ cup	1¹/₂ ounces, 42 g	Bean sprouts
For the Garnish		
20		Orange sections
2 tablespoons		Cilantro leaves
12		Cherry tomatoes, cut in half
¹/₂ cup	2 ounces, 56 g	Cashew nuts, roughly chopped

PROCEDURE

1 Bring the stock to a simmer with the ginger and garlic.

2   Add the chicken and simmer until the chicken is just cooked (do not overcook).

3   Remove the chicken from the liquid and let cool. Shred, cover, and set aside.

4   Place all the ingredients for the dressing in a blender and blend well.

5   Combine all the salad ingredients and toss together.

6   Combine the shredded chicken with $^1/_4$ cup (2 ounces, 55 ml) dressing.

7   Add remaining dressing to the salad ingredients and toss to coat.

8   Place the salad on cold plates and top with equal portions of shredded chicken. Garnish with the orange sections, cilantro, and cherry tomatoes. Top with cashew nuts.

Asparagus with Toasted Hazelnuts 4 SERVINGS

AMOUNT	MEASURE	INGREDIENT
$^1/_2$ cup	$2^1/_2$ ounces, 70 g	Hazelnuts
For the Vinaigrette		
3 tablespoons	$1^1/_2$ ounces, 42 ml	Hazelnut oil
3 tablespoons	$1^1/_2$ ounces, 42 ml	Corn oil
2 tablespoons	1 ounce, 28 ml	White wine vinegar
$^1/_4$ teaspoon	2 g	Salt
$^1/_8$ teaspoon		Pepper
	16 ounces, 453 g	Asparagus

PROCEDURE

1   Preheat the oven to 350°F (175°C).

2   Toast the hazelnuts for 5 to 8 minutes.

3   Remove, rub off skins, and coarsely chop. Set aside.

4   Combine both oils, vinegar, salt, and pepper. Whisk well. Set aside.

5   Peel the asparagus and boil in salted water until just tender, 3 minutes.

6   Drain the asparagus. Serve warm with the vinaigrette, sprinkled with the toasted hazelnuts.

Garden Pasta Salad

Garden Pasta Salad 4 SERVINGS

AMOUNT	MEASURE	INGREDIENT
For the salad		
1 tablespoon	1/2 ounce, 14 ml	Vegetable oil
1 teaspoon	5 g	Salt
4 cups	8 ounces, 226 g	Fusili or small shell pasta (dried)
3 cups	12 ounces, 336 g	Vegetables (carrots, zucchini, broccoli, sugar snap peas, or other vegetables of choice), julienned
For the Dressing		
2 tablespoons	1 ounce, 28 ml	Grainy mustard
2		Garlic cloves, minced
1 1/2 tablespoons	21 ml	Lemon juice
1 1/2 tablespoons	21 ml	Sherry vinegar
6 tablespoons	3 ounces, 84 ml	Olive oil
to taste		Salt and black pepper
1 1/2 tablespoons		Basil, chopped
1/2 cup	1 1/2 ounces, 42 g	Parmesan cheese, grated

PROCEDURE

1 Add the oil and salt to a pot of boiling water; add the pasta and cook to al dente.

2 Drain, shock in ice water, drain, and dry thoroughly.

3 Blanch the vegetable, until crispy-tender. Drain and shock in ice water. Drain and dry thoroughly.

4 Combine mustard, garlic, lemon juice, and sherry vinegar.

5 Whisk in the olive oil. Season with salt and pepper. Add the basil and Parmesan cheese.

6 Toss the pasta, vegetables, and dressing just before serving.

Oven-Roasted Potatoes 4 SERVINGS

AMOUNT	MEASURE	INGREDIENT
3 cups	16 ounces, 452 g	Red Bliss potatoes
2 tablespoons	1 ounce, 28 ml	Olive oil
1		Garlic clove, minced
1/2 teaspoon	1 g	Rosemary or thyme, chopped
to taste		Salt and black pepper

PROCEDURE

1   Preheat the oven to 375°F (190°C).

2   Wash and dry the potatoes. Cut a ring of skin from the middle of each potato, then cut the potatoes in half.

3   Combine the oil, garlic, and herbs with the potatoes in a roasting pan. Roast until tender, about 30 to 40 minutes.

Rosemary Focaccia 4–6 SERVINGS

AMOUNT	MEASURE	INGREDIENT
For the Sponge		
1 cup	8 ounces, 235 ml	Water, warm (100°F, 38°C)
1 teaspoon	2 g	Active dry yeast
1 cup	4 ounces, 113 g	All-purpose flour
For the Focaccia		
1/2 cup	4 ounces, 115 ml	Water
1/3 cup	2 1/2 ounces, 78 ml	Dry white wine
1/3 cup	2 1/2 ounces, 78 ml	Olive oil
2 tablespoons	1 ounce, 28 g	Yellow cornmeal, fine-grind
1 1/2 teaspoons	5 g	Kosher salt, more to taste

2³/₄ cups	12 ounces, 340 g	All-purpose flour
5 teaspoons	25 ml	Extra-virgin olive oil
1		Garlic clove, minced
to taste		Black pepper
1¹/₂ teaspoons	2 g	Rosemary, minced

PROCEDURE

1   Combine the warm water and yeast and let stand 2 minutes; stir to dissolve.

2   Stir in the flour until the mixture is smooth. Cover and let stand at room temperature for 24 hours.

3   Place the sponge in the bowl of a mixing machine with dough hook attachment; mix at low speed. Slowly add the water, wine, olive oil, cornmeal, and 1¹/₂ teaspoons (7.5 ml) salt. Mix until thoroughly incorporated.

4   Gradually mix in the flour, and mix on low speed until the dough is formed. Increase mixer to medium speed and work dough for 5 minutes.

5   Remove from mixer to a greased bowl. Cover and let rise at room temperature for approximately 1¹/₂ hours or until it doubles in size.

6   Grease a sheet pan with olive oil. Transfer the dough to the baking sheet and stretch it, using oiled fingers, until the dough completely fills the pan. Let the dough rest 5 minutes; the dough will shrink.

7   Restretch the dough to completely cover the pan. If it is still too elastic, let the dough rest longer and try again. Let dough rise in pan at room temperature for 1 hour.

8   Preheat the oven to 450°F (225°C).

9   Brush the focaccia with olive oil and sprinkle with rosemary and more kosher salt to taste. Bake for approximately 15 to 20 minutes or until nicely browned.

Steamed Asian Vegetables 4 SERVINGS

AMOUNT	MEASURE	INGREDIENT
1/2 cup	4 ounces, 115 ml	Chicken stock
2 cups	8 ounces, 226 g	Baby bok choy, split lengthwise
2 cups	4 ounces, 113 g	Snap peas, trimmed
1 cup	4 ounces, 113 g	Red bell peppers, seeded, julienned
1 cup	4 ounces, 113 g	Yellow bell peppers, seeded, julienned
1 cup	3 ounces, 85 g	White mushrooms, sliced
2		Garlic cloves, minced
1 tablespoon	3 g	Cornstarch
1 tablespoon	1/2 ounce, 14 ml	Water
1 teaspoon	5 ml	Soy sauce
1 teaspoon	5 ml	Sesame oil
to taste		Salt and black pepper

PROCEDURE

1 Bring the chicken stock to a boil. Add the bok choy, cover, and steam for 1 minute.

2 Add the snow peas, bell peppers, mushrooms, and garlic. Cover and steam for 1 minute.

3 Mix the cornstarch with the water, soy sauce, and sesame oil to make a slurry.

4 Add the cornstarch slurry to the vegetables. Cook over high heat for about 30 seconds, tossing constantly until the sauce thickens and the vegetables are nicely coated with the sauce.

5 Season with salt and black pepper; serve immediately.

Steamed Asian Vegetables

Stuffed Pork with Apples or Pears and Prunes   4 SERVINGS

AMOUNT	MEASURE	INGREDIENT
For the Stuffing		
I cup	4 ounces, 113 g	Apple (firm, tart) or pear, peeled, cored, coarsely chopped
3/4 cup	3 ounces, 85 g	Dried prunes
1/4 cup	2 ounces, 55 ml	White wine
1/2 cup	4 ounces, 115 ml	Apple brandy
For the Pork		
	16 ounces, 453 g	Pork roast (eye of loin), boned, tied
I tablespoon	1/4 ounce, 7 g	Butter
2 tablespoons	I ounce, 28 ml	Vegetable oil
1/4 cup	2 ounces, 55 ml	Heavy cream
to taste		Salt and white pepper

PROCEDURE

1   Combine the apples or pears and prunes.

2   Bring the wine and brandy to a simmer for 2 minutes, and then pour over the apple and prune mixture. Let it macerate for 30 minutes.

3   Preheat the oven to 375°F (190°C).

4   Stuff the fruit into the hole in the center of the pork by pushing it through with the handle of a wooden spoon. Truss the roast. Reserve remaining fruit and marinade.

5   Heat the butter and oil over medium-high heat. Add pork and brown evenly on all sides.

6   Remove the pork to a rack in a roasting pan; pour out excess fat from the pan.

7   Add reserved marinade to pan, stirring and scraping the bottom of pan. Pour the sauce into the roasting pan with the pork.

8   Cover pork and bake for approximately 45 minutes, until the meat is tender and cooked to 160°F (71°C). Remove the pork. Cover, and keep warm.

9   Add cream to roasting pan and simmer 5 minutes. Correct seasoning.

10   Slice the pork into 1/2-inch (1.2 cm) slices and serve with the fruit sauce.

The Cuisine of the Pacific Northwest

Stone fruits, apples and pears, berries and wild mushrooms, salmon and shellfish. The moist weather conditions and volcanic soil in Oregon and Washington help create one of the most fertile growing regions in the nation. And with the Pacific coastline, the abundant and varied fish and seafood of the area are the hallmarks of the region's cuisine. With a long harvest season and an accommodating climate, these areas support some of the most impressive local ingredients and offer yields unlike that found in other parts of the country. Driven by a strong mandate to save their valuable marine and forest resources, and to practice sustainable farming methods, locals hope to continue to provide future generations with the riches of the Pacific Northwest table.

Alaska, America's last frontier and "Land of the Midnight Sun," shares the bounty of the Pacific Ocean and, by an extraordinary combination of environmental and human factors, produces vegetables that grow to enormous sizes in the Alaskan floodplain.

Alaska Here, the state fish is the king salmon, the state bird is the willow ptarmigan, the state land mammal is the moose, the state marine mammal is the bowhead whale, the state tree is the Sitka spruce, and the state flower is the forget-me-not. the state sport is dog mushing.

Oregon "The Beaver State," where the state flower is the Oregon grape, the state fish is the Chinook salmon, the state mammal is the American beaver, the state nut is the hazelnut, the state bird is the Western meadowlark, and the state tree is the Douglas fir.

Washington "The Evergreen State," where the state fruit is the apple; the state fish is the steelhead trout; the state flower is the coast, or western, rhododendron; the state tree is the Western hemlock; and the state grass is bluebunch wheatgrass.

History and Major Influences

WASHINGTON AND OREGON

The people of the Pacific Northwest, like all Americans, are a mixture of histories and traditions. The first arrivals—mountain men from France, England, Russia, and Canada—found opportunities in fur trapping and trading. Since these newcomers were unfamiliar with the local ingredients, the Native American Indians taught them how to sustain themselves. The nomadic hunter-gatherers of the Quinault, Quileute, Chinook, and Tillamooks tribes introduced the settlers to the varieties of oysters, clams, crab, shrimp, and salmon from the Puget Sound. The Nez Perce, Cayuse, and Spokane tribes taught the new arrivals about the local berries and how to forage for mushrooms. The European settlers were also taught how to smoke their foods. They learned about the *potlach*. This Chinook word meaning "to give away" is used to describe a ceremonial feast connected with native rituals and important events. For the feast, each family would bring a contribution that might include salmon, clams, wild berries, greens, or other foods in season. This feast continues to be an important tradition in the area today.

Though the first settlers came to the Pacific Northwest for the valuable fur of the sea otter and beaver, they soon realized the potential of the region. Other industries such as mining, timber, fishing, cattle raising, and farming were established. In the early 1800s, Thomas Jefferson sent the party of Lewis and Clark to explore the Northwest; about the same time, Captain George Vancouver sailed into Puget Sound through the Straits of Juan de Fuca seeking safe harbor in what is now called Port Townsend. The opening of the Oregon Trail led settlers from the Central Plains to the Pacific Northwest, many of whom were first-generation Americans still with deep roots in Europe. Discoveries of gold on the coast and in the high country led to additional exploration and settlements.

Because Oregon and Washington are so large and mountainous, the railroads did not reach the Pacific Northwest states until 1883. The offers of work building the railroads brought people from China, Italy, and Greece. They were mostly young men who planned to earn as much money as they could before returning to their homelands. But many of those who came never left. Instead, they brought over their families from the homeland or married other settlers and raised families. Large numbers of Chinese settled in Oregon and east of the Cascade Mountains. Many of them eventually opened laundries, stores, and restaurants. By the late 1800s, immigration of Chinese laborers was prohibited, and social and political discrimination forced the Chinese immigrants to live together in areas called "Chinatowns."

Immigrants from southern European countries—mainly Italy and Greece—settled in the Portland area during the late 1800s. German settlers established their farm traditions in eastern Washington, planting vast wheat fields between the Cascade Mountains and Rocky Mountains. They were the first to grow the nation's supply of hops and barley, and to initiate the beer industry. A beer-making tradition called "microbrewing" began in the mid-1800s. Microbreweries were originally breweries that produced fewer than 10,000 barrels each year, and hundreds of small breweries opened throughout the remainder of the 1800s. As technology improved and production levels increased, the definition was increased to 15,000 barrels. Scandinavian settlers brought their dairy-farming expertise to the inland valleys and hillsides of that same area and continue to produce large amounts of milk. Realizing it was difficult to transport fresh milk and butter, the settlers reproduced the distinctive cheese-making processes developed in Europe. Basque and Mexican sheepherders settled in Oregon and eastern Washington. Cattle and livestock production increased dramatically owing to demand by hungry gold miners, as well as the availability of the transcontinental railroad connections to ship the cattle across the country.

In the late 1800s and early 1900s, after a series of massive earthquakes, volcanic eruptions from Mt. Fuji, and flooding that devastated homes and farmlands, a number of Japanese immigrants arrived to work on small farms. They created a strong social network to help those who lived and worked in the area. Many eventually acquired their own land and established the first berry and vegetable farms in Washington's Puget Sound area. They also brought their native Pacific and Kumamoto oysters and Manila, or Japanese Littleneck, clams to the coast.

The Asian influence in the Northwest has been strong, and most major cities in the Northwest have flourishing Asian communities. Immigrants used the ingredients native to the Pacific Northwest but prepared them using the cooking styles of their homeland. This fusion of techniques and ingredients is now known as Pacific Rim cooking. The first to populate open-air markets, the Asians brought fresh coriander, colorful basils, ginger, bitter melon, and exotic greens. Although many of these markets are no longer in operation, the influence they had on the region's cuisine continues today. Seattle's Chinatown is known today as the International District owing to the influences of its Filipino, Thai, Korean, and Vietnamese communities.

ALASKA

Since 1867, when the United States purchased Alaska from Russia, it has been a vast unknown country to the average American citizen. Frequently referred to as America's Last Frontier, it is one-fifth the size of the United States, with extremes of temperature, precipitation, sunlight, and wind.

A considerable percentage of Alaska's population has come from countries other than the United States. Many whose ancestors were Swedish, Norwegian, Danish, English, German, Russian, or Finlanders now call themselves Alaskans. These people came in the early days, when small communities were formed—when gold camps were being built during a "Goldrush to the Klondike." Travel was tedious then. Mail was carried by dog team, and meat was available only if there was a good hunter or trapper in the family.

Alaska suffered during the Great Depression of the 1930s. The price of fish and minerals dropped. Almost half of the people in the United States were out of work, and those who did work did not get paid well. President Franklin Roosevelt had the idea that if people moved to Alaska, they could start over again in a new place. They could farm and make a living. About 1,000 people moved from northern states like Michigan and Minnesota to Alaska during this time, and the first farm colony settled in the rich and fertile Matanuska Valley.

Every year at the Alaska State Fair in the Matanuska Valley town of Palmer, the giant vegetables are the main attraction. The challenge was begun during the Great Depression of the 1930s, when the government-relocated farmers discovered that, while the growing season is short—just three months—it is offset by nearly 24 hours of sunlight. The soil is a fine mix of glacial silt and loam, and the giant vegetable competitors carefully germinate their seed, monitor moisture, and prune strategically to direct all the plant's energy into a single vegetable. This results in vegetables like Swiss chard that grow 9 feet tall, broccoli 3 feet tall and 7 feet wide, 98-pound cabbages, and 25-pound mushrooms. Even with this rapid growth, these giants are considered to still have all the flavor of normal-size vegetables.

The most significant berry-growing regions are in the lower foothills of Alaska and western Oregon and Washington. Lingonberries and salmonberries are found along with blueberries, huckleberries, blackberries, red raspberries, and strawberries.

Alaska is home to nearly all of the wild salmon that is brought to market. And here, as well as up and down the coast of the Pacific Northwest, other seafood such as halibut, rockfish, Arctic char, all types of trout, sea urchins, octopus, squid, king crabs, and scallops can be found.

A Diverse Landscape

While the other regions of America have been significantly influenced by the history and culture of the people who live in the area, the Pacific Northwest regional cuisine is defined by the native ingredients that flourish in this diverse landscape.

PALOUSE

Along the edge of eastern Washington and western Idaho lies an area known as the Palouse (the name derives from the French word meaning "green lawn"). This region is generally considered to be the best in the world for growing lentils, peas, and chickpeas. Crop rotation of peas and lentils with soft, white winter wheat allows a second harvest of the land and organically enriches the soil. Over 200 million pounds of lentils are produced annually, and they are exported all over the world, mostly to India and the Middle East.

YAKIMA VALLEY

West across the extensive Columbia River plateau is the Yakima Valley, an active agricultural area often called the "Fruit Bowl of the Nation." A system of canals and wells supplies growers in this dry valley with ample water to carefully control irrigation of the land. In the 1880s, the first commercial apple orchards began production in the Yakima Valley. The availability of water has transformed this area into one of the largest and most productive wine regions in the Northwest. The cool temperatures also allow for an exceptional harvest of asparagus.

THE HOOD RIVER VALLEY

Mt. Hood, the tallest of Oregon's Cascade peaks, towers over the Columbia River Gorge. Runoff from its volcanic slopes enriches soil in the valleys below, which are famous for their production of pears, peaches, plums, sweet cherries, apricots, and apples. The leading cherry is the Bing cherry, developed in 1875 by Seth Luelling of Milwaukie, Oregon. The cherry was named after the owner's Chinese orchard manager and is now one of the most significant regional crops.

THE WILLAMETTE VALLEY

For the thousands of pioneers who came across the Oregon Trail, this lush valley was the promised land that they had been seeking. Nestled between the Cascade Mountains and the Coastal Ranges south of Eugene, Oregon, the valley takes its name from the river that flows through it. Historic cities and towns, settled more than century ago by people from all over the world, are found throughout the region. But this area is best known for its diverse agriculture, which includes a wide variety of fruits, dairy, vegetables, and hops. This is also Oregon's top berry-growing region, with blackberries, loganberries, raspberries, and strawberries found in the region. Over 90 percent of the country's hazelnuts are produced here, and the hazelnut takes the place of pecans in many of the regional recipes. Today, the valley's wine country is gaining worldwide attention as one of the Pacific Northwest's finest wine appellations, consistently turning out internationally acclaimed Pinot Noir, Pinot Gris, and Riesling.

THE COASTAL RANGES

This area is known for its rainy climate. The high precipitation supports coniferous forests along the coastal inlets, and many varieties of mushroom thrive in these conditions, as do elk, deer, and game birds. Mushroom hunting is on the rise owing to the high prices paid at market for matsutakes, morels, and porcini. The region is also known for its native truffles. White truffles as well as two varieties of black truffles are found in the undergrowth of the Douglas fir trees during the early fall through early spring. Corvallis, a small town in Oregon, is headquarters of the North American Truffling Society, and the truffles not consumed by the locals are sent to upscale restaurants around the country.

THE PACIFIC COASTLINE

Rivers and inlets lend their names to the region's trademark fish and shellfish. Pacific oysters are also known by their places of origin such as Yaquina, Wescott, Shoalwater, Quilcene, and Canterbury. The best known oyster bed is in Willapa Bay, a large estuary in southern Washington. The native Olympia oyster was farmed nearly to extinction in the 19th century. Today, the Japanese Pacific oyster dominates Willapa Bay, though Olympia and another Japanese oyster, the Kumamoto, are becoming more available. Shrimp, scallops, geoduck, clams, and crabs flourish along the Washington, Oregon, and Alaska coasts. The nation's oldest mussel farm, Penn Cove Mussels, is found on Whidbey Island in Washington's Puget Sound. The Olympic Peninsula is home to the popular Dungeness crab. Though this crustacean lives along much of the coast from Northern California to Alaska, this area is where it was first commercially harvested. Pacific cod, lingcod, black cod, halibut, and petrale sole are some of the fishes found along the coast. The Columbia, Rogue, Copper, and Yukon Rivers flow into the Pacific, and these rivers are an important thoroughfare for the five varieties of wild salmon, the river smelt, and the mild white sturgeon.

PIKE PLACE MARKET

Seattle's Pike Place Market was founded on August 17, 1907. Started as an experiment as a response to the city's high food prices, the Pike Place Market eliminated intermediaries and allowed consumers to purchase foods directly from growers. The concept proved successful, as the farmers typically sold all of their products and the consumers enjoyed the benefits of significantly lower prices. It also became a gathering place for all the food grown in the region, including foods that represent the mix of people and the ethnic groups that lived there.

In 1930, Pike Place Market reached its height of operation by issuing over 600 permits to sell local products. But in 1942 and the beginning of World War II, the Japanese Americans, who represented nearly half of the farmers, were placed in internment camps. Many never returned, and in 1949, only 53 farmers applied for permits to sell their goods. This decline continued into the 1950s as the flight to the suburbs left the cities vacant. In the late 1960s, downtown business interests formed a plan to demolish the neglected market to make way for modern commercial development. These interests were opposed, however, by a grassroots group who sought to preserve the market for its historic and cultural values. These activists were successful, and in 1971, the citizens of Seattle voted

Salmon

Nearly all of the nation's wild salmon is harvested in Alaska. Native Indians recognized five "tribes" of salmon, each having its own particular characteristics. They looked upon the salmon as life, as the salmon have been a physical and spiritual source since the days when people first came to the area. Spawned in freshwater streams, the young salmon travel to the ocean where they live and grow for three or four years. In the spring, after they reach maturity, the adult salmon return to their native streams to spawn. As the salmon return home, they stop eating and live mainly on the oils stored in their bodies. They travel great distances, leaping over obstacles such as dams and waterfalls, and are able to return to the exact spot where they were hatched. The salmon were once so plentiful that the Indians would spear or club them from the river banks, and the fish would be eaten fresh, air-dried to create jerky, or smoked. Today, wild salmon are threatened and the health of the salmon runs influence the health of the area's economy.

The fish are caught two ways: in nets and on hooks during trolling. Netted salmon are caught in larger quantities, thus making the fish less expensive to purchase. However, the flesh can be damaged in the process, resulting in lower quality fish. Trolling for salmon results in the highest quality fish, as only one fish at a time can be caught on each hook. Typically, salmon caught by trolling are labeled as such and bring a higher price at market.

Salmon is prepared using numerous techniques. It is said the Alaskans have as many preparations for salmon as people in the lower 48 have for beef. Descriptions of salmon indigenous to the region include:

CHUM This variety of salmon weighs about 7 pounds and is referred to by many other names, including "fall," "dog," "silverbrite," and "calico" salmon. Chum salmon has a

to place the market under public ownership and preserve and restore it to its place as the "Heart and Soul of Seattle."

The first Starbucks store was opened in Pike Place Market in 1971, and this company reflects Seattle's passion for coffee and the city's influence on coffee trends around the country. Espresso, cappuccino, latte, short, tall, and skinny have all become a familiar language, and "coffee breaks" have a new and significant importance in American culture.

pale flesh, with moderate fat content and mild flavor. It is commonly used to produce smoked salmon via both hot and cold smoking techniques.

KING The largest of the salmon varieties, weighing between 15 and 20 pounds. King salmon, sometimes referred to as "Chinook" salmon, has a high oil content and a rich, full flavor, making it excellent for grilling. Some king salmon have no pigmentation of the flesh and are called "white king" salmon. White king salmon are expensive because they are rare; however, they have the same flavor and texture as normal king salmon.

PINK This variety of salmon is the smallest, weighing only 3 to 5 pounds each. Pink salmon are found in huge numbers in the Alaskan waters and are also referred to as "hump-back" or "humpy" salmon. Their flesh is light and moist but is more delicate than that of other varieties of salmon. Most pink salmon is canned and used much like canned tuna.

SILVER This variety usually weighs 7 pounds and is also referred to as "coho" or "hooknose" salmon. It has a red flesh, similar to the king salmon, but a much lower fat content, making it not quite as flavorful as other salmon. Silver salmon are often canned and used much like canned tuna.

SOCKEYE These fish generally weigh 6 pounds and have an intensely red-colored flesh. Sockeye salmon are also referred to as "red" and "bluejack" salmon. The Japanese purchase the majority of the sockeye catch, as red is the color of celebration in Japan. This makes the fish more difficult to find in the United States, as well as more expensive than the other varieties of salmon.

Pike Place Market today offers the best introduction to the elements of Pacific Northwest cuisine. Artisinal products and specialty foods including smoked Pacific salmon, "handmade" and "farmstead" cheese, wild mushrooms, dried cherries, organic produce, and rustic breads are proudly produced and reflect the passion of the region.

Typical Pacific Northwest Ingredients and Dishes

Alaskan Halibut The largest member of the flounder family, Alaskan halibut are known to grow as large as 500 pounds and have firm, white flesh with a mild flavor, making them excellent for grilling, baking, or sautéing. Halibut fishing in the Pacific Northwest begins in the spring and continues until mid-November. Halibut cheeks, resembling large sea scallops, are a delicacy and can weigh up to 1 pound. The most common preparation of halibut cheeks is to dredge them in flour, pan-fry them, and serve them with a simple sauce.

Apples Washington's rich lava ash soil and plentiful sunshine create perfect conditions for growing apples. Today, Washington is the largest apple-growing region in America, producing between 10 and 12 billion apples per year. Although more than half of the orchards are dedicated to producing Red Delicious apples, other varieties are grown. Some of the most common varieties are those best for eating—the Fuji, Gala, and Red Delicious—and others that are also good for cooking and baking—Golden Delicious, Granny Smith, Jonagold, Jonathan, Newton Pippin, Rome Beauty, and Winesap.

Asparagus The Yakima and Columbia River valleys of Washington produce over 80 million pounds of asparagus annually. The asparagus season runs from April to early June and comes in both green and a milder (but more expensive) white form, the white having been blanched by being covered with soil. The most popular asparagus is called "pencil" asparagus for its long, thin shape, but the fatter, thicker asparagus are considered to be more tender and flavorful.

Berries

Blueberries With over 160 varieties, each has its own degree of flavor and sweetness. Generally the smaller the berry, the sweeter and more flavorful it is. Huckleberries are one of the more common varieties found in the region.

Blackberries The largest commercial crop of blackberries is a variety also known as the marionberry. Developed in Marion County, Oregon, this variety is a cross between wild and domestic blackberries. It is aromatic with a good balance of acid and sugar and is good for pies, cobblers, and jams. Other varieties include the loganberry, a highly acidic cross between a raspberry and a blackberry, and the boysenberry, a cross between the raspberry, blackberry, and loganberry. All of these are excellent for baking.

Cranberries Similar to the cranberries of the New England region, these very tart berries grow in the bogs along the Northwest Pacific coastline. Although the region grows only a small fraction of America's cranberries, they are sought after for their high quality, excellent flavor, and deep red color. The annual harvest takes place in October.

Lingonberries A tart, red berry related to the cranberry and indigenous to Alaska.

Raspberries Washington and Oregon are the top producers of red raspberries in the United States. Though not as common, wild red and black raspberries are grown in the region.

Salmonberries Plump red orange berries that resemble clusters of salmon eggs. They are related to wild raspberries.

Strawberries The largest commercial berry harvest in Oregon. Tiny, wild strawberries are also found in the coastal regions.

Brewpub Different from a microbrewery, the term "brewpub" indicates a pub that that makes its own beer on the premises. Typically a brewpub also serves light, casual American cuisine to accompany its beer products.

Caviar The salted eggs of the sturgeon fish. Pacific Northwest caviar is made in the same tradition as Russian and Iranian sturgeon caviar. The egg sacs are passed along a mesh to separate the eggs, then treated by a professional experienced in how much and how long to salt the eggs. Despite an abundance of female sturgeon in the Columbia River, many regulations concerning the collection of the roe make Pacific Northwest caviar rare as well as expensive.

Cherry Bing cherries have a sweet flavor with a dark red to almost black color and are America's most popular variety. The Rainier cherry, larger in size and gold with a reddish hue, was developed in Washington and has a more delicate flavor than the Bing cherry. Other varieties common to the region are the Meteor cherry (sour and usually used for pies, cobblers, and jams) and the Lambert cherry (which has a unique heart shape). Cherries are seasonal in nature and available only in the summer months.

Cheese The Pacific Northwest is noted as an exceptional producer of cheeses. "Farmstead cheese" is the term for handmade cheeses produced by people who raise their own goats, sheep, or cows. The region is noted for exceptional gouda, manchego, goat cheese, and blue cheese.

Cougar Gold Cheese A sharp, nutty white Cheddar cheese that is the result of an experiment by students on the campus at Washington State University in the 1930s. Using excess milk from the university's agricultural program, they developed this hard cheese that could be packaged in tin cans. Their goal was to create a recipe that did not produce the gases resulting from aging that caused the packaging to explode. Cougar Gold was named after the university's mascot and comes in a variety of flavors that continue to be sold in 30-ounce tins.

Tillamook Cheese "Tillamook," a Native American word meaning "land of many waters" is the name of a county in northwestern Oregon where the milk of Holstein, Jersey, and Guernsey cows is converted into a premier Cheddar cheese. Canadian cheesemaker Peter McIntosh came to the area in the late 1800s to teach the latest production techniques. A few years later, ten dairies banded together to ensure the high-quality standards established by McIntosh. Today, this 196-member dairy cooperative, known as the Tillamook County Creamery Association, produces over 50 million pounds of this name-brand natural cheese.

Clams Found in the muddy tidelands of Oregon and Washington, clams taste best when spawning, in the early summer. When purchasing clams, the shells should be tightly closed. Varieties of clams include:

Geoduck From the Native American word for "digging deep," pronounced GOOey-duck, this famous Pacific Northwest clam is large, sometimes growing up to 10 pounds, with a long siphon that looks like a neck. It burrows deep in the sand and is difficult to find. The neck meat can be tough and is chopped up to be used in chowder or made into fritters, or sliced into "clam steaks," pounded and pan-fried. The meat from the interior, referred to as the "breast," can be sautéed or served raw as an ingredient in sushi or as sashimi.

Manila Clam Originating in Asia, the Manila clam was introduced to the Pacific Northwest by Asian immigrants in the late 1800s. This small clam, only 1 inch in diameter, is the most common variety in the region, and is generally eaten in chowder or served steamed. It grows well in the wild and in oyster farms.

Razor Clam Long and slightly curved, resembling the straight razor used by barbers, this clam is served steamed, chopped, or used in chowder. The razor clam is a favorite among the Japanese and is used for sushi and sashimi preparations.

Crabs Crabs are some of the most profitable commercial seafood of the Northwest. The crab season in the Pacific Northwest is in the winter months, when the water is coldest. All of these crabs are typically purchased precooked and frozen.

Dungeness Crab Common along coastal waters from Mexico to the Aleutian Islands of Alaska, Dungeness crabs have unusually sweet tasting, tender meat.

King Crab The largest of the crab species, typically found in the waters of Alaska. Most king crabs grow to about 6 pounds; however, they have been known to exceed 25 pounds in weight, with a leg span of over 6 feet. The legs are generally steamed and served either hot or cold with drawn butter. King crab is fished in the rough, icy waters off the Alaskan coast, and the danger involved with fishing these crabs is one reason they are so expensive. The legs of the king crab are the only part of the crab utilized in commercial food-service operations.

Snow Crab A smaller relative of the king crab, found in the icy waters of Alaska. Unlike the king crab, the body meat is utilized as well as the leg meat. The meat is available in many forms—body meat only, leg meat only, and combinations of body and leg meat. It is used as an ingredient in other dishes but can also be prepared by steaming, as with king crab.

Hazelnut Nearly all of America's hazelnuts are grown in the Willamette and Umpqua Valleys of Oregon. Hazelnuts can be eaten whole as a snack but are more commonly used as an ingredient in cooking and in the production of baked goods and pastries. The oil derived from grinding, heating, and pressing the hazelnuts is highly regarded, and when combined with a more neutral flavored oil, is excellent for use as a salad dressing. Hazelnuts are also used in such specialty products as paste, butter, and flour. Once known as the filbert, the Oregon nut-growing industry voted to discontinue use of the name owing to the confusion it caused among consumers and industry professionals.

Lamb The most popular variety in the region is known as Ellensburg lamb, from eastern Washington. It is known for its excellent balance of flavor, tenderness, and fat content owing to the lamb's primary diet of grass and wild herbs instead of the more common grain.

Mussels The native mussel of the Pacific Northwest is the blue mussel, which grows in abundance attached to rocks and pilings along the coast. Most blue mussels are Penn Cove mussels, named after the bay where they are commonly grown. Recently, the Mediterranean mussel was introduced to the Pacific Northwest waters. This species is generally larger than the blue mussel and has plumper meat. Mussels deteriorate very rapidly and the beards, or stringy tendrils that protrude from the shell, must be removed before cooking.

Nettle A perennial plant indigenous to the forests of the region and gathered by foragers in the spring. Nettles have a peppery flavor and are used as an ingredient in cooking in a manner similar to that of sorrel and spinach. Care must be taken when picking nettles, as their stems are a skin irritant.

Oysters There are four main varieties of oysters found in the Pacific Northwest. Because oysters filter about 100 gallons of water every day, their flavor tends to take on the flavor and characteristic of the water in which they grow. They include:

> *Pacific Oyster* The most common in the area and often marketed under the name of the bay from which it came. Planted in the region by the Japanese, who emigrated to the area in the late 1800s, the Pacific oyster is identified by its oblong, oval shape and its deeply cupped, lightly ridged shell.

> *Kunamoto Oyster* Originating in southern Japan, it is small and known for its deep cup, sweet flavor, and buttery texture.

> *Olympia Oyster* The only oyster native to the Pacific Northwest. It is very small, measuring only about 2 inches in diameter. The shell is round in shape and the meat has a mild, delicate flavor.

> *European Flat Oyster* Also known as the "Belon," originally from France has a flat, round shell. Its meat has a pronounced flavor that is usually much stronger than that of the Pacific oyster.

Pears Summer pears include Bartlett and Red Bartlett (bell shaped, good for cooking and eating raw). Winter pears are Comice (softest, juiciest, with a smooth texture), Anjou (the most common pear, crisp, sweet, and juicy, and good for cooking or eaten raw), Bosc (especially good with cheese, but also the best pear for poaching), and Seckel (very sweet and smaller than other pears, good for eating or cooking).

Plums Oregon and Washington are among America's top five plum-producing states. Freestone plums, also known as "Italian plums," are usually cooked and are commonly used in pies, tarts, and jams. (Freestone plums get their name because the pit is not attached to the flesh of the plum and is easily removed.) The region also produces numerous varieties of plums that are eaten raw or used in fruit salad. Plums are seasonal in nature and available from June to August.

Rockfish This fish is common to the waters along the Pacific Coast, from Baja California all the way to the Gulf of Alaska. Although dozens of varieties of rockfish exist, the most common has a bright orange skin and yellow eye. Pacific rockfish are commonly referred to as Pacific red snapper even though the fish is only remotely related to the red snapper of the Atlantic Ocean. The meat is lean and flaky, with a mild flavor, and is generally sautéed. Other varieties of rockfish common to the region include black rockfish, quill-back rockfish, canary rockfish, and Pacific Ocean perch.

Smoked Salmon Originally developed to preserve salmon throughout the winter. In the Pacific Northwest, the hot smoking technique, also referred to as "kippering," is preferred to the cold smoking technique, which leaves the salmon virtually raw. Hot-smoked salmon is usually prepared by brining the fish in a wet or dry brine; the salmon is then rinsed and cooked very slowly over a smoking hardwood fire.

Stone Fruit A fruit containing a single pit or seed. Types of stone fruit include cherry, plum, peach, and apricot.

Sturgeon One of the oldest fish still thriving today. It is found in the waters of the Pacific Northwest. The sturgeon is a survivor of prehistoric times and can be identified by its long snout and a bone structure that is on the surface of the flesh rather than within the fish itself. Sturgeon is a meaty white fish available in the fall. It is excellent sautéed, grilled, or smoked. The egg sac of the female sturgeon is made into caviar.

Thai Black Rice A highly glutinous rice, black in color. Thai black rice is known for its nutty flavor and distinctly pleasing aroma.

Truffle A rare fungus that grows underground among the roots of certain trees—primarily Douglas fir in the Pacific Northwest, as opposed to oak in France and Italy. Truffles indigenous to the Pacific Northwest include the *tuber gibbosum,* similar to the white truffles of Umbria, Italy, and two varieties of black truffles—the *tuber magnatum* and the *melanogaster carthusianum*—both commonly found in Perigord, France. Truffles are known for their unique flavor and aroma. Truffles from the Pacific Northwest are quite rare and very expensive, seldom reaching the commercial markets of the United States

Walla Walla Onion Sweet onions grown in Oregon. Walla Walla onions are as prized as other special onions with distinguishing flavors, such as Vidalia onions from Georgia and Maui onions from Hawaii.

Wild Mushrooms Of the over 2,500 varieties of wild mushroom common to the Pacific Northwest, only about 35 are considered to be of choice edible quality. The prime locations for gathering wild mushrooms are in western Oregon and Washington, as well as in many areas of Alaska. The spring and fall seasons are when the vast majority of wild mushrooms become available, starting with morels in April and ending with chanterelles as late as December.

Chanterelle Mushroom The most plentiful of the wild mushrooms found in the area. Chanterelles are yellow or white in color. They appear as early as July and may be available as late as December. Chanterelles have a strongly characteristic flavor and are best cooked in a simple manner that allows their flavor to be fully appreciated.

Chicken of the Woods These mushrooms are available in fall and early winter. They are flat and do not have a stem. Their name comes from their texture and flavor, which is similar to chicken meat.

Matsutaki Mushroom Favorites in Japanese cooking, this mushroom grows within the decaying leaves and branches that cover the forest floor. Available in mid-fall, they are noted for their rich, earthy flavor. Their shape resembles the shiitake mushroom, only with a thicker and lumpier cap.

Meadow Mushroom This wild mushroom, when mature, is tan in color with a large, flat cap and resembles a portobello mushroom. Meadow mushrooms grow in field grasses and are available from May through June. When they are immature, they are slightly pink in color and are called "pinkbottoms."

Morel A mushroom with an earthy flavor, generally found April through May. Morels are tan to black in color and have a cone-shaped, umbrella-capped stem. Their growing patterns are inconsistent and unpredictable, making them scarce as well as expensive. The wrinkled caps are attached to a woody stem with a hollow center that lends itself well to stuffing.

Oyster Mushroom Grayish in color, growing in clusters on cottonwood trees at lower elevations along rivers and lakes, this mushroom is cultivated first in May and June, and then again in September and October.

Puffball A large, spherical mushroom found in the fall. Its large size and firm texture make it well suited for cutting into steaks and either grilling or sautéing.

Porcini Mushroom Also known as *cepes* in France, these mushrooms have red caps and a white, bulbous base. Normally associated with French and Italian cooking, porcini grow in the region from July through mid-September.

Menus and Recipes from the Cuisine of the Pacific Northwest

MENU ONE

Red Lentil Soup with Walla Walla Marmalade

Mussels in Thai Coconut Broth

Pear and Hazelnut Salad with Oregon Blue Cheese

Sautéed Halibut with Warm Apple and Dried Cherry Compote

Gai Lan (Chinese Broccoli) with Crispy Garlic

MENU TWO

Broccoli Soup with Tillamook Cheese and Toasted Hazelnuts

Roasted Lamb with Thyme-Merlot Sauce

Grilled Cod with Cucumbers and Ginger Salad

Brussels Sprouts with Hazelnuts

Zucchini and Snow Peas with Basil

Savory Bread Pudding

Strawberry Brûlée

MENU THREE

Pea Soup with Crabmeat and Mint

Hot-Smoked Apricot Salmon on Mushroom-Soba Noodle Salad

Blackberry Barbecued Chicken

Cranberry Beans with Fresh Oregano

Walla Walla Onion Rings

Chocolate Flourless Cake with Coffee Cream Anglaise

OTHER RECIPES

Alaskan King Crab Legs with Champagne Sauce

Blackberry Yogurt Soup

Red Lentil Soup with Walla Walla Marmalade 4 SERVINGS

AMOUNT	MEASURE	INGREDIENT
I cup	7 ounces, 220 g	Red lentils, picked over, misshaped beans or stones discarded, rinsed
6 cups	48 ounces, 1.5 l	Chicken or vegetable stock
$^1/_2$ cup	3 ounces, 94 g	Carrots, peeled, finely diced
$^1/_2$ cup	2 ounces, 32 g	Celery, finely diced
I		Garlic clove, finely diced
I		Bay leaf
to taste		Salt
$^3/_4$ teaspoon	I g	Black pepper
3 tablespoons	I $^1/_2$ ounces, 42 g	Unsalted butter
8 cups	I $^1/_2$ pounds, 750 g	Onions, Walla Walla or other sweet, chopped
I teaspoon	5 g	Granulated sugar
2 teaspoons	2 g	Thyme, chopped
I tablespoon	$^1/_2$ ounce, 15 ml	Sherry vinegar

PROCEDURE

1 Combine the lentils and stock, and bring to a boil. Cook for a few minutes at a gentle boil and remove any foam that comes to the surface.

2 Add the carrots, celery, garlic, and bay leaf. Reduce the heat and simmer, uncovered, until very soft, 30 to 35 minutes.

3 Remove from heat and discard bay leaf.

4 Puree the soup; if the soup is too thick, thin with additional stock. Season with salt and $^1/_2$ teaspoon (2.5 ml) pepper.

5 While the lentils are cooking, make the marmalade. Melt the butter and add the onions, sugar, and thyme. Cook, stirring often, until very soft and caramelized, 25 to 35 minutes.

6 Stir in the vinegar and correct seasoning with additional salt and remaining pepper.

7 Ladle into warm bowls and top each serving with warm onion marmalade.

Mussels in Thai Coconut Broth 4 SERVINGS

AMOUNT	MEASURE	INGREDIENT
2 pounds	1 kg	Mussels, in shell, washed, debearded
1/2 cup	4 ounces, 125 ml	Dry white wine
1 tablespoon	28 ml	Vegetable oil
2 cups	8 ounces, 226 g	Baby bok choy, trimmed, cut into 1-inch (2.5 cm) pieces
2 1/2 cups	10 ounces, 28 g	Red bell pepper, seeded, finely julienned
6 tablespoons	3 ounces, 84 g	Shallots, thinly sliced
1 tablespoon	1/2 ounce, 15 g	Ginger and garlic
2 teaspoons	10 g	Light brown sugar
1 teaspoon	2 g	Curry powder
1/8 teaspoon		Cayenne
1 can	13 ounces, 430 ml	Coconut milk (unsweetened), well shaken
1/4 cup	1/2 ounce, 15 g	Cilantro
4		Lime wedges

PROCEDURE

1. Place the mussels in a saucepan; discard any that fail to close to the touch. Add the wine and bring to a boil over high heat. Cover and cook, shaking, until the mussels open, about 5 minutes.

2. Save the liquid and transfer the mussels to a bowl, discarding any that failed to open; cover and keep warm.

3. Pour the liquid through a fine-mesh sieve lined with cheesecloth (muslin) and set aside.

4. Wipe out pan; add the oil and heat over medium heat.

5. Add the bok choy, bell pepper, sh. / , ginger and garlic. Cook, stirring, for 5 minutes or until vegetables are almost soft.

6. Stir in the brown sugar, curry powder, and cayenne; cook 1 minute.

7. Pour in the coconut milk and reserved mussel cooking liquid; bring to a boil.

8. Divide the mussels and vegetables among warmed bowls and ladle the broth over the top.

9. Sprinkle with cilantro and serve immediately with lime wedges on the side.

Pear and Hazelnut Salad with Oregon Blue Cheese 4 SERVINGS

AMOUNT	MEASURE	INGREDIENT
4 cups	8 ounces, 226 g	Butter lettuce

For the Vinaigrette

AMOUNT	MEASURE	INGREDIENT
I cup	4 ounces, 113 g	Roasted pear, ripe, peeled cored, chopped
1/4 cup	2 ounces, 55 ml	Rice vinegar
I teaspoon	5 g	Granulated sugar
1/4 cup	2 ounces, 55 ml	Hazelnut oil
to taste		Salt and white pepper
2		Roasted pears, ripe (Red Bartlett, preferably), peeled
1/4 cup	I ounce, 28 g	Hazelnuts, roasted, peeled, chopped
1/2 cup	2 ounces, 56 g	Oregon blue cheese

PROCEDURE

1 Wash and spin-dry the lettuce, breaking the larger leaves into 4-inch (10.2 cm) pieces.

2 Add pear to blender along with rice vinegar, to prevent pear from browning. Add the sugar, salt, pepper, and hazelnut oil and puree until smooth.

3 Place the cleaned, torn lettuce in a bowl and lightly toss with some dressing.

4 Arrange the dressed lettuce on chilled plates.

5 Slice each pear in half and spoon out the cores. Lay the halves on a cutting board, flat side down, and slice each half on a bias into 7 or 8 even slices. Press the sliced pear halves lightly to fan them out and carefully transfer the pear fan to the lettuce.

6 Scatter hazelnuts and crumbled blue cheese over each salad and serve.

Pear and Hazelnut Salad with Oregon Blue Cheese

Sautéed Halibut with Warm Apple and Dried Cherry Compote 4 SERVINGS

AMOUNT	MEASURE	INGREDIENT
$^1/_3$ cup	2 ounces, 56 g	Dried cherries
$^1/_4$ cup	2 ounces, 55 ml	Apple brandy
$^1/_4$ cup	2 ounces, 56 g	Unsalted butter
2 cups	6 ounces, 170 g	Walla Walla onions, thinly sliced
1 $^1/_2$ cups	6 ounces, 170 g	Granny Smith apples, $^1/_2$ inch (1.2 cm) dice
2		Garlic cloves, minced
1 tablespoon	$^1/_2$ ounce, 15 ml	Lemon juice
$^1/_2$ teaspoon	2 g	Salt and black pepper
4	5-ounce portions	Halibut fillets, boneless, skinless
1		Egg, beaten with a little water
as needed		All-purpose flour, for dredging
2 tablespoons	1 ounce, 28 ml	Hazelnut oil

PROCEDURE

1. Rehydrate the cherries in the brandy over a slow boil. Remove from the heat and set aside.

2. Heat the butter over medium heat and cook the onions until translucent, about 3 minutes.

3. Add the apples and garlic. Continue to cook and stir occasionally until the apples are soft and the onions are golden brown.

4. Stir the lemon juice into the cherries and brandy. Add the cherries to the apples; warm thoroughly and correct seasoning. Keep warm.

5. Season the fillets with salt and pepper. Dip fillets into beaten egg and then into flour.

6. Heat the oil over medium-high heat and sauté the fillets until golden brown on both sides, 3 minutes on one side, 2 minutes on the second side. (Turn only once, if necessary, finish in oven.)

7. Serve each halibut fillet topped with the warm compote.

Gai Lan (Chinese Broccoli) with Crispy Garlic 4 SERVINGS

chef tip *Gai lan* is also known as "Chinese broccoli." If *gai lan* is not available, substitute bok choy, broccoli, or broccoli rabe.

AMOUNT	MEASURE	INGREDIENT
2 tablespoons	I ounce, 55 ml	Vegetable oil
3		Garlic cloves, thinly sliced
¹/₄ teaspoon	I g	Red pepper flakes
I¹/₂ pounds	750 g	Gai lan, tough stem ends trimmed
3 tablespoons	I¹/₂ ounces, 42 ml	Rice wine or dry white wine
2 tablespoons	I ounce, 55 ml	Tamari (soy sauce)

PROCEDURE

1 Heat a large pan or wok over high heat. When hot, add oil and swirl to coat bottom.

2 When oil is hot but not smoking, add the garlic and red pepper flakes. Cook, stirring constantly, until the garlic is golden, about 3 minutes. Do not overcook the garlic.

3 Remove the garlic to paper towels to drain, but keep the oil in pan.

4 Add the gai lan and 2 tablespoons (28 ml) of the wine and cook, tossing and stirring to prevent scorching, until tender, about 5 minutes.

5 Add the tarmari and the remaining wine; cook 1 minute.

6 Transfer to a warm serving platter and sprinkle with the reserved garlic.

Broccoli Soup with Tillamook Cheese and Toasted Hazelnuts 4 SERVINGS

AMOUNT	MEASURE	INGREDIENT
2 tablespoons	1 ounce, 28 g	Unsalted butter
1 cup	4 ounces, 113 g	Leeks, halved lengthwise, cleaned, chopped
1 cup	4 ounces, 113 g	Onion, chopped
1 tablespoon	1/2 ounce, 15 g	Garlic, chopped
5 cups	16 ounces, 453 g	Broccoli, chopped, stalk peeled
1 cup	5 ounces, 141 g	Carrots, peeled, chopped
1 quart	32 ounces, 1 l	Chicken stock
1 cup	8 ounces, 235 ml	Half-and-half
to taste		Salt and black pepper
2 cups	8 ounces, 226 g	Tillamook Cheddar cheese
1 cup	4 ounces, 113 g	Hazelnuts, toasted, chopped

PROCEDURE

1 Melt the butter over medium heat and add the leeks and onion. Cook, stirring occasionally, for 8 minutes. Add the garlic and cook for 2 minutes more.

2 Combine the leek-onion mixture with the broccoli, carrots, and stock. Bring to a boil, reduce the heat, cover, and simmer for 20 minutes or until the vegetables are tender.

3 In batches, puree the vegetable mixture in a blender.

4 Return the pureed soup to the heat and stir in the half-and-half; season with salt and pepper.

5 Stir in the cheese and heat until melted. Do not boil. Correct seasoning.

6 Serve hot, sprinkled with hazelnuts.

Roasted Lamb with Thyme-Merlot Sauce 4 SERVINGS

AMOUNT	MEASURE	INGREDIENT
2 pounds	907 g	Leg of lamb
to taste		Salt and black pepper
2 tablespoons	1 ounce, 28 ml	Vegetable oil
1/4 cup	2 ounces, 55 ml	Dijon mustard
1 tablespoon	1/2 ounce, 15 g	Garlic, minced
1 teaspoon	1 g	Parsley, minced
1 teaspoon	1 g	Thyme, minced
1 cup	3 ounces, 85 g	Panko (Japanese bread crumbs)
2 tablespoons	1 ounce, 28 g	Shallots, minced
1/2 cup	4 ounces, 115 ml	Merlot red wine
1/2 cup	4 ounces, 115 ml	Brown stock
1 tablespoon	3 g	Thyme, chopped
1/4 cup	2 ounces, 56 g	Unsalted butter

PROCEDURE

1 Preheat the oven to 450°F (225°C).

2 Truss and season the lamb roast.

3 Heat the oil over high heat and sear the lamb on all sides until thoroughly browned. Remove the pan from the heat and brush the top side of the meat with the mustard.

4 Combine the garlic, parsley, and minced thyme with the bread crumbs and pat gently on top of the mustard until the meat is coated with crumbs.

5 Roast the lamb until desired temperature is attained, about 145°F (63°C) for medium. Remove lamb from roasting pan and allow the meat to rest in a warm place while the sauce is prepared.

6 Discard all but about 1 tablespoon (14 ml) of fat from the roasting pan and add the shallots. Cook 1 to 2 minutes or until they are translucent.

7 Deglaze the pan with the wine, add the stock and chopped thyme, and reduce the liquid by half.

8   Remove the pan from the heat and finish the sauce by briskly whisking in the butter, a little at a time, until smooth. (Strain if desired.)

9   Season with salt and black pepper.

10 Slice lamb and serve with sauce.

Grilled Cod with Cucumbers and Ginger 4 SERVINGS

AMOUNT	MEASURE	INGREDIENT
2 cups	9 ounces, 225 g	Cucumbers, English or hothouse, thinly sliced
I cup	4 ounces, 113 g	Red onion, very thinly sliced
2 teaspoons	10 g	Salt
3 tablespoons	2 ounces, 56 g	Pickled ginger, chopped
I tablespoon	$^1/_2$ ounce, 14 ml	Rice vinegar
3 tablespoons	10 g	Green onion tops, chopped
3 tablespoons	$1^1/_2$ ounces, 42 ml	Vegetable oil
4	5-ounce servings	Cod fillets, boneless, skinless
to taste		Salt and black pepper

PROCEDURE

1   Combine cucumbers and red onion and sprinkle with $1^1/_2$ teaspoons (8 g) of salt. Let stand 15 minutes; drain any liquid.

2   Combine the ginger, vinegar, and green onion tops with the cucumbers and red onions.

3   Add 2 tablespoons (1 ounce, 30 ml) oil; set aside.

4   Brush fish fillets with remaining oil and season both sides.

5   Grill fish skin side down to start, 3 minutes. Turn and finish cooking, 1 minute.

6   Transfer the fillets to warmed plates and serve with cucumber salad.

Grilled Cod with Cucumbers and Ginger

Brussels Sprouts with Hazelnuts 4 SERVINGS

AMOUNT	MEASURE	INGREDIENT
4 cups	12 ounces, 340 g	Brussels sprouts, cleaned
2 tablespoons	1 ounce, 28 g	Unsalted butter
1/4 cup	1 ounce, 28 g	Onion, 1/4 inch (.6 cm) dice
1 tablespoon	1/2 ounce, 14 g	Hazelnuts, finely chopped
to taste		Salt and white pepper

PROCEDURE

1 Remove the blemished outside leaves and score an X that is 1/2 inch (1.2 cm) deep in each stem end of the Brussels sprouts.

2 Par-boil the Brussels sprouts in simmering salted water until they are fork-tender. Drain and reserve.

3 Heat the butter over medium heat, add the onion, and cook for 2 minutes or until golden.

4 Stir in the chopped hazelnuts and continue to cook for an additional 1 minute.

5 Add the Brussels sprouts and toss, coating them thoroughly. Season with salt and pepper.

Zucchini and Snow Peas with Basil 4 SERVINGS

AMOUNT	MEASURE	INGREDIENT
1 cup	4 ounces, 113 g	Snow peas
1 tablespoon	$^1/_2$ ounce, 14 ml	Olive oil
1 teaspoon	5 ml	Peanut oil
3 cups	12 ounces, 340 g	Zucchini, $^1/_2$ inch (1.2 cm) dice
1 tablespoon	14 ml	Water
to taste		Salt
1 tablespoon	3 g	Basil leaves, torn or finely sliced
1 teaspoon	1 g	Mint leaves, finely sliced

PROCEDURE

1 Remove string from snow peas.

2 Heat the oils over medium-high heat.

3 Add the zucchini and snow peas along with water. Season and add half the basil. Cook until vegetables are tender.

4 Add remaining basil and the mint leaves; correct seasoning.

Savory Bread Pudding · 4 SERVINGS

AMOUNT	MEASURE	INGREDIENT
2 tablespoons	1 ounce, 28 g	Unsalted butter
2 ounces	56 g	Bacon, 1/4 inch (.6 cm) dice
1 cup	4 ounces, 113 g	Onion, 1/4 inch (.6 cm) dice
1		Garlic clove, minced
1		Egg
1/2 cup	2 ounces, 115 ml	Heavy cream
1/2 cup	4 ounces, 115 ml	Milk
1/2 cup	4 ounces, 115 ml	Chicken stock
1/4 teaspoon		Rosemary (dried)
4 cups	16 ounces, 453 g	French bread, 1/2-inch (1.2 cm) cubes
to taste		Salt and black pepper

PROCEDURE

1   Preheat the oven to 350°F (175°C).

2   Heat the butter over medium heat. Add the bacon, onion, and garlic; cook until lightly brown. Remove from pan and reserve.

3   Combine the egg, cream, milk, stock, and rosemary; stir to incorporate thoroughly.

4   Stir in the bacon and onion mixture.

5   Add the bread to the mixture and let sit to absorb liquid.

6   Grease the baking molds and add the bread pudding mixture. Cover with foil and bake for approximately 20 to 30 minutes or until the pudding is set.

7   Cut into servings and serve hot.

Strawberries Brûlée

Strawberries Brûlée 4 SERVINGS

AMOUNT	MEASURE	INGREDIENT
3 cups	18 ounces, 510 g	Strawberries, hulled and split
I tablespoon	$^1/_2$ ounce, 14 ml	Lemon juice
$^1/_4$ cup plus I tablespoon	$^1/_2$ ounce, 15 g	Granulated sugar
I cup	8 ounces, 235 ml	Heavy cream
2 tablespoons	I ounce, 28 g	Confectioners' sugar
I teaspoon	5 ml	Vanilla extract

PROCEDURE

1   Preheat the broiler.

2   Combine the strawberries, lemon juice, and 1 tablespoon (14 ml) granulated sugar; toss well.

3   Divide the mixture evenly among four 1-cup (235 ml) soufflé dishes; set aside.

4   Whip the cream, then add confectioners' sugar and vanilla.

5   Cover the strawberries with whipped cream and flatten the tops of the dishes.

6   Sprinkle about 1 tablespoon (14 ml) of sugar over the top of each and place the dishes directly under broiler or use a butane torch to bubble up cream until it browns slightly. The sugar will form a paper-thin layer of caramel. Serve at once.

Pea Soup with Crab and Mint 4 SERVINGS

AMOUNT	MEASURE	INGREDIENT
2 tablespoons	I ounce, 28 g	Unsalted butter
1 1/2 cups	6 ounces, 170 g	Leeks, halved lengthwise, cleaned, chopped
2 cups	10 ounces, 315 g	Shelled fresh or frozen English peas
2 1/2 cups	20 ounces, 587 ml	Chicken stock
1/2 teaspoon	3 g	Salt
1/2 teaspoon	I g	Black pepper
5 ounces	142 g	Dungeness crab, picked over for shell fragments
1 1/2 tablespoons	5 g	Mint, chopped

PROCEDURE

1 Over medium heat, melt half the butter.

2 Add the leeks and sauté until wilted, 3 to 4 minutes.

3 Add the peas, stock, and seasoning and bring to a boil; reduce heat to medium low, and simmer 5 to 10 minutes.

4 Puree the soup until smooth and return to pan.

5 In a separate pan, melt remaining butter and add crab; cook gently until warm through, about 1 minute.

6 Fold the mint into crab.

7 Ladle soup into warmed bowls. Top each serving with equal portions of crab.

Hot-Smoked Apricot Salmon 4 SERVINGS

AMOUNT	MEASURE	INGREDIENT
I tablespoon	$^1/_2$ ounce, 14 ml	Vegetable oil
I tablespoon	$^1/_2$ ounce, 15 g	Shallots, minced
I tablespoon	$^1/_2$ ounce, 15 g	Ginger, minced
3 tablespoons	$1^1/_2$ ounces, 42 g	Apricots (dried), $^1/_4$ inch (.6 cm) dice
2 tablespoons	I ounce, 28 ml	Rice wine vinegar
2 tablespoons	I ounce, 28 ml	White wine
$^1/_4$ cup	2 ounces, 56 g	Apricot jam
4	$4^1/_2$-ounce portions	Salmon fillets
as needed		Apple or cherry wood chips

PROCEDURE

1   Heat the oil and add the shallots and ginger; cook until shallots are transparent but take on no color.

2   Add the apricots and sauté for 2 minutes.

3   Add the vinegar and reduce to almost dry.

4   Add the wine and reduce by half.

5   Add the apricot jam and simmer 10 to 15 minutes. Cool.

6   Spread mixture evenly over salmon and let marinate for 2 hours.

7   Prepare smoker and preheat the oven to 350°F (175°C); see Braggin' Rights Brisket recipe (page 330).

8   Smoke the salmon for 3 minutes, then remove from smoker and finish cooking in oven. The smoke taste should be subtle and not too dominant. Use apple or cherry wood chips.

Mushroom-Soba Noodle Salad 4 SERVINGS

chef tip

For all types of mushrooms, look for clean caps free of blemishes, slimy spots, or signs of decay. Allow $^1/_4$ to $^1/_2$ pound per serving when used as a vegetable.

Store mushrooms, unwashed, in plastic or paper bags. Keep away from strawberries and vegetables in the produce refrigerator, as the spores can hasten the destruction of these fruits and vegetables.

AMOUNT	MEASURE	INGREDIENT
2$^1/_2$ cups	10 ounces, 312 g	Buckwheat soba noodles (dried)
1$^1/_2$ tablespoons	$^3/_4$ ounce, 21 ml	Roasted sesame oil
2 cups	12 ounces, 340 g	Asparagus, tough stems removed, cooked until tender, cut on bias into $^1/_2$-inch (1.2 cm) pieces
1 tablespoon	$^1/_2$ ounce, 14 ml	Rice vinegar
1 teaspoon	5 ml	Soy sauce (light)
1 teaspoon	5 g	Brown sugar
1		Garlic clove, minced
1 teaspoon	5 g	Ginger, grated
3 cups	8 ounces, 226 g	Cremini mushrooms (fresh), brushed clean, quartered
3 cups	8 ounces, 226 g	Wild mushrooms (fresh), such as chanterelle, shiitake, or oyster, rinsed quickly or brushed clean, cut into $^1/_2$-inch (1.2 cm) pieces
$^1/_4$ cup	1 ounce, 28 g	Almonds, sliced, toasted
1 tablespoon		Sesame seeds, roasted

PROCEDURE

1 Boil the soba noodles in salted water until barely cooked; drain and run under cold water.

2 Toss noodles with the sesame oil and asparagus; set aside.

3 Mix the vinegar, soy sauce, brown sugar, ginger, and garlic.

4   Cook mushrooms in a dry pan over medium-low heat for about 5 minutes, until their liquid has reduced.

5   Add the rice wine mixture and sauté until the mixture has been absorbed; remove from heat and set aside to cool.

6   Divide noodles and asparagus onto serving plates. Divide mushrooms on top of noodles.

7   Sprinkle with almonds and sesame seeds. Top with one piece of hot smoked salmon.

Blackberry Barbecued Chicken 4 SERVINGS

AMOUNT	MEASURE	INGREDIENT
I tablespoon	$^1/_2$ ounce, 14 ml	Vegetable oil
I cup	4 ounces, 113 g	Sweet onion, $^1/_4$ inch (.6 cm) dice
$^1/_2$ cup	4 ounces, 115 ml	Dry red wine
2 pints	I pound, 453 g	Blackberries (fresh or frozen)
$^1/_4$ cup	2 ounces, 56 g	Light brown sugar, firmly packed
I teaspoon	5 ml	Soy sauce
$3^1/_2$ pounds	1.75 kg	Chicken, cut into 8 pieces
$^1/_2$ teaspoon	3 g	Salt
$^1/_2$ teaspoon	I g	Black pepper

PROCEDURE

1   Heat the oil, add the onion, and cook, stirring frequently, until soft, about 5 minutes.

2   Add the wine, berries, brown sugar, and soy sauce. Cook until slightly thickened, 20 to 25 minutes.

3   Remove from heat and pass through a food mill.

4   Season the chicken with salt and pepper.

5   Grill chicken skin side down for 5 minutes. Baste with sauce, and cook 5 minutes.

6   Turn chicken and again baste with sauce. Cook until juices run clear.

7   Baste one more time before removing from heat. Serve immediately with additional sauce.

Cranberry Beans with Fresh Oregano 4 SERVINGS

AMOUNT	MEASURE	INGREDIENT
2¹/₂ pounds	1.25 kg	Cranberry (borlotti) beans (fresh)
or		
1¹/₄ cups	9 ounces, 280 g	Cranberry beans (dried)
2		Bay leaves
3		Garlic cloves
1¹/₄ teaspoons	8 g	Salt
3 tablespoons	1¹/₂ ounces, 42 ml	Extra-virgin olive oil
¹/₂ teaspoon	1 g	Black pepper
1 tablespoon	3 g	Oregano, chopped

PROCEDURE

1 If using fresh beans, shell them and cover with 2 inches (5 cm) of water. Add bay leaves and garlic. If using dried beans, pick them over, discarding any misshapen beans or stones. Rinse well, and soak over night. Drain soaked beans and cover with water; add bay leaves and garlic.

2 Bring beans to a boil, reduce heat, and simmer gently, uncovered, until beans are tender, 30 minutes for fresh beans and 1 hour for dried.

3 Remove from heat and add 1 teaspoon (5 ml) salt. Stir well and let stand 10 minutes.

4 Drain beans. Discard bay leaves; mash garlic.

5 Stir in the olive oil, pepper, oregano, and garlic. Mix well. Best if served at once while still warm.

Walla Walla Onion Rings 4 SERVINGS

AMOUNT	MEASURE	INGREDIENT
as needed		Vegetable oil, for deep-frying
1	14 ounces, 397 g	Sweet onion, sliced $^1/_4$ inch (.6 cm) thick
$^2/_3$ cup	5 ounces, 156 ml	Water
$^2/_3$ cup	$3^1/_2$ ounces, 100 g	All-purpose flour
$1^1/_2$ cups	$3^1/_2$ ounces, 100 g	Panko (Japanese bread crumbs)
1 tablespoon	10 g	Lime zest
1 teaspoon	5 g	Salt
2 tablespoons	6 g	Cilantro, chopped
4		Lime wedges

PROCEDURE

1 Preheat the oil to 375°F (190°C). Line baking pan with paper towels to drain onion rings.

2 Separate the onion slices into rings.

3 Whisk together the water and flour until smooth.

4 Dip onion rings into flour batter, lift out, let excess drip off, and then dip the rings into the panko, coating evenly.

5 Fry until golden brown, 1 to 2 minutes. Drain on paper towels. Repeat until all the rings are cooked.

6 To serve, sprinkle lime zest, salt, and cilantro over fried onion rings. Serve immediately with lime wedges.

Chocolate Flourless Cake 1 CAKE, 6 SERVINGS

AMOUNT	MEASURE	INGREDIENT
2 cups	8 ounces, 224 g	Chocolate, semisweet, chopped
1/2 cup	4 ounces, 113 g	Butter
6		Eggs, separated
1/2 cup plus 2 tablespoons	4 ounces, 113 g	Granulated sugar

PROCEDURE

1. Preheat the oven to 350°F (175°C). Cut a piece of parchment into a circle to fit the bottom of six 8-ounce (226 g) timbales or ramekins. Butter both the parchment and the sides of the ramekins.

2. Combine the chopped chocolate and butter; melt over low heat, stirring constantly. Cool slightly.

3. Whisk together the egg yolks with 1/2 cup (113 g) sugar until thick and pale yellow in color.

4. Stir chocolate into the egg yolk mixture.

5. Separately whisk the egg whites until thick. Add the remaining sugar gradually and beat to a light meringue.

6. In several additions, fold meringue into chocolate mixture.

7. Pour batter into prepared pan. Bake in a hot-water bath until puffed and tester inserted into center comes out with moist crumbs attached, about 30 minutes.

8. Transfer pan to rack. Cool 10 minutes.

9. Using small sharp knife, cut around edge of cake. Invert cake onto rack. Peel off parchment. Serve with Coffee Cream Anglaise (page 472).

Coffee Cream Anglaise   4 SERVINGS

AMOUNT	MEASURE	INGREDIENT
1/2 cup	4 ounces, 115 ml	Milk
1/2 cup	4 ounces, 115 ml	Heavy cream
1/2 cup	3 1/2 ounces, 100 g	Granulated sugar
1 teaspoon	5 ml	Vanilla extract
3		Egg yolks
1 tablespoon	15 g	Instant espresso coffee, dissolved in 1/2 tablespoon (7 ml) of water or dark rum

PROCEDURE

1   Combine the milk, cream, and sugar. Stir to begin dissolving the sugar.

2   Place the yolks in a 1-quart (1 l) bowl and whisk just enough to break them.

3   Bring the milk mixture to full rolling boil over medium heat. Remove the pan from heat.

4   Whisk about one-third of the boiling liquid into the yolks, Remember to begin whisking before pouring in the hot liquid. Return the saucepan to medium heat and return the remaining liquid to a full boil.

5   Whisk the yolk mixture into the boiling liquid. Continue whisking until the cream thickens slightly, about 30 seconds.

6   Continue to whisk, remove pan from heat. Immediately pour the sauce through a fine strainer.

7   Cool quickly over a bowl of ice water, stirring occasionally.

8   Stir in vanilla and espresso.

Alaskan King Crab Legs with Champagne Sauce · 4 SERVINGS

AMOUNT	MEASURE	INGREDIENT
1 1/2 pounds	680 g	King crab legs (frozen), split
1/4 cup	1 ounce, 28 g	Shallots, finely diced
2 tablespoons	1 ounce, 28 ml	White wine vinegar
1/4 cup	2 ounces, 55 ml	Dry Champagne
1/2 cup	4 ounces, 113 g	Butter
to taste		Salt and white pepper
1 tablespoon	3 g	Chives, minced

PROCEDURE

1 Rinse the frozen legs in cold water.

2 Steam the legs over boiling water in a covered pot for approximately 5 to 10 minutes or until heated thoroughly.

3 Combine the shallots and vinegar in a saucepan and bring to a boil. Reduce the volume by half.

4 Add the Champagne and reduce the volume of liquid by half again.

5 Add the butter, whisking constantly until all the butter is incorporated. Correct seasoning.

6 Serve the king crab legs on a hot plate with the sauce in a side dish. Sprinkle with the chives.

Blackberry Yogurt Soup 4 SERVINGS

AMOUNT	MEASURE	INGREDIENT
2¹/₂ cups	12 ounces, 340 g	Blackberries
¹/₄ cup	2 ounces, 55 ml	Dry white wine
¹/₄ cup	3 ounces, 55 ml	Honey
2 tablespoons	1 ounce, 28 ml	Lemon juice
1¹/₂ cup	12 ounces, 352 ml	Yogurt (plain)
¹/₄ cup	2 ounces, 55 ml	Half-and-half
4 tablespoons	2 ounces, 55 ml	Sour cream

PROCEDURE

1 Combine the blackberries, wine, honey, and lemon juice in a stainless steel saucepan.

2 Bring to a boil, cover, and reduce the heat. Slowly simmer the mixture for 15 minutes.

3 Puree the blackberry mixture in a blender or food processor and strain. Chill thoroughly.

4 Stir in the yogurt and half-and-half; refrigerate until needed.

5 To serve, carefully ladle the soup into chilled soup bowls or plates.

6 Garnish each portion with a small dollop of sour cream.

The Cuisine of Hawaii

The Hawaiian Islands are some of the most recent and some of the most isolated islands on Earth. Before the arrival of the first populations, the islands essentially grew nothing edible. Everything that the people of Hawaii eat has been brought in or introduced since then. From the Pacific Islanders that first reached the Hawaiian Islands, followed by the European voyages of discovery, to the migration of laborers to the sugar plantations, and now the focus on foods grown in the Islands, Hawaii offers a transparent look at the development of a society and a cuisine.

Hawaii "The Aloha State." The word "aloha" means both "hello" and "good-bye." The state bird is the nene, or Hawiian goose; the state flower is the yellow hibiscus; and the state tree is the kukui or candlenut tree. The state gem is black coral, and the state marine mammal is the humpback whale. The state fish is the humuhumunukunuku apuaa (the Hawaiian alphabet has only 12 letters: a, e, i, o, u, h, k, l, m, n, p, and w), also known as the rectangular triggerfish.

History of the Islands

The people who first lived in this part of the world are called "Polynesians"; the name means "people of the many islands." Hawaii is a chain of 132 islands that extends for more than 1,500 miles. The eight main islands are Hawaii (the Big Island), Maui, Oahu, Kauai, Molokai, Lanai, Nihau, and Kahoolawe. Almost all of the Hawaiian populations lives on seven of these eight islands.

The islands have absorbed wave after wave of immigrants bringing bits and pieces from their homelands to create a unique people of blended ancestry. In addition to those of Polynesian descent and whites and blacks from the mainland United States, Hawaii's population includes people of Chinese, Filipino, Japanese, Korean, and Portuguese ancestry. All have contributed customs to what has become Hawaiian culture.

The First Visitors

It is believed that the first voyagers to Hawaii were from the Marquesas Islands and Tahiti, and they arrived in approximately A.D. 800. Expert navigators, these Polynesians explored immense stretches of ocean in sailboats made by lashing two huge canoes together and raising a sail. The early sailors used the stars, clouds, ocean currents, and even seabirds to find their way from island to island. Kings ruled separate kingdoms scattered over the Hawaiian Islands, and many chiefs ruled under each king.

In the late 1700s, Captain James Cook of the British Navy, searching for the Northwest Passage to lead from Europe to Asia, discovered Hawaii. He named it the Sandwich Islands, after the Earl of Sandwich, the First Lord of the British admiralty. Merchant vessels from all over the world stopped in the Hawaiian Islands en route to China. For many years, Hawaiians earned more money by providing whalers and traders with goods than from any other business.

During the early 19th century, the Hawaiian Islands were ruled by four chiefs. But in the 1780s, Kamehameha I—the ruling chief of Hawaii Island—defeated the other chiefs and united the islands. During Kamehameha's rule, Hawaii began to trade with other countries. Settlers, sailors, and merchants came from England, the United States, France, Portugal, Korea, the Philippines, and Russia to take advantage of Hawaii's natural resources. When King Kamehameha died in 1819, his son Liholiho ruled as

Kamehameha II. As trade grew, Christian missionaries came to the islands. Political struggles between the missionaries and the Hawaiian natives weakened the established religious and social systems. In 1893, Queen Liliuokalani, a descendant of King Kamehameha, was removed from the throne by powerful U. S. and European landowners, and the Hawaiian monarchy was ended. On July 7, 1898, while pursuing the U.S. policy of manifest destiny, President William McKinley formally authorized American annexation of the Republic of Hawaii. In 1900, Hawaii was made a U.S. territory. After World War II, statehood became a major issue, and in 1959, Hawaii became the 50th state.

A Most Diverse Culture

The Polynesian natives who came to Hawaii found tropical vegetation, fertile soil, and many species of fish and wildlife. On return visits, they brought their own foods, such as taro, breadfruit, coconuts, sweet potatoes, sugarcane, pineapples, and bananas. They also brought small pigs to start their new lives in Hawaii. When sailors traveling from the Americas to Asia stopped in Hawaii, they could rest, eat, and resupply their ships in the middle of the vast Pacific Ocean. The sailors, traders, and whalers brought with them salted meats and fish, sea biscuits, and a limited supply of fruit and vegetables. Later, in the 1820s, missionaries from the East Coast of the United States came to Hawaii in an attempt to Christianize the natives. They brought staples they were accustomed to in New England, such as potatoes, apples, salt cod, corned beef, cheese, and butter.

SUGAR AND PINEAPPLE

By the end of the 19th century, sugar and pineapple plantations run by American businessmen had taken over much of Hawaii's land, and the crops were the two most important sources of revenue for the Hawaiian economy. As the sugar crops grew, so did the demand for labor, encouraging tens of thousands of people to emigrate to Hawaii. The plantation owners hired contract workers, and substantial numbers of Chinese, Japanese, Filipinos, Koreans, and Portuguese came to work. Each group demanded its own food on the plantations, and small farms, market gardens, and fishing operations were established. The Chinese replaced the poi—the thick, gray paste pounded from the taro root—with rice and relied on their own herbs and spices. The Japanese brought their favorite vegetables, noodle soups, and stir-fry techniques. They packed their lunches to take to the fields, and plate lunches or *bento* (box lunch) became common. Though many of the familiar vegetable seeds they had carried with them from Japan would not grow in Hawaii's climates, the Japanese succeeded in making tofu and soy sauce. The Portuguese introduced their favorite foods with an emphasis on pork, tomatoes, peppers, souring agents and spices, and sausages. They also built their traditional Portuguese beehive bread oven, or *forno,* which allowed them to make their *pao doce* (sweet bread). It is said they also introduced the Japanese to tempura and the Koreans to hot chiles. The Koreans brought their giant crocks of *kim chee* and adobo stews, and built their barbecue pits to cook their marinated meats.

The massive Hawaiian pineapple industry began when James Dole planted his first pineapple trees on the island of Oahu in 1901. In 1922, he purchased the island of Lanai for the purpose of large-scale production, and by 1950, his was the largest pineapple company in the world. But since the 1970s, with crops grown more cheaply in places such as Southeast Asia, Hawaii has taken a much more diverse posture with regard to its agricultural output. The soil in Hawaii is fertile and productive, and the climate, which offers plenty of sunshine and rain, provides excellent growing conditions for agricultural products including livestock, squash, peppers, tomatoes, and lettuce.

HAWAIIAN FOOD, LOCAL FOOD, AND THE HAWAIIAN REGIONAL FOOD MOVEMENT

When those first voyagers from the South Pacific landed on the Hawaiian Islands, they found fish, shellfish, salt, birds, and fresh water, but few edible plants. To survive and flourish, they had to bring their own edible plants. Most important to them was taro. For centuries, it was the main staple of their diet, and it is still served at luaus and important ceremonial occasions. According to a popular legend, the Hawaiian sky god Wakea and the earth god Papa produced two children. The first child died and was buried. From this spot, the taro plant grew. Their second child became the ancestor of the Hawaiian people. *Ohana,* the Hawaiian word for "family," is derived from the word *oha,* the word for the taro cormlets that branch from the stem, or corm, of the plant. The entire taro plant is edible, and there are hundreds of different varieties. The corm of the wetland taro makes the best poi, as well as taro starch or flour. The dry-land variety has a crispy texture and is used for making taro chips, and the smaller Japanese variety is used in stewed dishes. The heart-shaped, deep green leaves and stalks can be cooked as a vegetable, much like turnip greens or other leaf vegetables, or used to wrap other ingredients. The tops of the taro are saved for replanting. Where taro would not grow, sweet potatoes were planted and many varieties are available. In addition, the Marquesan settlers brought the breadfruit and the Tahitians brought the baking banana. The new settlers also introduced coconuts, sugarcane, and pineapples.

"Local food" is the term used in Hawaii to describe how the immigrants adapted to their new lives by using what were new foods to them on the sugar plantations. The food they found was unfamiliar and they had to adapt their cooking methods to create their meals from what was provided and what they brought with them. As a result, their traditional cuisines were transformed. Local Food is best exemplified in the plate lunch, which is served from a plate lunch wagon that can be found around the islands, outside of office buildings, in parks, or by the beaches. Made up of two scoops of rice, a scoop of salad (usually potato salad or macaroni salad), and meat, chicken, or fish heaped on a plate to be eaten with chopsticks, salt and pepper, and soy sauce. The meat could be a large portion of kalua pig (pit-cooked pork), curry stew, Shoyu chicken (chicken simmered in soy sauce), or fried fish. Other favorites such as Portuguese sausage, Chinese sausage, SPAM, sweet and sour pork, teriyaki beef, chicken katsu (a breaded and fried cutlet), Kal bi (Korean barbecued short ribs), char siu (Chinese roast pork), manapua (savory stuffed buns), and musubi (rice ball) exemplify local food. Teenagers in Hawaii consider themselves responsible for the frequently found *loco moco*. Designed to replace sandwiches and typical Asian foods, loco moco is now found in small local restaurants. It is two scoops of rice topped with a hamburger patty and a fried egg, then topped with a generous serving of gravy over the entire meal. Saimin, the Hawaiian version of an Asian noodle soup, is prepared many ways, typically using the somen noodle, broth, and any choice of additional ingredients and seasoning and is served for breakfast, lunch, or dinner. The Hormel Company's canned meat product SPAM (spiced ham) is still considered an important protein, a result of wartime rationing after fishing around the Islands during World War II was prohibited. Most commonly fried and served with rice, it can also be wrapped in ti leaves and roasted, used as a stuffing for wontons, skewered and deep-fried, or used in stir-fry dishes. A SPAM musabi is made by using a rectangle of sticky rice, topped with a fried slice of SPAM, and wrapped with a piece of dried seaweed. The most frequent snack food is any choice of preserved fruits that may be sweetened, or salted and called "crack seed." Brought by the Chinese immigrants, it refers to the *seed* of the fruits that are often left in, and *crack* for the cracking of the seed to expose the kernel.

In 1992 a group of chefs—Sam Choy, Roger Dikon, Amy Ferguson Ota, Mark Ellman, Beverly Gannon, Jean-Marie Josselin, George Mavrothalassitis, Peter Merriman, Philippe Padovani, Gary Strehl, Alan Wong, and Roy Yamagucchi—came together to sponsor a cookbook to be sold for charity. Before they came along, visitors to Hawaii

The Fish of Hawaii

All the ethnic cuisines rely on Hawaii's coastal and offshore fisheries. Hawaiian fish are defined in four categories:

TUNA Tuna is the most important commercial fish in Hawaii. Varieties include skipjack or bonito (*aku*), the big eye or yellowfin tuna (*ahi*), and albacore (*tombo*). A large part of the catch goes to Japan to be sold for sashimi. Tunas range up to several hundred pounds in weight and their silvery bodies are darker on the top than on the bottom. In Hawaii, they are favored for sashimi or poke but are also good grilled or sautéed.

BILLFISH Most common during the summer, these sport fish are known locally as *au*. On the mainland they are known as marlins and swordfish. Like tuna, they can be very large, from 100 to 300 pounds. The Pacific blue marlin (known as *kajiki*) has amber flesh that turns white when cooked. It is good barbecued or grilled, but because this fish has a very low fat content, it should not be overcooked. The broadbill swordfish (*shutome*) is very popular and shipped all over the continental United States. The flesh is white to pinkish, and the meat is tender and mild to the taste. This fish is high in fat and steaks may be grilled, broiled, or used in stir-fries.

BOTTOM FISH The groupers or sea bass, known as *hapuu,* are noted for their clear white flesh and delicate taste. They are most often steamed. The ruby snapper (*onaga*) is small with a delicate flavor when steamed, poached, or baked. The pink snapper (*opakapaka*) is very popular, with a higher fat, light pink flesh, often steamed or baked and served with a light sauce.

OTHER OPEN OCEAN FISH The best known are the wahoo (known as *ono*), with its moist, white flesh that is good grilled or sautéed, the dolphin fish (*mahimahi*), which is usually cut into steaks and fried or grilled, and the moonfish (*opah*) with large grained flesh ranging from pink to red, and is good for broiling, smoking, and making sashimi. The moonfish is considered by the Hawaiians to be a good-luck fish and they will often give it away as a gesture of goodwill, rather than sell it.

were likely to get canned pineapples or frozen fish at Island restaurants. The goal of this new group of chefs was to create farm goods and be a link with the agricultural community and for Hawaiian Regional Cuisine to be a reflection of the community. They took an uninspired international hotel restaurant cuisine, based on imported products, and replaced it with a cuisine based on foods grown in the Islands. They prepared local produce, fish, and meats in the Asian, Pacific, American, and European styles they had experience with. They have been able to redefine dining; create a new agriculture, new books and products, and a new culinary vocabulary; and give the Aloha State a new profile as a new culinary destination.

Typical Hawaiian Ingredients and Dishes

Adobo Spanish for "marinade," it refers to the method of preparing meat or seafood in a marinade and to the dish itself. The Mexican version is hot with chiles, the Portuguese and Philippine versions pungent with vinegar.

Azuki Beans A dried red bean prized for its sweet flavor, mashed to make a filling for mochi, doughnuts, and other confections.

Bitter Melon A gourd vegetable, sour in flavor, with a ridged, warty rind. They are seeded and sliced, parboiled, and then used in a variety of dishes such as stir-fries, braises, and soups. They may also be stuffed.

Bok Choy A member of the cabbage family with thick, white stems and tasty green leaves. Most often used in soups, dumplings, or in stir-fried dishes.

Butter Mochi Local cake made of sweet rice flour (*mochiko*), sugar, eggs, butter, and coconut milk.

Char Sui Chinese barbecued pork sold in almost every Chinese delicatessen, it is reddish and slightly sweet, and is used in many Chinese dishes and for topping saimin (Japanese noodle soup).

Chop Suey Yam The local description of the root vegetable jicama. Eaten raw or used as a substitute for water chestnuts in Chinese dishes.

Crack Seed A popular local snack of preserved fruits, such as rock salt plum or dried mango.

Daikon a large mild white or sometimes black radish used in either raw or cooked form, for salads, stir-fries, and garnishes. Essential for local Japanese cooking it is steamed or pickled.

Dashi Clear stock made from dried bonito flakes and seaweed.

Fish Cake The paste of fresh fish of Chinese origin, and the processed fish cake of the Japanese.

Fish Sauce Light brown to amber seasoning sauces prepared from salted, fermented fish. Known to bring all the flavoring elements into balance, the fishy smell disappears in cooking.

Five Spice Powder A Chinese preparation with the number five possessing symbolic potency for health. It may contain star anise, fennel seeds, Sichuan peppercorns, clove, cinnamon, or nutmeg. It is used for roasted meat and poultry.

Guava A tropical shrub with fragrant berrylike fruit. It is used for jam and jelly. The juice may be mixed with other tropical fruit juices.

Hawaiian Sea Salt Coarse local sea salt, sometimes colored red by clay.

Hawaiian Sweet Bread (Pao Doce) Slightly sweet Portuguese festival bread.

Hawaiian Vintage Chocolate Using criollo cocoa beans from Venezuela, Jim Walsh founded Hawaiian Vintage Chocolate believing that cocoa beans are like wine grapes and that different varietals result in distinct flavors and textures and differences in soil and climate produce differences in the resulting product. Labeled by variety and when and where grown, this premium chocolate is shipped around the world.

Hoisin Sauce A sweet and spicy brown paste of ground beans, garlic, sugar, vinegar, and sesame oil.

Imu A traditional underground pit oven, lined with rocks and ti leaves (or banana leaves), for cooking meats such as chicken and pig.

Kale A member of the cabbage family with dark green, crinkled leaves. Sometimes referred to as "Portuguese cabbage" because of their liking for it, particularly in their soup, caldo verde.

Kalua Pig Pork cooked in an underground earth oven until very tender and then shredded.

Katsu A breaded pork or chicken cutlet. Often served as a plate lunch item.

Kim Chee A pungent Korean condiment of pickled shredded vegetables that may include Chinese cabbage, radishes, cucumber, greens, onions, garlic, and chiles, seasoned with fermented shellfish and salt. This condiment varies widely in its strength.

Kona Coffee The only coffee commercially grown in the United States. It is prized for its wonderful, mellow aroma and robust flavor. It is hand-picked, sun-dried, and named for the area where the coffee farms are located.

Kukui Nut From the Kukui tree, this nut was used by the early Hawaiians for oil, lighting, and other purposes. It is also still used as a relish known as inamona (the nut is roasted, pounded, and salted and served with raw fish). Not available commercially, it is very similar to macadamia nuts, which can be used as a substitute.

Lemon Grass A type of grass with long, tapered, fibrous leaves and a small tender white bulb. It is used to flavor curries, soups, and other dishes. The thick bulb can be finely chopped or ground to a paste to add to stir-fries, braises, and raw dishes.

Limu Edible seaweed, also called "sea vegetables." Used in soups, noodle dishes, or relishes.

Loco Moco A local fast-food menu item consisting of a hamburger patty on two scoops of rice, topped by a fried egg, and covered with brown gravy.

Lomi To rub, press, or massage. Used for fish that has been kneaded with the fingers.

Lomilomi Salmon Salt salmon massaged between the fingers and served chilled with tomatoes and onions as an appetizer or side dish.

Lotus Root The root of a plant in the water lily family that in cross-section has a delicate, lacy, starlike pattern. Thin slices of the peeled root may be used in Asian stir-fries and salads or, when fried, used as a garnish.

Luau Traditional Hawaiian feast. The word is also used for the large green leaves of the taro plant and for the dish of chopped taro leaves with coconut milk and chicken or octopus.

Lumpia In Philippine cooking, this thin pastry wrapper encloses a savory filling, either fresh and wrapped in a lettuce leaf, or deep-fried like an egg roll.

Lychee The fruit of a small tree, also called the "Chinese plum." The exterior of the nut-like fruit has a thin, red, scaly shell with soft, white, fleshy interior that surrounds a pit. The fruit is eaten fresh, dried, canned, or preserved in syrup both as a fruit dessert and as an accompaniment to savory foods.

Macadamia Nut A nut from the tree native to Australia, but now cultivated mostly in Hawaii. Usually shelled and roasted before purchase, the round nut is white, sweet, and high in fat. It is used mainly for cookies, cakes, and pies.

Malasadas Deep-fried, yeast-raised doughnuts, from the Portuguese.

Manapua A steamed Chinese bun, usually stuffed with sweetened pork (char sui).

Mango A tropical evergreen tree with fruit that varies in size, shape, and color. It is usually a deep green to orange color and pear shaped, with smooth orange flesh. Mangos are eaten fresh, or if still green, cooked in preserves, pickles, salads, and chutneys.

Mirin Japanese sweet rice wine used for cooking.

Miso Fermented soybean paste. Used in many Japanese dishes, it ranges from a mild white version to a stronger red version.

Mochi A "cake" made of cooked, pounded mochi rice or steamed sweet rice flour. It may be filled or flavored with red azuki bean paste and eaten as a dessert.

Musubi Rice cooked and shaped into a ball, triangle, or block, sometimes wrapped in nori, and eaten as a snack or fast-food-style item.

Maui Onion Sweet onion, grown on the island of Maui on the slopes of Mount Haleakala. The flavor is much like the Vidalia onion from Georgia, the Walla Walla onion from Oregon, or the 1015 onion from Texas.

Nori Thin black sheets of seaweed, used either toasted or untoasted for wrapping sushi, rice balls, and crackers, and for coating food to be deep-fried. It may also be crushed as a garnish for other Japanese dishes.

Panko The Japanese version of bread crumbs (*pan* from the Portuguese word for "bread," and *ko*, meaning "derived from"). The larger irregular shapes make a light yet crispy coating.

Papaya A tall tropical plant with large pear-shaped fruit that has a thin skin that turns yellow when ripe, a smooth yellow or orange flesh, and many black seeds resembling peppercorns. Unripe papaya can be cooked as a vegetable like squash; the sweet ripe fruit is eaten in many ways, like melon. It is widely used for breakfast with a squeeze of lime juice.

Passion Fruit (Lilikoi) A climbing vine or shrub with egg-sized fruit that turns deep purple and wrinkled with ripeness. Its greenish orange flesh, aromatic, lemony, and intense, is eaten raw with the seeds or squeezed and bottled for juice.

Pilot Crackers (Saloon Pilots, Hardtack, Ship Biscuits) A hard cracker that was often used for military rations because of its excellent keeping qualities. Most likely brought by the New England seamen, it is a favorite dessert when softened in hot water soaked in condensed milk and a little butter, and sprinkled with sugar.

Pineapple Brought to Hawaii from South America in the early 1800s by the Spaniards, but the industry boomed with the importation of plants from Jamaica in 1885. Once a very important industry in Hawaii, the pineapple plantations are unable to compete with fruit grown in countries with cheaper labor.

Plate Lunch Island lunch of the local residents consisting of two scoops of sticky rice, potato or macaroni salad, and some kind of meat.

Poi The traditional Hawaiian porridge of cooked taro root, pounded smooth, thinned with water to the desired thickness, fermented to attain a sour flavor, and eaten with the fingers on its own or as a condiment. One of the most digestible foods, it is said to be an acquired taste.

Poke To cut in blocks or slice crosswise. Now used to refer to fresh raw fish usually seasoned with soy salt, sesame seed paste, chiles, or seaweed. Different from sashimi, as it is rough cut and piled onto a plate and can be made with less expensive pieces of fish.

Portuguese sausage A spicy pork sausage. Eaten with rice, this is one of the most popular Island breakfasts.

Potstickers Chinese meat dumplings steamed and fried in a pan, and usually served with a dipping sauce.

Pupu A Hawaiian word used to refer to cocktail snacks or hors d'oeuvres.

Rice One of the first major crops grown by and for the plantation workers in Hawaii to replace taro. The preferred rice is known as "Calrose rice," after a variety developed for the area. When cooked, the medium to short grains cling together. It is sometimes called "sticky rice" and is easy to eat with chopsticks.

Saimin Noodles in a Japanese dashi or chicken broth with a variety of toppings such as green onions, strips of omelet, char sui, fishcake, or Spam. Bamboo skewers of barbecued chicken or pork may be served on the side.

Sashimi Literally translated as "fresh slice," in Japanese it is actually raw fish expertly sliced according to the particular variety and served with garnishes, condiments, and sauces.

Shave Ice A Japanese favorite snack made from ice thinly shaved off a large block, mounded into a paper cone, and topped in sweet fruit-flavored syrup. It is sometimes topped with bean paste or ice cream.

Shoyu Commonly used Japanese word for soy sauce.

Soba A Japanese buckwheat and wheat flour noodle, brownish in color. In some parts of Japan where rice was difficult to grow, soba was the staple.

Somen A Japanese fine wheat noodle.

SPAM Most commonly fried and served with rice or made into a musubi (a slice of teriyaki-flavored SPAM fried and wrapped sushi style with rice). Hawaii consumes 5 million pounds of SPAM every year, the most in the nation.

Sushi Japanese rice flavored with a sweet vinegar. Formed into fingers or rounds, seasoned with wasabi (Japanese horseradish) or other condiment, sometimes rolled in seaweed, and garnished with raw seafood or fish, or perhaps a vegetable.

Sweet Potato One of the first foods brought to the Islands by the first voyagers, sweet potatoes have a prominent place in the diets of different ethnic groups.

Tamarind The pod or fruit of a large tropical tree. When fresh, its pulp is white, crisp, and sweet-sour, but when dried it turns reddish brown and very sour. It is used both as a souring agent and as a red coloring used in curries, chutneys, pickles, sauces, and refreshing drinks.

Taro A tropical and subtropical plant used for its spinachlike leaves, asparaguslike stalks, and potatolike root. One of the most important crops in Hawaii, it can be used in soups and stews; fried into chips; or cooked, kneaded and fermented into poi. Poi is often given to babies as their first whole food, as it is easily digested and high in nutrients.

Tempura In Japanese cooking, seafood and vegetables dredged in a light batter and quickly deep-fried in oil. Served with a dipping sauce.

Teriyaki Japanese for poultry, fish, or meat marinated in a sweet soy sauce preparation and grilled over charcoal so that the marinade forms a glaze.

Ti Leaves for wrapping. Ti plants were planted close to Hawaiian underground ovens *(imus)*. The smooth, pearl-shaped leaves are used to wrap food and add flavor.

Tofu Bean curd widely used throughout Asia. High in protein, low in calories, and free of cholesterol, tofu is made from dried soybeans processed into a "milk" that is coagulated like cheese; the molded tofu curds are kept fresh in water. Of the many types, momen (cotton) is the most common fresh tofu in the United States as well as in Japan; kinu (silk) has a finer texture. Chinese tofu is firmer than the Japanese tofu.

Udon A thick Japanese wheat noodle.

Wasabi A plant often called "Japanese horseradish," whose root is used as a condiment for raw fish dishes; it comes fresh, powdered, and as a paste. It is very hot in flavor and green in color.

Water Chestnut The fruit of a long-stemmed water plant that grows inside irregularly shaped thorns beneath the floating leaves. This starchy fruit has a crisp texture and delicate taste and is widely used in Chinese dishes.

Winter Melon A melon with hard, smooth, or furrowed skin and white to pale green or orange flesh. Varieties include casaba, honeydew, crenshaw, Santa Claus; called winter melons because they keep and travel well. Often used for soup.

Menus and Recipes from the Cuisine of Hawaii

MENU ONE

Ahi Poke

Spam Musubi

Daikon Cakes with Salad Greens and Spicy Plum Dressing

Saimin with Teriyaki Meat Sticks

Char Siu

Deep-Fried Calamari Salad

Pineapple Fritters with Maui Mango Sauce

MENU TWO

Butternut Squash and Pumpkin Ginger Soup

Baby Artichoke Salad with Tomato-Chile Vinaigrette

Caramelized Salmon with Orange-Shoyu Glaze

Lemongrass Beurre Blanc

Balsamic-Soy Glaze

Fried Basil Leaves

Sautéed Mixed Vegetables

Steamed Japanese Rice

Asian Pear and Macadamia Wontons

MENU THREE

Coconut-Ginger-Carrot Soup

Kalua Pig Spring Rolls with Pineapple Dipping Sauce

Macadamia Nut–Crusted Mahimahi with Wasabi Cream Sauce

Vegetable Tempura

Chicken Long Rice

Mango Bread

OTHER RECIPES

Sweet Potato Puree

Chinese-Style Steamed Snapper

Miso Soup with Taro and Butterfish

Sautéed Pacific Snapper with Curry Kamuela Tomato Sauce

Taro Root Cakes

Ahi Poke   4 SERVINGS

AMOUNT	MEASURE	INGREDIENT
3 cups	16 ounces, 453 g	Sushi-grade tuna, cut in 1-inch (2.5 cm) cubes
¹/₄ tablespoon	4 g	Hawaiian salt or kosher salt
1 cup	6 ounces, 170 g	Tomato, peeled, seeded, ¹/₄ inch (.6 cm) dice
¹/₂ cup	2 ounces, 56 g	Maui sweet onion, ¹/₄ inch (.6 cm) dice
2 tablespoons	1 ounce, 28 ml	Soy sauce
1 teaspoon	7 ml	Roasted sesame oil
¹/₂ teaspoon	3 g	Granulated sugar
¹/₂ teaspoon	1 g	Red pepper flakes
2 tablespoons	8 g	Green onions, sliced, for garnish

PROCEDURE

1   Combine all ingredients except green onions and allow flavors to blend for 1 hour.

2   Serve chilled. Garnish with green onions.

Ahi Poke

SPAM musubi 4 SERVINGS

AMOUNT	MEASURE	INGREDIENT
2 sheets		Nori, cut in quarters lengthwise
2 cups	13 ounces, 360 g	Cooked rice
6 ounces	170 g	SPAM
3 tablespoons	1 1/2 ounces, 42 ml	Soy sauce
2 tablespoons	1 ounce, 28 ml	Mirin
2 tablespoons	1 ounce, 28 g	Granulated sugar

PROCEDURE

1 Open the SPAM on both sides. Remove the SPAM and cut into 8 slices.

2 Fry until slightly crispy. Remove and drain on paper towels.

3 Combine the soy sauce, mirin, and sugar. Bring the mixture to a simmer over medium-high heat, and reduce to low.

4 Add the SPAM slices, coating them in the mixture. When the mixture has thickened, remove the SPAM from pan and cool.

5 Lay a piece of nori lengthwise on a dry cutting board. Moisten the lower half of musubi maker (see Note) and place on lower third of nori.

6 Fill musubi maker with rice and press flat until the rice is 3/4 inch (1.9 cm) high.

7 Top with a slice of SPAM.

8 Remove the musubi maker and keep it in a bowl of warm water to keep it clean and moist.

9 Starting at the end toward you, fold nori over the SPAM and rice stack, and keep rolling until wrapped in the nori, like a ribbon. Slightly dampen the end of the nori to seal it. Repeat with the other 7 slices of SPAM, making sure to rinse off musubi maker after each use.

Note: You can use the empty SPAM can that has been opened on both sides for the musubi mold, using your hands (or a piece of SPAM) to press down on the rice.

SPAM Musubi

Daikon Cakes with Salad Greens 4 SERVINGS

AMOUNT	MEASURE	INGREDIENT
4 cups	1 1/2 pounds, 680 g	Daikon, peeled, shredded
1/4 cup	1 ounce, 28 g	Rice flour
1/2 cup	3 ounces, 85 g	Lup cheong (sweet Chinese sausage; if not available, sliced baked ham can be used)
1/2 cup	2 ounces, 56 g	Shiitake mushrooms, 1/2 inch (1.2 cm) dice
1		Shallot, minced
2		Garlic cloves, minced
1 tablespoon	1/2 ounce, 15 g	Ginger, minced
2 tablespoons	6 g	Cilantro, minced
2 tablespoons	1/2 ounce, 15 g	Green onions, chopped
to taste		Salt and pepper
2 tablespoons	1 ounce, 28 g	Butter
1 tablespoon	1/2 ounce, 14 ml	Sesame oil
8 cups	16 ounces, 453 g	Spinach (fresh), washed, dried
1 bunch	12 ounces, 340 g	Curly endive, washed, dried

For the Asian Dressing

AMOUNT	MEASURE	INGREDIENT
1/4 cup	2 ounces, 55 ml	Soy sauce
2 tablespoons	1 ounce, 28 ml	White wine vinegar
2 tablespoons	1 ounce, 28 ml	Vegetable oil
6 tablespoons	3 ounces, 84 ml	Sake
6 tablespoons	3 ounces, 85 g	Shallots, minced
1 tablespoon	1/2 ounce, 14 ml	Passion fruit concentrate
1/2 tablespoon	8 g	Ginger, grated
1/4 teaspoon	1 g	Sesame oil

PROCEDURE

1   Squeeze the moisture out of the daikon by wringing it in a towel.

2   Combine daikon, flour, sausage or ham, mushrooms, shallot, garlic, ginger, cilantro, and green onions. Correct seasoning.

3 Form into 4 or 8 patties by hand like potato pancakes. (You can also use individual serving-size ring mold to form them, which will allow for more height and smooth edges.) If the mixture is watery when you begin to form the cakes, squeeze more liquid out and, if necessary, add more rice flour.

4 Sauté patties in the butter and oil until golden brown.

5 Combine ingredients for dressing.

6 Toss the salad greens with Asian Dressing. Put on plates.

7 Place daikon cakes on salad greens and drizzle with Spicy Plum Dressing (page 494).

Daikon Cakes with Salad Greens and Spicy Plum Dressing

Spicy Plum Dressing 4 SERVINGS

AMOUNT	MEASURE	INGREDIENT
1/4 cup	2 ounces, 55 ml	Plum sauce
3 tablespoons	1 1/2 ounces, 42 ml	Lime juice
3 tablespoons	1 1/2 ounces, 42 ml	Rice wine vinegar
2 tablespoons	1 ounce, 28 g	Granulated sugar
1 tablespoon	1/2 ounce, 14 ml	Sesame oil

For the Spicy Fish Sauce

4 tablespoons	2 ounces, 55 ml	Red wine vinegar
2 tablespoons	1 ounce, 28 ml	Water
1/4 cup	2 ounces, 56 g	Granulated sugar
4 tablespoons	2 ounces, 55 ml	Thai fish sauce
1		Thai chile, minced

PROCEDURE

1   Mix plum sauce, lime juice, and vinegar until thoroughly blended, leaving any plum pieces intact.

2   Combine ingredients for fish sauce. Add to plum mixture.

3   Stir in the sugar and sesame oil. Stir well.

Saimin 4 SERVINGS

AMOUNT	MEASURE	INGREDIENT
4 cups	16 ounces, 453 g	Fresh saimin, somen, or other fine white flour noodles
2 teaspoons	4 g	Dashi powder
4 cups	8 ounces, 226 g	Spinach, washed, dried, cut into 2-inch (5 cm) pieces
1 cup	4 ounces, 113 g	Kamaboko (Japanese fish cake), thinly sliced
1¼ cups	8 ounces, 226 g	Char sui (Chinese glazed pork roast), thinly sliced
1 tablespoon	½ ounce, 14 ml	Soy sauce
½ cup	1 ounce, 28 g	Green onions, thinly sliced

PROCEDURE

1 Cook the fresh noodles in boiling water for 3 minutes or until just done.

2 Drain and divide among 4 warm soup bowls.

3 Make the dashi by mixing powder mixed with 4 cups (32 ounces, 1 l) water; heat over medium heat and bring almost to a boil. Do not boil.

4 Divide spinach among the bowls of noodles.

5 Pour a cup of dashi over the noodles and spinach in each bowl.

6 Divide remaining ingredients evenly among the bowls. Scatter green onions on top,

7 Serve hot with Teriyaki Meat Sticks (page 496).

Teriyaki Meat Sticks 4 SERVINGS

chef tip

Teri- anything is a plate lunch favorite, distinctly different from the Japanese origins. In Japan, combining soy sauce and mirin, the Japanese sweet cooking wine, makes teriyaki, and it is used to marinate fish and as a basting sauce for broiling. The term came from "glazed" *(teri)* and "seared with heat" *(yaki)*. In Hawaii, the brown sugar is substituted for mirin, and ginger and green onions were added. The addition of substantial amounts of sugar to soy sauce would have been natural where mirin was virtually unobtainable but where sugar was king. Ginger and garlic may have been Chinese additions. Hawaiian-style teriyaki sauce has become one of the culinary symbols of the Islands.

AMOUNT	MEASURE	INGREDIENT
1/4 cup	2 ounces, 55 ml	Soy sauce
1 1/2 tablespoons	3/4 ounce, 21 g	Brown sugar
1 1/2 teaspoons	7 ml	Sherry
1 teaspoon	5 g	Ginger, minced
1		Garlic clove, minced
1 cup	6 ounces, 170 g	Beef top round, sliced 2 inches (5 cm) long, 1/2 inch (1.2 cm) thick

PROCEDURE

1 Combine the soy sauce, brown sugar, sherry, ginger, and garlic. Stir over low heat until the sugar is dissolved. Cool.

2 Marinate the meat slices in soy mixture for 30 minutes.

3 Thread the meat onto skewers and grill until done.

Chicken breast meat can be substituted for the beef.

Char Siu 4 SERVINGS

To shorten the total cooking time, cut the meat into small chunks.

AMOUNT	MEASURE	INGREDIENT
2 pounds	907 g	Boneless pork butt
I tablespoon	$1/2$ ounce, 15 g	Hawaiian sea salt or kosher salt
$1/4$ cup	2 ounces, 55 ml	Soy sauce
2 tablespoons	I ounce, 28 ml	Dry Sherry
2 tablespoons	I ounce, 28 g	Granulated sugar
I tablespoon	$1/2$ ounce, 14 ml	Honey
I teaspoon	2 g	Chinese five-spice powder
$1/2$ cup	2 ounces, 56 g	Ginger, sliced, crushed with side of a cleaver
$1/2$ teaspoon		Red food coloring (optional)

PROCEDURE

1 Rub the pork with salt and refrigerate for 1 hour.

2 Combine the remaining ingredients. Heat in a saucepan for 1 minute to dissolve the sugar. Cool. Rub the pork with the marinade.

3 Marinate the pork in the refrigerator for 24 hours or at room temperature for 2 hours. Drain meat and reserve the marinade.

4 Preheat the oven to 350°F (175°C).

5 Place meat on a rack over $1/4$ inch (.6 cm) of water in a shallow roasting pan. Roast in the oven for 30 minutes.

6 Turn meat over, reduce heat, and continue roasting for 1 hour at 325°F (163°C), brushing occasionally with the reserved marinade. Remove from oven and let rest for 10 minutes.

7 Cut meat into thin, bite-size slices that can be eaten with chopsticks.

Deep-Fried Calamari Salad · 4 SERVINGS

AMOUNT	MEASURE	INGREDIENT
As needed		Vegetable oil, for deep-frying
2 cups	9 ounces, 255 g	All-purpose flour
2 tablespoons	1 ounce, 30 g	Paprika
2 2/3 cups	16 ounces, 453 g	Calamari, cleaned, cut into rings
to taste		Salt and black pepper

For the Cilantro Vinaigrette

AMOUNT	MEASURE	INGREDIENT
2 tablespoons	6 g	Cilantro leaves
1/2 cup	4 ounces, 115 ml	Orange juice
1/2 tablespoon	7 ml	Rice wine vinegar
1/2 tablespoon	7 ml	Lime juice
1/4 cup	1 1/2 ounces, 42 g	Honey
1		Garlic clove
1 teaspoon	5 g	Ginger, minced
1/4 cup	2 ounces, 58 ml	Vegetable oil
to taste		Salt and pepper

For the Salad

AMOUNT	MEASURE	INGREDIENT
4 cups	8 ounces, 225 g	Spring salad greens
1/2 cup	2 1/2 ounces, 70 g	Red bell pepper, julienned
1/2 cup	2 1/2 ounces, 70 g	Yellow bell pepper, julienned
1/2 cup	2 ounces, 56 g	Sweet Maui onion, julienned
1 1/2 cups	9 ounces, 255 g	Cucumbers, peeled, seeded, sliced
3/4 cup	4 ounces, 113 g	Tomato, peeled, seeded, cut into wedges

PROCEDURE

1. Heat the oil to 350°F (175°C).
2. Combine the flour and paprika.
3. Season calamari with salt and pepper.
4. Toss the calamari in flour and paprika mixture. Dust off the excess flour.
5. Deep-fry until golden brown.

6   Combine ingredients for dressing.

7   Toss salad greens with vinaigrette, then arrange greens, peppers, onion, cucumber, and tomato on cold plates.

8   Place calamari on top. Serve additional dressing on the side.

Deep-Fried Calamari Salad

Pineapple Fritters with Maui Mango Sauce   4 SERVINGS

AMOUNT	MEASURE	INGREDIENT
For the Maui Mango Sauce		
I cup	6 ounces, 170 g	Mango, sliced
$^1/_2$ cup	$3^1/_2$ ounces, 99 g	Granulated sugar
I tablespoon	$^1/_2$ ounce, 14 ml	Lemon juice
For the Pineapple Fritters		
$^1/_2$ cup	$1^1/_2$ ounces, 42 g	Panko (Japanese bread crumbs)
$^1/_4$ cup	I ounce, 28 g	Graham cracker crumbs
$^1/_2$ teaspoon		Cinnamon
8		Pineapple slices (fresh), $^1/_4$ inch (.6 cm), cored
2 tablespoons		All-purpose flour
I		Egg, beaten with I tablespoon water
$^3/_4$ cup	$5^1/_4$ ounces, 148 g	Granulated sugar
as needed		Vegetable oil, for frying

PROCEDURE

1   Puree mango for the sauce. Pass through a sieve.

2   Add the sugar and lemon juice. Set aside.

3   Mix panko, graham crumbs, and cinnamon.

4   Dip the pineapple slices first into the flour, then into the egg, and then into panko.

5   Heat oil to 350°F (175°C).

6   Deep-fry the pineapple slices until golden brown.

7   Sprinkle with sugar and serve with mango sauce.

Pineapple Fritters with Maui Mango Sauce

Butternut Squash and Pumpkin Ginger Soup 4 SERVINGS

AMOUNT	MEASURE	INGREDIENT
3 cups	16 ounces, 453 g	Butternut squash
3 cups	16 ounces, 453 g	Pumpkin
1 tablespoon	1/2 ounce, 14 ml	Vegetable oil
2 tablespoons	1 ounce, 28 g	Ginger, minced
1 1/2 cups	6 ounces, 210 g	Maui Sweet onions, 1/4 inch (.6 cm) dice
1 tablespoon	1/2 ounce, 15 g	Garlic, minced
1 cup	5 ounces, 141 g	Carrots, 1/4 inch (.6 cm) dice
1 cup	4 ounces, 113 g	Celery, 1/4 inch (.6 cm) dice
1/2 teaspoon	1 g	Fennel seeds
1 teaspoon	2 g	Cumin seeds
1/2 teaspoon	1 g	Hot pepper flakes
1		Bay leaf
1		Star anise
2 tablespoons	6 g	Basil, chopped
1 teaspoon	5 g	Salt
1/2 cup	4 ounces, 115 ml	Dry white wine
2 cups	16 ounces, 470 ml	Chicken stock
2 slices		Ginger
1		Kaffir lime leaf or regular lime leaf
1 cup	8 ounces, 235 ml	Heavy cream
1 cup	2 ounces, 56 g	Enoki mushrooms
2 tablespoons	6 g	Parsley, chopped

PROCEDURE

1   If using small squash or pumpkins, cut in half, remove seeds, and roast at 375°F (190°C) until the meat is soft, about 1 hour. Or peel, seed, and cut the squash and pumpkin into large cubes, then bake, covered, in oven until soft.

2   Heat the oil and sauté the ginger, onions, garlic, carrots, and celery until soft, 3 to 5 minutes.

3   Add the fennel seeds, cumin seeds, hot pepper flakes, bay leaf, star anise, basil, and salt. Cook 1 minute.

4   Add the wine and cook 1 minute.

5   Add the squash and pumpkin. Add the stock and simmer 30 minutes. After 15 minutes, add lime leaf and ginger slices.

6   Remove lime leaf and ginger slices. Puree the soup.

7   Add the cream. Bring almost to a boil and correct seasoning.

8   Heat the mushrooms and use as garnish. Serve sprinkled with parsley.

Baby Artichoke Salad with Tomato-Chili Water Vinaigrette 4 SERVINGS

AMOUNT	MEASURE	INGREDIENT
2 cups	4 ounces, 113 g	Frisée lettuce, cleaned
2 cups	3 ounces, 84 g	Watercress, cleaned
2 tablespoons	1 ounce, 28 ml	Olive oil
to taste		Salt and black pepper
as needed		Vegetable oil, for frying
$1/2$ cup	2 ounces, 56 g	Maui Sweet onion, sliced paper-thin
$1/2$ cup	2 ounces, 56 g	All-purpose flour, for coating onions
4		Baby artichokes, blanched, quartered
8		Asparagus tips, blanched
$1/2$ cup	3 ounces, 85 g	Tomato, peeled, seeded, $1/4$ inch (.6 cm) dice
1 tablespoon	$1/2$ ounce, 15 g	Shallot, minced
1 teaspoon	1 g	Basil, chopped
1 teaspoon	1 g	Parsley, chopped
1 teaspoon	1 g	Chives, minced
1 tablespoon	$1/2$ ounce, 14 ml	Olive oil
$1/2$ tablespoon	7 ml	Lemon juice
1		Artichoke bottom, shaved as thin as possible

PROCEDURE

1 Toss the frisée and watercress with olive oil. Season with salt and pepper. Divide among 4 cold plates.

2 Heat oil to 375°F (190°C).

3 Toss the onion in flour to coat. Shake off excess flour. Deep-fry 1 minute, until brown and crispy. Drain well and place on top of greens.

4 Toss the baby artichoke quarters, asparagus tips, tomato, shallot, and herbs in oil and lemon juice. Season to taste and place on top of greens and onions.

5   Deep-fry the sliced artichoke bottom until crisp and sprinkle over the salad.

6   Spoon Tomato-Chile Vinaigrette (page 506) around the salads on the plate.

Baby Artichoke Salad with Tomato-Chile Vinaigrette

Tomato-Chile Vinaigrette 4 SERVINGS

AMOUNT	MEASURE	INGREDIENT
For the Chile Water		
1 teaspoon	5 g	Salt
1 teaspoon	5 ml	Rice wine vinegar
1		Garlic clove, crushed
6		Thai chiles (red, dried)
2 cups	16 ounces, 470 ml	Water
For the Vinaigrette		
1/2 cup	4 ounces, 112 g	Tomato puree
2 tablespoons	1 ounce, 28 ml	Olive oil

PROCEDURE

1   Sterilize a 16-ounce (453 g) bottle by boiling in water for a few minutes and allow it to cool.

2   Place the salt, vinegar, garlic, and chiles into the bottle. Bring the water to a boil and pour into bottle. Stir with a chopstick and leave for 3 days under refrigeration to mature.

3   In a blender, emulsify the tomato puree, 4 tablespoons (2 ounces, 56 ml) chile water, and oil to make Tomato-Chile Vinaigrette.

Caramelized Salmon with Orange-Shoyu Glaze 4 SERVINGS

AMOUNT	MEASURE	INGREDIENT
1/2 cup	4 ounces, 113 g	Ginger, peeled, chopped
1 tablespoon		Sichuan peppercorns
1/4 cup	2 ounces, 56 ml	Orange juice
1/2 cup	1 ounce, 28 g	Cilantro
4	16 ounces, 453 g, total	Salmon fillets
1/2 cup	3 1/2 ounces, 99 g	Granulated sugar
2 tablespoons	1/2 ounce, 15 g	Black pepper, coarse ground
1 tablespoon	1/2 ounce, 14 ml	Peanut oil
2 tablespoons	1 ounce, 28 ml	Soy sauce
2 tablespoons	1 ounce, 28 ml	Grand Marnier

PROCEDURE

1. Combine the ginger, peppercorns, orange juice, and cilantro in a food processor and finely chop.

2. Roll the salmon in the mixture; cover and marinate at room temperature for up to 2 hours.

3. Mix the sugar and black pepper.

4. Heat the peanut oil in a sauté pan over medium heat.

5. Press the salmon presentation side into the sugar-pepper mixture. Sauté, seasoned side down first, to caramelize the sugar, about 2 to 3 minutes. Do not let the sugar begin to burn.

6. Add the soy sauce and Grand Marnier, swirling and stirring well to dissolve the caramelized sugar. Turn the salmon skin side down, lower heat, and let the salmon finish cooking.

7. Place the salmon on a plate, add Lemongrass Beurre Blanc (page 509) around the salmon. Drizzle a few drops of Balsamic-Soy Glaze (page 509) over the sauce on the plate. Serve with Sautéed Mixed Vegetables (page 510). Garnish with Fried Basil Leaves (page 510).

Caramelized Salmon with Orange-Shoyu Glaze and Steamed Japanese Rice

Lemongrass Beurre Blanc 4 SERVINGS

AMOUNT	MEASURE	INGREDIENT
$^1/_2$ cup	4 ounces, 115 ml	White wine
1		Shallot, minced
1 stalk		Lemongrass, cut into 2-inch (5 cm) pieces, then mashed
$^1/_2$ cup	4 ounces, 113 g	Butter, cut into 8 pieces
to taste		Salt and white pepper

PROCEDURE

1. In a nonreactive saucepan, combine the wine, shallot, and lemongrass. Let the mixture soak for 30 minutes to soften the lemongrass.

2. Boil until the liquid is almost evaporated. Strain the liquid—you should have about 2 tablespoons (1 ounce, 28 g).

3. Return the liquid to a clean saucepan and bring to a boil. Remove the pan from heat. Start whisking the butter into the liquid, 2 pieces at a time. As one piece of butter is almost melted, add the next 2. If the pan gets too cool, return it to the heat and whisk in all the butter. Season to taste.

Balsamic-Soy Glaze 4 SERVINGS

AMOUNT	MEASURE	INGREDIENT
1 cup	8 ounces, 235 ml	Balsamic vinegar
$^1/_2$ cup	4 ounces, 115 ml	Soy sauce

PROCEDURE

Combine the vinegar and soy sauce in a nonreactive pan and reduce to a syrup, about 15 minutes.

Fried Basil Leaves 4 SERVINGS

AMOUNT	MEASURE	INGREDIENT
12–18		Basil leaves
as needed		Vegetable oil, for deep-frying

PROCEDURE

1   Rinse and thoroughly dry the basil leaves.

2   Heat the oil to 350°F (175°C).

3   Fry the basil leaves for a few seconds, until they turn crisp and translucent. Remove them from oil and drain well. (This can be done up to 1 hour in advance.)

Sautéed Mixed Vegetables 4 SERVINGS

AMOUNT	MEASURE	INGREDIENT
2 tablespoons	1 ounce, 28 ml	Olive oil
1 cup	4 ounces, 113 g	Green beans, blanched
1 cup	4 ounces, 113 g	Zucchini, cut in 2-inch (5 cm) sticks
1 cup	4 ounces, 113 g	Red bell pepper, julienned
1 cup	4 ounces, 113 g	Yellow bell pepper, julienned
to taste		Salt and white pepper

PROCEDURE

1   Heat the oil in a sauté pan over medium heat. Add the vegetables and sauté until heated through, but not brown.

2   Season with salt and pepper to taste.

Steamed Japanese Rice 4 SERVINGS

chef tip

Japanese nonglutinous short-grain rice (Calrose, Tomaki) brand is the kind most often served in the Islands. When cooked, the rice should end up moist but not mushy, the grains distinct but clinging, making it easier to be lifted on chopsticks. Because it is traditionally eaten with flavorful accompaniments, usually sour, sweet, salty, or spicy, it is cooked without salt.

AMOUNT	MEASURE	INGREDIENT
2 cups	13 ounces, 368 g	Japanese short-grain rice
2 cups	16 ounces, 470 ml	Water

PROCEDURE

1 Place the rice in a bowl and cover with cold water. Rub the rice with your hand and swirl it vigorously, drain the water. Repeat this step 3 or 4 times until the water is clear.

2 Drain the rice into a sieve and let it dry for 30 minutes.

3 Combine the rice and water, and bring to a simmer over high heat. Cover the pan, reduce the heat to moderate, and cook for 15 minutes.

4 Without opening the lid, reduce the heat to its lowest point and simmer for another 5 minutes.

5 Without opening the lid, let the rice rest off the heat for another 5 minutes or until ready to serve, before removing the lid.

6 Fluff the rice with a fork before serving.

Asian Pear and Macadamia Wontons 4 SERVINGS

AMOUNT	MEASURE	INGREDIENT
1		Asian pear, peeled, seeded, $^1/_4$ inch (.6 cm) dice
2 tablespoons	$^1/_2$ ounce, 14 g	Macadamia nuts, finely chopped
	4 ounces, 115 ml	Coconut milk
1 tablespoon	14 ml	Lemon juice
24		Wonton wrappers, cut into circles
as needed		Confectioners' sugar
as needed		Honey

PROCEDURE

1 Combine the pear, macadamia nuts, coconut milk, and lemon juice. Simmer this mixture until it is almost dry, about 20 minutes. Set aside to cool.

2 Place a spoonful of the filling on 1 wonton circle and moisten the exposed wonton wrapper with water. Top with another wonton circle, crimping the edge all the way around to seal it. Repeat with the remaining wonton circles to make 12 wontons. Place them on sheet pan and freeze them for a few minutes to firm up.

3 Heat the oil to 375°F (190°C).

4 Deep-fry the wontons until browned and cooked through.

5 Drain well on paper towels. Dust with sugar and serve with honey.

Asian Pear and Macadamia Wontons

Coconut-Ginger Carrot Soup 4 SERVINGS

AMOUNT	MEASURE	INGREDIENT
2 tablespoons	1 ounce, 28 ml	Vegetable oil
1/2 cup	2 ounces, 56 g	Onion, 1/4 inch (.6 cm) dice
3 cups	16 ounces, 453 g	Carrots, 1/4 inch (.6 cm) dice
2 tablespoons	1 ounce, 28 g	Ginger, minced
2 cups	10 ounces, 283 g	Sweet potatoes, peeled, 1/2 inch (1.2 cm) dice
3 cups	24 ounces, 705 ml	Vegetable or chicken stock
to taste		Salt and white pepper
1 tablespoon	1/2 ounce, 14 ml	Lemon juice
1 tablespoon	1/2 ounce, 15 ml	Honey
1/2 can	2.8 ounces, 78 ml	Coconut milk, warm
2 tablespoons	6 g	Cilantro, chopped

PROCEDURE

1   Heat the oil. Add the onion and cook over medium heat for about 5 minutes.

2   Add the carrots and ginger, and cook another 5 minutes. Add the sweet potatoes, stock, salt, and pepper. Bring to a boil, then reduce to a simmer. Cook until the carrots and potatoes are tender, about 25 minutes.

3   Puree until smooth. Reheat on low.

4   Add the lemon juice, honey, and coconut milk. Mix thoroughly. Add more vegetable stock or chicken stock if the soup is too thick.

5   Garnish with the cilantro.

Kalua Pig 8 SERVINGS

AMOUNT	MEASURE	INGREDIENT
2¹/₂ pounds	1.3 kg	Boneless pork butt
2 tablespoons	1 ounce, 28 g	Hawaiian or kosher salt
2 tablespoons	1 ounce, 28 ml	Liquid Smoke
2		Garlic cloves, minced
8		Ti leaves, ribs removed (or aluminum foil)

PROCEDURE

1 Preheat the oven to 400°F (205°C).

2 Score the pork on all sides with ¹/₄-inch (.6 cm)-deep slits about 1 inch (2.5 cm) apart.

3 Combine the salt, Liquid Smoke, and garlic.

4 Rub mixture all around the pork butt. Wrap the pork butt in ti leaves and tie with string to hold in place. Place in appropriate pan and cover tightly with lid or foil.

5 Bake for 1 hour. Lower temperature to 350°F (175°C) and cook for 2 hours until tender.

6 Remove from pan. Let cool slightly and shred meat.

Kalua Pig Spring Rolls with Pineapple Dipping Sauce

Kalua Pig Spring Rolls 4 SERVINGS

AMOUNT	MEASURE	INGREDIENT
I tablespoon	14 ml	Vegetable oil
I cup	6 ounces, 170 g	Kalua Pig (see recipe)
1/4 cup	I ounce, 28 g	Onion, 1/4 inch (.6 cm) dice
I teaspoon	5 g	Garlic, minced
3/4 cup	3 ounces, 85 g	Water chestnuts, 1/2 inch (1.2 cm) dice
2 cups	5 ounces, 141 g	Napa cabbage, shredded
1/2 cup	I 1/2 ounces, 42 g	Red cabbage, shredded
1/4 cup	1/2 ounce, 14 g	Green onion, chopped
I tablespoon	1/2 ounce, 14 g	Carrot, finely grated
I tablespoon	1/2 ounce, 15 g	Oyster sauce
to taste		Salt and white pepper
10		Spring roll wrappers
I		Egg, beaten with I tablespoon water (egg wash)
as needed		Vegetable oil, for frying

PROCEDURE

1 Heat the oil and sauté the pork, onion, and garlic for 2 minutes.

2 Add the water chestnuts, cabbages, green onion, carrot, and oyster sauce, and cook 3 minutes, until cabbage is tender. Remove from the heat. Adjust seasoning. Drain excess liquid. Cool.

3 Separate the spring roll wrappers and keep under a slightly damp towel.

4 Place 2 tablespoons (28 ml) of filling on a wrapper. Fold the nearest edge of wrapper over filling; fold left and right corners toward the center. Roll tightly and seal with the egg wash.

5 Heat the oil to 375°F (190°C).

6 Deep-fry the spring rolls until golden brown. Place on paper towels to drain.

7 Serve with Pineapple Dipping Sauce (page 518).

Pineapple Dipping Sauce   4 SERVINGS

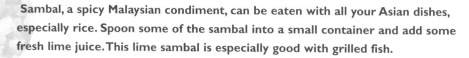

chef tip   Sambal, a spicy Malaysian condiment, can be eaten with all your Asian dishes, especially rice. Spoon some of the sambal into a small container and add some fresh lime juice. This lime sambal is especially good with grilled fish.

AMOUNT	MEASURE	INGREDIENT
For the Sambal		
10		Hot chiles (Long Hots or 15 to 20 serranos)
2 tablespoons	1 ounce, 28 g	Shrimp paste (toasted)
³/₄ teaspoon	8 g	Salt
For the Sauce		
¹/₂ cup	3 ounces, 85 g	Pineapple, peeled, ¹/₄ inch (.6 cm) dice
¹/₄ cup	2 ounces, 56 g	Granulated sugar
4 tablespoons	2 ounces, 55 ml	Cider vinegar
4 tablespoons	2 ounces, 55 ml	Water
1 tablespoon	14 ml	Fish sauce

PROCEDURE

1   Wash chiles and discard stems. Allow to air-dry or use papers towels to dry them off.

2   Roughly cut up the chiles and place in a blender with shrimp paste and salt. Process until ingredients are in very small pieces.

3   Spoon into a clean container and keep refrigerated.

4   Combine remaining ingredients, add 1 tablespoon (¹/₂ ounce, 15 ml) sambal, and chill for 1 hour before serving.

Macadamia Nut–Crusted Mahimahi 4 SERVINGS

AMOUNT	MEASURE	INGREDIENT

For the Macadamia Nut Crust

AMOUNT	MEASURE	INGREDIENT
1 cup	4 ounces, 113 g	Macadamia nuts
1¼ cups	4 ounces, 113 g	Panko (Japanese bread crumbs)
to taste		Salt and white pepper
4	4–6 ounces, 113–170 g, each	Mahimahi fillets, skinned
to taste		Salt and white pepper
as needed		All-purpose flour
1		Egg, lightly beaten with a little water
as needed		Vegetable oil, for frying

PROCEDURE

1 In a food processor, combine the macadamia nuts, panko, salt, and pepper. Blend until the mixture is finely ground.

2 Season and dredge the fish in flour, egg wash, and the nut mixture, coating each fillet on both sides.

3 Heat oil and pan-fry the fish over medium-high heat until golden brown on both sides. Remove and drain on paper towels. Serve with Wasabi Cream Sauce (page 520).

Wasabi Cream Sauce   4 SERVINGS

AMOUNT	MEASURE	INGREDIENT
I tablespoon	$^1/_2$ ounce, 15 g	Shallot, finely dice
$^1/_2$ cup	4 ounces, 115 ml	Dry white wine
$^1/_2$ cup	4 ounces, 115 ml	Fish stock
$^3/_4$ cup	6 ounces, 174 ml	Heavy cream
I tablespoon	$^1/_2$ ounce, 7 g	Wasabi powder
2 tablespoons	I ounce, 28 ml	Water
I tablespoon	$^1/_4$ ounce, 7 g	Cornstarch
to taste		Salt and white pepper

PROCEDURE

1   Combine the shallot and wine over medium heat; reduce until almost dry.

2   Add the stock and reduce by one-third.

3   Add the cream and wasabi powder. Reduce by one-third.

4   Combine the water and cornstarch and use to thicken the sauce, if necessary. Stir in.

Vegetable Tempura 4 SERVINGS

AMOUNT	MEASURE	INGREDIENT

For the Tempura Batter

AMOUNT	MEASURE	INGREDIENT
¹/₂ cup	2 ounces, 56 g	All-purpose flour
¹/₂ cup	2 ounces, 56 g	Cornstarch
1		Egg
¹/₂ teaspoon	3 g	Salt
¹/₂ cup	4 ounces, 115 ml	Cold water
as needed		Vegetable oil, for deep-frying
2¹/₂ cups	12 ounces, 340 g	Sweet potatoes, peeled, julienned (keep in water to prevent discoloration; pat dry just before using)
1		Japanese eggplant, cut lengthwise into ¹/₄-inch (.6 cm) slices
¹/₂ cup	1 ounce, 28 g	Mushrooms, sliced lengthwise into ¹/₄-inch (.6 cm) thickness
1 cup	3 ounces, 84 g	Zucchini, sliced lengthwise into ¹/₄-inch (.6 cm) slices

PROCEDURE

1 Stir batter ingredients together. Do not overstir; batter should be lumpy. Let sit 15 minutes.

2 Heat the oil to 375°F (190°C).

3 Dip vegetable strips into batter (it does not matter if a few stick together).

4 Fry until light golden brown, then drain on paper towels.

5 Serve with soy sauce or Tempura Dipping Sauce (page 523).

Vegetable Tempura with Tempura Dipping Sauce

Tempura Dipping Sauce 1¹/₂ CUPS

AMOUNT	MEASURE	INGREDIENT
¹/₄ cup	2 ounces, 55 ml	Mirin
¹/₄ cup	2 ounces, 55 ml	Soy sauce
1 cup	8 ounces, 235 ml	Dashi
1 tablespoon	¹/₂ ounce, 15 g	Granulated sugar

PROCEDURE

Mix all ingredients.

Chicken Long Rice

Chicken Long Rice · 4 SERVINGS

AMOUNT	MEASURE	INGREDIENT
1 1/2 pounds	24 ounces, 680 g	Chicken thighs, bone-in
1 1/2 quarts	1.5 l	Chicken stock
5 teaspoons	3/4 ounce, 21 g	Ginger, thinly sliced
1 tablespoon	1/2 ounce, 15 g	Salt
	6 ounces, 170 g	Bean thread noodles (sai fun or mung bean noodles)
1 tablespoon	14 ml	Vegetable oil
1 1/2 cups	6 ounces, 170 g	Maui Sweet onion, thinly sliced
1		Garlic clove, minced
1 1/2 tablespoons	21 ml	Soy sauce
3 tablespoons		Green onions, chopped

PROCEDURE

1   Cover the thighs with stock. Add 1 1/2 tablespoons (21 ml) ginger and the salt. Cover and simmer until just cooked (do not boil).

2   Allow the chicken thighs to cool in the broth. Remove the chicken thighs, bone the meat, and discard the skin. Cut the chicken into 1-inch (2.5 cm) cubes.

3   Strain the chicken stock and reserve.

4   Soak the bean thread noodles in warm water for 10 minutes, or in cold water for 1 hour. Drain.

5   Heat the oil. Sauté the onion, garlic, and remaining ginger until lightly browned.

6   Add the noodles and enough reserved chicken stock to cover. Add soy sauce and simmer for 5 minutes. Turn off heat and let stand for 10 minutes.

7   Cut the bean thread noodles into approximately 3-inch (7.6 cm) lengths, if desired. Add the chicken meat and reheat. Top with green onions before serving.

Mango Bread 4 SERVINGS

AMOUNT	MEASURE	INGREDIENT
1 cup	4 ounces, 113 g	All-purpose flour
1 teaspoon	4 g	Baking soda
1/2 teaspoon	1 g	Cinnamon
1/4 teaspoon	2 g	Salt
3/4 cup	5 1/4 ounces, 148 g	Granulated sugar
1 cup	6 ounces, 170 g	Mango, ripe, 1/2 inch (1.2 cm) dice
2		Eggs, beaten
6 tablespoons	3 ounces, 84 ml	Vegetable oil
1/2 teaspoon	2.5 ml	Vanilla extract
1/2 cup	2 ounces, 56 g	Macadamia nuts, chopped

PROCEDURE

1. Preheat the oven to 350°F (175°C). Grease and flour a loaf pan.

2. Sift the flour, baking soda, cinnamon, and salt together. Set aside.

3. Combine the sugar, mango, eggs, oil, and vanilla in a separate bowl.

4. Add the dry ingredients to the wet ingredients, and blend together for about 1 minute. Do not overmix.

5. Add the macadamia nuts and distribute evenly in the batter.

6. Pour the mixture into pan. Bake for about 40 to 45 minutes, or until a toothpick comes out clean.

7. Let the bread cool before serving.

Sweet Potato Purée 4 SERVINGS

AMOUNT	MEASURE	INGREDIENT
4 cups	16 ounces, 453 g	Sweet potatoes (orange-flesh)
2 tablespoons	1 ounce, 28 g	Butter, unsalted
to taste		Salt and black pepper
1/4 cup	2 ounces, 55 ml	Heavy cream, warm

PROCEDURE

1   Peel the sweet potatoes and cut into 1-inch (2.5 cm) pieces.

2   Cover with water, bring to a boil, and cook until they are soft.

3   Drain well. Run through a food mill and return to a warm pan.

4   Combine butter, salt, pepper, and enough heavy cream to make a smooth purée.

Chinese-Style Steamed Snapper   4 SERVINGS

AMOUNT	MEASURE	INGREDIENT
1	2–3 pounds, 907 g–1.36 kg	Red snapper, whole
to taste		Salt and white pepper
1³/₄ cups	4 ounces, 113 g	Shiitake mushrooms, ¹/₂-inch (1.2 cm) slices
2 tablespoons	1 ounce, 28 g	Ginger root, thinly sliced
¹/₂ cup	2 ounces, 56 g	Green onions, sliced
¹/₂ cup	1 ounce, 28 g	Cilantro, coarsely chopped
¹/₄ cup	2 ounces, 55 ml	Soy sauce
¹/₄ cup	2 ounces, 55 ml	Vegetable oil
1 tablespoon	¹/₂ ounce, 14 ml	Sesame oil

PROCEDURE

1   Clean and scale the fish. Rinse and pat dry; rub with salt and white pepper.

2   Scatter shiitake mushrooms over the fish.

3   Steam fish for 15 minutes or until done. Remove to platter.

4   Sprinkle with ginger, green onions, and cilantro. Pour soy sauce over the fish.

5   Heat the vegetable and sesame oils until smoking. Pour hot oil over the steamed fish and serve immediately.

Miso Soup with Taro and Butterfish   4 SERVINGS

chef tip

Butterfish is also known as black cod or sablefish.

AMOUNT	MEASURE	INGREDIENT
3 cups	24 ounces, 705 ml	Water
³/₄ cup	3 ounces, 85 g	Maui Sweet onion, ¹/₄ inch (.6 cm) dice
¹/₂ cup	3 ounces, 85 g	Tomato, peeled, seeded, ¹/₄ inch (.6 cm) dice
¹/₂ tablespoon	¹/₄ ounce, 7 g	Ginger, slivered
I cup	4 ounces, 113 g	Taro root, peeled, ¹/₄ inch (.6 cm) dice
¹/₄ ounce	7 g	Dried shrimp
I tablespoon	¹/₂ ounce, 14 g	Dried dashi konbu (kelp), soaked and cut into ¹/₄-inch (.6 cm) strips
I³/₄ cups	4 ounces, 113 g	Shiitake mushrooms, ¹/₂-inch (1.2 cm) slices
¹/₄ teaspoon	I g	Dashi powder, prepared, or ¹/₄ pkg (0.17 oz, 5 g) hondashi (Japanese fish-flavored soup granules)
I tablespoon	¹/₂ ounce, 14 g	White miso (Japanese fermented soybean paste)
I cup	5 ounces, 141 g	Tofu, firm, drained, in 1-inch (2.5 cm) cubes
I cup	4 ounces, 113 g	Butterfish, skinned, in 1-inch (2.5 cm) cubes
I teaspoon	5 g	Granulated sugar
to taste		Salt and white pepper

PROCEDURE

1 Bring the water, onion, tomato, and ginger to a boil. Reduce heat; simmer for 20 minutes.

2 Put the taro root in a saucepan, cover with water, and cook until tender. Drain and then add to the soup mixture.

3 Add the dried shrimp, konbu, mushrooms, and dashi powder. Simmer for 10 minutes.

4 Add the miso, tofu, butterfish, sugar, salt, and pepper. Cook for 1 minute.

5 Let the soup stand for 5 minutes before serving.

Sautéed Pacific Snapper with Curry Kamuela Tomato Sauce 4 SERVINGS

AMOUNT	MEASURE	INGREDIENT
2 tablespoon	1 ounce, 28	Olive oil
2		Garlic cloves, $1/4$ inch (.6 cm) dice
1 tablespoon	$1/2$ ounce, 15 g	Ginger, minced
1 stalk		Lemongrass, chopped
1 tablespoon	6 g	Fennel seeds
1 tablespoon	$1/2$ ounce, 15 g	Red curry paste
4 tablespoons	2 ounces, 55 ml	Dry white wine
3 cups	18 ounces, 510 g	Tomatoes, peeled, seeded, $1/4$ inch (.6 cm) dice
$1/2$ cup	4 ounces, 115 ml	Heavy cream
to taste		Salt and black pepper
4	4–6 ounces, 113–170 g each	Snapper fillets

PROCEDURE

1 Heat 1 tablespoon ($1/2$ ounce, 14 ml) oil over medium heat.

2 Add the garlic, ginger, lemongrass, fennel seeds, and curry paste. Cook and stir 2 minutes.

3 Add the wine and reduce by half.

4 Add the tomatoes; cook 10 minutes.

5 Add the cream and bring to a boil.

6 Puree the sauce and strain through a fine-mesh sieve. Correct consistency (if too thin, reduce by cooking further). Season with salt and pepper. Keep warm.

7 Heat remaining oil and sauté fish.

8 Place each fillet on a warm plate and serve with the sauce.

Taro Root Cakes 4 SERVINGS

AMOUNT	MEASURE	INGREDIENT
1 1/2 cups	8 ounces, 224 g	Taro root, peeled, 1/4 inch (.6 cm) dice
1 1/2 cups	8 ounces, 224 g	Russet potatoes, peeled, 1/4 inch (.6 cm) dice
2 tablespoons	1 ounce, 28 g	Butter
1 cup	4 ounces, 112 g	Maui Sweet onions, 1/4 inch (.6 cm) dice
2 tablespoons	6 g	Parsley, chopped
to taste		Salt
as needed		Flour

PROCEDURE

1   Boil the taro root and potatoes in salted water until tender. Drain, dry, and run through a ricer.

2   Heat a sauté pan over medium heat. Add the butter and sweat the onions until translucent.

3   Stir in the parsley. Add the taro root and potato mixture, and combine well.

4   Season with salt and shape into 2-ounce (56 g) patties. Roll in flour and pan-fry until golden brown. Serve immediately.

Brown Stock — 1 GALLON (3.8 L)

Brown stock is a flavorful liquid made from caramelized beef, veal, chicken, or game bones and vegetables, simmered in water with seasonings for 6 to 8 hours (3 to 4 hours for chicken). This stock should be a rich, dark color, highly aromatic, and gelatinous when finished. The standard ratio of ingredients for brown stock is 8 pounds (3.6 kg) of beef, veal, poultry, or game bones, 6 quarts (5.7 l) of cold water, 1 pound (60 g) of mirepoix, and 1 sachet d'épices or bouquet garni per gallon of finished stock.

AMOUNT	MEASURE	INGREDIENT
8 pounds	128 ounces, 3.6 kg	Beef, veal, chicken, or game bones
1/4 cup	2 ounces, 55 ml	Vegetable oil
6 quarts	192 ounces, 5.7 l	Water, cold

for the mirepoix

AMOUNT	MEASURE	INGREDIENT
2 cups	8 ounces, 240 g	Onions, in large dice
1 cup	4 ounces, 120 g	Carrots, in large dice
1 cup	4 ounces, 120 g	Celery, in large dice
1/2 cup	4 ounces, 120 g	Tomato paste

for the sachet d'épices

AMOUNT	MEASURE	INGREDIENT
1/2 teaspoon	1 g	Thyme leaves
1/2 teaspoon	1 g	Black peppercorns, cracked
3–4		Parsley stems
1		Garlic clove, crushed

PROCEDURE

1   Preheat the oven to 400°F (204.4°C).

2   Coat the bones with the oil and roast them, stirring frequently, until well browned.

3   Place the bones in a 10-quart (9.5 l) stockpot and cover with the cold water (keep roasting pan at hand). Bring to a simmer. Skim the surface, removing and discarding any impurities.

4   While the stock comes to a simmer, heat the roasting pan used to brown the bones to clarify the fat. Drain the fat and reserve.

5   Deglaze the roasting pan with 2 cups (8 ounces, 240 ml) of the liquid from the stockpot. After the roasting pan is deglazed, add the remaining liquid to the simmering stock.

6   For the mirepoix, lightly coat the onions, carrots, and celery with some of the reserved fat, place them in the roasting pan, and brown thoroughly, stirring regularly.

7   Combine the tomato paste with the vegetables and return to the oven. Continue to roast the vegetables, stirring regularly, until the tomato paste starts to brown.

8   Add the roasted, browned vegetables to the simmering stock.

9   Deglaze the roasting pan again with ¹/₂ cup (4 ounces, 120 ml) of the liquid from the stockpot and add to the simmering stock.

10 To create the sachet d'épices, place the thyme, peppercorns, parsley, and garlic in a small square of cheesecloth and tie with twine. Add the sachet to the simmering stock.

11 Continue to simmer gently for 6 to 8 hours (3 to 4 hours for chicken). Skim the surface regularly, discarding the impurities. Add water as needed to keep the bones from becoming exposed as the stock evaporates.

12 Degrease the stock and strain through several layers of cheesecloth that have been rinsed in cold water and placed in a conical strainer.

chef tip   **For any type of brown stock, be careful to thoroughly and evenly brown the bones and mirepoix. Remember, the difference between browned and burned bones is only a brief amount of time.**

White Stock   I GALLON (3.8 L)

White stock is a flavorful liquid made from beef, veal, or chicken bones simmered in water with vegetables and seasonings for 6 to 8 hours (3 to 5 hours for chicken bones). The resulting liquid should be clear and without color, highly aromatic, and gelatinous. For a neutral flavor, veal bones are suggested. The standard ratio of ingredients used to prepare white stock is 8 pounds (3.6 kg) of beef, veal, or poultry bones; 6 quarts (5.7 l) of cold water; 1 pound (460 g) of mirepoix; and 1 sachet d'épices or bouquet garni per gallon of finished stock.

AMOUNT	MEASURE	INGREDIENT
6 quarts	192 ounces, 5.7 l	Water, cold
8 pounds	3.6 kg	Beef, veal, or chicken bones
for the mirepoix		
2 cups	8 ounces, 240 g	Onions, in large dice
1 cup	4 ounces, 120 g	Carrots, in large dice
1 cup	4 ounces, 120 g	Celery, in large dice
for the sachet d'épices		
1/2 teaspoon	2 g	Thyme leaves
1/2 teaspoon	2 g	Black peppercorns, cracked
3–4		Parsley stems
1		Garlic clove, crushed

PROCEDURE

1   Bring the water to a boil in a 10-quart (9.5 l) stockpot. Place the bones in the stockpot, return to a boil, then immediately remove from the heat.

2   Strain the bones, discard the liquid, and rinse the bones under cold running water.

3   Clean the stockpot, add the rinsed bones and water to cover, bring to a boil, and simmer over low heat. Skim the surface, removing and discarding any impurities. Simmer the stock for 6 to 8 hours (3 to 4 hours for chicken bones). Continue to skim the surface regularly, discarding the impurities.

4   Add the mirepoix ingredients.

5   Place the sachet d'épices ingredients in a small square of cheesecloth, tie with twine, and add to the simmering stock.

6   Continue to simmer gently for 1 additional hour.

7   Strain the stock through several layers of cheesecloth that have been rinsed in cold water and placed in a conical strainer.

chef tip

Blanching the bones before making a white stock is an optional step. Chefs today disagree on whether or not this is necessary; the question has to do with the loss of flavor during the blanching process. Although the process does take away a little flavor from the resulting product, blanching the bones gives the finished stock extra clarity. If the bones are very fresh, blanching is certainly not necessary, as extremely fresh bones provide both maximum flavor and clarity to stocks made with them. If the bones are frozen or a few days old, they should be blanched. If you choose to blanch the bones, do so with water that is boiling so that as little flavor as possible is lost.

Fish Stock

Fish stock is a flavorful liquid made from fish or shellfish bones simmered with vegetables in water and seasonings for approximately 30 to 45 minutes. Good-quality fish stock is highly aromatic and colorless. The standard ratio of ingredients used to prepare fish or shellfish stock is 176 ounces (5 kg) of bones or shells, 5 quarts (160 ounces, 4.7 l) of cold water, 1 pound (454 g) of mirepoix, and 1 sachet d'épices or bouquet garni per gallon of finished stock.

AMOUNT	MEASURE	INGREDIENT
11 pounds	176 ounces, 5 kg	Fish bones
1 cup	4 ounces, 120 g	Celery, in large dice
2 cups	8 ounces, 240 g	Onions, in large dice
1 cup	4 ounces, 120 g	Leeks, green portion only, chopped
3 cups	10 ounces, 300 g	Mushroom stems
5 quarts	160 ounces, 4.8 l	Water, cold

for the sachet d'épices

1/2 teaspoon	1 g	Thyme leaves
1/4 teaspoon	1 g	Black peppercorns, crushed
1		Bay leaf
3–4		Parsley stems
2–3		Leeks, green portion only, cut into 2-inch (5 cm) pieces

PROCEDURE

1 Rinse the fish bones thoroughly under cold running water.

2 In a small stockpot, combine the bones, celery, onions, leeks, mushroom stems, and cold water.

3 Place the ingredients for the sachet d'épices in a small square of cheesecloth, tie with twine, and add to the liquid.

4 Slowly bring the stock to a gentle simmer and continue to simmer for 30 to 45 minutes while regularly skimming the surface, removing and discarding any impurities.

5 Strain the stock through several layers of cheesecloth that have been rinsed in cold water and placed in a conical strainer.

Vegetable Stock 1 GALLON (3.8 L)

Vegetable stock is a flavorful liquid made from vegetables that are simmered in water, wine, and seasonings for approximately 45 minutes. The resulting liquid should be clear, with a light color, and highly aromatic. Including just two or three vegetables in addition to mirepoix produces better results than a vegetable stock made with a larger variety of vegetables.

AMOUNT	MEASURE	INGREDIENT
	2 ounces, 58 ml	Vegetable oil

for the mirepoix

AMOUNT	MEASURE	INGREDIENT
4 cups	16 ounces, 480 g	Onions, in small dice
2 cups	8 ounces, 240 g	Carrots, in small dice
2 cups	8 ounces, 240 g	Celery, in small dice
2 cups	8 ounces, 240 g	Leeks, white and green parts, chopped
1/2 cup	2 ounces, 60 g	Turnip, in small dice
1/2 cup	2 ounces, 60 g	Tomato, diced
4		Cloves garlic, chopped
1 gallon	128 ounces, 3.8 l	Water, cold
1 cup	8 ounces, 240 ml	Dry white wine

for the sachet d'épices

AMOUNT	MEASURE	INGREDIENT
1/2 teaspoon	2g	Thyme leaves
1		Bay leaf
6–8		Parsley stems
1/4 teaspoon	1g	Black peppercorns, crushed

PROCEDURE

1. Heat the oil in a medium saucepot.
2. Sweat the mirepoix, leeks, turnip, tomato, and garlic until the onions are translucent, approximately 8 to 10 minutes.
3. Add the water and wine.
4. Place the sachet d'épices ingredients in a small square of cheesecloth, tie with twine, and add to the liquid.

5   Slowly bring the stock to a gentle simmer and continue to simmer for 45 minutes while regularly skimming the surface, removing and discarding any impurities.

6   Strain the stock through several layers of cheesecloth that have been rinsed in cold water and placed in a conical strainer.

chef tip

Any type of vegetables can be used for vegetable stock, but the number of vegetable types in a single stock should be limited. Too many vegetables can create a confusing flavor. The selection of vegetables should complement the intended purpose or finished product of the stock. If the vegetable stock is being used to make a mushroom sauce, for example, mushroom stems would be an excellent choice to include as one of the flavors in the stock. Fennel, however, would not be appropriate because its strong flavor would overpower the taste of the mushrooms.

Hollandaise Sauce   1 QUART (946 ML)

One of the five grand sauces, hollandaise sauce is a rich, hot emulsion sauce made from egg yolks and butter flavored with vinegar and lemon juice. A variety of small sauces are made from hollandaise sauce, the most common being béarnaise sauce. An example of hollandaise sauce used in American regional cuisine is demonstrated in the recipe for Braised Leeks, featured in Cajun and Creole Cuisines (page 221).

AMOUNT	MEASURE	INGREDIENT
for the reduction		
1 teaspoon	5 g	Black peppercorns
4 tablespoons	2 ounces, 58 ml	Water, cold
2 tablespoons	1 ounce, 28 ml	Distilled vinegar
1/2 teaspoon	2 g	Salt
for the sauce		
5		Egg yolks
2 1/2 cups	18 ounces, 504 ml	Butter, clarified, warm (not hot)
to taste		Lemon juice
to taste		Salt

PROCEDURE

1 Crack the peppercorns in the bottom of a saucepan.

2 Add the water, vinegar, and salt. Bring to a boil and reduce the volume of liquid by two-thirds. Remove from the heat and reserve until needed.

3 Place the egg yolks in a stainless-steel bowl. Strain the liquid from the reduction into the bowl with the egg yolks.

4 Cook over a double boiler, whisking constantly and vigorously. Cook the egg yolks until the mixture reaches a minimum of 150°F (65°C). This process takes only 3 to 5 minutes. Typically, the egg mixture thins, then starts to thicken. At 160°F (71°C), the egg mixture should have a nappé consistency. Be careful to stir constantly so the eggs do not congeal.

5 Once the egg yolks are cooked, immediately remove the bowl from the double boiler.

6 Whisk in the warm clarified butter, 1 ounce (28 ml) at a time, with a vigorous back-

and-forth motion, in order to incorporate as much air as possible. Make sure the clarified butter is warm, as hot butter will cause the emulsion to break down.

7   Season the sauce to taste with lemon juice and salt. If the sauce is too thick, adjust the consistency with a little warm water. If the sauce appears to have small pieces of congealed egg in it, strain it through a chinois before using.

chef tip

A well-made hollandaise sauce is smooth and free of lumps. The flavor is primarily of butter, but not so much that the butter overpowers the egg and lemon flavors. The consistency of hollandaise should not be heavy but rather light and fluffy. Many professionals choose to use softened whole butter instead of clarified butter in their hollandaise sauce because whole butter has much more flavor. If using whole butter, make sure that the initial reduction is cooked until almost dry because whole butter contains a lot of natural moisture, which can lead to a thinner sauce. This problem is countered by cooking the reduction longer to decrease liquid. Hollandaise sauce is an emulsion sauce, which means the fat molecules of the butter are temporarily suspended in the eggs. This emulsion is not permanent and is subject to breaking down. A hollandaise may break for a variety of reasons, including exposure to heat, exposure to cold, the technique used to prepare the sauce, or simply because the sauce was not stirred from time to time.

RECOVERY INSTRUCTIONS

Before attempting to recover a broken hollandaise, perform a few diagnostics. First, feel the bottom of the bowl to determine whether the sauce is too hot or too cold. If the hollandaise is too cold, reheat it over a double boiler before following the recovery instructions. If the sauce is too hot, let it cool slightly and add an egg yolk to the water in the recovery instructions. If the hollandaise is the correct temperature, follow the recovery instructions as written. Place 1 tablespoon (15 ml) of warm water in a stainless steel bowl and whisk in the broken sauce, 1 ounce (30 ml) at a time, with a vigorous back-and-forth motion until all the broken hollandaise has reemulsified. This process is highly effective in recovery of broken hollandaise sauce.

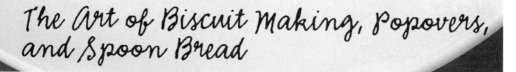

The Art of Biscuit Making, Popovers, and Spoon Bread

Biscuits do not fall into a single category. There are two distinct varieties of biscuits: soft and fluffy, or flaky and high rising. Each type requires different ingredients and techniques.

KEY INGREDIENTS

The flour that is used has a great effect on the biscuit. For a fluffy biscuit, the key is to use soft flour, such as White Lily, or a blend of low-protein, all-purpose flour and plain cake flour, which is extremely soft. For a flaky biscuit, you need high-protein all-purpose flour, which will give the biscuit structure.

Butter can be used for fluffy biscuits. Because flaky biscuits are handled a fair amount, the gluten is activated and the result is a less tender product. To counteract this, some shortening needs to be added with the butter to provide tenderness. When it comes to mixing, it is critical that the fat remain cold and firm. This requires that you move quickly when rubbing the fat into the dry ingredients. A food processor can make this task fast and nearly foolproof.

Biscuits are always at their best when served as soon as they come out of the oven. The dough, however, may be made some hours in advance, stored in the refrigerator, and baked when needed. Even after refrigeration they will still rise well.

Fluffy Biscuits 12 BISCUITS

Make sure that your oven rack is set at the center position. If baked at too low a temperature, the biscuits will likely end up with burned bottoms.

AMOUNT	MEASURE	INGREDIENT
1 cup	4 1/2 ounces, 124 g	All-purpose flour
1 cup	4 ounces 110 g	Cake flour
2 teaspoons	8 g	Baking powder
1/2 teaspoon	2 g	Baking soda
1 teaspoon	5 g	Granulated sugar
1/2 teaspoon	3 g	Salt
1/2 cup	4 ounces, 115 ml	Unsalted butter, chilled, cut into 1/4-inch (.6 cm) pieces
2 tablespoons	1 ounce, 28 g	Unsalted butter, melted
3/4 cup	6 ounces, 170 ml	Buttermilk, cold

PROCEDURE

1 Set oven rack at middle position. Preheat the oven to 450°F (225°C).

2 Mix or pulse first 6 ingredients in a large bowl or the work bowl of a food processor fitted with steel blade. With your fingertips, a pastry blender, 2 knives, or steel blade of the food processor, mix, cut, or process chilled butter into the dry ingredients until mixture resembles coarse meal with a few slightly larger butter lumps.

3 If making by hand, stir in buttermilk with a rubber spatula or fork until mixture forms into soft, slightly sticky ball. If dough feels firm and dry bits are not gathering into a ball, sprinkle dough clumps with additional tablespoon of buttermilk. Be careful not to overmix. If using a food processor, pulse until dough gathers into moist clumps. Remove the dough from food processor bowl and form into rough ball.

4 With lightly floured hands, divide dough into 12 equal portions. Lightly bat a portion of dough back and forth a few times between floured hands until it begins to form a ball, then pat lightly with cupped hands to form a rough ball. Repeat with remaining dough, placing formed dough rounds 1 inch (2.5 cm) apart on ungreased cookie sheet or pizza pan. Brush dough tops with melted butter or milk. (May be covered with plastic wrap and refrigerated for up to 2 hours.) Bake until biscuit tops are light brown, 10 to 12 minutes. Serve immediately.

Flaky Biscuits 16 BISCUITS

AMOUNT	MEASURE	INGREDIENT
2 cups	8 3/4 ounces, 249 g	All-purpose flour
1 tablespoon	1/2 ounce, 10 g	Baking powder
3/4 teaspoon	4 g	Salt
5 tablespoons	2 1/2 ounces, 70 g	Unsalted butter, chilled, cut into 1/4-inch (.6 cm) cubes
3 tablespoons	1 1/2 ounces, 42 ml	Vegetable shortening or lard, chilled
2 tablespoons	1 ounce, 28 g	Unsalted butter, melted
3/4 cup	6 ounces, 170 ml	Milk, cold

PROCEDURE

1 Adjust oven rack to center position. Preheat the oven to 450°F (225°C).

2 Mix first 3 ingredients in a large bowl or the work bowl of a food processor fitted with steel blade. Add the chilled butter; with your fingertips, a pastry blender, 2 knives, or steel blade of a food processor, mix, cut, or process butter and shortening into dry ingredients, until the mixture resembles dry oatmeal. (Transfer food processor mixture to a large bowl.)

3 Stir in the milk with a rubber spatula or fork until dry ingredients are just moistened. Let dough rest for 1 minute, then transfer it to a well-floured work surface.

4 Roll the dough into a rough 6 x 10 inch (15 x 25 cm) rectangle. With the long edge of the dough facing you, fold in both short ends of the dough so that they meet in the center; then fold the dough in half by width, forming a package of dough 4 layers thick. Once again, roll the dough into a 6 x 10 inch (15 x 25 cm) rectangle 1/2 inch (1.2 cm) thick.

5 Using a lightly greased and floured 2-inch (5 cm) cutter, stamp, with one decisive punch per round, 4 rows of 3 dough rounds, cutting them close together to generate as few scraps as possible. Dip cutter into flour before each new cut. Push the scraps of dough together so that their edges join; firmly pinch the edges with fingertips to make a partial seal. Pat the dough into small rectangle, fold it as before, and re-roll 1/2 inch (1.2 cm) thick. Cut out 3 or 4 more biscuits.

6 Place dough rounds 1 1/2 inches (3.8 cm) apart on an ungreased baking sheet; brush dough tops with melted butter or milk. (May be covered with plastic wrap and refrigerated up to 3 hours.)

7 Bake until biscuits are lightly browned, 10 to 12 minutes. Serve immediately.

Cheddar Biscuits Decrease the butter called for in Fluffy Biscuits to 5 tablespoons (2¹/₂ ounces, 70 g), or that in Flaky Biscuits to 3 tablespoons (1¹/₂ ounces, 42 ml). After the fat has been cut or processed into the flour, add 1 cup (235 ml) shredded extra-sharp Cheddar cheese; toss lightly, then stir in liquid.

Herb Biscuits Make Fluffy Biscuits, adding 3 tablespoons (9 g) minced parsley or 2 tablespoons (6 g) parsley and 1 tablespoon (3 g) of either minced fresh tarragon or dill after the fat has been cut or processed into the flour. Split these and use them as a base for rich scrambled eggs or creamed chicken or seafood, or serve them as biscuits plain and simple.

Strawberry Shortcake Follow the directions for Flaky Biscuits, but increase the butter to (4 ounces, 112 ml) and the shortening to ¹/₄ cup (2 ounces, 56 ml). With a 3-inch (7.6 cm) cutter, stamp out 8 dough rounds. Brush tops with melted butter and sprinkle with about 1 tablespoon (¹/₂ ounce, 15 g) sugar. Toss 1 quart (1 l) hulled and sliced strawberries with ¹/₄ cup (2 ounces, 55 g) sugar. Let stand at room temperature for about 30 minutes. Split shortcakes in half and spread with a bit of unsalted butter. Arrange bottoms on plates, cover with berries, and replace the tops. Top with 2 to 3 tablespoons (28–42 ml) of heavy cream.

POPOVERS

Popovers seem like magic. Made from a simple, thin batter of eggs, flour, milk, and melted butter, they pop up in the oven to triple their original height with no help from leavening of any sort. This amazing feat is the result of two factors; a hot oven and a pan that is deeper than it is wide, which causes the steam released during baking to make a giant bubble. The steam is contained by a structure created by the starches and proteins in the batter. The ideal popover pops up high with a thin, crusty exterior and a relatively dry interior with threads of custardy dough.

The Best Popovers   1 DOZEN, IN A MUFFIN TIN

This batter can be made ahead and refrigerated for up to 4 days. If you're making it ahead, bring it to room temperature and stir well before pouring it into a hot pan.

AMOUNT	MEASURE	INGREDIENT
1 cup	4 ounces, 113 g	All-purpose flour
1/4 teaspoon	2 g	Salt
1 cup	8 ounces, 235 ml	Milk (whole)
2		Eggs (extra-large)
1 tablespoon	1/2 ounce, 14 g	Unsalted butter, melted

PROCEDURE

1 Adjust oven rack to low position and heat the oven to 450°F (225°C). Place empty muffin or popover tin in oven to heat while making batter.

2 Whisk the flour and salt together in a medium bowl. Lightly whisk together the milk, eggs, and butter. Pour wet ingredients into dry ingredients all at once; whisk until just blended. (Batter can be made ahead and refrigerated in sealed container for up to 4 days.) Pour batter into measuring cup for easy pouring.

3 Remove hot pan from oven; lightly grease interior of each cup and pan rim.

4 Fill each cup half full with batter. Bake without opening oven door for 20 minutes. Lower heat to 350°F (175°C) and continue to bake until popovers are rich brown in color, 15 to 20 minutes longer. Serve warm. (Popovers can be frozen in airtight plastic bags, and warmed in 325°F [163°C] oven until heated through, 5 to 10 minutes.)

SOUTHERN SPOON BREAD

For light, tender spoon bread, choose fine-grind cornmeal and use beaten egg whites instead of baking powder for lift.

To make spoon bread, you must first whisk cornmeal into a simmering liquid and let it thicken into a "mush," as though you were cooking oatmeal or farina. To the cooled mush add eggs, salt, butter, and other ingredients. The mixture is poured into a baking dish and baked. The resulting dish should be light and airy with a tender, rich crumb. As with many historic dishes, however, ingredients and cooking techniques vary enormously.

The act of stirring cornmeal into simmering milk can be tricky. If you don't do it properly, the meal can separate from the liquid and turn into a bunch of lumps rather than a smooth mush. Start whisking vigorously and continuously and do not stop until the mush is thickened, about 2 to 4 minutes. The oldest recipes for spoon bread call for whole eggs, not separated; however, using eggs separated and beaten will produce a light, high soufflé. The most important element, however, is the type of cornmeal used. Yellow corn, more common in the North, and white corn, more common in the South, are both fine, the major difference being that the white produces a spoon bread that is slightly milder in flavor. Most important is that the corn is a fine grind, which produces a considerably smoother texture.

Classic Spoon Bread   6 TO 8 SERVINGS

A standard 8-inch (20 cm) soufflé dish, but any straight-sided, heavy pan will work, even an iron skillet. Because the spoon bread soon falls from its spectacular height, serve it as quickly as possible; even in its deflated state, though, spoon bread still tastes delicious. Serve leftovers with maple or cane syrup.

AMOUNT	MEASURE	INGREDIENT
3 cups	24 ounces, 705 ml	Half-and-half
I teaspoon	5 g	Salt
I cup	6¹/₄ ounces, 178 g	White or yellow cornmeal, fine-ground
2–3 tablespoons	1–1¹/₂ ounces, (28–42 ml)	Unsalted butter, melted
3		Eggs (large), at room temperature, separated

PROCEDURE

1   Preheat the oven to 350°F (175°C). Butter a 1¹/₂-quart (1.5 l) soufflé dish.

2   Bring the half-and-half and salt to a simmer in large, heavy saucepan. Reduce heat to low.

3   Slowly whisk in the cornmeal. Continue whisking until cornmeal thickens and develops satin sheen, 2 to 4 minutes. Turn off heat and stir in butter; set mush aside.

4   Whisk yolks and 1 to 2 teaspoons (5 to 10 ml) water together in small bowl until lemon-colored and very frothy. Stir them into cooled mush, a little at a time to keep yolks from cooking.

5   Beat egg whites to stiff but not dry peaks; gently fold them into mush mixture.

6   Pour mixture into buttered soufflé dish. Bake until spoon bread is golden brown and risen above dish rim, about 45 minutes. Serve immediately.

Spoon Bread with Cheddar Cheese Follow recipe for Classic Spoon Bread, stirring in I cup (2 ounces, 56 ml) grated sharp Cheddar cheese along with the butter.

Basic Culinary Vocabulary

Al dente Cooked firm, not soft or mushy. Another way of saying al dente is "to the bite."

Albumin The primary protein found in egg whites. Albumin is available powdered and granulated and is frequently used as an edible glue for sealing foods together.

Allumette A classic vegetable cut that results in shapes measuring $1/8$ x $1/8$ x 2 inches (.3 x .3 x 5 cm). The term is used in reference to potatoes only. All other vegetables cut into this shape are referred to as *julienne.*

Appareil A prepared mixture of ingredients used by itself or as an ingredient in other preparations. Examples of appareils are *due duxelles* and *pâte à choux.*

Aromatics Spices, herbs, and certain vegetables added to preparations to enhance their flavor or aroma.

Aspic A clear jelly made from clarified stock and thickened with gelatin. Aspic is sometimes referred to as *aspic jelly* and *aspic gelée* and is used primarily to coat foods. In some cases, aspic is cut into uniform shapes and used as a garnish for pâtés and other charcuterie items.

Au gratin Describes foods finished under a broiler or salamander and served with a browned top. Frequently, the topping for gratinée items is made from bread crumbs, cheese, or sauce.

Au sec Describes food cooked until almost dry.

Bain marie A container that holds foods in a hot-water bath. *Bain marie* is also the name for a hot-water bath used to slowly cook foods or to hold them at a hot temperature until needed.

Base A widely used, commercially produced flavor base usually available in powdered, granulated, and paste forms. Bases are typically mixed with water to create instant stock or used in small quantities to enhance the flavor of soups and sauces. A number of convenient food bases are available today. The application of these convenience products is highly dependent on the type of food-service establishment and the desired flavor outcomes. Some factors to consider when using bases are time, cost, storage, and flavor. Be sure to read the product's label carefully so that you know its ingredients. Taste the product to ensure that its flavor meets your expectations.

Batonnet A classic vegetable cut that results in shapes measuring $^1/_4$ x $^1/_4$ x 2 inches (.6 x .6 x 5 cm).

Blanching The process of quickly and partially cooking food items in boiling water or hot fat. Blanching is generally done as a part of a combination cooking method or to aid in the preparation of a food item. Examples of blanching uses are to remove the skin from tomatoes, to prepare french fries for final cooking, to ready food items for freezing, and to remove undesirable flavors from foods.

Bouillon French for "broth." (See *Broth*.)

Bouquet garni A selection of fresh vegetables and herbs tied into a bundle with twine. A bouquet garni is typically submerged in stocks, sauces, soups, and stews and used as a flavoring agent.

Broth The culinary definition of broth is "a flavorful liquid derived by simmering meat, vegetables, and aromatics in water." To make beef, veal, or chicken broth, simmer meat in water with vegetables and seasonings.

Brunoise A classic vegetable cut that results in shapes measuring $^1/_8$ x $^1/_8$ x $^1/_8$ inch (.3 x .3 x .3 cm).

Brunoise fine A classic vegetable cut that results in shapes measuring $^1/_{16}$ x $^1/_{16}$ x $^1/_{16}$ inch (.1 x .1 x .1 cm).

Caramelization The process of browning the sugars found on the surface of many foods to enhance their flavor and appearance. Browning vegetables or protein items is also referred to as caramelizing.

Carryover cooking What happens when roasted foods, small or large, continue to cook after being removed from the oven. Carryover cooking is normal and can dramatically alter the degree of doneness once the product is removed from the oven. The larger the food item, the greater the amount of heat it retains and the more its internal temperature rises.

Château A classic vegetable cut resulting in a small seven-sided football shape approximately 1$^1/_2$ inches (3.8 cm) in diameter.

Cheesecloth Cotton gauzelike cloth with a number of culinary uses, including straining liquids, enclosing spices, herbs, and other flavoring agents to be applied in a cooking process, and binding ingredients together during the cooking process. The cloth's loose weave allows for the distribution of flavor and moisture during cooking while the structural integrity of the product it encloses is maintained.

Chiffonade A vegetable cut applied to leafy greens and herbs, such as spinach and basil. It results in long, very thin strips typically used as a garnish or as a bed on which other food items are placed. This cut is accomplished by stacking the leaves, rolling the stack into a cylinder, and slicing the roll into fine strips.

Chinois A conical strainer. While this term applies to all such strainers, it is generally used to describe those that use a fine mesh rather than perforated metal to strain.

Clarification The process of turning a cloudy liquid into a clear one by removing the solid impurities or sediment from it. This process turns broth or stock into consommé by trapping the impurities in a mixture of ground meat, egg whites, and acidic product and aromatics. The term *clarification* is applied to this clarifying mixture, or clear meat, as well as the process itself.

Clarified butter Pure butterfat rendered from whole butter (a process that removes milk solids and water). Clarified butter has a higher smoking point, or temperature at which it burns, than whole butter. This property makes it suitable for cooking food at higher temperatures and for cooking processes such as sautéing. Clarified butter has less butter flavor than whole butter and may be kept for a longer period without becoming rancid.

Clearmeat The mixture of egg white, ground meat, acidic ingredient, mirepoix, and other aromatics used in the process of clarifying stock or broth into consommé. (See *Clarification.*)

Cocotte A classic vegetable cut that results in a small seven-sided football shape approximately ³/₄ inch (1.9 cm) in diameter.

Compote A preparation of chilled fresh or dried fruit previously cooked slowly in a sugar syrup. Compotes are often flavored with spices or liqueur.

Concassée To pound or coarsely chop. The term is most often applied to peeled, seeded, and coarsely chopped tomatoes. The term describes the result as well as the action. For example, a chef may concassée a tomato to produce tomato concassée.

Confit Meat or poultry slowly cooked and preserved in its own fat. Classically, goose, duck, and, sometimes, pork is used to make confit.

Conical strainer Specifically, a conical strainer made of perforated metal rather than mesh. (See *Chinois.*)

Consommé A rich, clear soup made by clarifying broth or stock. Consommés are served hot or cold. A consommé reduced by half to intensify its flavor is known as a double consommé.

Coulis A thick sauce made from raw or cooked fruit or vegetables. The term *puree* is sometimes used interchangeably.

Deglaze To add a liquid, usually stock or wine, to a pot or pan after it has been used to cook a food item in order to remove the cooked food particles and their flavor from the surface of the cooking vessel. These flavorful food particles are called the *fond* and, once lifted from the pan, are used to enhance the flavor of a stock or sauce. (See *Fond.*)

Degraisse A French term referring to the process of removing the fat from the surface of a stock, soup, or sauce.

Depouillage A French term referring to the process of skimming the surface of a stock to remove the impurities that naturally rise to the surface while simmering.

Double and triple stocks Stocks made with a prepared stock rather than water. Double and triple stocks are not recommended, as the product cost increases significantly and the flavor is not much different from that of a properly made regular stock.

Dredge To dip or submerge an item in a dry ingredient in order to coat it. Food products are often dredged in flour to coat them prior to sautéing, pan-frying, or deep-frying.

The coating keeps the product from sticking to the pan and promotes the development of a crust on the surface of the product. This crust may enhance the product by developing an appealing brown appearance and by encasing the product in a way that retains flavor and moisture.

Duxelles An appareil composed of mushrooms, shallots, and butter. The mushrooms and shallots are finely chopped and cooked in the butter until a dry, thick paste forms. Duxelles are often used to flavor items such as soups or sauces or as stuffing or a component of stuffing.

Emulsion The suspension of one liquid within another when those liquids generally do not mix. The combination of oil (or fat) and water-based liquids into a smooth mixture is the classic culinary emulsion. An emulsion has a thicker consistency than that of either liquid separately. This characteristic provides mouthfeel, cling, and general structural benefits. Emulsions may be temporary, permanent, or semipermanent. Emulsions are often aided by the addition of emulsifiers or stabilizers such as mustard or the lecithin found in egg yolks.

Enriched stock A stock made with meat as well as bones, creating a hybrid of stock and broth. For 1 gallon (128 ounces, 5.8 l) of chicken stock, it is recommended that 2 whole chickens be added to the recipe. When done, the chickens should be reserved and utilized in another recipe or preparation. For beef or veal stock, it is recommended that a 2-pound (1.8 kg) piece of shank meat be added to enrich the stock. Enriched stock yields a much richer flavor than plain stock and, as long as the meat is utilized in another preparation, should not increase cost.

Essence The fusion of a particular flavor, such as mushrooms or fennel, into a stock to derive a characteristic flavor or aroma.

Fond French for "base." In French cooking, *fond* refers to a stock, typically the basis for many classic and modern recipes. *Fond* is also used to describe the residue attached to the bottom of a cooking vessel after a food ingredient has been roasted or sautéed. A great deal of flavor is usually retained in the fond, which is removed from the cooking vessel through the process of deglazing. (See *Deglaze*.)

Fondant A classic vegetable cut that results in a small seven-sided football shape approximately 2 inches (5 cm) in diameter.

Garnish A food item added for appearance, taste, and texture. Garnish can be integral to the dish or added as an embellishing accompaniment. The term also applies to the act of adding a garnish to a dish.

Gelatin A mixture of proteins derived from boiling bones, connective tissues, and other animal parts. Gelatin, when dissolved and cooked in a hot liquid, adds a jellylike texture to the product. It is flavorless and odorless and comes in granular and sheet forms. It is used to thicken and stabilize food products.

Gelatinous Describes a liquid with jellylike properties. A gelatinous product is semisolid when cold and liquid when hot. Gelatinous properties are important for stocks and sauces due to the characteristics of richness, body, substance, and mouthfeel they provide to the food products.

Glace A quality stock reduced slowly over a prolonged period until it reaches a thick and syrupy consistency. Glace can be used to enhance or enrich soups and sauces and as a glaze to add a sheen to broiled and grilled proteins. Although some commercial food bases have a similar appearance, they may or may not achieve the same results as a fresh-made glace. Today, glace can be purchased already made, but the products vary widely in flavor and quality by manufacturer.

Glazing The process of adding sheen to a food item. Glazing can be accomplished by many means. Examples include brushing a grilled steak with glace before serving, coating an hors d'oeuvre with aspic gelée, and sautéing foods in butterfat and granulated sugar.

Grand sauce A basic classic sauce from which a number of small sauces are produced. There are five recognized grand sauces: espagnole (brown), velouté, béchamel (white), hollandaise, and tomato. In recent years, many culinarians argue that demi-glace has replaced espagnole in common use as the foundation sauce, though classic demi-glace is made from espagnole. Grand sauce is also known as *mother sauce* and *lead sauce.*

Griswold A cast-iron skillet. This heavy-gauge pan requires a seasoning process to seal it, which involves coating the pan with oil and heating it to a high temperature. The griswold is important to the production of many regional dishes. For example, it is the traditional pan used for blackening Cajun dishes, baking corn breads, and pan-frying Southern fried chicken. Its heavy gauge maintains temperature evenly once heated.

Julienne A classic vegetable cut that results in shapes measuring $^1/_8$ x $^1/_8$ x $^1/_2$ inches (.3 x .3 x 1.2 cm).

Julienne fine A classic vegetable cut that results in shapes measuring $^1/_{16}$ x $^1/_{16}$ x $^1/_2$ inches (.1 x .1 x 1.2 cm).

Large dice A classic vegetable cut that results in cubes measuring 3/4 x 3/4 x 3/4 inch (1.9 x 1.9 x 1.9 cm).

Liaison A mixture of cream and egg yolk used to finish soups and sauces. The use of a liaison enriches, slightly thickens, and gives sheen to the completed soup or sauce. A liaison must be carefully incorporated into the hot product through tempering. A product containing a liaison cannot be boiled or the yolk will scramble and the item will have a curdled or broken appearance.

Marmite A stockpot, often made of earthenware. This large pot is taller than it is wide to allow prolonged periods of simmering while minimizing evaporation. Marmites sometimes have legs.

Matignon An edible mirepoix. Matignon uses the same ratio and variety of vegetables as a traditional mirepoix, but because it is intended to be consumed, the matignon should be cut into uniform shapes before cooking.

Medium dice A classic vegetable cut that results in cubes measuring $^1/_2$ x $^1/_2$ x $^1/_2$ inch (1.2 x 1.2 x 1.2 cm).

Mince To cut or chop into very small pieces.

Mirepoix A combination of vegetables frequently used in cooking. Mirepoix typically includes 2 parts onion, 1 part carrot, and 1 part celery. The size to which mirepoix ingredients are cut varies with the intended use and is determined by the amount of time the mirepoix will be cooked. For a brown stock that cooks for 6 to 8 hours, a large dice is preferred, but for a fish stock, which cooks for 45 minutes only, a small dice yields better results.

Mise en place A culinary term meaning "everything in its place." It connotes a state of preparedness. *Mise en place* applies to the assembly of ingredients and equipment prior to undertaking food production. It is also a mindset brought about by thorough forethought and planning.

Nappé A liquid consistency that just coats a spoon. The term *nappé* also refers to the act of lightly coating a food item with sauce.

Oblique A classic vegetable cut made by cutting the vegetable on a bias. Between each cut, the vegetable is rolled 180 degrees. This cut is used primarily for carrots, but other vegetables, such as broccoli stems and asparagus, can be prepared this way.

Olivette A classic vegetable cut resulting in a small seven-sided football shape approximately $1/2$ inch (1.2 cm) in diameter.

Onion brûlée A peeled onion cut in half and charred on the sliced side. Onion brûlée is added to stocks, soups, and sauces for added caramel color and enhanced flavor. French for "burnt onion."

Onion piqué A whole peeled onion to which a bay leaf is tacked with whole cloves. Another approach is to make a slice into the onion and secure the bay leaf within the slice, then stick cloves into the onion separately. Onion piqué is used to flavor sauces, generally white sauces such as béchamel and velouté, and soups. French for "pricked onion."

Parboil To par-cook food in boiling or simmering water.

Par-cook To partially cook a food by any method. This technique is used to bring food to a state where it can be quickly cooked to finish, especially in the case of dense foods. Par-cooking is also used to prepare a number of individual foods, which take various amounts of time to cook, to a degree of doneness whereby they can be completed together in the same amount of time.

Parisienne A classic vegetable cut resulting in perfectly round shapes. No diameter is specified, but it is very important that each of the vegetables used for the same preparation is uniform in size.

Pâte à choux A paste or batter made of milk or water, flour, butter, and eggs. It is also known as choux paste, cream-puff dough, and éclair paste. Pâte à choux is used to produce a number of hollow pastries that are often filled. It is also used as a binder or appareil for other preparations.

Paysanne A classic vegetable cut that results in shapes measuring $1/2 \times 1/2 \times 1/8$ inch (1.2 × 1.2 × .3 cm). Paysanne cuts can be round, triangular, or square.

Peel To remove the outer layer or peel from fruits and vegetables. The term also describes a long-handled, spade-shaped tool used by bakers to remove baked items from the oven.

Pincé To caramelize a product by sautéing. This term is most often applied to tomato products.

Puree A sauce or soup made from ingredients, especially fruits or vegetables, that have been blended, processed, or sieved until a thick smooth consistency is achieved. The term also refers to the act of blending, processing, or sieving a food item to such a consistency.

Raft Congealed clearmeat that settles at the top of a consommé during clarification.

Reduction The product resulting when a liquid, such as a stock or sauce, is simmered or boiled to evaporate its water, reduce its volume, and concentrate its flavor. Stocks and sauces made with commercial food bases, which do not contain gelatin, will not benefit from the process of reduction.

Refresh To submerge or run a blanched product under cold water to stop the cooking process and set the color. This is also known as *shocking*.

Remouillage French for "rewetting." Remouillage is a stock made with bones previously used to make stock. The procedure for making remouillage is the same as for a regular stock, but the product is not as clear or flavorful. Remouillage is frequently used to make glace and, in the past, was used instead of regular stock to make double-strength stocks. (See *Double stock, Glace*.)

Rendering The process of heating fatty animal products to melt and separate the fat from the remaining tissue. This process produces clear liquid fat, useful for many cooking applications, and brown, crisp connective tissue. This crisp tissue is often crumbled or cut and used as a garnish known as *cracklings*.

Rondeau A heavy, wide, shallow, straight-sided pot with two loop handles.

Rondelle A classic vegetable cut that results in round shapes, $1/8$ inch (.3 cm) thick. The rondelle cut is sometimes referred to as *coins*.

Roux A mixture of cooked fat and flour used to thicken soups and sauces. Often, the fat used is butter. Other fats, such as rendered animal fat and various oils, are sometimes used for their flavor and temperature characteristics. The general ratio of fat to flour is 1:1 by weight. A roux may be cooked to various degrees of doneness for desired flavor and color characteristics.

Sachet d'épices A bag of spices used to flavor soups, stocks, and sauces. The spices are generally wrapped in a piece of cheesecloth, tied with a long string, and fastened with one end of the string to the pot of the product to which it is applied. This allows the sachet ingredients to be easily added and removed when desired. A standard sachet d'épices contains cracked black peppercorns, parsley stems, bay leaf, dry thyme, and, sometimes, a crushed clove of garlic.

Sauteuse A single-handled sauté pan with rounded, sloping sides.

Sautoir A single-handled sauté pan with straight sides.

Shock To submerge or run a blanched product under cold water to stop the cooking process and set the color. This is also known as *refreshing*.

Sieve A wire mesh kitchen utensil used to strain liquids or sift dry ingredients, such as flour. The term also applies to the act of straining liquid or particles through a sieve.

Small dice A classic vegetable cut that results in cubes measuring ¹/₄ x ¹/₄ x ¹/₄ inch (.6 x .6 x .6 cm).

Small sauce A derivative sauce made by altering a grand sauce with additional ingredients. Many classic small sauces can be made from each of the grand sauces.

Standard breading procedure The sequential process of coating a food product with bread crumbs by first dredging it in flour, then egg wash, and, finally, the crumbs. This process is also used with other dry coatings, such as cracker crumbs, ground nuts, and cornmeal. Such a coating is often applied to an item before it is pan- or deep-fried.

Stir-frying A hot, quick, dry-heat cooking method done in a skillet on the stovetop with very little fat. Traditionally, this method employs a wok as the cooking vessel. Larger items to be stir-fried are generally cut into small pieces. The method is similar to sautéing, but the food is constantly kept moving.

Sweating The process of cooking food in a pan without browning or adding color to the food. Sweating should be done over low heat until the items are tender and begin to release moisture. The purpose of sweating is to help the food release its flavor quickly when combined and cooked with other foods. Onions are an example of a food item commonly sweated. They turn almost translucent when properly sweated.

Tempering A process of adjustment employed when heat or acid may cause an ingredient or combination of ingredients to curdle. Heat or acid is applied to the ingredients gradually in order to adapt them to the change. Hot liquids are added slowly to a liaison, for example, to bring the temperature of the eggs up slowly so they do not scramble. This term also applies to the stabilization of chocolate through a melting and cooling process.

Tomato concassée A rough cut or chop of peeled and seeded tomato.

Tourné A classic vegetable cut that results in a small football shape with seven even sides.

Tranche An angled portion slice from a fillet of fish.

Translucent Semitransparent. The term often describes the appearance of onion products cooked to the point where they are somewhat limp.

Tuber A fleshy, usually oblong or rounded thickening or outgrowth of a root, stem, or shoot beneath the ground. A common tuber is the potato.

Whisk A looped wire kitchen utensil, also called a *whip*, used for whipping and stirring. The term also applies to the action of whipping vigorously to incorporate ingredients or air into ingredients.

White mirepoix Standard mirepoix in which the proportion of carrots is replaced with parsnips, leeks, and mushrooms. White mirepoix is used in fish stock and fish fumet and is sometimes used in white stock when a lighter product is desired. (See *Mirepoix*.)

Zest The thin outer layer of the peel of citrus fruit. Zest is used as a flavoring agent. The term also refers to the action of cutting the zest from the citrus fruit.

References

THE CUISINE OF NEW ENGLAND

Heinrichs, Ann. *Vermont.* New York: Children's Press, 2001.

Kent, Deborah. *Maine.* New York: Children's Press, 1999.

McNair, Sylvia. *Connecticut.* New York: Children's Press, 1999.

———. *Massachusetts.* New York: Children's Press, 1998.

———. *Rhode Island.* New York: Children's Press, 2000.

Mariani, John. *The Encyclopedia of American Food and Drink.* New York: Lebhar-Friedman Books, 1999.

White, Jasper. *Jasper White's Cooking from New England.* New York: Harper & Row, 1989.

THE CUISINE OF THE MID-ATLANTIC STATES

Blashfield, Jean. *Delaware.* New York: Children's Press, 2000.

———. *Virginia.* New York: Children's Press, 1999.

Burgan, Michael. *Maryland.* New York: Children's Press, 1999.

Fazio, Wende. *West Virginia.* New York: Children's Press, 2000.

Heinrichs, Ann. *New York.* New York: Children's Press, 1999.

———. *Pennsylvania.* New York: Children's Press, 2000.

Stein, R. Conrad. *New Jersey.* New York: Children's Press, 1988.

THE CUISINE OF THE DEEP SOUTH

Davis, Lucille. *Alabama.* New York: Children's Press, 1999.

George, Linda. *Mississippi.* New York: Children's Press, 1999.

Hintz. Martin. *North Carolina.* New York: Children's Press, 2000.

Kent, Deborah. *Tennessee.* New York: Children's Press, 2001.

Lewis, Edna, and Scott Peacock. *The Gift of Southern Cooking.* New York: Alfred A. Knopf, 2003.

Masters, Nancy. *Georgia.* New York: Children's Press, 1999.

McNair, Sylvia. *Arkansas.* New York: Children's Press, 2001.

Stein, R. Conrad. *Kentucky.* New York: Children's Press, 1999.

———. *South Carolina.* New York: Children's Press, 1999.

FLORIBBEAN CUISINE

Heinrichs, Ann. *Florida.* New York: Children's Press, 1998.

Rodriguez, Douglas. *Nuevo Latino.* California: Ten Speed Press, 2002.

Susser, Allen. *New World Cuisine and Cookery.* New York: Doubleday, 1995.

CAJUN AND CREOLE CUISINES

Harris, Jessica B. *Beyond Gumbo.* New York: Simon and Schuster, 2003.

Hintz, Martin. *Louisiana.* New York: Children's Press., 1998.

THE CUISINE OF THE CENTRAL PLAINS

Blashfield, Jean. *Wisconsin.* New York: Children's Press, 1998.

Blue, Anthony Dias. *America's Kitchen.* Georgia: Turner Publishing, Inc., 1995.

Heinrichs, Ann. *Indiana.* New York: Children's Press, 2000.

———. *Ohio.* New York: Children's Press, 1999.

Hintz, Martin. *Iowa.* New York: Children's Press, 2000.

———. *Michigan.* New York: Children's Press, 1998.

———. *Minnesota.* New York: Children's Press, 2000.

———. *Missouri.*New York: Children's Press, 1999.

———. *North Dakota.* New York: Children's Press, 2000.

Masters, Nancy. *Kansas.* New York: Children's Press, 1999.

McNari, Sylvia. *Nebraska.* New York: Children's Press,.

Santella, Andrew. *Illinois.* New York: Children's Press, 1998.

Sheperd, Donna Walch. *South Dakota.* New York: Children's Press, 2001.

TEXAS

DeWitt, Dave, and Nancy Gerlach. *The Whole Chili Pepper Book.* Canada: Little, Brown & Company, 1990.

Griffith, Dottie. *The Contemporary Cowboy Cookbook: Recipes from the Wild West to Wall Street.* Texas: Lone Star Books, 2003.

Heinrichs, Ann. *Texas.* New York: Children's Press, 1999.

Raichlen, Steven. *BBQ USA.* New York: Workman Publishing, 2003.

Reedy, Jerry. *Oklahoma.* New York: Children's Press, 1998.

SOUTHWESTERN CUISINE AND THE ROCKY MOUNTAIN STATES

Blashfield, Jean. *Arizona.* New York: Children's Press, 2000.

———. *Colorado.* New York: Children's Press, 1999.

George, Linda. *Idaho.* New York: Children's Press, 2000.

———. *Montana.* New York: Children's Press, 2000.

Kent, Deborah. *New Mexico.* New York: Children's Press, 1999.

———. *Utah.* New York: Children's Press, 2000.

———. *Wyoming.* New York: Children's Press, 2000.

Stein, R. Conrad. *Nevada.* New York: Children's Press, 2000.

THE CUISINE OF CALIFORNIA

Heinrichs, Ann. *California.* New York: Children's Press, 1988.

Jordan, Michele Anna. *California Home Cooking.* Boston: The Harvard Common Press, 1977.

THE CUISINE OF HAWAII

Hintz, Martin. *Hawaii.* New York: Children's Press, 1999.

Laudan, Rachel. *The Food of Paradise: Exploring Hawaii's Culinary Heritage.* Hawaii: University of Hawaii Press, 1996.

THE CUISINE OF THE PACIFIC NORTHWEST

Blashfield. Jean. *Washington.*New York: Children's Press, 2001.

Ingram, Scott. *Oregon.* New York: Children's Press, 2000.

Nicholas, John F. *The Complete Cookbook of American Fish and Shellfish.* New York: Van Nostrand Reinhold, 1990.

Shepherd, Donna. *Alaska.* New York: Children's Press, 1999.

Index